Shakespeare

IN PERFORMANCE

Shakespeare

IN PERFORMANCE

CONSULTANT EDITORS

KEITH PARSONS & PAMELA MASON

a Salamander book

Published by Salamander Books Limited
LONDON

A SALAMANDER BOOK

Published by Salamander Books Ltd
129-137 York Way
London N7 9LG
United Kingdom

Distributed by Random House Value Publishing, Inc.
40 Englehard Avenue
Avenel, New Jersey 07001

A CIP catalog record for this book is available from the Library of Congress.

Printed in Italy

ISBN 0-517-14091-8

CREDITS

Commissioning Editor: Tony Hall
Designer: Pedro Prá-Lopez, Kingfisher Design Services
Picture research: Juliet Duff
Four-color and line artwork: Hugh Dixon
Half-title Globe artwork: Vana Haggerty
Typesetting/DTP: Frances Prá-Lopez, Kingfisher Design Services
Color reproduction: Pixel Tech Ltd, Singapore

9 8 7 6 5 4 3 2 1

For Edmund, Elinor and Elizabeth

Publisher's Note
The publishers would like to give special thanks to the following picture sources and archives
for their great help in supplying pictures for this book:
James Shaw of the Shakespeare Birthplace Trust; Donald Cooper; Richard Mangan of Mander and Mitcheson;
Sue Harris and Chris Hay of the Birmingham Central Library; Ann Daniels of the RSC Collection.

A note on the text
All quotations from Shakespeare's plays have been standardised to the New Penguin Editions –
except for references to *Cymbeline* and *Titus Andonicus* which use the older Penguin texts.

CONTENTS

INTRODUCTION

What excites us most about Shakespeare is the theatrical vitality of his plays. It is performance which releases their potential and what may be a puzzle on the page can leap into life on the stage. The best productions make us hear lines that we have not registered before and will new-mint those words which we thought were familiar.

But Shakespeare offers us more than text. There are the essentially theatrical dangers and delights of overhearing scenes and slapstick comedy, of duels and disguises. Silence on stage can read eloquently. Whenever we see *Hamlet*, the play is recreated afresh at every performance and wherever Elsinore is located the pressure of moment-by-moment experience can prompt insight and inspiration, compassion,

perspective, and even spiritual awareness. The immediacy of performance enables Shakespeare's plays to transcend critical analysis and reverberate with contemporary truth.

We adopted Nick Bottom's advice to Peter Quince and simply asked our contributors to 'say what the play treats on'. We hope that their individual voices can be heard clearly and that their views stimulate both those who have yet to see a particular play and those who can share memories of how triumphantly Shakespeare's text works in performance. Above all, our hope is that our enthusiasm and that of our contributors will prove infectious.

Keith Parsons and **Pamela Mason**

CONTRIBUTORS

Romana Beyenberg teaches at Irmgardis Grammar School, Cologne. She has published work on the women in Shakespeare's late plays.

Janet Clare is Lecturer in English, University College, Dublin. She has written articles on Renaissance drama and a book on Elizabethan and Jacobean censorship.

Rebecca Flynn is Deputy Head of Education at The Shakespeare Birthplace Trust, Stratford-upon-Avon. She has prepared educational material to accompany sets of slides of RSC productions.

Etsuko Fukahori is Associate Professor of English at Kwassui Women's Junior College, Nagasaki, Japan. She has contributed several articles to *The Kwassui Review*.

Andrew Gurr is Professor of English at the University of Reading. He has written several books on Shakespeare and is chairman of the Academic Advisory Committee to the Bankside Globe project.

Suzanne Harris is developing a career in theatre management and is involved in Royal Shakespeare Company project work at The Other Place in Stratford-upon-Avon.

Pamela Mason is a Fellow of The Shakespeare Institute and Lecturer in

English at The University of Birmingham. She has written on *Much Ado about Nothing* and has edited criticism of Shakespeare's early comedies.

Tom Matheson was formerly Deputy Director and is now an Honorary Fellow of The Shakespeare Institute, The University of Birmingham. He has lectured on Shakespeare, particularly in relation to modern literature and drama, throughout the world.

Keith Parsons is Tutor in Literature at Wroxton College and Visiting Lecturer in the School of Continuing Studies, The University of Birmingham. He has written educational material for The Birmingham Royal Ballet.

Mike Paterson is Head of Drama at the Royal Grammar School, Guildford. He has directed many productions and is currently researching the stage history of *Romeo and Juliet*.

Susan L. Powell is Lecturer in English and Media Studies at Hertford College. She is embarking upon a course in Creative Writing at the University of East Anglia.

Niky Rathbone is The Shakespeare Librarian at Birmingham Shakespeare Library. She compiles the annual listing of Shakespeare productions for *Shakespeare Survey*.

James Shaw is Assistant Librarian at The Shakespeare Centre Library, Stratford-upon-Avon. He has contributed stage histories to recent RSC programmes.

Elizabeth Schafer is Lecturer in Drama and Theatre Studies at Royal Holloway College, University of London. She has edited Thomas Middleton's *The Witch* for the New Mermaid series.

Helen J. Schaffer Snow is Assistant Professor of Literature at Harlaxton College, the British campus of the University of Evansville. Her research has explored issues of gender in Shakespeare's plays.

Robert Wilcher is Senior Lecturer in English at The University of Birmingham. His publications include articles on Shakespeare and books on Andrew Marvell and Arnold Wesker.

Richard Johnson made his professional acting debut in Sir John Gielgud's theatre company at the age of 16. He appeared frequently in leading rôles in the London theatre before becoming a Founder Member and Associate Artist of the Royal Shakespeare Company. His Shakespearean rôles have included Antony, Cassius, Orlando, Hamlet, Laertes, Othello and Sir Andrew Aguecheek.

FOREWORD

As a Shakespearean actor, it has seemed to me, on occasion, that the interests of scholars, critics, teachers and performers have been too exclusive. It is a very great pleasure, therefore to welcome this beautiful book which encompasses the experience of all these groups in a most authoritative and satisfying manner. It also gives me an opportunity to sound off, a little, on what Shakespeare means to me.

I have pondered this question many times over the years that I have spent as a professional interpreter of his work. I remember, in my first acting job as a 16 year old spear-carrier and understudy, haunting the wings of the Haymarket Theatre night after night to watch Gielgud perform Hamlet, as the buzz bombs and rockets flew noisily or silently towards London; of the extraordinary power that tremendous poetry and that great actor exercised on my young mind; of thinking that if I had to to die now, then I would rather go with those lines in my head. Later, at Stratford in the Fifties, I thought that to play Orlando in As you Like It and Posthumous Leonatus in Cymbeline opposite Peggy Ashcroft (whose Ophelia and Titania I had adored in that Haymarket season a decade earlier) was as near as one could get to heaven without actually going through the pearly gates. And, recently, as I approached the fiftieth year of my quest, I have had the marvellous opportunity, at the Royal Shakespeare Company's theatres, of rethinking the role of Antony in Antony and Cleopatra, in the light of a perspective coloured by another 20 years of experience since I first played the part in 1972.

And so it has gone on to this day: for me, to act in Shakespeare has been to be in love. And with what a lover! Always stimulating; always contributing to the relationship; but demanding, too, of the very best one has to offer. Once, in the Sixties, I was sharing the dissatisfactions of daily life with a fellow player; we whined on for a while over our lunchtime Guinness at The Dirty Duck; finally my companion polished off his glass and rose purposefully: "Oh, come on, Richard, let's go down to the theatre and face reality." I've never forgotten those words, for in that seeming contradiction lies, I think, the nub of the theatrical experience: that we actors, through our insubstantial pageant, can illuminate and interpret the lives of our audiences, can hold the mirror up to nature.

Of all playwrights, Shakespeare's all-round understanding of the world and its suffering, its beauty and diversity, has never been, and perhaps never will be matched; but I feel he prized above all the capacity (if not always the ability) of mankind to forgive, to show mercy, to love his friend or his enemy. It is that quality, expressed in language of sublime beauty, which draws me back, again and again, to his work.

Richard Johnson

ONE MAN IN HIS TIME

*The nature and origin of Shakespeare's genius must be sought
beyond the circumstances of his life in Stratford-upon-Avon.*

The two most important and influential books in the English language appeared within just twelve years of each other, at the beginning of the seventeenth century in London. The Authorised or King James Version of the Bible in English, published in 1611, is the collective product of generations of biblical scholars and a committee of translators, whereas *Mr William Shakespeare's Comedies, Histories and Tragedies*, published in the so-called First Folio of 1623, is ultimately the product of a single imagination. The one is supposedly divine in origin and specifically religious in application; the other is human and secular. As the two greatest collections of character and story in any language, both the Bible and Shakespeare's First Folio have remained in print, in one form or another, ever since, and have remained a continuous source of inspiration, instruction and entertainment. Historically, they also signal the end of an unprecedented, explosive phase in the English language, unfettered by systematic grammars, dictionaries and reference books, incorporating new words and phrases from every linguistic source, both ancient and modern.

Shakespeare's First Folio is the first exclusive collection of plays by a single author in English. In preparation probably since Shakespeare's own death on 23 April 1616, it represents a unique act of rescue and restoration on the part of its editors, Shakespeare's actor-executor friends, John Heminge and Henry Condell. The volume contains thirty-six plays, presented not in any chronological

Above: William Shakespeare, 1564–1616
The Chandos Portrait, possibly by John Taylor, has proved to be a popular and enduring image of the dramatist, but it has a limited claim to authenticity. It can be seen in the National Portrait Gallery, London.

order, but arranged into three generic categories: fourteen comedies, ten histories and twelve tragedies. It excludes, without explanation, the two narrative poems *Venus and Adonis* and *The Rape of Lucrece* (published with formal dedications in 1593 and 1594 respectively); the collaborative plays *Pericles* (first published in a separate Quarto in 1609,

attributing it to Shakespeare), and *The Two Noble Kinsmen* (attributed to Shakespeare and John Fletcher in 1634); the *Sonnets* (published, probably without the author's agreement, in 1609); and other shorter poems.

The Folio, although naturally addressed 'To the Great Variety of Readers', is quite clearly a commemoration of Shakespeare as a poet of the theatre, for his command of expressive language is repeatedly praised. Of the thirty-six plays in the volume, eighteen are printed here for the first time, including, for example, some of Shakespeare's most famous and characteristic works: *The Tempest, Julius Caesar, Macbeth, Antony and Cleopatra, Twelfth Night* and *Cymbeline*. The other eighteen already existed in print, sometimes in multiple editions, in the smaller separate-play, almost pocket-sized format of Quarto. The need to rescue so many plays from oblivion seems to indicate either Shakespeare's own lack of interest in putting the plays into print or a deliberate resistance on the part of the owners of his plays, his theatrical company, the King's Men, to release them for the profit of publishers.

But even before the Folio, for any of those other eighteen plays which *were* previously published, there is no evidence that Shakespeare either prepared them directly for the press or supervised them in the process of printing. This does not mean that Shakespeare had no interest in the texts of his plays as scripts for live performance. As we can see from the variations in early editions of plays that were reprinted, he did prepare the plays for theatrical performance, and in some of them made changes amounting to actual revision during their performance history on stage. It is now thought that at least *Hamlet, Lear, Othello* and *Troilus and Cressida* were revised, reinforcing the view that for Shakespeare performance of his plays always took priority over print.

The Folio title-page and the preface by Heminge and Condell, stress the completeness and accuracy of the texts presented 'according to the True Originall Copies' and 'absolute in their numbers'. This may be

A
Moſt pleaſaunt and
excellent conceited Co-
medie, of Syr *Iohn Falſtaffe*, and the
merrie Wiues of *Windſor*.

Entermixed with ſundrie
variable and pleaſing humors, of Syr *Hugh*
the Welch Knight, Iuſtice *Shallow* , and his
wife Couſin M. *Slender*.

With the ſwaggering vaine of Auncient
Piſtoll, and Corporall *Nym*.

By *William Shakeſpeare*.

Asit hath bene diuers times Acted by the right Honorable
my Lord Chamberlaines ſeruants. Both before her
Maieſtie, and elſe-where.

LONDON
Printed by T. C. for Arthur Iohnſon,and are to be ſold at
his ſhop in Powles Church yard, at the ſigne of the
Flower de Leuſe and the Crowne.
1602.

Above: The inviting title page for the shortest of the Shakespearean 'Bad' Quartos: *The Merry Wives of Windsor,* 1602

Right: The impressive title page for The Authorised or King James Bible, 1611

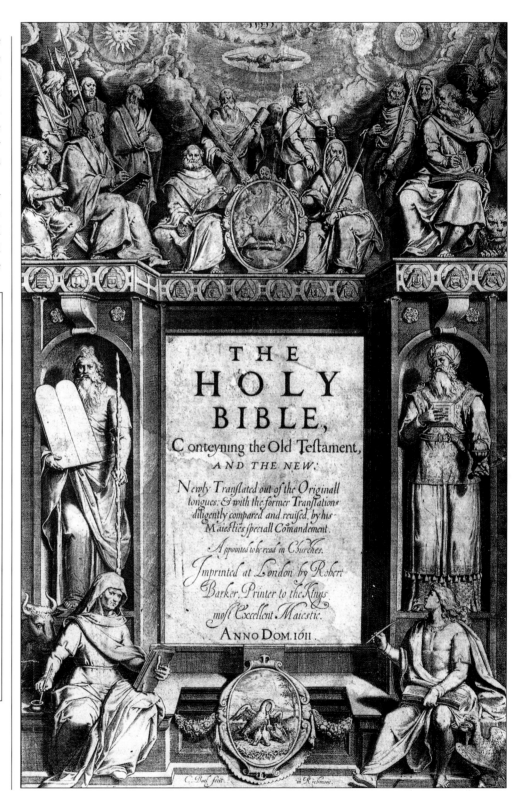

The Tragedy of Hamlet

Hor. A trowant disposition, my good Lord,
Ham. Nor shall you make mee truster
Of your owne report against your selfe:
Sir, I know you are no trowant:
But what is your affaire in *Elsenoure?*
Hor. My good Lord, I came to see your fathers funerall.
Ham. O I pre thee do not mocke mee fellow studient,
I thinke it was to see my mothers wedding.
Hor. Indeede my Lord, it followed hard vpon.
Ham. Thrift, thrift, *Horatio,* the funerall bak't meates
Did coldly furnish forth the marriage tables,
Would I had met my deerest foe in heauen
Ere euer I had seene that day, *Horatio;*
O my father, my father, me thinkes I see my father.
Hor. Where my Lord?
Ham. Why, in my mindes eye *Horatio.*
Hor. I saw him once, he was a gallant King.
Ham. He was a man, take him for all in all,
I shall not looke vpon his like againe.
Hor. My Lord, I thinke I saw him yesternight,
Ham. Saw, who?
Hor. My Lord, the King your father.
Ham. Ha, ha, the King my father keyou.
Hor. Ceasen your admiration for a while
With an attentiue eare, till I may deliuer,
Vpon the witnesse of these Gentlemen
This wonder to you.
Ham. For Gods loue let me heare it.
Hor. Two nights together had these Gentlemen,
Marcellus and *Bernardo,* on their watch,
In the dead vast and middle of the night,
Beene thus incountered by a figure like your father,
Armed to poynt, exactly *Capape*
Appeeres before them thrise, he walkes
Before their weake and feare oppressed eies
Within his tronchions length,
While

Prince of Denmarke.

As any the most vulgar thing to sence,
Why should we in our peuish opposition
Take it to hart, fie, tis a fault to heauen,
A fault against the dead, a fault to nature,
To reason most absurd, whose common theame
Is death of fathers, and who still hath cryed
From the first course, till he that died to day
This must be so : we pray you throw to earth
This vnpreuailing woe, and thinke of vs
As of a father, for let the world take note
You are the most immediate to our throne,
And with no lesse nobilitie of loue
Then that which dearest father beares his sonne,
Doe I impart toward you for your intent
In going back to schoole in *Wittenberg,*
It is most retrograd to our desire,
And we beseech you bend you to remaine
Heere in the cheare and comfort of our eye,
Our chiefest courtier, cosin, and our sonne.
Quee. Let not thy mother loose her prayers *Hamlet,*
I pray thee stay with vs, goe not to *Wittenberg.*
Ham. I shall in all my best obay you Madam.
King. Why tis a louing and a faire reply,
Be as our selfe in Denmarke, Madam come,
This gentle and vnforc'd accord of *Hamlet*
Sits smiling to my hart, in grace whereof,
No iocond health that Denmarke drinkes to day,
But the great Cannon to the cloudes shall tell,
And the Kings rowse the heauen shall brute againe,
Respeaking earthly thunder; come away. *Florish. Exeunt all,*
Ham. O that this too too sallied flesh would melt, *but Hamlet.*
Thaw and resolue it selfe into a dewe,
Or that the euerlasting had not fixt
His cannon gainst seale slaughter, ô God, God,
How wary, stale, flat, and vnprofitable
Seeme to me all the vses of this world?
Fie on't, ah fie, tis an vnweeded garden
That growes to seede, things rancke and grose in nature,
Possesse it meerely that it should come thus
C. But

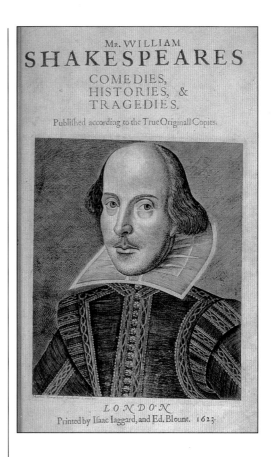

MR. WILLIAM
SHAKESPEARES
COMEDIES,
HISTORIES, &
TRAGEDIES.

Published according to the True Originall Copies.

LONDON
Printed by Isaac Iaggard, and Ed. Blount. 1623.

partly a commercial incentive to buy, and their preface is initially a sales-pitch, but comparison of the Folio texts of plays with those Quartos printed earlier does seem to suggest that Heminge and Condell did attempt to compare and correct some of the earlier variant versions. Their metaphor for the text of some of the earlier Quartos is as a disabled body 'maimed, and deformed by the frauds and stealthes of injurious impostors, that expos'd them', suggesting incompetent piracy. Their task as editors is conceived, in almost evangelical terms, as the restoration and resurrection of the mangled limbs of a human body, as at the day of judgement. It used to be thought that they were categorising all earlier Quartos as thoroughly defective, but their reference to a class of 'diverse stolne, and surreptitious copies' seems to distinguish

Above far left: A page from the 'Bad' Quarto of *Hamlet*, 1603
Above left: A page from the 'Good' Quarto of *Hamlet*, 1604/5
Above: The title page from the First Folio, prepared by Heminge and Condell, with its engraving by Martin Droeshout, 1623
Below left: An extract from the MS. of *Sir Thomas More*, c.1594

some so-called 'bad' Quartos from others whose text may be regarded as 'good'.

Even this distinction has now been called in question, although it is hard to regard as anything but 'bad' a Quarto (such as the 1602 *Merry Wives of Windsor* or the 1603 *Hamlet*) which is only half as long as other versions of the play; in which speeches are omitted, abbreviated, or paraphrased; in which scenes are transposed and motivation altered; and which appears to be the result of a reconstruction from memory by subverted actors. None of the true original copies of Shakespeare's plays – in the form of an autograph manuscript (so-called 'foul papers'), a scribal transcript (a fair copy made by a professional scribe) or theatre prompt-book – survives. As specimens of Shakespeare's handwriting we have six variously-spelt signatures (three on his will, three on other legal documents), and a controversial fragment contributed to the revision of a censored and unpublished manuscript play on the life of Sir Thomas More. We have to conjecture the nature of his manuscripts from the printed texts of those plays which appear to have been printed directly from the author's own copy, such as the 1600 *Much Ado*, incorporating into its speech-prefixes not only the names of the characters Dogberry and Verges, but those of the actors Will Kemp and Richard Cowley, who played them.

Heminge and Condell seem almost to overstate the accessibility and universality of the author's works in the Folio, offering them to the whole literate population ('from the most able, to him that can but spell'), as well as testifying to what were felt to be Shakespeare's most characteristic qualities throughout the seventeenth and eighteenth centuries, a creative power as strong as a force of nature and an instinctive facility and inventiveness as a writer. For Heminge and Condell censure and dissent are already irrelevant: 'these Playes have had their triall alreadie, and stood out all Appeales' – on the stage.

To the natural frustration of modern biographers, there is no reference in the Folio to the private, personal or domestic life of the author. The author's presence and persona as a writer is fully acknowledged, but that he might have had a wife, children and a home in Stratford-upon-Avon is carefully ignored.

Nevertheless, it is chiefly the First Folio which asserts the identity of Shakespeare as the author of the plays and which ties that author to William Shakespeare, citizen of Stratford, solving, technically at least, what to

Above: A woodcut of a tavern scene such as at The Boar's Head.

Left: Gheerart Janssen's monument in Holy Trinity Church, Stratford-upon-Avon, is one of the very few representations of Shakespeare that have any substantial claim to be true likenesses.

many people has been a mystery: how could a commoner have written plays which show such insight into complex questions of monarchy and government? And how could the comparatively uneducated son of a Stratford wool-dealer be that commoner? It is Ben Jonson, Shakespeare's friend and fellow-dramatist, who testifies to the accuracy and authenticity of Martin Droeshout's title-page portrait, in his facing poem 'To the Reader': 'Wherein the Graver had a strife with Nature, to out-doo the life.' It is also Ben Jonson, in the most eloquent eulogy in the language: 'To the memory of my beloved, The AUTHOR, Mr. William Shakespeare: And what he hath left us', who links Shakespeare to Stratford. The use of the word 'beloved' seems extravagant, but is matched by Jonson's admiration of Shakespeare's genius, here unqualified by his complaints elsewhere of 'small Latin, and less Greek'. It is Jonson too, with his description of Shakespeare as 'Sweet Swan of Avon!' who confirms the identification earlier provided by the bequests to actors in Shakespeare's

Stratford will of 1616, and the assertion that Shakespeare of Stratford was a genius comparable to Socrates and Virgil on the inscription to Gheerart Janssen's monumental bust in Holy Trinity Church, sculpted and installed shortly after 1616.

By themselves, nothing in the circumstances of Shakespeare's life in Stratford can explain the nature and origin of his genius. Only a combination of forces and factors – genetic, cultural, linguistic and historical, inherently difficult to unravel – can have contributed to his emergence at that time and place. The search for life experiences and personality, however natural and inevitable, given human curiosity, may even be misguided. As with most other authors, it is likely that Shakespeare's true life, the life of thought and imagination, is embedded in his works: sometimes perhaps on the surface, when he describes plants and animals familiar from his native countryside; though more often perhaps commonly disguised, even when he seems to write personally about the agonies of sexual desire, as in the *Sonnets*. Further, the craft of dramatist imposes reticence and impersonality. Plays are generally

Above: An embroidered scene of hunting and hawking, c.1585
Above right: The image of the Elizabethan family (here Lord Cobham's) was portrayed by artists such as Hans Eworth, c. 1550 to 1574
Right: Woodcut from *The Praise, Antiquity and Commodity of Beggary, Beggars and Begging* by John Taylor, 1621

the least autobiographical and confessional of literary forms, requiring their author to sublimate and project his own thoughts into those of his characters. No doubt Shakespeare's private life and personality are buried somewhere in the works. The difficulty is to identify and isolate them. And, many would argue, what would be the point and value in any case? The personality, even if we could isolate it, would not provide a key to the works or a detailed explanation of their composition. Undoubtedly, Shakespeare is both a product of his own time, and a natural genius with the capacity to transcend its limits and confines.

Stratford-upon-Avon in the sixteenth century was a small market town, important locally because of its position at a bridging point of the River Avon, with about 2000 inhabitants at the turn of that century. The stresses and tensions within sixteenth-century rural society were certainly felt: the legacy of religious division between Catholic and Protestant; the continuous inflation of prices; periodic food shortages; the shift from pastoral to arable farming; the consequent enclosure of land and impoverishment of many common people; the increasing numbers of beggars, rogues and vagabonds; the developing distance between rich and poor in the community. It has been estimated that in 1600, out of Stratford's population of 2000, no less than 700 should be classed as destitute poor, relying on the charity of the parish for their maintenance.

This is at a time when Shakespeare himself had become the owner of the second largest house in Stratford, the splendid three-storeyed, five-gabled New Place. The deed of purchase, dated 4 May 1597, records a payment of £60 in silver. Later, Shakespeare bought 107 acres (43 hectares)of arable land and 20 acres (8 hectares) of pasture; later still he invested £440 in Stratford tithes (the right to collect rents on specified land or produce), receiving from them an annual income of £60. It is impossible to give an exact equivalence for this amount in modern money, but it undoubtedly represents a sum of several thousand pounds. By that time he was already famous and wealthy from his career as actor, playwright and shareholder in the King's Men

Above: An eighteenth century sketch of New Place made after the house was demolished in 1759

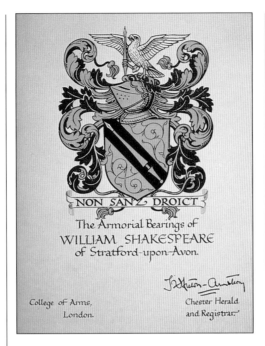

Above: A development of the coat of arms originally applied for by John Shakespeare and granted in 1596
Above right: The house in Wilmcote that is taken to be the girlhood home of Shakespeare's mother, Mary Arden
Right: John Shakespeare became a householder in Henley Street, Stratford-upon-Avon. In 1552 he was fined for creating an unauthorised dung-heap there.

theatre company in London. Criticism of Shakespeare's prosperity is irrelevant; that prosperity is the product of his own extraordinary achievements and his apparent caution in managing his business. But it does throw light on the many passages in those bitter plays (such as *King Lear, Timon of Athens* or *Coriolanus*) when the conflict between rich and poor in society becomes a central issue, not easily resolved. Shakespeare's likely satisfaction at and enjoyment of his own prosperity was, on the evidence of these and other plays, undoubtedly tempered by his vivid sense of what it meant to be, and have, nothing.

The coincidence of birth and death on 23 April, St George's Day, is suggestive, but meaningless, implying no special destiny. We

know quite a lot from public records about the life, family and property of Shakespeare, but nothing that is private or intimate, except by very conjectural inference. His father John was a glover, wool-dealer and sometime money-lender, who made a prosperous marriage to a farmer's daughter, Mary Arden. His fortunes rose, taking him to the positions of bailiff (or mayor) and Justice of the Peace, before later casting him down again, possibly for Catholic sympathies, although in 1596 he had been granted a coat-of-arms as a

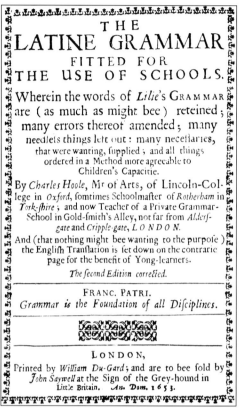

Above: The schoolroom in Church Street, Stratford-upon-Avon, where it is likely that William Shakespeare received free tuition
Right: The title page of a later Latin grammar based upon William Lily's *Short Introduction* which is the basis for a scene in *Merry Wives* in which Master William's knowledge is tested

Above: The cottage in Shottery where Anne Hathaway, the woman Shakespeare married in 1582, grew up

THE
LATINE GRAMMAR
FITTED FOR
THE USE OF SCHOOLS.

Wherein the words of *Lilie's* GRAMMAR are (as much as might bee) reteined ; many errors thereof amended ; many needlets things left out : many neceffaries, that were wanting, fupplied ; and all things ordered in a Method more agreeable to Children's Capacitie.

By *Charles Hoole*, Mr of Arts, of Lincoln-College in *Oxford*, fomtimes Schoolmafter of *Rotherham* in *Tork-fhire* ; and now Teacher of a Private Grammar-School in Gold-fmith's Alley, not far from *Alderf-gate* and *Cripple-gate*, L O N D O N.

And (that nothing might bee wanting to the purpofe) the Englifh Tranflation is fet down on the contrarie page for the benefit of Yong-learners.

The fecond Edition correfted.

FRANC. PATRI.
Grammar is the Foundation of all Difciplines.

LONDON,
Printed by *William Du-Gard*; and are to bee fold by *John Saywell* at the Sign of the Grey-hound in Little Britain. *An. Dom.* 1 6 5 3.

gentleman. There were eight children of the marriage, only four sons and one daughter surviving, William being the eldest. The presence in so many plays of elder sons threatened by the envy of younger brothers (for example, *Richard III, As You Like It, Much Ado About Nothing, Hamlet, King Lear* and *The Tempest*) causes one to wonder about the home life of Shakespeare and his own three brothers; but nothing domestic is known, although the freely-named villain in *Lear* is given the name of Shakespeare's own younger brother Edmund, also an actor, later to be buried in Southwark, in London.

Shakespeare presumably attended the King's New (or grammar) School in Church Street, Stratford, acquiring some familiarity with the Latin language and his obvious love of literature, both ancient and modern. We assume he left school aged about fifteen. There is no evidence of education at university. He is clearly, on the evidence of extensive reference within his plays, one of the most

widely-read authors of his time. His favourite books seem to have included Ovid's *Metamorphoses* (in Arthur Golding's translation of 1567) and Plutarch's *Lives of the Noble Grecians and Romans* (translated by Sir Thomas North from the French version in 1579), indicating an equal interest in legendary mythology and in authenticated history. Ovid's is the only identified book brought on stage as a property: once in *Titus Andronicus*, at the start of his career, and again in *Cymbeline*, at the end; on each occasion in connection with the rape of a principal female character. But he was equally responsive to English contemporaries such as the popular, bohemian dramatist and pamphleteer Robert Greene, who introduced the London street-life of prostitutes and criminals into his 'cony-catching' pamphlets of

1591; or to learned Europeans like Frenchman Michel de Montaigne, whose speculative essays were translated into English in 1603 by John Florio, who shared with Shakespeare a common patron in the Earl of Southampton: The Bible, of course, is ever present; the Gospel of St Matthew even providing a title for Shakespeare's play *Measure for Measure* about a corrupt judge:

Judge not, that ye be judged. For with what judgment ye judge, ye shall be judged: and with what measure ye mete, it shall be measured to you again.

[St Matthew 7.1-2]

The wide range of his reading is partly to meet the theatre's demand for virtually two new plays a year over two decades of a professional career. Shakespeare rarely invents the plots or main characters of his plays. What he does invent are speeches which bring them to life, scenes which bring them into passionate confrontation and a structure which carries them to an inevitable destiny. But whatever is borrowed, is always radically transformed.

As far as this kind of reading is concerned, Shakespeare is not only a practical professional dramatist and poet, but also a reflective intellectual, assimilating experience through literature on a continuous basis. No information or example seems useless; his metaphorical habit of thought made constant connections across widely different fields of knowledge. One reason, in fact, why there may be so little evidence of Shakespeare's private life, is that most of it, like that of many equally prolific authors, was spent reading and writing. There is no evidence that he travelled, except in the mind. The rich, largely Mediterranean culture of the Renaissance, he encountered through reading. His private life was essentially his professional life – a life of words.

Sexual experience and paternal responsibility came early, however, with his bond to marry Anne Hathaway, issued on 28 November 1582, when he was eighteen and she twenty-six, and pregnant. Their daughter Susanna was baptised on 26 May 1583 and the twins Hamnet and Judith on 2 February 1585. Over the years, as in all families, there were deaths (Hamnet died, aged eleven, in 1596); marriages (Susanna to the physician John Hall in 1607, Judith to Thomas Quiney in 1616); a grandchild (Elizabeth, born to Susanna in 1608); even the peripheral anxieties, involving the children or their husbands, of adultery and illegitimacy. Shakespeare's will, signed on

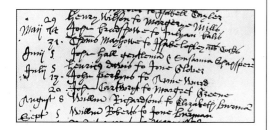

Above: The entry in the register of Holy Trinity Church for the marriage of Shakespeare's elder daughter, Susanna, in 1607

25 March 1616, leaving only a second-best bed to his widow, was once thought to indicate marital alienation, but it now seems clear that she would have inherited a substantial proportion of her husband's property automatically, and that the supposedly significant second-best bed may simply have been the one she preferred to sleep in, being accordingly set aside. We can read neither passion nor indifference into these bare facts. Even the story that Shakespeare met his death from a fever contracted after a Stratford drinking bout with his literary friends Michael Drayton and Ben Jonson is merely anecdotal.

What is clear is that at some time before 1592 Shakespeare had left his family in Stratford to begin a career as actor, playwright and shareholder in a London theatre company. In that year Robert Greene, in his valedictory pamphlet *A Groatsworth of Wit*, scathingly refers to him as an 'upstart crow, beautified with our feathers', seemingly implying emulation if not deliberate plagiarism. Henry Chettle, another playwright, immediately apologised for the part he had played in editing Greene's scurrilous pamphlet, by testifying to his personal knowledge of Shakespeare's civil demeanour, uprightness and honesty of dealing, and excellence and grace in writing – the first of numerous subsequent tributes, others referring to Shakespeare's gentleness, openness, and freedom of nature.

Ironically, twenty years later Shakespeare turned Greene's accusation into a prophecy, by using the plot and characters of Greene's most famous story *Pandosto* (1588) as the basis for his own play *The Winter's Tale*, but changing the fate of King Pandosto, Greene's incest-driven suicidal hero, into the reconciled and repentant life of his own equivalent, King Leontes. How Shakespeare had managed to insert himself into the London theatrical scene by 1592 has never been discovered. The

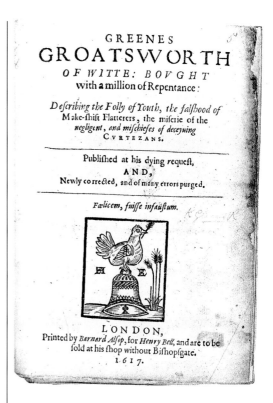

Above: The title page of a 1617 reprint of Robert Greene's *A Groatsworth of Wit* published 'at his dying request' in 1592

likeliest explanation is that at some point, following a natural aptitude or inclination, he attached himself to a theatre company passing through Stratford or Oxford on tour.

It is worth emphasising how recent a development was professional theatre in London when Shakespeare arrived. The first two public theatres and the first private theatre were all built in Liberties (districts outside the jurisdiction of the Sheriff and the City Corporation) on the north bank of the Thames in 1576. These were James Burbage's Theatre and Henry Laneman's Curtain in the Liberty of Holywell, Shoreditch, and Richard Farrant's first Blackfriar's theatre for the Chapel Children in the Liberty of Blackfriars, lying roughly between Ludgate Hill and the river, on the site of a disused Dominican priory. The Fortune Theatre, for which a

contract and measurements survive (indicating a square construction), was also on the north bank.

The persistent opposition to plays by the Corporation and the City reminds us that however free Shakespeare may have been from internal inhibition, external restraints were numerous – from the threat of arrest for vagabondage to players without aristocratic patronage, to the requirement that all plays be subject to the censorship of the Lord Chamberlain's Master of the Revels before performance, and to the licensing system of the Stationers' Company before printing. It may be that these external restraints also liberated the inventiveness of Shakespeare and his fellow-playwrights in finding both new subject-matter (such as England's fifteenth-century Wars of the Roses, as chronicled by historians Edward Halle and Raphael Holinshed) and new ways of dealing with contentious political questions such as republicanism or the assassination of a ruler (by disguising them within the framework of ancient Roman history).

Elizabethan audiences certainly saw parallels between the incidents in some of Shakespeare's plays and recent historical events. The prime example is *Richard II*, probably first performed in front of Queen Elizabeth's minister Sir Robert Cecil in a private house on 9 December 1595. The deposition of King Richard by Henry Bolingbroke was perceived as a possible encouragement to contemporary dissent. The deposition scene in Shakespeare's play was censored and was not printed or publicly performed, except on one occasion, until her successor King James was on the throne. That exceptional performance was at the Globe on 7 February 1601, specially commissioned by the Earl of Essex's supporters, on the day before his planned overthrow of Queen Elizabeth, and was clearly intended to raise support among the populace. It did not encourage any general uprising; the rebellion failed and Essex himself was executed on 25 February. After an explanation of the circumstances, no action was taken against the actors, who even performed before the Queen at Whitehall on the day before Essex's execution.

The Globe was one of a group of more famous theatres on the south bank of the Thames. They include the Swan, probably built in 1595, of which a Dutch visitor to London, Johannes De Witt, made a drawing in 1596. A copy by his friend Arend van Buchell (only discovered in 1888) depicts a circular building with three rows of seats in each of the three galleries; an apron stage, half covered by a canopy projecting into the arena or yard; two doors, but no central recess in the rear wall (elsewhere known as 'the discovery space'); and six boxes, apparently for spectators, above the stage. There is neither scenery nor curtains, and only one property, a bench. De Witt, in his Latin description, speaks of the theatre as the biggest and finest in London, holding 3000 people. The foundations of the Rose and Globe theatres have recently been identified and excavated; those of the Rose revealed a surprisingly small theatre, with the inner 'yard' or 'pit' and the stage area having a diameter of only 14.5 yards (13 metres).

The playing conditions of the Elizabethan public theatres, while differing in detail, seem to have in common several important elements, some of them inherited from the old inn-yards. These included a galleried auditorium, based on an amphitheatre of narrow diameter, as well as a canopied platform stage projecting into an uncovered yard and entrance doors in the rear wall of the stage. Performances were held in the after-noons, with elaborate costumes and little fixed scenery. The audience would generally be close to the actors, around and above them on three sides at least. Men and boys would play all the parts, including the women's. Other common features would have been the machinery for lowering the 'gods' from above, as well as a trap in the stage to indicate a nether world. Most theatres would provide incidental accompaniment to the perfor-mance with music and sound effects.

Modern theorists argue that theatre essen-tially requires only one person to perform, one person to watch and an empty space to play in. The experience may be rich and rewarding, but the means are minimal. Elizabethan theatre cannot properly be regarded as minimalist, despite the undoubted primacy given to the actor's body and voice. That primacy is nowhere more evident than in the Prince's advice to the visiting players in *Hamlet*. Apart from Horatio, the players seem to be Hamlet's only friends, and his views on acting must mirror Shakespeare's own:

> **Suit the action to the word, the word to the action, with this special observance, that you o'erstep not the modesty of nature. For anything so o'erdone is from the purpose of playing, whose end, both at the first and now, was and is to hold, as 'twere, the mirror up to nature, to show virtue her own feature, scorn her own image, and the very age and body of the time his form and pressure.**

[III.2.17-24]

This principle of deeply felt, truthful and eloquently expressed emotion remains as valid in the modern theatre as it is in *Hamlet*, although the interpretation of 'nature' will vary from age to age. The Elizabethan theatre developed as perhaps the first form of sensa-

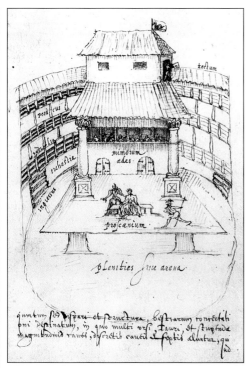

Above left: Bull and bear baiting in Germany
Above: The interior of the Swan Theatre as interpreted in a copy by Arend van Buchell of a lost drawing made by Johannes De Witt: '…built of a mass of flint stones and supported by wooden columns painted in such excellent imitation of marble…' c. 1596

tional mass entertainment, showing *all* its action, including violent death, to the audi-ence, rather than narrating it in the third person, as in classical theatre. In its appeal, it seems too, like the modern medium of televi-sion, to transcend all barriers of age, class, gender and education.

The theatre company with which Shakespeare can first be definitely associated is the Lord Chamberlain's under the patronage of Henry Carey, Baron Hunsdon. By 1595, Shakespeare is already named in accounts for payment for performances given before the Queen at Greenwich over Christmas. By that date at least two of his plays were in print: *The First Part of the Contention betwixt the two famous Houses of Yorke and Lancaster* (now known as *Henry VI Part Two*) and *The Most Lamentable Romaine Tragedie of Titus Andronicus*, both dated 1594. Shakespeare the actor is listed as one of ten 'principal comedians' in Ben Jonson's *Everyman In His Humour*, 1598, and as one of

eight 'principal tragedians' in Jonson's *Sejanus*, 1603. In 1598 Shakespeare became a shareholder in the Chamberlain's Men, being one of the co-operative syndicate building and running the Globe Theatre, with a tenth share. By 1603 he is one of the nine members of the newly-constituted King's Men, and in 1608 he is named as one of seven sharers in the lease of the Blackfriars private, indoor theatre, for which – with its opportunities for the effect of artificial lighting, music and the greater scenic spectacle associated with the court masque – many of his later plays must have been conceived. Records of his partici-pation in any company cease by 1613 when the first Globe was destroyed by fire.

It is hard to conceive of a more active professional and artistic involvement in every

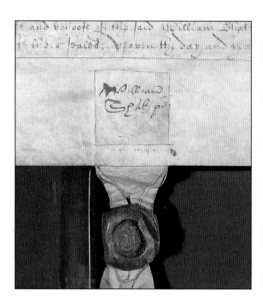

Above: Shakespeare's signature on the conveyance paper for a house in Blackfriars bought for £140 in 1613

aspect of the life of the theatre over two decades, at a crucial period of its development. Plays which he wrote, acted in, and probably, in our sense, directed, were performed at every available venue – in large public theatres, in small private theatres, at Court in command performances before Queen Elizabeth or King James I, and on tour in the provinces or abroad. Some eye-witness accounts of early performances do survive, although, frustratingly, they concentrate more on the details of plot and action than on stage effects. Simon Forman's manuscript *Booke of Plaies,* now in the Bodleian Library, contains notes of his visits to three of Shakespeare's plays – *Macbeth, The Winter's Tale* and *Cymbeline* – at the Globe, probably all in 1611.

One reason for our continuing interest in Shakespeare may be that as a writer he never seems to condition or pre-determine the meaning of his plays. The outcome of the action may always be the same, but every reading reveals new possibilities of interpre-

tation, every performance provides a unique and unrepeatable experience. Reading the text of a play isolates the reader; it allows and even encourages us to stop and interrogate the text for meaning at every point; it gives priority to our individual understanding and sensibility, stimulating reflection, reconsideration and interpretation. Seeing a play in performance requires a degree of surrender to a shared experience, in which the instantaneous impressions of our senses and our instinctive emotional responses are paramount and in which we are not given time to think, until it is all over, and too late.

By 1616 Shakespeare had died, aged only 52, and by 1623 his plays had been collected in the First Folio and permanently preserved. Individually they continued to be performed and printed as Quartos, and in 1632 the Folio itself was reprinted. The future King Charles I saw a performance of *Benedicte and Betteris* (or *Much Ado About Nothing*) given at Court by the King's Men in 1612; twenty years later he wrote this alternative title into his copy of the reprinted (Second) Folio. By 1642, the real conflict of the English Civil War had begun to drive the fictional conflicts of dramatic literature from the stage. On 2 September 1642, Parliament issued the *First Ordinance against Stage Plays and Interludes*, effectively closing all playhouses. The second Globe was pulled down on 15 April 1644, the Blackfriars on 6 August 1655, both to make tenements. The Bible, at least as interpreted by the Puritans, had achieved a temporary triumph. But when the political crisis was over, Shakespeare's plays returned to the centre of post-Restoration cultural life, providing, often in adapted form, a continuing opportunity both for the ephemeral excitement of live performance, and for the calmer pleasures of the text.

Tom Matheson

Redeeming time

Shakespeare wrote 38 plays between 1590 and 1614.

Henry VI Part Two
Henry VI Part Three
The Two Gentlemen of Verona
Titus Andronicus
Henry VI Part One
Richard III
The Comedy of Errors
The Taming of the Shrew
Love's Labour's Lost
Romeo and Juliet
King John
Richard II
A Midsummer Night's Dream
The Merchant of Venice
Henry IV Part One
Henry IV Part Two
Much Ado About Nothing
Henry V
Julius Caesar
The Merry Wives of Windsor
As You Like It
Hamlet
Twelfth Night
All's Well That Ends Well
Troilus and Cressida
Measure for Measure
Othello
King Lear
Macbeth
Antony and Cleopatra
Coriolanus
Timon of Athens
Pericles
Cymbeline
The Winter's Tale
The Tempest
Henry VIII
The Two Noble Kinsmen

Attempts to determine the order in which the plays were written are contentious because there is little documentary material and judgements must interpret internal evidence such as contemporary reference and stylistic development.

THE GLOBE RECONSTRUCTED

*On 23rd April 1988 building work eventually began. It was
directed towards the fulfilment of an international dream.*

The Globe and the eight comparable open-air theatres which were built to their own unique design between 1567 and 1614 were an oddly short-lived feature of England's theatre life. They could accommodate as many as three thousand spectators, when the biggest enclosed halls in London could hold barely half that number. They were short-lived, though, for two reasons. First, the players as well as the audiences came to prefer roofed theatres. Second, in the early years of professional acting there was a large proportion of citizens who hated plays. The Globe was pulled down in 1644, and its land and its bricks and timbers were re-used to make tenements.

The old open-air theatres were fringe activities located in the suburbs. The only illustrations of the Globe made in its own time are contained on a tiny inset map of Southwark done by a Londoner, John Norden, in 1660. It shows three broad circular arenas, each with what look like thatched roofs topping the ring of galleries. Norden's inset was put into his larger engraving of London as seen from the church which is now Southwark Cathedral, done in 1593. That shows the Rose as a tall six-sided theatre with a flag flying and a cover over its stage, on the northern side of the circle of galleries. The excavation of the Rose's foundations in 1989 show that it was in fact a fourteen-sided polygon. The early illustrations were vague and impressionistic.

For many years it was thought that the only clear illustration of the first Globe was in an engraving of London done by the Dutchman

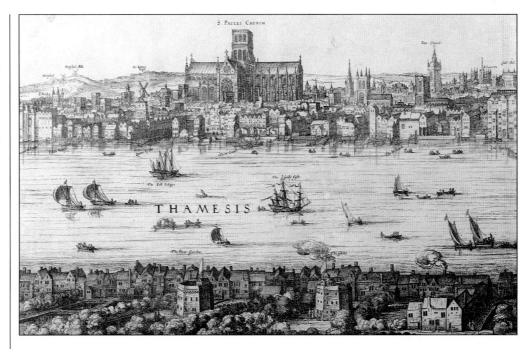

THAMESIS

Cornelius Visscher. Issued in Amsterdam in 1616, it shows a tall eight-sided structure with inward-sloping sides and windows at three levels. This picture is still regularly used as the only depiction of the original Globe, which burned down in 1613. In his famous 'Long View' of London, done like Norden's panorama from the tower of Southwark Cathedral, in the 1630s, the Bohemian Wenceslas Hollar gave a very different impression of the second Globe, built in 1614 on the same foundations to replace the original theatre. His theatre was three times as broad as it was high, and had a double-gable front to its stage cover, which faced in almost the opposite direction to the Rose's.

Above: View of London, 1616
An engraving by C.J. Visscher showing the Bear Garden and the Globe as tall octagonal buildings

Visscher's illustration, however, was shown in 1948 to be based on a copper engraving of 1572, before even the original Globe was built in London; it even featured some fairly fanciful inserts based on hearsay to fill in more recent structures. Thus his depiction of the Globe was largely imaginary, and certainly unreliable. In fact only the most rudimentary picture of the original Globe survives, in the shape of Norden's crude and tiny inset of a circular, squat, thatched theatre.

Hollar's second Globe looks a much more plausible shape for a large theatre than

19

Constructing a playhouse

The frame of the saide howse to be sett square and to conteine ffowerscore of lawfull assize everye waie square withoutt and fiftie fiue foote of like assize everye waie within, with a good suer and a strong foundacion of pyles, brick, lyme and sand bothe without & within, to be wroughte one foote of assize att the leist aboue the grounde; And the saide fframe to conteine three Stories in heighth …

The contract for the Fortune Theatre

The theatrical experience

Nay, when you look into my galleries,
How bravely they're trimm'd up, you all shall swear
You're highly pleas'd to see what's set down there:
Stories of men and women, mix'd together,
Fair ones with foul, like sunshine in wet weather;
Within one square a thousand heads are laid
So close that all of heads the room seems made …

Middleton & Dekker, *The Roaring Girl*, 1611

The cost of theatre-going

… anyone who remains on the level standing pays only one English penny: but if he wants to sit, he is let in at a further door, and there he gives another penny. If he desires to sit on a cushion in the most comfortable place of all, where he not only sees everything well, but can also be seen, then he gives yet another English penny at another door. And in the pauses of the comedy, food and drink are carried round …

Thomas Platter, 1599

Cornelius Visscher's. In the 1980s, moreover, Hollar's whole panorama was proved to be a remarkably accurate piece of drawing. The scholar John Orrell laid his panorama on a modern Ordnance Survey map, picking out the buildings in Hollar's scene that are still there, and found his positioning remarkably precise. The second Globe stood only a few hundred yards from his observation point, so his was clearly the best of the few illustrations. Although it was not of Shakespeare's original theatre but its replacement, a legal testimony that the second Globe was built on the foundations of the first at least suggested that measuring Hollar carefully would give an accurate set of dimensions for the first Globe. When in the autumn of 1989 a fragment of the Globe's foundations was dug up, it confirmed Hollar's general accuracy. It was on that basis that the designers of the new Globe made their plans.

Work began on the reconstruction of Shakespeare's Globe in Southwark on 23 April 1988. It was the culmination of years of fund raising and energetic campaigning by enthus-iasts led by the inspired commitment of Sam Wanamaker. Plans for a replica building had started to gain support a hundred years earlier, but they were delayed by the disruption of two World Wars and scholarly debate about architectural detail. The new Globe's design has used the archaeological evidence and Hollar's picture as faithfully as possible, but there are still many uncertainties. There are other bits of evidence which give some help, notably a contract made out in 1600 for the Fortune playhouse, built by the carpenter who erected the Globe the year before. It gives the exact height for each gallery level, and specifies that the stage should project out from the gallery tiring house to 'the middle of the yard'. The Fortune was built square, whereas the Globe was a twenty-sided polygon made to look circular. But it seems that the Fortune's auditorium was designed to have twenty bays. There is a remarkable consistency in the basic evidence provided by the archaeologists, by the early illustrators, and finally by the modern architects who have studied and used the traditional sixteenth-century carpentry techniques to fix the design of the reconstruction.

Andrew Gurr

Below: The first theatre to be built on London's Bankside was Philip Henslowe's Rose in 1587. The photograph shows an aerial view of its excavation in 1989.
Below right: The new theatre under construction at the International Shakespeare Globe Centre.

Theories of the Globe's Shape

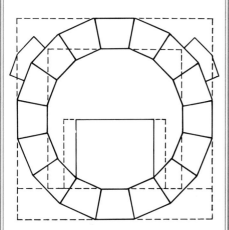

Above: Inconsistencies in early panoramic views may be explained by the representation of theatres as polygons being merely a device of perspective drawing. However, what we know of Elizabethan constructional techniques makes it unlikely that the buildings were perfectly round.

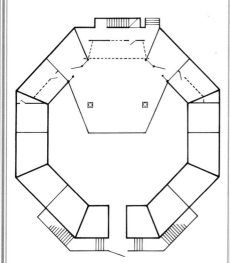

Above: Basing his interpretation upon Visscher's engraving and upon theories of an 'inner stage', John Cranford Adams made precisely detailed calculations that influenced thinking in the 1930s. His plan was effectively discredited in 1948.

THE CHANGING STAGE

Despite shifts in cultural and theatrical fashion, succeeding generations have rediscovered the excitement of Shakespeare's plays in performance.

Much of what we know about the circumstances of production and the staging of Shakespeare's plays in his own time has been gleaned from the plays themselves. His theatre offered relatively little to interest the eye; there was a much greater emphasis upon the spoken word. In the Prologue to *Romeo and Juliet* Shakespeare urges his audience to attend 'with patient ears' [13]. Similarly, he suggests that an ambitious visual dimension can be created through listening:

> Think, when we talk of horses, that you see
> them
> Printing their proud hoofs i'th' receiving earth;
> For 'tis your thoughts that now must deck our
> kings,
> Carry them here and there, jumping o'er times,
> Turning th' accomplishment of many years
> Into an hour-glass: for the which supply,
> Admit me Chorus to this history,
> Who Prologue-like your humble patience pray,
> Gently to hear, kindly to judge, our play.
> [*Henry V*, Prologue, 26-34]

The Elizabethan open, or thrust, stage requires more time for exits and entrances but allows more flexible, fluid action, draws audiences into the conspiracies of overhearing (in *Love's Labour's Lost, Much Ado, Othello* for instance) and permits the convention of relocation once the stage has been cleared of actors, as is reflected in the scene divisions marked by Shakespeare's first editors in 1623. But above all, it invites the imaginative participation of an audience:

> Work, work your thoughts...
> And eke out our performance with your mind.
> [III.25 & 35]

Other features of the Elizabethan theatre form an integral part of the plays. The balcony forces the physical separation between Romeo and Juliet which makes their words so necessary for communicating passion and feeling. The raised platform stage offers more exciting possibilities than that of mere convenience for a grave-trap. The Ghost of Hamlet's father can roam disturbingly in the midst of the audience:

> Well said, old mole! Canst work i'th'earth so
> fast?
> [I.5.162]

The cue for 'Music of hautboys under the stage' in *Antony and Cleopatra* draws the audience into sharing the eerie uncertainty of the four anonymous soldiers stationed 'in every corner of the stage' [IV.3.9].

The discovery space permits the intimacy of the bed-chamber and makes possible revelations such as Falstaff sleeping, Hermione's statue or Ferdinand and Miranda discovered playing the mating game of chess. A scene which was established in this intimate interior space could then spill out to occupy the whole of the thrust stage. Audience participation, therefore, was an integral dimension in the creative process. There was no expectation of naturalism and the audience would respond to the verbal cues for location and

Above: A wildly imaginative nineteenth century reconstruction of a perfomance of *Henry IV* at 'the Old Globe in Shakespeare's Day' featuring an audience of 'masked and pipe-smoking ladies'.

setting. The daylight made no distinction between the play-world and the audience, and so darkness too would have to be imagined. Calling for or carrying lights makes gloom implicit and allowed Shakespeare to exploit not just the passage of time but more powerfully the intrigue, mystery, romance or danger of scenes at night.

The strongest position for an Elizabethan

actor was what today might be described as downstage, though the term reflects the later practice of using raked stages that slope down towards an audience seated on just one side. On Shakespeare's stage an actor standing at the front of a thrust stage with his audience on three sides was at the hub of the theatrical experience, and the proximity to more members of the audience creates a sense of privileged intimacy that can lend force to the function of soliloquy. A king or a beggar could share his thoughts with a diverse audience.

During the reigns of James I and Charles I there were shifts in public taste and a growing interest in the effects made possible by the stage machinery that was used in the development of court masques. However, any gradual evolution of new theatrical forms was prevented by the English Civil War, which caused the closing of the theatres from 1642 to 1660. The disruption that occurred during just 18 years of what is now a 400-year tradition of Shakespearean production, might superficially seem no more than an historical hiccough. In fact it proved more significant.

Puritan disapproval of stage representations had been voiced before Shakespeare began his career, but attacks upon what was presented on the Jacobean and Caroline stage gained in frequency and vehemence. Parliament's *First Ordinance against Stage Plays and Interludes* was issued in September 1642. Though it was resisted and had to be reinforced by a second ordinance in 1647, habits of popular entertainment were modified. Soldiers were employed in raids upon the Cockpit and Red Bull in 1643; the Globe theatre that had been rebuilt in 1613 was pulled down in 1644, as were the Fortune and Phoenix in 1649, the Blackfriars in 1655 and the Hope or Bear Garden in 1656 after seven of its bears had been shot. There were a few private performances during the period of the Commonwealth but the popular appeal of

Above: Sir Thomas Killigrew, manager of the first Theatre Royal, Drury Lane, from 1663 (in a portrait by Sir Anthony Van Dyck)
Right: Prince James Duke of York playing royal or 'real' tennis, 1641

theatre was lost.

With the Restoration of King Charles II in 1660 there was suddenly a very different spirit. In the post-war world an aristocratic society was eager to redefine itself and explore new attitudes towards morality and sexual relationships. When one of James Shirley's plays was revived it was provided with a new Prologue which acknowledged that:

> **In our Old Plays, the humor Love and passion**
> **Like Doublet, Hose, and Cloak, are out of**
>   **fashion:**
> **That which the world call'd Wit in Shakspears**
>   **Age,**
> **Is laught at, as improper for our Stage.**
>
> *Love Tricks*, 1667

The eagerness of the aristocracy to indulge their new-found liberty and laughter was reflected in the Letters Patent that were

THE HIGH BORNE PRINCE IAMES DVKE OF YORKE. borne October = the 13. 1633.

Sould by Tho: Ienner at the South Entry of the Exchange.

granted to Sir William Davenant and Thomas Killigrew to establish two companies. No longer was the theatre to be the focus for a brand of popular entertainment that might share premises with spectacles such as bear-baiting or cock-fighting. Whereas in Elizabethan times the weekly audience had been perhaps 24,000, the new theatre buildings had a capacity of about 400. They were to cater exclusively for the court circle and the new plays held the mirror up to a narrow, somewhat self-regarding segment of society. The Duke's Men first performed at Salisbury Court, then in a converted tennis court near Lincoln's Inn Fields before moving into the purpose-built and much grander Dorset Garden Theatre in 1671. It had seats for just over a thousand people. The Theatre Royal, Drury Lane, was built for the King's Men in 1663. It was an explicit condition of the Royal Warrants that actresses be cast in the women's rôles and the plays by Shakespeare that were most readily absorbed into the repertory were those which offered 'breeches parts'. The opportunities that Shakespeare provided for his boy actors to play girls playing boys ('What, shall we turn to men?' says Nerissa in *The Merchant of Venice*) were eagerly seized upon by actresses relishing the opportunity to show rather more than a well-turned ankle. The theatre offered opportunities for social advancement to such as Moll Davis and Nell Gwynn. A King who was prepared to lend his coronation robes as theatrical costume was eager to take something in return.

Greater concern for the audience's creature comforts and a developing interest in the possibilities of scenic display led to the development of stage-shapes and theatre buildings in which the demarcation line between audience and actors would eventually be more sharply drawn. Side and stage boxes were created for those members of the audience who visited the theatre primarily to be seen and to enhance their own social status. The wish to project a thoroughly modern image led to the revision and refinement of the old plays. The rights to perform Shakespeare's plays were divided between the two companies and in 1662 Davenant conflated *Measure for Measure* and *Much Ado*. Two years later his *Macbeth* was a considerable success. The witches flew across the stage and Macbeth was given a clarifying, deathly line:

Farewell vain World, and what's most vain in it, Ambition.

Davenant and John Dryden were uneasy collaborators on an adaptation of *The Tempest* which was performed in 1667. They sought to establish a pattern of symmetry, introducing Hippolito as 'a Man who had never seen a Woman' as well as sisters for Miranda and Caliban and a lover for Ariel. The production proved enormously successful, holding the stage until the late eighteenth century. Dryden's *Troilus and Cressida* (1679) cut through what is complex or ambivalent in Shakespeare's play, preferring a certainty of moral judgement:

I new model'd the Plot; threw out many unnecessary persons; improv'd those characters which were begun, and left unfinish'd: as Hector, Troilus, Pandarus and Thersites… I made with no small trouble, an Order and Connection of all the Scenes…no leaping from Troy to the Grecian Tents, and thence back again in the same Act; but a due proportion of time allow'd for every motion…
Dryden's *Preface*

Enthusiasm for sensation-seeking prompted the inclusion of scenes of attempted rape in *Cymbeline, Coriolanus* and *King Lear*. Edward Ravenscroft's *Titus Andronicus* (1678) included the on-stage torture of Aaron, the gruesome revelation of 'the head and hands of Demetrius and Chiron hanging up against the wall' and, after Tamora had stabbed her baby, Aaron offered to eat it. Shakespeare had incorporated elements of the masque in plays such as *As You Like It, Timon of Athens, Cymbeline* and *The Tempest*, but the recent exile of the English Court also prompted the pursuit of fashions of visual spectacle adopted from France. In reworking *Timon of Athens* (1678), Thomas Shadwell claimed: 'I can truly say, I have made it into a Play'. For Timon's feast he devised a full-length masque of Cupid and Bacchus with music written by Henry Purcell. The same partnership had contributed to an operatic and scenically elaborate development of the

Above:
Nell Gwynn, actress and King's mistress (in a portrait by Peter Lely)

Above: Thomas Betterton, whose performances as Hamlet and Othello were especially notable for their intensity of feeling and for the emotional demands they made upon his audience

Davenant/Dryden *The Tempest* in 1674 and Purcell's *Dido and Aeneas* would be incorporated into a production of *Measure for Measure, or Beauty the Best Advocate* in 1699. The imperative that promoted adaptation is reflected in:

> **Shakespeares sublime in vain entic'd the**
> **Throng,**
> **Without the charm of Purcels Syren Song.**
>
> Granville, *The Jew of Venice*, 1701

In 1681 Nahum Tate adapted *King Lear* and his version was to hold the stage for 150 years. It was approved by Dr Johnson and acted by Thomas Betterton, David Garrick (with further modifications), John Philip Kemble and Edmund Kean. Tate regarded Shakespeare's play as: 'a Heap of Jewels, unstrung and unpolisht yet…dazling in their Disorder'. He 'seiz'd the Treasure' and set about 'to rectifie what was wanting in the Regularity and Probability of the Tale', promising that he 'us'd less Quaintness of Expression' in his 'Revival…with Alterations'. Lear, Gloucester and Kent survive, the Fool is

omitted altogether and Tate introduces a new character, Arante, who serves as a Nurse and confidante for Cordelia. The focus of the story became:

> **A Love betwixt Edgar and Cordelia… This**
> **renders Cordelia's Indifference and her**
> **Father's Passion in the first Scene probable…**
> **The Distress of the Story is evidently**
> **heightened by it; and it particularly gave**
> **Occasion of a New Scene or Two… This**
> **Method necessarily threw me on making the**
> **Tale conclude in a Success to the innocent**
> **distrest Persons: Otherwise I must have**
> **incumbred the Stage with dead Bodies,**
> **which Conduct makes many Tragedies**
> **conclude with unseasonable Jests.**
>
> Dedication to *The History of King Lear*, 1681

Tate's ending is resonantly confident with Edgar, now married to Cordelia, saying:

> **Thy bright example shall convince the World**
> **(Whatever Storms of Fortune are decreed)**
> **That Truth and Virtue shall at last succeed.**
>
> *The History of King Lear*, 1681

Above far left: An unfinished portrait of David Garrick by Johan Zoffany c. 1770
Above left: *A sentence; come prepare*
Charles Macklin as Shylock, 1775
Above: John Philip Kemble, actor-manager at Drury Lane from 1788 and at Covent Garden from 1803
Right: *Does any here know me?*
Edmund Kean as Lear, 1820

When the two patent companies amalgamated in 1682, it gave Thomas Betterton access to a wider range of parts. From several accounts his Hamlet was remarkable. His countenance was said to turn:

> **instantly on the Sight of his Father's Spirit, as**
> **pale as his Neckcloth, when every Article of**
> **his Body seem'd to be affected with a Tremor**
> **inexpressible.**
>
> *The Laureate*, 1740

Few of the early Restoration actors and none of the actresses could learn their craft by watching more experienced members of their profession, but it was necessary for them to study the manners and deportment of the audience they sought to reflect. In 1695 Betterton led a breakaway group of actors to re-establish a second company. A manual of what had presumably worked for him, was published in Betterton's name:

> You must lift up or cast down, your eyes, according to the nature of the things you speak of; thus if of heaven, your eyes naturally are lifted up; if of earth, or hell, or any thing terrestrial, they are as naturally cast down… In swearing, or taking a solemn oath, or attestation of any thing, to the verity of what you say, you turn your eyes, and in the same action lift up your hand to the thing you swear by, or attest.
>
> *The History of the English Stage*, 1741

Shakespeare's plays became a focus for the virtuoso skills of actors with the talent to hold and sway an audience for whom the play might be less important than the social opportunities that visiting the theatre afforded. An emphasis upon the statuesque pose and strut favoured by society led to the mannered, declamatory style of acting developed by James Quin.

In 1741 Charles Macklin chose to play Shakespeare's text rather than George Granville's adaptation of *The Merchant of Venice* and he broke with the tradition of playing Shylock in a vein of broad comedy; instead he stressed the sullen villainy of the character. In the trial scene he presented implacable resolution, tinged with malevolence of a frightening intensity. Later that year Garrick played Richard III, moving from hypocrite and politician to warrior and hero. He was an immediate sensation. In the following seven months he played 18 different parts. In contrast to the sonorous, heavyweight Quin, Garrick was graceful and harmonious in voice and movement, earning praise as a man among puppets. It was recognised that he represented a turning point in theatrical tradition:

> Garrick, then young and light and alive in every muscle and in every feature, [came] bounding on the stage… – heavens what a transition! – it seemed as if a whole century had been stept over in the transition of a single scene; old things were done away, and a new order at once brought forward, bright and luminous, and clearly destined to dispel the barbarisms and bigotry of a tasteless age, too long attached to the prejudices of custom, and superciliously devoted to the illusions of imposing declamation. This heaven-born actor was then struggling to emancipate his audience from the slavery they were resigned to…
>
> Richard Cumberland, *Memoirs*, 1806

He adapted Shakespeare's text where he judged it necessary and his version of *Hamlet* 'rescued that noble play from all the rubbish of the fifth act' removing the gravediggers, the fencing match and the deaths of Rosencrantz, Guildenstern and Ophelia. Rather than die of poison Gertrude was driven mad with remorse. Accounts of his own performance as Hamlet testify to his ability to hold a packed theatre in total silence, so powerfully did he convey the depths of his terror as he turned and saw the Ghost.

When Macklin appeared as Macbeth at Covent Garden in 1773 he was in his seventies. He broke with the tradition of wearing the suit of scarlet and gold and the tail wig appropriate to a contemporary general. Although his Lady Macbeth appeared in modern dress, he:

> whose eye and mind were ever intent on his profession, saw the absurdity of exhibiting a Scotch character, existing many years before the Norman Conquest, in this manner, and therefore very properly abandoned it for the old Caledonian habit. He showed the same attention to the subordinate characters as well as to the scenes, decorations, music and other incidental parts of the performance.
>
> William Cooke, *Memoirs of Charles Macklin*, 1806

The public's appetite for realistic devices in pantomime and more elaborate effects of scenery and stage lighting created pressure to increase the size of the two theatres. Covent Garden had been built in 1732 and was enlarged in 1784 and again in 1791. Garrick's improvements to Drury Lane in 1762 excluded the audience from the stage and back-stage areas and increased the size of the auditorium so that it held about 2000. The building that had been constructed in 1672 was eventually condemned and pulled down in 1793. The new theatre which opened the following year had a capacity of 3611:

> Since the stages of Drury Lane and Covent Garden have been so enlarged in their dimensions as to be henceforward theatres for spectators rather than playhouses for hearers, it is hardly to be wondered at if their managers and directors encourage those representations, to which their structure is best adapted. The splendour of the scenes, the ingenuity of the machinist and the rich display of dresses, aided by the captivating charms of music, now in a great degree supersede the labours of the poet.
>
> Richard Cumberland, 1806

Covent Garden was rebuilt in 1809 to accommodate just under 3000.

The first production in the enlarged Drury Lane theatre was *Macbeth* in March 1794 and although John Philip Kemble cut the appearance of Banquo's ghost, he presented the witches in a radically new way, restoring for them something of the disturbing ambivalences of Shakespeare's text. The tradition was for them to be comic human figures bedecked in mittens, caps and lace-edged aprons but

Above left: The auditorium of the Theatre Royal, Drury Lane, in 1775. It would be rebuilt in 1793 with five tiers.
Above: Kemble and Sarah Siddons in *Macbeth*
Below left: The first Theatre Royal, Covent Garden, on its reopening in 1792. The horse-shoe tiers and cast-iron columns were decorated in pearl-white and red with gilt ornament. The theatre was destroyed by fire in 1808.

Kemble made them preternatural beings; black, white, blue, grey spirits who were unearthly figures of disturbing power. As Hamlet, Kemble was solemn and deliberate and indeed generally he displayed a formal, statuesque dignity, working to craft his skill as an actor. His sister, Sarah Siddons, displayed a more instinctive, natural talent. Accounts of her performances glow in praise of her magnificence and grandeur as well as affirming her capacity to convey a compelling truthfulness. She excelled in tragedy and was particularly effective in conveying wronged suffering which evoked both tears and respect. She was the first actress to emphasise Lady Macbeth's protective love for her husband. Twenty-five years' experience convinced her that although Lady Macbeth's driving ambition is substantially responsible for Macbeth's killing of Duncan, her sleep walking scene is evidence of the remorse she suffers. Audiences claimed they could smell the blood. She refused to allow the dictates of fashion to influence her costume, preferring gowns inspired by Greek statues.

The early nineteenth century theatres were huge spaces more conducive to spectacle than to hearing the actors' words, yet though many struggled in a hostile environment Edmund Kean triumphed. His emotionally committed, passionate and dangerous style captured the mood of romanticism that prevailed. 'To see Kean act', Coleridge wrote, was 'like reading Shakespeare by flashes of lightning' and Byron praised his Richard III as 'Life, nature, truth, without exaggeration or diminution'. Hazlitt described the final scene:

> He fought like one drunk with wounds: and the attitude in which he stands with his hands stretched out, after his sword is taken from him, had a preternatural and terrific grandeur, as if his will could not be disarmed, and the very phantoms of his despair had a withering power.
>
> *A View of the English Stage*, 1818

Shylock also allowed Kean to exploit his talent for the presentation of active villainy. Tribute was paid to his capacity to convey depths of humanity in Macbeth as he looked at the blood on his hands and realised what he had done. His style of acting contrasted starkly with that of Kemble. Leigh Hunt declared: 'It was as sure a thing as Nature against Art, or tears against cheeks of stone' [*The Tatler*, 1831].

William Charles Macready served as manager of Covent Garden and later Drury Lane, bringing greater discipline to the rehearsal process. He was determined to rehearse with the same earnestness as he acted. Macready went back to the original texts and although he cut and shaped the

Above: Portrait of William Charles Macready
Right: The playbill reflects the priorities of popular taste in the eighteenth century.

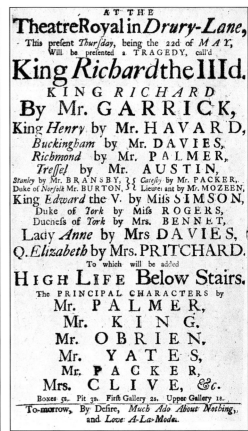

plays he did instil a fresh integrity into Shakespearean production. Whilst earning praise for the intelligent worthiness of his performances, he did not match the monumental dignity of Kemble nor the inspired unpredictability of Kean. However, in scenes of domestic intensity he was supreme. His willingness to adopt a low-toned whisper worked well as he confided to Lady Macbeth that he had killed Duncan.

The two patent theatres had jealously guarded their monopoly but competition did develop from some half-dozen minor theatres whose efforts to circumvent the law created variety theatre with animal acts and melodramatic dumb-shows where the dialogue was presented on placards. Straight plays could only be performed with the insertion of interludes and the addition of not fewer than six songs. In 1741 *Richard III* had been presented 'At the late Theatre in Goodman's Fields' during the interval of a concert.

An immediate consequence of the Theatre

Regulation Act of 1843 which repealed the monopoly of Covent Garden and Drury Lane was the transformation of Sadler's Wells from being a home for aquatic melodrama into a legitimate theatre dedicated to Shakespeare. Thirty-four of his plays were presented during the eighteen years from 1844 in which Samuel Phelps was manager. He sought to make the scenic displays that his audience expected serve the playwright's text and his staging of *A Midsummer Night's Dream* in 1853 was praised for judicious rather than extravagant expenditure. The action in the wood near Athens was played behind a gauze. There was no scene-shifting, but 'as in dreams one scene is made to glide insensibly into another'. The same critic wrote of Phelps' productions generally:

Above: Samuel Phelps played Macbeth as a 'half-barbarous warrior chief' in 1864.
Above right: Charles Kean was criticised for the 'diminution of regal pomp' in his production of *Macbeth* at the Princess's Theatre, 1853

The scenery is always beautiful, but it is not allowed to draw attention from the poet, with whose whole conception it is made to blend in the most perfect harmony. The actors are content also to be subordinated to the play, learn doubtless at rehearsals how to subdue excesses of expression that by giving undue force to one part would destroy the balance of the whole, and blend their work in such a way as to produce everywhere the right emphasis.

Henry Morley,
Journal of a London Playgoer, 1851-66

The ending of the monopoly of the two patent theatres also allowed a focus upon Shakespeare at the Princess's Theatre where Charles Kean took pride in the historical and scholarly detail of his research. In his 1857 production of *Richard II*, he inserted a scene before the Westminster Hall abdication. Taking his cue from York's later description he presented a living repetition, portrayed with scrupulous accuracy, of the arrival of Richard and Bolingbroke in London. He used music, bells and dancing to greet Bolingbroke and for Richard's processional entrance there were murmurs and groans from what was described as a cast of five or six hundred people. It won praise as the most marvellous scenic illusion ever attempted. Kean argued that such scenes were not for mere show or idle spectacle and he defended the way in which he had presented *Henry V*:

let me refer to the siege of Harfleur, as presented on this stage ... it was a correct representation of what actually had taken place; the engines of war, the guns, banners, fire balls, the attack and defence, the barricades at the breach, the conflagration within the town, the assault and capitulation, were all taken from the account left to us by a priest who accompanied the army, was an eye-witness, and whose Latin MS. is now in the British Museum.

Charles Kean's farewell address, 1859

As actor-manager of the Lyceum from 1878, Henry Irving showed a similar enthusiasm for the visual impact of his productions. When he revived *Macbeth* in 1888, the noble pictures presented by the scenery and costumes were highly praised. However, there is no doubting the emotional magnetism of his performance and that of Ellen Terry which thrilled the audience with suspense and dread. As Irving gave his explanation of why he had killed the grooms, Lady Macbeth encouraged him with small involuntary gestures and inarticulate movements of her lips before she collapsed and was carried out, red hair flowing in the torchlight. Their earlier performances in *The Merchant of Venice* (1879) and in *Much Ado* (1882) had been acclaimed as true to life, and the reviews are characterised by an attention to textual detail which suggests that audiences had started listening to Shakespeare again.

The academic inquiry and historical reconstruction favoured by Charles Kemble, Charles Kean and Henry Irving paradoxically prompted a diametrically opposed style of presentation. By bringing similar earnestness and scholarship to the recreation of Elizabethan acting conditions, William Poel necessarily adopted a much sparer and more economical approach to performance. Freeing the theatre from oppressive, expensive and restrictive settings, he was committed to a rapid delivery of the verse and he was sensitive to the patterning of scenes. Defending the function of Lady Macduff and her children, he argued that if she had been Lady Macbeth then Duncan would not have been murdered. In April 1881 Poel staged the First Quarto text of *Hamlet*. Ophelia's funeral was traditionally a state occasion of pomp and procession, but he observed the text's instruction of 'maimed rites' and had just a single priest officiating. His efforts drew mockery, derision and pedantic quibbling, but George Bernard Shaw recognised the integrity of the approach:

The more I see of these performances by the Elizabethan Stage Society, the more I am convinced that … any play performed on a platform amidst the audience gets closer home to its hearers than when it is presented as a picture framed by a proscenium.

Saturday Review, 2 July 1896

Harley Granville-Barker developed Poel's work but he felt that it was necessary to temper the commitment to an Elizabethan world picture with an awareness of contemporary culture. He removed the footlights because of the unnatural effects and shadows they produced, preferring down-lighting with its surgical evenness. Granville-Barker shared Poel's belief in the primacy of the words and he saw the task of directing as analogous to orchestrating the musical patterns of the drama. His productions of *The Winter's Tale* and *Twelfth Night* in 1912, and *A Midsummer Night's Dream* two years later, challenged convention and tradition by removing all pomp, pageantry and stage embellishment. To some extent Granville-Barker's work anticipated Bertolt Brecht's theory and practice, providing the basis for many productions in the second half of the twentieth century. In arguing for a socially committed theatre Brecht developed techniques to discourage an audience from the uncritical empathy that picture-frame staging invites. Constant lighting, choric commentary and an audience grouped around an acting area, so that they register each other's responses, take us back to Shakespeare's time.

The great rivalry that existed between John Philip Kemble and Edmund Kean at the beginning of the nineteenth century has been paralleled in the twentieth century by the achievements of John Gielgud and Laurence Olivier. Gielgud has brought sensitivity and distinction to Shakespeare's poetry, triumphing in the line of noble characters, such as Richard II and Prospero. Olivier attempted neither of those but the impact of

Below far left: Henry Irving
Below left: Ellen Terry
Below: William Poel's production of the First Quarto *Hamlet* was revived for a single perfomance in the Carpenters' Hall, 1900

Above: Bertolt Brecht developed theories of theatre for a scientific age.

Above: John Gielgud as Prospero at the Shakespeare Memorial Theatre, 1957

Above: Olivier first played Richard III in 1944 and directed himself in his 1955 film.

his Richard III and Othello prompted comparison with the excitement of Kean. Olivier's achievement within the medium of film is some measure of how his theatrical performances transcended the limitations of the proscenium arch stage.

The Shakespeare Memorial Theatre (now the Royal Shakespeare Theatre) in Stratford-upon-Avon has been the proving ground for the aspirations of Shakespearean actors and directors since the present building was opened in 1932. It was constructed with a picture-frame arch and a narrow, stepped forestage that could distance the audience even further from the action. From about 1960 principles of continuous staging have led to infrequent use of a front curtain and there have been various attempts to establish a more Elizabethan relationship between actor and audience. This follows the interest engendered by Tyrone Guthrie's work from 1953 at The Shakespearean Festival Theatre, Stratford, Ontario. In Stratford, England, the stage has been built further forward, and in 1972, a white box sought to create a one-room experience. For the 1976 season, timbered balconies were wrapped round the stage in an attempt to create something more like a

Shakespearean thrust-stage. Experimental work in a hut that had once been a rehearsal space (The Other Place) has allowed Royal Shakespeare Company actors to work in something like the close-up detail of the television studio and audiences have been encouraged to be variously voyeurs, observers, participants, fellow travellers or shocked conspirators.

In April 1986 Stratford's third theatre, the Swan, was created within the shell of the original 1879 theatre. The relationship between actor and audience is both intimate and yet capable of an epic scale. The height and the placing of the balconies demand an extra dimension from actors more used to showing a part to an audience or to providing the kind of minimalist performance that works so well on screen. The shape of the building puts the actor at the hub of the experience and the thrust stage provides an open platform which gives an uncluttered view from all sides. There is no single perspective. The strength of the design is that, as the audience wraps around the stage, a range of experience is provided. The view of the stage puts the action not in the fixed visual context of 'setting' but in the human arena of an embracing audience.

What takes place on the stage is tempered, intensified, modified, qualified and complicated by members of the audience reading the response of others. The use of artificial light does not negate our bond with audiences of 400 years ago because the shape of the Swan stage resists exclusive lighting. We can never quite forget where we are, nor with whom we share the experience.

Perhaps it is fondness that encourages us to think that Shakespeare might recognise something of the theatres that he knew in the vitality of theatrical experience that the Swan and similar stages can offer. From what the plays suggest about Shakespeare's development as a dramatist, we also believe that he would have been excited by the potential (not least financial) of film, television and multimedia ventures. Technology that makes possible analysis and replication of intonation and vocal textures, precise comparison between the printed text and its visualisation in different video versions and most recently Karaoke *Macbeth* on CD-ROM does essentially promote an emphasis upon the words that are the dramatist's building blocks. Nowadays the text may be treated with varying degrees of respect, paraphrased or re-ordered, but such is its primacy for so many in an audience that it cannot be disregarded. That is not to deny the function of spectacle, for ballet adaptations such as those by Ashton and MacMillan show that sometimes Shakespeare's words can be heard more clearly when they are unspoken. But crucially it is his words and the need to listen to them to which we must return:

What, a play toward? I'll be an auditor –
An actor too, perhaps, if I see cause.
A Midsummer Night's Dream, [III.1.72-3]

Keith Parsons and Pamela Mason

'TO MAKE THE EVEN TRUTH IN PLEASURE FLOW'

The Early Production History of *All's Well That End's Well*

All's Well That Ends Well was probably written between 1601 and 1604 and may well have been performed around this time. There are no records of any subsequent performances until March 1741, when it was added to the list of Shakespeare's plays in production at Henry Gifford's theatre in Goodman's Fields, in what was probably a relatively full version. The play was ousted, however, because of Gifford's desire to give young David Garrick as much opportunity as possible to play Shakespeare's tragedies. The play was not performed again as Shakespeare wrote it until Benson's 1916 production at Stratford-upon-Avon.

On 24 February 1756, Garrick, now manager at Drury Lane, produced an adaptation of the play that quickened the pace and strongly focused attention on Parolles, the 'braggart-soldier', and the farcical elements in the play. This was at the expense of the poetry, dramatic structure and several significant characters. Helena was reduced to passive sentimentality. After Garrick's production, *All's Well That Ends Well* was not seen again at Drury Lane until John Philip Kemble's adaptation in 1794. Garrick had emphasised farce; Kemble shaped the play into a sentimental comedy. Helena was more important yet she was not the strong woman of Shakespeare's vision but selfless, placid and docile. Kemble's version with Helena as 'Virtue Rewarded' was immensely popular.

There were no productions of note between Kemble's and Benson's. There was an extraordinary extravaganza, where Helena was acted and *sung* by a 'Miss Inverarity' and a mediocre performance in 1895 by the Irving Dramatic Club, which was witnessed by George Bernard Shaw. In Helena, Shaw found his 'New Woman'; the Countess he saw as 'the most beautiful woman's part ever written'. The play began its return to theatrical popularity in 1953 with a production that preserved textual integrity: Tyrone Guthrie's lavish production at Stratford, Ontario, transferred to Stratford-upon-Avon six years later and was a great success.

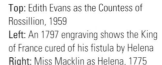

Top: Edith Evans as the Countess of Rossillion, 1959
Left: An 1797 engraving shows the King of France cured of his fistula by Helena
Right: Miss Macklin as Helena, 1775

ALL'S WELL THAT ENDS WELL

*A resourceful woman cures a king and wins a husband,
but she must do more before the promise of the title can be fulfilled.*

*A*ll's Well That Ends Well has some myste-rious and obscure avenues. It also offers wonderful moments of humour, the wisdom of experience and poetry that has the richness and eloquence of autumn. It gives us an exceptional heroine in Helena, a resourceful and determined woman of humble birth who wins a husband by curing a king. When rebuffed and abandoned, she wins the reluc-tant young man a second time by faith, inge-nuity and the help of a loving conspiracy of women. As was often the case, Shakespeare found his source in someone else's story and made it incomparably his own; this time it was a tale by Giovanni Boccaccio. The play reverberates with folk-tale motifs but also offers a truly human drama. In its conclusion, it holds an ambiguous magic that anticipates the themes and resolutions of Shakespeare's late plays.

Though *All's Well* can seem oddly unap-proachable on the page, it rewards our atten-tion in the theatre with a heroine who intrigues, a plot that entertains, and language and humour that resonate more deeply and wittily the nearer we approach. Peter Hall's production at the Swan, beautifully illustrated this. The enhancing effect of proximity was even more obvious when the production transferred to the smaller space of The Pit: the play acquired the eloquence and intimacy of chamber music. As the eye noted the fine and intricate patterns in costumes, the lines in faces, the delicate tracery of lace collars, so the ear could tune in to the subtlest nuances and details of language. The impeccable care

taken over the language was illustrated, for example, in the character of Lavatch, the cryptic clown at the Countess' house in Rossillion. It is a part rarely understood and often rigorously or completely cut. In Hall's production, however, Anthony O'Donnell established a mutually tolerant rapport with the audience. This rotund and gaudy Lavatch vividly signalled the play's bawdy.

The play has scarcely begun before we find ourselves involved in the passionate and intense emotions of its heroine, Helena. Where a few moments before, we had believed her to be crying for the death of her

Above: *– So now they come …*
*–   Yond's that same knave
That leads him to these places.*
Harriet Walter, Gillian Webb as the Widow and Cheryl Campbell watch the army arrive in Florence, 1981

father, we now grasp that she is desperately in love with Bertram, the young man whom we have just seen bid his mother, the Countess, farewell. Helena's sense of loss is so acute that it is a kind of death:

**I am undone: there is no living, none,
If Bertram be away.**

[I.1.83-4]

In Trevor Nunn's production, Harriet Walter gave a religious edge to the sexual longing she expressed in soliloquy and she fondly touched material objects as if they held a tangible residue of Bertram's dear presence. Hers was a taut and deeply earnest Helena; her low social status seemed more like a wound than simply an impediment. The character's self-definition in the early part of the play is through extraordinary and brooding soliloquies; Helena is disconcertingly inward in these scenes.

This obscurity, this introspection of Helena – indeed, the inwardness of the whole play – are beautifully evoked in the BBC-tv production. The viewer sees sets reminiscent of Dutch interiors, of Vermeer or Samuel van Hoogstraten's trick perspectives, often providing a stillness and a mood of contemplation in which the words move evocatively and with wonderful poise. One sees faces pause in light or shadow, meditative or occasionally illuminated by flickering red flames from a fire. Helena's soliloquies are deeply self-communing and through them we follow clues to her inmost nature. The potential of television is used in this production with great sensitivity. The intimacy of close-up and the use of voice-over work especially well, for example, when Helena plays a poignant air on the virginals as she muses. We are drawn into an exceptionally close relationship with the character by the silently approaching lens. The virginals Helena has been playing lead us to Parolles' interruption of her reverie: 'Are you meditating on virginity?' [109]. The banter which follows, part comic, part earnest, reveals Helena as a strongly sexual woman and somehow seems to launch her out of depression and into action.

The Countess' love for Helena is a strong element in the play; the relationship between the two is a subtle and rich alliance, unusual

in that later, the older woman takes sides with Helena and disowns her son, Bertram. Perhaps the wisest, most beautiful Countess ever, was Peggy Ashcroft, who was, it seems, crucial to Trevor Nunn's concept of the play. She brought a world of wisdom to the part, enhancing the rôle with poise and a fund of experience. She introduced unexpected, gentle humour into the rôle and later poignantly conveyed the character's dilemma, torn between love for her wayward son and her adopted child, her new daughter-in-law:

> **Which of them both**
> **Is dearest to me I have no skill in sense**
> **To make distinction.**
>
> [III.4.38-40]

There can rarely have been this balance of compassion and distress expressed in so lovely a face.

Above: *And with this healthful hand, whose banished sense*
Thou hast repealed, a second time receive
The confirmation of my promised gift,
Which but attends thy naming.
John Franklyn-Robbins and Harriet Walter, 1981

Parolles, who impels Helena to action and Bertram to the wars, is the 'braggart-soldier' so loved by eighteenth century audiences that during that time all other characters were neglected. He seduces Bertram into believing him 'of very valiant approof' [II.5.2]. When the King rewards Helena for curing him by granting her choice of husband, Parolles encourages Bertram in his plan to run away to war before the marriage is consummated. After Helena's return to Rossillion, she receives a letter from her husband, intimating that her death would be welcome news to him and setting his despised wife, his 'clog' [53] as he calls her, an apparently impossible challenge:

*When thou canst get the ring upon my finger,
which never shall come off, and show me a child
begotten of thy body that I am father to, then call
me husband; but in such a 'then' I write a
'never'.*

[III.2.56-9]

Helena leaves Rossillion. Unable to help herself, it seems, she gravitates towards Florence, where Bertram is. The next news received by all those who know her, is of her death. In Florence, both Bertram and Helena discover the treacheries of men but Helena finds the support and loyalty of a loving band of women, centred on the Widow and her daughter, Diana.

While Helena's friendship with the women deepens, Bertram's alliance with Parolles begins to crack. There is a delightful, brief scene where Parolles – having promised with his usual empty bravado, to recover the company's drum – is tricked by his fellows into thinking he has been captured by the enemy. It was marvellously funny to see urbane Stephen Moore (1981) and grainy-voiced Michael Siberry (1992), quake and tremble in terror while their captors bandied words in an entirely improvised language: '*Throca movousus, cargo, cargo, cargo … Manke revania dulche … Oscorbidulchos volivorco*' [IV.1.63,77-8]. It was less funny when we saw Parolles later brought before Bertram, proving his treachery by blurting out every military secret his brain could muster. Bertram's illusions are thoroughly destroyed.

Bertram, however, has dishonesties of his own. He is led to believe that he has seduced Diana into going to bed with him by promises of marriage. This scene of persuasion had great intensity in Peter Hall's production and the sharp ironies of the exchange were wittily delivered. In the BBC-tv production the erotic charge was almost palpable between the players, their faces flushed by flickering light.

Above: – *Will you be mine now you are doubly won?*
– *If she, my liege, can make me know this clearly*
I'll love her dearly, ever, ever dearly.
Sophie Thompson, Barbara Jefford and Toby Stephens, 1992

When the war is over, Bertram, thinking Helena dead, returns home. As a result of the bed-trick, Helena becomes pregnant. Able now to fulfil the terms of Bertram's letter, she returns to Rossillion and has Diana petition the King.

There was especially strong emphasis on the women in Barry Kyle's production. Not only the Widow, Diana and Mariana followed the heroine back to the estate, but several others made the journey too, including one with a baby. They thus manifested strong female allegiances, camaraderie and love. The fatherless baby in arms seemed at once a reminder of the deceptions of men and an intimation of the birth to come. Suzan

Sylvester's Diana had real moral authority, her virtue was vigorous and her allegiance to Helena absolute. Set against the close and validated unity of the women in this production, was the spurious vanity of the men in earlier scenes. Their desire for war came out of nursery childishness with toy soldiers and a rocking horse; when they prepared to parade before the King, they were narcissistic peacocks, preening in front of full-length mirrors.

NOTABLE PRODUCTIONS OF *ALL'S WELL THAT ENDS WELL*

	THEATRE	DIRECTOR	DESIGNER	PRINCIPALS
1980	BBC-tv	Elijah Moshinsky	David Myerscough-Jones	Angela Down ....*Helena* Ian Charleson ....*Bertram* Celia Johnson ....*Countess* Donald Sinden ....*King of France* Peter Jeffrey ....*Parolles* Pippa Guard ....*Diana* Paul Brooke ....*Lavatch*
1981	Royal Shakespeare Theatre, Stratford-upon-Avon	Trevor Nunn	John Gunter	Harriet Walter ....*Helena* Mike Gwilym ....*Bertram* Peggy Ashcroft ....*Countess* John Franklyn-Robbins ....*King of France* Stephen Moore ....*Parolles* Cheryl Campbell ....*Diana* Geoffrey Hutchings ....*Lavatch*
1989	Royal Shakespeare Theatre, Stratford-upon-Avon	Barry Kyle	Chris Dyer	Patricia Kerrigan ....*Helena* Paul Venables ....*Bertram* Gwen Watford ....*Countess* Hugh Ross ....*King of France* Bruce Alexander ....*Parolles* Suzan Sylvester.........................*Diana* Geoffrey Freshwater ....*Lavatch*
1992	Swan Theatre, Stratford-upon-Avon	Peter Hall	John Gunter	Sophie Thompson ....*Helena* Toby Stephens ....*Bertram* Barbara Jefford ....*Countess* Richard Johnson ....*King of France* Michael Siberry ....*Parolles* Rebecca Saire ....*Diana* Anthony O'Donnell ....*Lavatch*

Above: *Stand no more off,*
But give thyself unto my sick desires
Suzan Sylvester and Paul Venables, 1989

All roads meet where many of them started, at Rossillion; Bertram's trial takes place and he proves far more perfidious than Parolles. Bertram becomes totally enmeshed in a web of his own desperate dishonesties. There is only one person who can save him from the King's anger and she now appears. Bertram joins the others in amazement at the miraculous entry of Helena returned, it seems, from the dead. There is lovely detail here, in the BBC-tv production as the camera's eye adopts Helena's perspective and we see a mixture of warm and wondering emotions in individual faces as she encounters each in turn. Bertram, perceiving that his wife has brought him safety, release and a child to come, is 'doubly won' [V.3.312] and seems at last ready to accept her. The play ends. All seems well. There is a reconciled, if tentative future. As the light dimmed on Nunn's production a couple began to turn in a slow, cautious waltz.

Susan L. Powell

ANTONY AND CLEOPATRA

*The world's greatest love story frames the conflict between
rational responsibility and the pressure of a passionate relationship.*

The Roman soldiers who frame the first scene of *Antony and Cleopatra* are theatrically anonymous. They stand in opposition to the received view of the greatest love story the world has seen, and they reject vehemently the present behaviour of a pair of lovers whose reputation must inevitably precede their entrance. The soldiers' perspective is emotionally committed and the first words of the play declare their opposition to what they can only regard as Antony's aberrant behaviour:

**Nay but this dotage of our general's
O'erflows the measure…**

[I.1.1-2]

Their world is one of order and military discipline. In the 1972 production at Stratford the Roman soldiers clustered together in a knot of blackness on a stage splashed with colour. They were ill at ease in an alien environment. Antony had betrayed his military calling by adopting Egyptian robes and worst of all was his readiness to make an exhibition of himself in public. The video version of that production boldly disconcerts its television audience as a monochrome panorama of soldiers' faces registers implacable distaste for the cavortings of their general. The distinction between Antony as seen through Roman eyes and the sincerity of his emotional need to demonstrate his commitment to Cleopatra is strongly drawn.

Right: *Eternity was in our lips and eyes,
Bliss in our brows' bent.*
Richard Johnson and Janet Suzman, 1972

'NO GRAVE UPON THE EARTH SHALL CLIP IN IT A PAIR SO FAMOUS'

The Early Production History of *Antony and Cleopatra*

Antony and Cleopatra was entered in the Stationers' Register on 20 May 1608 and was probably written during the previous year with the *Life of Marcus Antonius* from North's Plutarch (1579) as its primary source. Publication was delayed until the First Folio of 1623 when the copy-text would seem to have been Shakespeare's own manuscript rather than a prompt-book. Indeed, there is no record of an early performance though a revised version of Samuel Daniel's *Cleopatra* published in 1607 includes a description of Antony being hoisted up to the monument that may have derived from seeing Shakespeare's play on stage.

John Dryden's more sentimental treatment *All for Love, or The World Well Lost* was first presented in 1677 at Drury Lane and was preferred for almost two hundred years. Garrick's extravagantly staged attempt to restore something of Shakespeare's text in 1759 lasted just six performances, and it was not until 1849 that Samuel Phelps staged a spectacular but more faithful revival. His well-studied bacchanalian attitudes won particular praise and Isabella Glyn was the first in a line of actresses to be acclaimed for the intense theatrical impact of Cleopatra's final scene. In Beerbohm Tree's

1906 production, a dissolving vision of the Sphinx framed the action.

The use of a permanent set at the Piccadilly Theatre in 1947 demonstrated how the pace of successive scenes can create a kaleidoscopic interplay of mood, and the subtlety within the partnership of Godfrey Tearle and Edith Evans like that between Laurence Olivier and Vivien Leigh four years later at the St James' Theatre eluded easy definition for those critics who came burdened with preconceptions. *Antony and Cleopatra* has resisted simplistic interpretation and has not easily accommodated fashions for updating or relocation. In 1953 Michael Redgrave was rugged and Peggy Ashcroft seductive, both achieving grandeur in a production that won praise for Egyptians who looked like Egyptians and Romans who looked like Romans.

Top: Michael Redgrave and Peggy Ashcroft, 1953
Left: Frontispiece to Dryden's *All for Love* in an edition of 1792
Right: Isabella Glyn, whose poses were 'severely statuesque', 1849

Janet Suzman demanded displays of affection with the proud confidence of a woman in love. Hers was an intelligent, joyous performance, matched by an Antony conscious of her worth but racked by his Roman sense of responsibility. The bed from which she would mime:

Give me my angle. We'll to th'river there…

[II.5.10]

exemplified the priority given to a drowsy, voluptuous wallowing in sensual experience in her Egypt. In 1978 Glenda Jackson was altogether more severe, a statuesque figure with maternal authority. Her Antony was a little boy cowed by the expectations thrust upon him. Four years later, at The Other Place, a wounded lion of an Antony was teased and taunted by a sex-kitten. Cleopatra makes less of an impression in Charlton Heston's film. Its emphasis is firmly upon Antony's predicament with low-angle shots exaggerating the craggy features of the Herculean Roman.

The play's method repeatedly encourages us to be wary of getting too involved in the passions and excitements. We are discouraged from identifying too closely with any individual character's point of view. Our rôle is to observe, 'Look where they come' [I.1.10] and to assess dispassionately 'Take but good note' [11]. It is reiterated for us with 'Behold and see' [13]. Rather than offer linear development the playwright exploits the technique of montage. Scene is set against scene to produce a series of juxtapositions and conflicting impressions. At Stratford in 1972, hydraulic stage machinery caused steps and podia to ripple up for the uncompromisingly business-like scenes in Rome. Egypt was initially a place of space, depth and openness but a huge pyramid reared up for the monument scenes. In 1987, on the open stage of the Olivier theatre, the set presented an image of

Above: – *If it be love indeed, tell me how much.*
– *There's beggary in the love that can be reckoned.*
– *I'll set a bourn how far to be beloved.*
Charlton Heston and Hildegard Neil, 1973

a fragmenting world and the action spilt into the auditorium. However, at the same time as we are being encouraged to distance ourselves, the play's method, involving crucially its succession of short scenes, is also working to complicate our response and make it difficult for us to establish a settled point of view. Brook offered a series of uncompromising oppositions with much of the action taking place on a mat that hinted at a boxing ring. The episodic nature of the play is reflected in the way Charlton Heston could radically rearrange the pieces in an attempt to create an organic narrative for his cinema audience.

In these first three scenes there is an intense focus upon the relationship between Antony and Cleopatra. We see the passion, the excitement, the tension of the relationship:

Cleopatra's shifts of mood (her infinite variety) and her ability to control Antony; Antony's awareness of what he should do and yet his difficulty in managing to break his 'strong Egyptian fetters' [I.2.117]. Judi Dench and Anthony Hopkins were older lovers, with a sense of their time being past. Yet she was resolutely life-assertive, capricious and consistently alluring for an exhausted man who needed the heady excitement of power. The development of a relationship that is larger than the play that the characters inhabit, then broadens to encompass the substance of Rome, as the action shifts across the Mediterranean and we see for ourselves the operation of Roman thinking upon Antony. We do not see Antony and Cleopatra together again until the middle of Act III.

Our first view of Rome shows us Caesar reading a report of Antony's conduct in Egypt. It is an observer's, a Roman observer's, view of what we have just witnessed and that view is further distanced by Caesar's perspective. Corin Redgrave's Caesar, employed the metallic tones and bright-eyed fanaticism of the political extremist. His lack of military experience was displayed by the whiteness of his knees when he appeared in uniform at Alexandria and it was clear that he depended for his authority upon his bully boys. John Castle is similarly youthful in the Heston film

with an astuteness thrown into relief by his grizzled advisers and by hooded eyes that habitually veil his thoughts. His meeting with Antony takes place as counterpoint to a gladiatoral contest. Tim Pigott-Smith was cold, quick to anger and, like Corin Redgrave, he did not like being touched. Jonathan Pryce was a shabbier, wheeling-dealing survivor.

The extent to which we agree with Caesar's view of Antony:

> **You shall find there**
> **A man who is the abstract of all faults**
> **That all men follow**

[I.4.8-10]

can depend upon whether we are ruled by our heads or our hearts, but Shakespeare encourages the debate by having Lepidus present an alternative interpretation which in turn is countered by Caesar's precise calculation, 'You are too indulgent' [16]. Lepidus will try to mediate between Rome, as epitomised by Caesar, and Egypt as seen in its influence upon Antony. He may be well-meaning, as in the 1992 production, or a buffoon for attempting the impossible. Similarly, Octavia's rôle requires her to reconcile the irreconcilable, and the nuances of her rela-

Below: *With thy sharp teeth this knot intrinsicate*
Of life at once untie.
Glenda Jackson and Paola Dionisotti as Charmian, 1978

THE PLAYS: *ANTONY AND CLEOPATRA*

tionship with her brother Caesar may suggest that she is a pawn, or as in Peter Brook's production, permit a more sultry interpretation. In 1992, Antony's decision to return to Egypt derived from a realisation that he had been outmanœuvred by Caesar, whereas Charlton Heston overhears Enobarbus' praise of Cleopatra and immediately sets sail from Rome. Crashing waves signal how passion conquers reason. Throughout the play there are various struggles to reconcile such opposing forces. Later, Enobarbus will also seek but fail to find a middle way. Within the framework of *Antony and Cleopatra* compromise and reconciliation on a human plane will not work – the solution must be found in something 'other'.

Much of the central section of the play is occupied with the debate as to whether the battle should take place on land or at sea. We see how Cleopatra spurs Antony, taunts him into taking the decision – the fatal, the wrong decision – to fight at sea. Canidius is amazed:

Why will my lord do so?

[III.7.29]

Enobarbus goes further:

Your ships are not well manned...

[34]

detailing the inadequacy of Antony's forces to the task. We know that what Enobarbus says makes sense, for the sea has not been Antony's natural element. By rejecting the solid basis of his own military achievement and the reasoned advice of his senior officer, Antony is betraying the Roman part of himself. In choosing to fight at sea he will depend upon the flimsy support of Cleopatra's 'sixty sails' [49].

Again and again in this play we are encouraged to take into account the perspective of

the ordinary soldier. There is a procession of minor characters who have little opportunity to establish any individuality. After the important characters' response to Antony's decision to fight at sea, Shakespeare gives us that of the ordinary man:

Enter a Soldier...

O noble emperor, do not fight by sea.
Trust not to rotten planks. Do you misdoubt
This sword and these my wounds?

[61-3]

In the 1973 film, the soldier puts his hand on Antony's arm. The depth of commitment that prompts the physical restraint is registered before Antony is again distracted by Cleopatra's presence. The scene ends in what has become a characteristic way – with further commentary upon what we have seen,

Above left: *I am fire and air.*
Helen Mirren, 1982
Above: *I must be gone.*
Michael Gambon, 1982

prompting us to assess and judge what we have witnessed. The soldier avows his belief in the truth of his conviction:

By Hercules, I think I am i'th'right.

[67]

choosing an ironically apt oath to swear by, and Canidius affirms this truth:

Soldier, thou art.

[68]

Heston has Canidius play the soldier and his Enobarbus adds considerable authority to the endorsement. Whereas Patrick Stewart played Enobarbus as a bluff, uncomplicated soldier

41

who shied away from comprehending the greater drama, frequent cut-away shots establish Eric Porter's watchful and increasingly troubled presence.

Heston's film gives particular prominence to the land versus sea debate both visually and through introduced verbal repetitions, but ultimately the argument is sterile for the course of events has been determined by history and to leave the debate is to abandon the baser elements of land and sea, earth and water, in favour of those elements that are more essentially elusive, evanescent and ethereal. The direction is signposted for us:

> Their preparation is today by sea
> We please them not by land...
> I would they'd fight i'th'fire or i'th'air,
> We'd fight there too.
>
> [IV.10.1-4]

Antony's words resound with more than rhetorical bluster, for the characters in this play have a remarkable ability to lift themselves above the rut of common experience. They seem to be aware of their own destiny and Antony will meditate on man's unstable hold of his very entity. Richard Johnson's earlier Antony had shown a strength and humanity, but when he returned to the part in 1992, he reached beyond impersonation to present the breadth of vision of a figure resonant with authority and experience. Anthony Hopkins gave a performance that went beyond the everyday world and Alan Howard had a sensitive vulnerability that set him apart from ordinary men.

In the last movement of the play Cleopatra transcends earthly reality, achieving an ethereal communion with:

Left: *But since my lord*
Is Antony again, I will be Cleopatra.
Judi Dench and Anthony Hopkins, 1987

42

I am fire and air; my other elements
I give to baser life...

[V.2.288-9]

Judi Dench had shown a huge, embracing humour, but here she was single-minded with an intensity of focus. Earlier in the play Clare Higgins had worn a series of wigs to suggest her consciousness of the image she presented to Antony and the world, but in the final scene all pretence and play-acting were stripped away. The asps were delivered by the soothsayer in a death-mask. In contrast, Janet Suzman's encounter with the 'rural fellow' [233] permitted a humour which emphasised the strength of her decision. She underwent a robing ceremony that became a ritual transformation into the icon by which the story reverberates through the ages.

Keith Parsons

Above: *The time of universal peace is near.*
Prove this a prosperous day
Jonathan Pryce, 1978

NOTABLE PRODUCTIONS OF *ANTONY AND CLEOPATRA*

	THEATRE	DIRECTOR	DESIGNER	PRINCIPALS
1972	Royal Shakespeare Theatre, Stratford-upon-Avon	Trevor Nunn	Christopher Morley	Richard Johnson ....*Antony* Janet Suzman ....*Cleopatra* Corin Redgrave ....*Octavius Caesar* Patrick Stewart ....*Enobarbus*

This production was recorded for television transmission in 1974 and has been released on video

	THEATRE	DIRECTOR	DESIGNER	PRINCIPALS
1973	Transac/Izaro/ Folie Films	Charlton Heston	Maurice Pelling	Charlton Heston ....*Antony* Hildegard Neil ....*Cleopatra* John Castle ....*Octavius Caesar* Eric Porter ....*Enobarbus*
1978	Royal Shakespeare Theatre, Stratford-upon-Avon	Peter Brook	Sally Jacobs	Alan Howard ....*Antony* Glenda Jackson ....*Cleopatra* Jonathan Pryce ....*Octavius Caesar* Patrick Stewart ....*Enobarbus*
1980	BBC-tv	Jonathan Miller	Colin Lowrey	Colin Blakely ....*Antony* Jane Lapotaire ....*Cleopatra* Ian Charleson ....*Octavius Caesar* Emrys James ....*Enobarbus*
1982	The Other Place, Stratford-upon-Avon	Adrian Noble	Nadine Baylis	Michael Gambon ....*Antony* Helen Mirren ....*Cleopatra* Jonathan Hyde ....*Octavius Caesar* Bob Peck ....*Enobarbus*
1987	National Theatre, London	Peter Hall	Alison Chitty	Anthony Hopkins ....*Antony* Judi Dench ....*Cleopatra* Tim Pigott-Smith ......*Octavius Caesar* Michael Bryant ....*Enobarbus*
1992	Royal Shakespeare Theatre, Stratford-upon-Avon	John Caird	Sue Blane	Richard Johnson ....*Antony* Clare Higgins ....*Cleopatra* John Nettles ....*Octavius Caesar* Paul Jesson ....*Enobarbus*

'WE THAT ARE TRUE LOVERS RUN INTO STRANGE CAPERS'

The Early Production History of *As You Like It*

Although *As You Like It* was first printed in the First Folio of 1623, it was to be over a hundred years before any performance was recorded. However, parts of the play were seen in 1723 in Charles Johnson's play, *Love in a Forest* at the Drury Lane Theatre, London.

The first production known to be faithful to Shakespeare's text took place in 1740, also at Drury Lane and was a great success. Indeed, by 1741 it was joined by a production at Covent Garden signalling the subsequent popularity of *As You Like It*.

Productions in the nineteenth century were presented with large casts and great attention to realistic settings – particularly the Forest of Arden – and substantial cuts to the text were often made to allow lavish

theatrical set-pieces. William Charles Macready's 1842 production at Drury Lane, for example, featured a cast of 97 and an exciting and realistic wrestling match.

It was to be after World War I before the full, uncut text of the play was seen. Nigel Playfair's 1919 production at the Shakespeare Memorial Theatre in Stratford-upon-Avon was a 'modern' production which outraged many traditionalists with its stylised medieval settings. As the twentieth century progressed, productions became increasingly dominated by their Rosalinds, attracting the great stars of each generation. Peggy Ashcroft played Rosalind to great acclaim in 1932, as did Edith Evans in 1936 and Vanessa Redgrave in 1961.

Top: Julia Neilson, 1896
Left: *Bear your body more seeming, Audrey*
Mrs H. Marston as Audrey and Mr F. Younge as Touchstone, c. 1850
Right: Vanessa Redgrave, 1961

AS YOU LIKE IT

*Tensions between the values of court and country test
the motivations and commitment of four pairs of lovers.*

Explorations of love lie at the heart of *As You Like It*. Set in two principal locations, the rigid hierarchical patriarchy of a usurped court and the unstructured and pastoral potentiality of the Forest of Arden, the play consistently and comically examines the social construction of romance and what it means to be both a man and a woman. In Johan Engels' design for the 1992 Stratford production, the dark austere court dominated by huge static thrones was transformed into a forest of seemingly real trees and grass, the stage washed by lights which made the auditorium glow with a beckoning, comforting green.

The play opens, however, at court, the metaphor for everything which will be interrogated in Arden. Orlando is heard railing against his brother, Oliver, and the patriarchal power he is exerting upon him:

he keeps me rustically at home.

[I.1.6-7]

Orlando is excluded from his rightful place by a brother who mistrusts and dislikes him, not because he is unlikeable, but precisely the opposite:

**he's gentle, never schooled and yet learned, full
of noble device, of all sorts enchantingly
beloved.**

[155-6]

Andrew Tiernan dressed in an overlarge overcoat, looking cold, unshaven, and fragile is the

image of a gentle, sensitive boy. As he waits for Oliver in the foyer of his opulent office block, Orlando is as inappropriate in his brother's world as a woman would be. It is one of the ironic twists of the play however, that it is not Orlando's sensitivity which eventually ensures his exclusion from court, but rather his spectacular success in the overtly masculine wrestling ring. Peter de Jersey, stripped to the waist, stole a remarkable victory against

Above: – *Well, this is the Forest of Arden.*
– *Ay, now am I in Arden, the more fool I.*
Nicky Henson, Fiona Shaw as 'Aliena' and Juliet Stevenson as 'Ganymede', 1985

an impossibly strong-looking opponent. His success seemed against the odds, its outcome superhuman. Orlando earns his banishment from this victory, but his swift transformation from fragile boyhood to manly success is just a hint of the magic which will occur when he leaves the court behind.

Rosalind too seems a misfit at court. Emma Croft, young, feminine and apparently at ease, charms everyone at her uncle's lavish cocktail party, but her attractive personality and gentle character unsettle the usurping Duke Frederick:

> **Her very silence, and her patience**
> **Speak to the people, and they pity her.**
>
> [I.3.76-7]

Like Orlando, Rosalind will be banished because her gentle success has created a threat to the male order of aggressive usurpation. But she does not face humiliation alone, she has Celia. Fiona Shaw was bright and vivacious, pacing the stage, attempting to cheer up Juliet Stevenson's Rosalind who was passive and withdrawn, her isolation symbolising her alienated position within the court. But when Celia chooses to accompany her into banishment, Stevenson suddenly became animated by the idea of disguise in Arden:

> **Were it not better,**
> **Because that I am more than common tall,**
> **That I did suit me all points like a man?**
>
> [112-14]

The power shifts here from Celia to Rosalind. Fiona Shaw delayed her response to this line – what would this male disguise mean within their intimate female friendship? Rosalind's ruse begins as an expedient measure, but Rosalind-as-Ganymede will become a new character who will challenge the foundations of gender rôle-play.

It is banishment into the forest which provokes and allows Rosalind's gender reversal. The place will allow almost anything to happen, and Juliet Stevenson and her party approached its fringes with excitement and trepidation. Bob Crowley's Arden consisted of white parachute silks which dominated the stage. He gave us a snow-covered landscape; cold, unfriendly, unwelcoming. This prospect provoked Juliet Stevenson's sarcastic 'Well, this is the forest of Arden' [II.4.12]. Christine Edzard's film seeks constantly to find contemporary resonances. Her forest is an inner-city wasteland surrounded by the office blocks which are the high-rise, encroaching court. Exile and banishment in this Arden echo contemporary homelessness and dispossession, emphasising the potential dangers of release from the court. Arden is a place which allows fantasy, but it is also a place of uncertainty and potential danger.

Orlando's entry into Arden is full of apprehension. Like the new Ganymede who must care for Celia, Orlando keenly feels the need to protect and nourish Adam, his old and loyal companion. Orlando fears for his safety but bravely challenges the exiled Duke for food:

Above: *To you I give myself, for I am yours.*
Juliet Stevenson and Hilton McRae embrace, watched by Lesley Manville, Roger Hyams, Alan Rickman, Fiona Shaw and Bruce Alexander as Oliver, 1985

> **He dies that touches any of this fruit**
> **Till I and my affairs are answered.**
>
> [II.7.99-100]

His violent intrusion on the peaceful picnic and aggressive demand for food at knifepoint are according to masculine stereotype. Andrew Tiernan appears like a waif at the wasteland gathering, his brave swagger poignantly out of place and swiftly diffused by the friendship of the forest. Edzard's Arden has an ugly exterior, but the mood of its inhabitants is unquestioningly warm. Orlando quickly finds that in the forest natural gentleness is valued and nurtured. Here the exiled Duke Senior and his companions have established a new court. Gathered around a campfire which provides a comforting warmth against the backdrop of waste and decay, theirs is an environment which is comfortable enough to allow philosophy and debate, and the reflective melancholy of Jaques is welcomed in their midst:

> All the world's a stage,
> And all the men and women merely players;
> They have their exits and their entrances,
> And one man in his time plays many parts.
>
> [140-4]

James Fox's Jaques smiles through this speech and his measured, calm delivery is comforting and wise. This Jaques is an ageing aristocrat, offering philosophical guidance through a topsy-turvy world.

Rosalind, however, grabs her Arden with both hands. No longer imprisoned by the ornate gowns and high heels of court, Juliet Stevenson enjoyed the freedom of Ganymede's baggy trousers, stealing centre-

Above:
Alas, he is too young; yet he looks successfully.
Tom Hollander and Adrian Lester watch the wrestling match in Cheek by Jowl's all-male production, 1991

Above: *There is a man haunts the forest that abuses our young plants with carving 'Rosalind' on their barks.*
Emma Croft, disguised as 'Ganymede', finds her forest in an urban setting, 1992

stage and infusing her speeches with a new-found excitement. In Arden, *As You Like It* becomes Ganymede's play and in choosing to remain in disguise with Orlando, Rosalind becomes an on-stage director of much of the rest of the action. She plays with Orlando's earnest romantic beliefs, promising to 'cure' [III.2.407] him of his emotional aberration. Cheek By Jowl's all-male production added comic complexity and, surprisingly, a sustained eroticism to this confusion of gender. Adrian Lester's exaggerated, feigned masculinity as Ganymede – he punched Patrick Toomey's arm in a gesture of male bonding and was nearly felled by its return – and his hesitant, 'feigned' femininity as his Ganymede pretended to be Rosalind, revealed not only the visual comedy of the artificiality of gendered behaviour, but also the essential similarity between men and women in their experience of love. Lester and Toomey played at being a heterosexual couple with a sexy freedom which liberated the play for a modern audience.

Whilst Rosalind and Orlando make love with words, Touchstone the court jester also finds romance in the forest. A well-groomed city gent, Griff Rhys-Jones is captivated by Miriam Margolyes' demure and buxom Audrey. The only character to find love across the class divide between court and forest, Rhys-Jones charms her away from her forlorn and lonely burger van with the excitement of wit and the promise of something new and exciting. Richard Cant's Audrey was altogether more assertive. Tall and willowy, wearing an absurdly short and glamorous white mini-dress, Cant delighted, excited and enthralled Peter Needham's Touchstone.

woman who falls in love with a man who treats her badly. Rosalind uses her new-found gender power and abuses another woman.

Fiona Shaw's Celia was increasingly irritated and then angered by Juliet Stevenson's behaviour. She became a powerful, yet silent, on-stage witness of Ganymede's manipulations of others, reminding the audience of Rosalind's potentially dangerous charade. When she finally burst out:

You have simply misused our sex in your love-prate. We must have your doublet and hose plucked over your head, and show the world what the bird hath done to her own nest

[IV.1.186-8]

Left: *Wedding is great Juno's crown*
Samantha Bond, Peter de Jersey, Phyllida Hancock and Adrian Lukis as Oliver, 1992
Below: Andrew Jarvis as Duke Frederick watches Peter de Jersey and Nick Holder as Charles, 1992

The success of Touchstone's wooing of Audrey is not matched by Silvius' approach to Phebe. Indeed Silvius' protestations are both melodramatic and unsuccessful:

Sweet Phebe, do not scorn me, do not, Phebe.
Say that you love me not, but say not so
In bitterness.

[III.5.1-3]

He behaves in a stereotypically feminine way, employing emotional blackmail in order for Phebe to take pity on him and relent. In Christine Edzard's film, Silvius valiantly ignores Phebe's steadfast and deliberate disdain which is made more cruelly comic by her calm and solitary meal of a bag of chips. This Phebe, glamorous and sophisticated, is bored, but when Rosalind intrudes without invitation and verbally attacks her, Phebe changes instantly. Her sexual attraction to Ganymede is immediate. She is a stereotype: a

she revealed all the disappointment and frustration of a woman who has lost a friend in favour of a lover.

At the romantic climax of the play Rosalind will shed her disguise and re-present herself to Orlando. The re-establishment of true gender identity allows love to become the dominant emotion and motive for the action, but the sudden reappearance of the real Rosalind in the Cheek By Jowl production was marked by a brief and powerful moment of anger and realism. Patrick Toomey knew that this Rosalind had been his friend and mentor Ganymede, and he strode to the back of the stage hurt and betrayed, taking some minutes to return and accept Lester's love. In Adrian Noble's production, Juliet Stevenson and Hilton McRae knelt together and stared at their reflections in a pool. It was as if Orlando saw his friend Ganymede magically transformed into his lover Rosalind. Giving up her disguise grants Rosalind the power to allow marriages to take place, enables a general forgiveness and permits the fractured court to be permanently reconstructed. The play ends happily, yet we leave the forest behind. But something of the magical, transient world of Arden lingers when Rosalind steps forward to speak the play's Epilogue:

> **If I were a woman, I would kiss as many of you**
> **as had beards that pleased me...**
>
> [Epilogue 211-12]

When Adrian Lester delivered these lines – a male actor playing a woman – they provided a poignant and funny reminder that what is at the heart of *As You Like It* is not Arden, but what Arden has allowed: the freedom to explore the similarities rather than the differences between men and women.

Helen J. Schaffer Snow

NOTABLE PRODUCTIONS OF *AS YOU LIKE IT*

	THEATRE	DIRECTOR	DESIGNER	PRINCIPALS
1985	Royal Shakespeare Theatre, Stratford-upon-Avon	Adrian Noble	Bob Crowley	Juliet Stevenson ....*Rosalind* Fiona Shaw ....*Celia* Hilton McRae ....*Orlando* Alan Rickman ....*Jaques* Mary Jo Randle ....*Audrey* Nicky Henson ....*Touchstone* Lesley Manville ....*Phebe* Roger Hyams ....*Silvius*
1991	Cheek By Jowl tour	Declan Donnellan	Nick Ormerod	Adrian Lester ....*Rosalind* Tom Hollander ....*Celia* Patrick Toomey.....................*Orlando* Joe Dixon ....*Jaques* Richard Cant ....*Audrey* Peter Needham ....*Touchstone* Sam Graham ....*Phebe* Mark Benton ....*Silvius*
1992	George Reinhart and Sands Films	Christine Edzard	Director of photography Robin Vidgeon	Emma Croft ....*Rosalind* Celia Bannerman ....*Celia* Andrew Tiernan ....*Orlando* James Fox ....*Jaques* Miriam Margolyes...................*Audrey* Griff Rhys-Jones...............*Touchstone* Valerie Gogan ....*Phebe* Ewen Bremner ....*Silvius*
1992	Royal Shakespeare Theatre, Stratford-upon-Avon	David Thacker	Johan Engels	Samantha Bond ....*Rosalind* Phyllida Hancock ....*Celia* Peter de Jersey.......................*Orlando* Michael Siberry ....*Jaques* Susan-Jane Tanner ....*Audrey* Anthony O'Donnell ....*Touchstone* Emma Gregory ....*Phebe* Andrew Cryer ....*Silvius*

'METHINKS YOU ARE MY GLASS, AND NOT MY BROTHER'

The Early Production History of *The Comedy of Errors*

The Gray's Inn Record of 28 December 1594 gives an account of a night of riot and disordered tumult on which 'it was thought good not to offer anything of Account, saving Dancing and Revelling with Gentlewomen; and after such Sports, a Comedy of Errors' presented by 'a Company of base and common fellows'. This would seem to be the first recorded performance of Shakespeare's play and, though its derivation from Plautus' tale of identical twins, *The Menaechmi*, was recognised, the reactions of its first critic signal centuries of academic disparagement.

The eighteenth century's enthusiasm for adaptation led to *Every Body Mistaken* in 1716, *See If You Like It* in 1734 and *The Twins*, a re-working by Thomas Hull with songs for 'Hermia', Adriana's cousin, in 1762. In various versions the last-mentioned proved a perennial favourite at Covent Garden and was the basis for Kemble's production in 1808. An operatic treatment by Frederick Reynolds in 1819 also proved popular.

In 1855 Samuel Phelps returned to Shakespeare's text and in 1864 at the Princess's Theatre, two brothers played the Dromio twins. Since then simply stressing the farcical aspects of the play has generally ensured box-office success for an increasing number of lively productions. In 1938 Komisarjevsky staged a burlesque in a Toytown set with music by Handel and Antony Bernard. In the same year New York saw *The Boys from Syracuse*, a musical comedy by Rodgers and Hart. The 1940 film used anachronistic gags such as taxi chariots and stone newspapers.

Since then enthusiasm for musical ingredients has led to a rock *Errors* in 1960, a production with bagpipes in 1971, a rag-time accompaniment in 1983 and in the same year translation to the Wild West with an abundance of country and western music. The Edinburgh audience of Frank Dunlop's 1971 production was told that any Englishman setting foot on Scottish soil would be arrested, but the warning came too late for Egeon.

Top: The Webb brothers as the two Dromios, 1864
Left: Thomas Hull, 1777
Right: Mr Dunstal as Dromio of Syracuse, 1762

THE COMEDY OF ERRORS

*Amidst the hilariously comic confusions caused by two sets
of identical twins, Shakespeare explores the nature of identity.*

Shakespeare chooses to relocate *The Comedy of Errors* in Ephesus rather than accept Plautus' Epidamnum. Ephesus had a reputation for debauchery and black magic and the visiting Antipholus nervously expresses his apprehension:

> They say this town is full of cozenage;
> As nimble jugglers that deceive the eye;
> Dark-working sorcerers that change the mind;
> Soul-killing witches that deform the body;
> Disguised cheaters, prating mountebanks;
> And many such-like liberties of sin.
>
> [I.2.97-102]

Clifford Williams' production began by stressing the theatricality of the piece and the potential that any play offers for disguise and deception. His actors gathered on and around a bare, steeply raked and stepped platform. They were dressed plainly and their patterned movements emphasised first the identity of an acting company and then developed through assuming the stereotypes of a *commedia dell'arte* troupe into a sense of the community of Ephesus as they bartered brightly coloured costume pieces. The BBC-tv production also seeks to establish the tradition of *commedia* as a context for the action of the play. A group of mimes enact Egeon's story on a map of the Mediterranean.

The fearsome image of the town can contribute to a more sombre opening. For a play that proclaims itself to be a comedy in its title, the opening lines of *The Comedy of Errors* are unpropitious:

> Proceed, Solinus, to procure my fall
> And by the doom of death end woes and all.
>
> [I.1.1-2]

In 1976 the force of the implacable sonorities with which the Duke of Ephesus responds to the pleadings of the condemned Egeon was heightened by his military uniform and use of a microphone. Even the more comic aspects of his police-state prompted contemporary resonances of the inflexible authority necessary to maintain a dictatorship. The visiting Antipholus and

Above: *I charge thee, Satan, housed within this man,
To yield possession to my holy prayers*
Francesca Annis, Nickolas Grace, Judi Dench and Mike Gwylim watch while Robin Ellis as Doctor Pinch attempts exorcism, 1976

Dromio quickly realised that it was not a good idea to wear T-shirts advertising that they came from Syracuse, and they left the stage before Griffith Jones' Egeon sought to give credence to the improbable tale of his family's separation at sea by producing photographs of his twin sons. Despite the aahs of sympathy, the public nature of the scene gives the Duke little room for clemency and though Egeon is the innocent victim of a mercantile dispute the declared sanctions must be enforced:

Hopeless and helpless does Egeon wend,
But to procrastinate his lifeless end.

[I.1.158-9]

The action of the play is contained within a single day and there is a series of references to time passing to remind an audience of the darker aspects of the play's narrative frame.

In going beyond his source to introduce not only Egeon's story but a second set of identical twins as servants to the Antipholus brothers, Shakespeare does more than double the potential for comic confusion. We are given an emblem of partnerships built on affection and loyalty rather than economic necessity. Yet the knockabout humour has a fierce physicality that threatens to go beyond the essential harmlessness of slapstick. Both Dromios endure beatings that are perceived as given with 'neither rhyme nor reason' [II.2.49], but we are encouraged to recognize the distress and confusion that provokes both Antipholus brothers to violent action.

The first opportunity that Antipholus of Syracuse has for reflection is used to express a deep-seated uncertainty about the direction and focus of his own life:

Below: Diana Rigg silently seeks to make her peace with Ian Richardson watched by Tony Steedman as the Duke, Pauline Letts as the Abbess, Tony Church as Egeon, Susan Maryott as Luciana and Alec McCowen.

I to the world am like a drop of water
That in the ocean seeks another drop,
Who, failing there to find his fellow forth,
Unseen, inquisitive, confounds himself.
So I, to find a mother and a brother,
In quest of them unhappy, lose myself.

[I.2.35-40]

The impulse of his search becomes a quest for identity. Roger Rees was equipped for the tourist trail with his guide-book and camera and proved a wide-eyed innocent abroad, easily shocked by the merest hint of 'liberties of sin' [102]. He took comfort in sharing his puzzled bewilderment with the audience. As his other self, Antipholus of Ephesus, Mike Gwilym displayed a veneer of assurance but there was an embittered sense of disillusion which eventually erupted in a frenzy born of emptiness and frustration. In 1962, Alec McCowen and Ian Richardson both made the audience aware of the thinness of the veneer that constitutes acceptable social behaviour. Playing both parts with the aid of some television trickery, Michael Kitchen discriminates sharply between the sensitive vulnerability of Antipholus of Syracuse and the more worldly-wise, cynical rough diamond who is his brother. The latter's latent savagery is glimpsed when he fashions the rope's end into a noose and creates an impromptu gibbet.

Amongst the play's images of potential bondage or chastisement, the chain was originally intended as a present from Antipholus of Ephesus to his wife, Adriana. Their marriage has deteriorated recently, but we may wonder whether there has ever been much of a relationship. In her scene with the man that she assumes is her husband but is his brother, Adriana through the cautious bewilderment shown by Diana Rigg or the more caustic chastisement of Judi Dench begins her journey of self-discovery. She wonders how he has become 'estrangèd'

[II.2.129] from himself and unconsciously she echoes an image the questing Antipholus had used to suggest his uncertainty about identity:

A drop of water in the breaking gulf.

[135]

His lack of response to her entreaties prompts her to look within herself and strive for self-definition.

When Antipholus of Ephesus finds himself locked out of his own house, the use in 1962 of a door simply constructed in mime allowed the audience a full view of what was happening both inside and out, whilst in 1976 a similar effect was achieved with an entry phone system. As frustration mounted the intercom unit was ripped from the wall and communication degenerated into the transmission of rude noises. In this production, there were clear indications that Adriana's determination to dine 'above' [217] with the man she thought her husband was a euphemism for her hunger for sexual fulfilment. After Antipholus of Syracuse had accompanied her to the bedroom, it would be easier for Judi Dench's termagant wife to forgive her husband's affair with the Courtesan.

Luciana represents what Adriana might have been before her marriage and since her idealism is so vehemently rejected by her sister we may suspect that it is shared and has been repressed by Adriana rather than lost. In Luciana the unmarried Antipholus finds what he has been seeking. She offers the excitement and wonder of discovery of that which is other and he willingly surrenders his sense of himself 'Smothered in errors' [III.2.35] to aspire to:

It is thyself, mine own self's better part…

[61]

In the recording of Trevor Nunn's production,

Above: *Will you go with me?*
Ingrid Pitt as the Courtesan and Michael Kitchen, 1983

Antipholus looks into a mirror and sees Luciana's image magically appear adjacent to his own. However, his experience of Ephesus soon lurches into a nightmare world. It was presented in 1962 with a masque of shadowy, threatening figures:

There's not a man I meet but doth salute me
As if I were their well-acquainted friend,
And everyone doth call me by my name.
Some tender money to me…
Sure, these are but imaginary wiles,
And Lapland sorcerers inhabit here.

[IV.3.1-11]

In 1976, Roger Rees' bewilderment at the multiplicity of greetings he received was expressed through song and the more surreal aspects of his confusion were suggested through lighting changes and choreography.

NOTABLE PRODUCTIONS OF *The Comedy of Errors*

	THEATRE	DIRECTOR	DESIGNER	PRINCIPALS
1962	Royal Shakespeare Theatre, Stratford-upon-Avon	Clifford Williams	John Wyckham	Alec McCowen ....*Antipholus of Syracuse* Ian Richardson ....*Antipholus of Ephesus* Barry MacGregor ....*Dromio of Syracuse* Ian Hewitson ....*Dromio of Ephesus* Diana Rigg ....*Adriana*

Originally mounted as a stop-gap production, it returned to Stratford in 1963, 1965 and 1972. It went on provincial and world tours, including visits to the USSR, Europe and the United States and was given a Royal Command Performance at Windsor. It survived many cast changes.

1976	Royal Shakespeare Theatre, Stratford-upon-Avon	Trevor Nunn (music by Guy Woolfenden)	John Napier	Roger Rees ....*Antipholus of Syracuse* Mike Gwilym.................*Antipholus of Ephesus* Michael Williams ....*Dromio of Syracuse* Nickolas Grace......*Dromio of Ephesus* Judi Dench.............................*Adriana*

A recording of this production was made for television transmission by ATV in 1978 and later released on video.

1983	BBC-tv	James Cellan-Jones	Don Homfray	Michael Kitchen ....*Antipholus of Syracuse & Antipholus of Ephesus* Roger Daltrey ....*Dromio of Syracuse & Dromio of Ephesus* Suzanne Bertish ....*Adriana*

Luciana and the charlatan Pinch compete for the soul of the wandering Antipholus and Guy Woolfenden transmuted the tawdry ritual of exorcism by the 'threadbare' conjuror into a show-stopping production number. One benefit of the Syracusan twins seeking sanctuary is that other characters gain time for reflection. The parallel pressures of experience upon Antipholus of Ephesus are suggested as the Abbess remonstrates with Adriana:

> **thy jealous fits**
> **Hath scared thy husband from the use of wits.**
> [V.1.85-6]

Although Luciana defends her sister, Adriana accepts responsibility for a marriage that is failing:

> **She did betray me to my own reproof.**
> [90]

Judi Dench reacted to the Abbess' rebuke with the shock of recognition.

Like their masters, the two Dromios are 'one in semblance' [349]. The BBC production presents an earlier confrontation in which the truth of appearances is tested through an empty mirror frame. Symmetrical patterning of the stage action in 1962 encouraged the audience to expect the mirror image that is formalised by one of the Dromios at the point where no-one need worry which is which:

> **Methinks you are my glass, and not my brother.**
> [418]

With the resolution of the action and a surprise revelation for the audience when the Abbess proclaims herself to be the wife of Egeon, there is the briefest debate between the Dromios about who should take precedence before they agree upon the emblem of partnership expressed in the final lines:

> **We came into the world like brother and brother,**
> **And now let's go hand in hand, not one before another.**
> [425-6]

In 1976 this was the cue for a song in which the whole company joined. A wave of happiness engulfed the curtain calls and swept over the front of the stage as the actors moved into the auditorium to shake hands with as many people as possible.

Keith Parsons

CORIOLANUS

*Glorious success in a military campaign proves to be
no preparation for the political skills necessary to earn public office.*

Coriolanus is a play about power, politics and conflict. Its principal protagonist, Caius Martius Coriolanus, is the focus for the unresolvable dichotomy between public and private perceptions of government, war and masculinity which lie at the heart of the play. In Michael Bogdanov's 1990 production, the epic nature of the play was consistently emphasised. Set in Eastern Europe during the turbulent days of the late 1980s, Bogdanov offered a specific politicised interpretation which achieved a frighteningly resonant realism. *Coriolanus* opens with the Roman citizens rebelling against their patrician leaders. Unfurling a banner across the stage with the word 'Democratie' written in red script reminiscent of the Polish banner 'Solidarity', Bogdanov's citizens were well organised; theirs was no mere protest - we were witnessing the birth of a new political movement. This focus on the 'people' was maintained throughout the production and it was highly sympathetic to their cause. The character of Coriolanus was deliberately marginalised and we felt little sympathy for him; he became an exemplar of everything against which 'Democratie' was fighting.

The interpretative focus of Elijah Moshinsky's production is on the private and personal. Using the unique intimacy and single viewpoint of the television camera, Moshinsky offers a play about individuals. Close-ups provide an opportunity for subtle characterisation – at no time do we ever see Moshinsky's citizens as an indistinct crowd, they are identifiable individuals. Quiet and

contemplative, their demands for corn seem a reasonable protest. They are polite, deferential and easily controlled by the governing Tribunes; these are childlike citizens, unused to power.

While the citizens' general public demand is for a functioning democracy, their specific focus is on the personality of Caius Martius (later called Coriolanus) and what he represents:

Above: *– The people's enemy is gone!*
– Our enemy is banished, he is gone! Hoo-oo!
The citizens rejoice, 1990

FIRST CITIZEN   **Though soft-conscienced men can be content to say it was for his country, he did it to please his mother, and to be partly proud, which he is even to the altitude of his virtue.**

[I.1.35-8]

'Now, as I live I will'

The Early Production History of *Coriolanus*

Coriolanus was written in 1608 and first published in the First Folio in 1623, but there are no records of performance until Nahum Tate's in 1681. Tate's production was an adaptation of Shakespeare's text entitled *The Ingratitude of the Common-Wealth*, and it was to be the first in a series of adaptations of the play which held the stage until William Charles Macready's productions of Shakespeare's original play at Drury Lane and Covent Garden seen between 1819 and 1839.

In 1901 Irving played Coriolanus to Ellen Terry's Volumnia at the London Lyceum, and as the twentieth century progressed the part of Coriolanus became a significant one in the Shakespearian repertoire. The most influential Coriolanus of recent times was Laurence Olivier's who first played the rôle in 1938. But it was Olivier's 1959 performance which was said to vindicate the play on the stage, and after this production the popularity of the play grew, particularly in repertory companies. *Coriolanus* has always been popular in translation, its political themes consistently finding contemporary resonances. It was performed in France and Russia in the 1930s and in Prague in 1960. But the play has been particularly significant in Germany. Between 1911 and 1920 it was performed more in Germany than in Britain, and in the 1930s it was used, particularly in schools, as a text which supposedly spoke of Nazi honour and valour. In 1963 Bertolt Brecht's adaptation of the play was performed by the Berliner Ensemble. This sought to diminish the value of Coriolanus' valour and heroism, focusing more on the democratic aspirations of the citizens.

Top: Henry Irving, 1901
Left: Brecht's *Coriolan*, 1963
Right: Edith Evans as Volumnia, 1959

Martius is seen as the emblem of a political regime which pursues its aims at the expense of its people and his first speech ironically echoes this perception:

> **What's the matter, you dissentious rogues,**
> **That rubbing the poor itch of your opinion**
> **Make yourselves scabs?**
>
> [162-3]

Alan Howard spits out his first line, his face contorted with distaste and we are confronted with a protagonist who is patently not a diplomat and resents his peacetime rôle as a politician. Here is a man who prefers the physical violence of the battlefield to the politics of verbal rhetoric. He swiftly embraces the chance to exchange debate with his own people for military combat with their enemies the Volsces. Tim Supple's production with its huge cast, including over 50 extras, emphasised with frightening realism the enormity of Martius' victory at the city of Corioles. The large Volscian army approached striking their huge shields making a threatening and fearful noise. Kenneth Branagh achieved victory facing apparently insurmountable odds. Martius is a spectacularly successful soldier and Rome's war becomes his personal, solitary battle. Rising with contempt above his fellow soldiers, the 'shames of Rome' [I.4.31], he dismisses ordinary men as inadequate and focuses his proud masculine extremism on Aufidius:

> **I'll fight with none but thee, for I do hate thee**
> **Worse than a promise-breaker.**
>
> [I.8.1]

Both Martius and Aufidius are consumed with the passion of hatred and ambition. Each sees the other as a trophy which will bring with it fame, honour, and masculine supremacy. Theirs is a powerful intimate rela-

tionship and in Robert Lepage's stylised interpretation it was overtly homosexual; they fought naked on a steeply raked stage in slow motion, the alienating cinematic strategy of the production adding to the self-absorbed exclusivity of their intense and private battle. This relationship became central to Lepage's conception of the whole play, providing a compelling reason for Martius' inability to function effectively away from the violence of the battlefield.

Tim Supple's production placed much of the explanation for Martius' masculine extremism on his mother, Volumnia. Whilst Martius is away securing victory at Corioles, Volumnia encourages his fearful, silent wife to glory in his martial valour:

> **If my son were my husband, I should freelier**
> **rejoice in that absence wherein he won honour**
> **than in the embracements of his bed where he**
> **would show most love.**
>
> [I.3.2-5]

Above left: *Rome hath such a soldier*
Kenneth Branagh, 1992
Above: *O, mother, mother!*
What have you done?
Judi Dench and Kenneth Branagh, 1992

Judi Dench infused motherly pride in her son's military supremacy with an uncompromising sincerity which was sinister and disturbing. Her voice was steely and terrifying; here was an insight into the upbringing of a man whose extremist dogmatism has become a symbol of patrician pride and self-indulgence. This was underlined by Volumnia's enthusiastic playing of war games with Martius' small and vulnerable-looking son.

Irene Worth's Volumnia is a more gentle, maternal mother. When Alan Howard returns from victory over Aufidius bearing the new name as a talisman of his victory she is almost speechless with tearful pride, 'What is it? – Coriolanus must I call thee?' [II.1.167]. As he kneels in supplication before her, Irene Worth

As for my country I have shed my blood,
Not fearing outward force, so shall my lungs
Coin words till they decay against those measles
Which we disdain should tetter us...

[III.1.76-8]

Alan Howard brings a calm, rational pragmatism to Coriolanus' speeches which make them persuasively convincing. As he speaks, the faces of the Senators and the wily Tribunes betray the truth, and even the kind and fatherly Menenius, played by Joss Ackland as a wise elder statesman, looks vaguely shamed. Spoken before a small committee of politicians sitting around a plain conference table, Howard's words seem to pierce the organised hypocrisy to which even the Tribunes are prepared to contribute. It is inevitable that however hard they try to dissuade him, Coriolanus will continue to speak his mind in public. A dangerous misfit in the Senate and a useful symbol of corruption for the Tribunes, Coriolanus becomes a dual scapegoat:

BRUTUS
There's no more to be said, but he is banished
As enemy to the people and his country.
It shall be so.

[III.3.117-9]

holds this moment, making it intensely private and calm amongst the pomp of Coriolanus' public welcome. Martius presents his new name as a gift to his mother.

The plan to elevate Coriolanus to the Roman Senate is the symbolic realisation of Volumnia's ambitions for her son, yet his election demands that he must go to the people, show his wounds, and feign sincerity. It is the public exhibition of private experience. In David Thacker's production set in a world reminiscent of revolutionary France, Toby Stephens exhibited a determined and deliberate contempt for citizens, Tribunes and Senators. Stephens' Coriolanus was an arrogant, overbearing aristocratic youth, his distaste for both democracy and people consistently emphasising the class-based

Above: *Did you perceive*
He did solicit you in free contempt?
The citizens are incited by the Tribunes, 1992

focus of the production. Mockingly wearing his plain Gown of Humility as if it were ridiculous fancy-dress, Stephens exposed the risky shallowness of a society which is governed and preserved by the playing of rôles. For Coriolanus to parade his masculine honour in front of the mutinous citizens has been both to secure order amongst the people and maintain the exclusivity of the ruling martial aristocracy; but Coriolanus' exposure of Rome's hypocrisy destabilises the entire political system. When called to speak before Senators and Tribunes, Coriolanus' contempt for democracy and the people is chilling and disturbing:

Coriolanus leaves Rome and banishment returns to him a sense of self-determination; by refusing to compromise himself he has retained his identity and his sense of honour. Essentially unchanged by what has happened, Coriolanus goes back to his old enemy, Aufidius, who is the only man who has offered him respect and a kinship born of common ambition. To present himself to Aufidius unsure of his reception is an act of private courage which contrasts starkly with the public act of hypocrisy he has avoided in Rome. Toby Stephens' Coriolanus arrived to face Aufidius physically exhausted. His cloak

bore a remarkable similarity to the Gown of Humility he had previously been forced to wear, but his pledge to revenge himself on Rome revealed that his pride and arrogance had been strengthened through exile. For Barry Lynch's Aufidius, Coriolanus' arrival was wondrous and almost unbelievable. Pacing around the stage, keeping Coriolanus at a distance, Lynch measured his response to this completely unexpected event before embracing Stephens, touching his scarred body to see if it was real:

Let me twine
Mine arms about that body.

[IV.5.109-10]

Stephens accepted this embrace as the symbol of a martial pact; he would go on to use Aufidius to achieve his spiteful goal. By contrast, Lepage's production presented this scene as the wondrous and magical reunion of two lovers; Aufidius and Coriolanus had at last found each other without having to fight.

This intimate, peaceful greeting serves to symbolise a public partnership which will be potentially catastrophic for Rome. In Michael Bogdanov's production, the news of Coriolanus' alliance with Aufidius against Rome arrived by telephone to the editorial office of the new 'Democratie' newspaper, stopping the Tribunes and the new party in its tracks. A moment of crisis has been reached, something must be done to save Rome, but as the pattern of the play has suggested, it must be a private act to serve a public purpose.

When Menenius fails to persuade Coriolanus to change his mind, Rome's last chance is to call upon his mother. Volumnia pleads for her life and the lives of his wife and son, but she also asks him to abandon everything she has brought him up to value: honour, valour and martial manhood. Judi Dench faced both Coriolanus and the audi-

ence, varying tone and position, pacing the stage, daring her son to defy her, until worn down Kenneth Branagh's Coriolanus gave in. When he roared the lines 'O, mother, mother!/What have you done? [V.3.183-4] in an ecstasy of despair which echoed around the theatre, Volumnia suddenly and with profound horror realised that in saving Rome she had sacrificed her son. When she returned to Rome to be hailed its saviour, she was consumed with grief. She was a mother who had murdered her son.

It is Coriolanus' final capitulation to his mother which ensures his downfall. In Aufidius' eyes Coriolanus has committed a double betrayal. He has given in to Rome's entreaties by listening to a woman. For a man to abandon self-determination at the behest

Left: *What would you have, you curs,*
That like nor peace nor war?
Toby Stephens, 1994
Below: Toby Stephens embraces Caroline Blakiston, Ivor Hill as Young Martius and Monica Dolan, 1994

NOTABLE PRODUCTIONS OF *CORIOLANUS*

	THEATRE	DIRECTOR	DESIGNER	PRINCIPALS
1983	BBC-tv	Elijah Moshinsky	Dick Coles	Alan Howard......................*Coriolanus* Joss Ackland ....*Menenius* John Burgess ....*Sicinius* Anthony Pedley ....*Brutus* Irene Worth ....*Volumnia* Joanna McCallum ....*Virgilia* Mike Gwilym..........................*Aufidius*
1990	English Shakespeare Company	Michael Bogdanov	Chris Dyer	Michael Pennington ....*Coriolanus* Bernard Lloyd ....*Menenius* Michael Cronin ....*Sicinius* Robert Demeger ....*Brutus* June Watson ....*Volumnia* Lynn Farleigh ....*Virgilia* Andrew Jarvis ....*Aufidius*
1992	Renaissance Theatre Company with Chichester Festival Theatre	Tim Supple	Bunny Christie	Kenneth Branagh ....*Coriolanus* Richard Briers ....*Menenius* Jimmy Yuill.............................*Sicinius* Gerard Horan...........................*Brutus* Judi Dench ....*Volumnia* Susannah Harker ....*Virgilia* Iain Glen ....*Aufidius*
1992	Théâtre Repère, Quebec	Robert Lepage	Robert Lepage	Jules Philip ....*Coriolanus*

Other rôles were not assigned in the programme. The play was performed as *Coriolan* in a translation and adaptation by Michel Garneau.

	THEATRE	DIRECTOR	DESIGNER	PRINCIPALS
1994	Royal Shakespeare Company	David Thacker	Fran Thompson	Toby Stephens ....*Coriolanus* Philip Voss ....*Menenius* Linal Haft ....*Sicinius* Ewan Hooper ....*Brutus* Caroline Blakiston ....*Volumnia* Monica Dolan.........................*Virgilia* Barry Lynch ....*Aufidius*

Above: *I have some wounds upon me, and they smart*
To hear themselves remembered.
Toby Stephens, 1994

of his mother is to betray his valour and masculine honour. Barry Lynch bellowed his attack on Coriolanus' manhood:

But at his nurse's tears
He whined and roared away your victory

[V.6.97-8]

Declaiming Coriolanus's betrayal to the Volscians with a fierce and angry rhetoric, he created a terrifying desire for public retribution which was echoed in the faces of his people who thronged the encircling balconies of the Swan Theatre. Suddenly the stage was filled by angry citizens and Coriolanus was brutally felled. Toby Stephens' Coriolanus was killed not just by Aufidius, but also by the people he had so recently conquered. There was no posthumous honour for this Coriolanus. As the citizens deserted the stage, Lynch was left, unable to carry Coriolanus' body by himself. As the lights faded, Aufidius remained alone, burdened by the corpse of the man who had betrayed him.

Helen J. Schaffer Snow

CYMBELINE

*The audience is transported to a world of long, long ago for
an amazing tale in which love and fidelity triumph over adversity.*

Cymbeline is an exciting experiment in dramatised romance, a challenging form with action that spans disparate times and places, and includes intricately woven sub-plots. The play's themes are appearance and reality, human relationships, court and country values, principles of government and codes of honour. The mature dramatist employs subtle characterisation and rich language to play on his audience's emotions. He juxtaposes tragedy and comedy and he toys with farce. The pattern of *Cymbeline* is one of deception followed by revelation, reconciliation and affirmation of the power of human goodness.

While seeking to embrace the play's remarkable diversity, directors have also striven to establish unifying themes. In Peter Hall's second production, a great golden zodiac symbolised the Jacobean cosmos. Bill Alexander explored the extraordinary emotional range of the play on a bare circular stage to the eerie accompaniment of steel drums, wind chimes and tubular bells. JoAnne Akalaitis chose to juxtapose the British Empire and Native American Indians. Robin Phillips presented the Court as the suffocatingly correct British monarchy between the wars. For both William Gaskill and John Barton the play was more simply a wonderful story. In Gaskill's production a single actor entered and whistled. Servants, who doubled as stage hands, gathered round to hear how Cymbeline, King of Britain, had rebelled against the Emperor Augustus. Emblems set against a grey cyclorama indi-

Above:
*I am nothing; or if not
Nothing to be were better.*
Barbara Jefford as 'Fidele' at the Old Vic, 1956

cated location: an heraldic lion for Britain, an eagle for Rome. Barton established the character of Cornelius as the play's narrator, allowing him to move through the action, book in hand. In this production Sebastian Shaw was a venerable King Cymbeline with his white hair flowing into his white beard. His anonymous Queen, Imogen's stepmother, herself articulates the fairytale context:

> **No, be assur'd you shall not find me, daughter,**
> **After the slander of most stepmothers,**
> **Evil-ey'd unto you.**
>
> [I.2.1-3]

In Barton's production she was played by Sheila Allen as an exotic bird of prey crowned with pheasant's curling feathers. Thirteen years later Julie Legrand, at The Other Place, would run blood-red finger nails over her collection of poisons.

For all the expense of directorial ingenuity and inventive stage design, audiences remember the play for the radiance of Imogen. Her single-minded, pure love for

'EMBRACED BY A PIECE OF TENDER AIR'

The Early Production History of *Cymbeline*

The plot of *Cymbeline* is taken from Holinshed's *Chronicles* and various old plays and popular romances. The 1623 First Folio is the earliest text, printing 'Imogen' for the 'Innogen' of Holinshed. Simon Forman saw the play before 1611 and it may have been written as early as 1608-9. The next recorded performance was in 1634 before Charles I. After the Restoration *Cymbeline* was adapted by Thomas D'Urfey as *The Injured Princess or, The Fatal Wager*. A second adaptation by William Hawkins in 1759 included music by Thomas Arne.

Garrick revived the original play in 1761, and Posthumus was one of his favourite parts. In 1827 Charles Kemble staged a carefully researched production 'displaying as accurately as stage effect will permit, the Habits, Weapons and buildings of the Gaulish and Belgic Colonists of the Southern Counties of Britain…'. In the

course of time Imogen became one of the most loved of Shakespeare's heroines with particularly fine performances from Sarah Siddons and Ellen Terry. George Bernard Shaw gave the latter detailed guidance on how to approach the rôle and also wrote a tongue-in-cheek alternative last act, *Cymbeline Refinished*, eliminating the 'surprises that no longer surprise anybody'. It is

occasionally performed.

Cymbeline has been seen less frequently in the twentieth century. The experimental 1920s modern dress production at Birmingham Repertory Theatre with Cedric Hardwicke as Iachimo was hailed as 'Shakespeare in plus fours'. Donald Wolfit in 1937 relished Iachimo's villainy, and Paul Scofield's Cloten (in 1946) was both malicious and royal. Michael Benthall's 1956 Old Vic production eliminated scenery and had figures emerge from darkness into the misty light of Britain or the sunshine of Italy. In 1957 Peter Hall and his designer Lila de Nobili achieved the timeless quality of romance, combining Roman soldiers with pastoral, Renaissance and Gothic elements.

Top: Peggy Ashcroft at the Shakespeare Memorial Theatre, 1957
Left: Thomas Arne, 1710–1778
Right: Robert Harris as Cymbeline, 1957

Above: Robert Arnold as Guiderius, Brian Bedford as Arviragus and Cyril Luckham as Belarius mourn the 'death' of Peggy Ashcroft as 'Fidele' at the Shakespeare Memorial Theatre, 1957

Posthumus and her spirited response to adversity rarely fails to elicit an audience's emotional commitment. Vanessa Redgrave was a golden Celtic princess and Susan Fleetwood was ethereal in pale floating robes. Judi Dench more robustly brought out the character's humour and courage, while Geraldine James and Harriet Walter, in very different productions, both exemplified her integrity and determination. It is to the barely concealed delight of Court and audience that Imogen has secretly married Posthumus. His banishment to Rome is the stuff of fairytale.

The BBC production seeks to establish a sense of the play being a story for all time by giving it the contemporary frame of Shakespeare's England. Cymbeline is a hot-tempered, powerful Jacobean ruler, with Claire Bloom's Queen a cold, calculating Machiavellian figure, black against Helen Mirren's pure white and gold Imogen. Michael Pennington's Posthumus is an honest English gentleman, as fair as his Imogen. He is banished not to classical Rome but to the sumptuously furnished courts of late Renaissance Italy, reflecting the implicit comparison between idealised Roman honour and Italian trickery. In such a setting Iachimo, 'slight thing of Italy' [V.4.64] in black leather with black gloved hands can cynically impugn Imogen's chastity and Posthumus can be reduced to wagering on her honour.

Imogen is tricked into taking Iachimo's trunk into her bedchamber. An enormous white bed which epitomised both her chastity and her sexuality dominated Barton's stage. Imogen sleeps, and in an unfailingly theatrical moment Iachimo emerges from the trunk beside the bed. Robert Lindsay, apparently naked, leans close over her:

> **Our Tarquin thus**
> **Did softly press the rushes 'ere he waked**
> **The chastity he wounded.**
>
> [II.2.12-14]

He lecherously fondles her bracelet, using it like a magnifying glass. Tim Pigott-Smith licked her hand to draw the bracelet off, lifting the sheet to peer at her naked body and note the mole beneath her breast, the damning detail which persuades Posthumus that Iachimo has seduced her.

In Rome, Michael Pennington's Posthumus slowly loses faith in Imogen's fidelity. Iachimo describes her chamber, finally drawing back his sleeve to show her bracelet. Trust struggles with misgiving as the camera closes in on Pennington's angry, betrayed eyes. Patrick Allen was a less mature, over-confident Posthumus, a tempting target for Eric Porter's mischievous trickery. Humiliated by Porter's mocking laugh and rendered vulnerable by his isolation in an alien culture he lost all faith in Imogen's fidelity. Posthumus turns from love to violent loathing which goes beyond an individual focus upon Imogen to become a fierce misogynist tirade:

> **...there's no motion**
> **That tends to vice in man but I affirm**
> **It is the woman's part...**
>
> [II.5.21-3]

His revenge will be Imogen's death and it is his hapless servant Pisanio who is ordered to kill her, with the first step being to trick her into leaving the court.

In the BBC-tv production an eagle circles

Above: *O sleep, thou ape of death, lie dull upon her.*
And be her sense but as a monument,
Thus in a chapel lying.
Vanessa Redgrave and Eric Porter, 1962

Pisanio with 'I false!' [III.4.46] and winning a laugh with her flat delivery of:

Most like
Bringing me here to kill me.

[117-18]

Imogen is followed to Milford Haven by Cloten. In the BBC-tv production Paul Jesson is an elegant fop with oiled, curled hair, tiny moustachios and beard, lisping 'Womans', while in 1962 Clive Swift played a stupid lout whose attendants treated him with bored disdain, and in 1974 Charles Keating swaggered, sure of his sexual attractiveness. At the National Theatre Ken Stott communicated Cloten's brute courage, human failings and patriotism. Earlier in the play Imogen had angrily rejected him for Posthumus, declaring:

His meanest garment
That ever hath but clipped his body is dearer
In my respect than all the hairs above thee,
Were they all made such men…

[II.3.133-6]

A production at the Manchester Royal Exchange in 1984 sought to emphasise the symbolic relationship between Cloten and Posthumus by doubling the parts. Cloten's desire to wear Posthumus' clothes when pursuing Imogen not only facilitates complication of the plot but more profoundly contributes to the play's exploration of psychological complexity. Cloten represents a dark, sexual violence (an 'other' male self) from which Imogen is saved by the intervention of her as yet unacknowledged brother. As played by Clive Swift, Cloten appeared almost psychopathic, justifying Guiderius' sudden violence. Keeping faith with a realistic truthfulness Imogen tires of her disguise, 'I see man's life is a tedious one' [III.6.1], and indeed she falls ill. The medicine she takes is,

slowly over the clean winter landscape of Milford Haven. At the National Theatre the transition from court intrigue to countryside was spectacularly accomplished by designer Alison Chitty. The circular playing area under the golden zodiacal heavens inverted to reveal the rocks and grass of Wales. The centre of the stage sank to create the cave from which Belarius enters: 'A goodly day' [III.3.1]. Basil Henson's paternal pride in his adopted sons was moving, their praise of the natural life fervent. Recent Stratford, Ontario, and New York productions have chosen to present the boys as 'noble savages', or Black and Native Americans. At The Other Place, by contrast,

the frustrated youths' less than enthusiastic responses to Belarius' lyric enthusiasm for pastoral life seemed credible.

Vanessa Redgrave's tomboyish Fidele impulsively cried, 'O for a horse with wings' [III.2.48] as she rushed to meet Posthumus. She faced disillusion bravely. Susan Fleetwood, with a tremulous smile at her plight, was transformed from fairytale princess to simple country boy. Harriet Walter remained essentially herself, confronting

however, straight out of fairytale and she falls into a sleep that has all the appearance of death. She is laid next to the headless corpse of Cloten and the dirge is spoken:

Golden lads and girls all must
As chimney-sweepers, come to dust.

[IV.2.262-3]

At the National Theatre Cloten's corpse was heaped with flowers which Geraldine James slowly brushed away as she built to a climax of poignant mourning. She cradled what Imogen assumes to be Posthumus' body in her arms. Vanessa Redgrave's audience moved between laughter and tears as, in a waking nightmare of misapprehension, at once ludicrous, moving and horrific, she caught up the body and smeared her face with its blood. Harriet Walter's performance drew on depths of emotional truthfulness to transcend any sense of contrivance or the absurd. She drew tears from an absorbed audience wholly bound up with the intensity of her suffering.

William Gaskill and John Barton both chose to direct the battle between the Romans and Britons as sequences of extended slow-motion mime. Gaskell choreographed the stage directions to music which swelled and receded with the fortunes of the armies. It was consistent with the rôle given him throughout Barton's production that Cornelius should narrate events. In 1979 the battle was symbolically presented. On a darkened stage soldiers waved flags to background battle music and Cymbeline stood in a pool of light upstage, the focus of the action. At the National Theatre Tim Pigott-Smith's Iachimo was overcome by guilt, his sexual cynicism re-evaluated. He was unable to fight Posthumus who, similarly overcome by remorse and stripped to filthy rags, wore the cloth that was supposedly steeped in Imogen's blood round his head.

Following the battle comes the play's

central revelation of divine providence, the descent of Jupiter. As Posthumus awaited execution and slept in a cage over the stage, the Leonati, in Gaskill's production, glided round him to intercede with the god. At The Other Place the outline of an eagle was projected onto the floor between the spirits of Posthumus' parents. On television the god is played by Michael Hordern who appears like a loving, patient father and delivers his judgement to the anxious family grouped round the manacled Posthumus. By contrast Gaskill, Barton and Hall all made full use of theatrical equipment for a traditional *deus ex machina*. As described in the text, to the crash of thunder, a spectacular golden eagle descends bearing Jupiter who dispenses his mercy:

Whom best I love I cross; to make my gift,
The more delayed, delighted...

[V.4.100-101]

Following this scene comes the virtuoso series of thirty or so revelations. Discovery follows

Below: *A mother to the birth of three?*
David O'Hara as Guiderius, David Bradley, Paul Webster as Belarius, Paul Spence as Arviragus, Nicholas Farrell and Harriet Walter, 1987

NOTABLE PRODUCTIONS OF *CYMBELINE*

	THEATRE	DIRECTOR	DESIGNER	PRINCIPALS
1962	Royal Shakespeare Theatre, Stratford-upon-Avon	William Gaskill	Rene Allio	Vanessa Redgrave....................*Imogen* Patrick Allen ....*Posthumus* Eric Porter ....*Iachimo* Tom Fleming ....*Cymbeline*
1974	Royal Shakespeare Theatre, Stratford-upon-Avon	John Barton with Barry Kyle, Clifford Williams	John Napier, Martyn Bainbridge, Sue Jenkinson	Susan Fleetwood ....*Imogen* Tim Pigott-Smith ....*Posthumus* Ian Richardson ....*Iachimo* Sebastian Shaw ....*Cymbeline*
1979	Royal Shakespeare Theatre, Stratford-upon-Avon	David Jones	Christopher Morley	Judi Dench ....*Imogen* Roger Rees ....*Posthumus* Ben Kingsley ....*Iachimo* Jeffrey Dench.....................*Cymbeline*
1982	BBC-tv	Elijah Moshinsky	Barbara Gosnold	Helen Mirren ....*Imogen* Michael Pennington ....*Posthumus* Robert Lindsay ....*Iachimo* Richard Johnson ....*Cymbeline*
1986	The Shakespearean Festival Theatre, Stratford, Ontario	Robin Phillips	Daphne Dare	Martha Burns ....*Imogen* Joseph Ziegler ....*Posthumus* Colm Feore ....*Iachimo* Eric Donkin ....*Cymbeline*
1987	The Other Place, Stratford-upon-Avon	Bill Alexander	Kit Surrey	Harriet Walter........................*Imogen* Nicholas Farrell ....*Posthumus* Donald Sumpter ....*Iachimo* David Bradley ....*Cymbeline*
1988	National Theatre, London	Peter Hall	Alison Chitty	Geraldine James ....*Imogen* Peter Woodward ....*Posthumus* Tim Pigott-Smith ....*Iachimo* Tony Church ....*Cymbeline*
1989	Public/Newman Theatre, New York	JoAnne Akalaitis	George Tsypin	Joan Cusack ....*Imogen* Jeffrey Nordling ....*Posthumus* Michael Cumpsty ....*Iachimo* George Bartenieff ....*Cymbeline*

Above: *I see a man's life is a tedious one.*
Geraldine James, 1988

discovery with bewildering speed. At The Other Place deliberate comic effects were introduced, varying the emotional tension. Cymbeline's lines: 'Does the world go round?' [V.5.233] and 'New matter still?' [244] were spoken by David Bradley with dry humour. Richard Johnson is, by contrast, a vigorous, commanding king, moved to wonder, anger and forgiveness. The play concludes with general reconciliation. John Barton's production culminated in a blaze of gold as King Cymbeline sloughed off his browns and greys and donned flowing golden robes in a dazzling return to his proper authority. The Other Place production drew its audience into an inward-looking harmonious circle affirming a deep sense of peace and spiritual calm.

Niky Rathbone

HAMLET

*A restless obsession with questions which procrastinate is translated
into a patient acceptance of the imperative to action.*

Hamlet's perception of Elsinore is characterised by paralysing disgust. Expressed early in the play in Hamlet's first soliloquy, this disgust springs from his mother's 'o'erhasty marriage' [II.2.57] to his uncle Claudius, from whom, as Hamlet's 'prophetic soul' [I.5.40] senses, emanates an all-pervading corruption. The set in Ron Daniels' production visualised the disturbed nature of the Danish court, with walls, doors and windows running at twisted angles, a court literally 'out of joint' [188]. A 'smiling, damnèd villain' [106] who can hide his guilt behind joviality, Claudius presides over a court where spying and hypocrisy are the order of the day, apparent in the courtiers' approval of Claudius' and Gertrude's marriage or Polonius' instructions for Reynaldo. To Robert Sturua, corruption in Elsinore was omnipresent. On a stage dominated by a T-shaped steel walkway and lit by harsh white light, this court emerged as a prison run by an austere Claudius followed by a sycophantic Polonius. Although less pervasively oppressive, the image of Elsinore as a prison is also conveyed in Grigori Kozintsev's film where gates are lowered and drawbridges pulled up to create an hermetically sealed space. Frequent shots of Hamlet on the shore establish the sea as a symbol of freedom and escape. Glimpsed through an upstage window, the sea served a similar purpose in Daniels' production.

Right: *– I did love you once.*
– Indeed, my lord, you made me believe so.
Laurence Olivier and Jean Simmons, 1948

'NOW CRACKS A NOBLE HEART'

The Early Production History of *Hamlet*

The first to play Shakespeare's most famous rôle was probably Richard Burbage. When Burbage died in 1619, Joseph Taylor took over, and his influence extended well into the Restoration – Betterton is said to have been instructed by Davenant, who saw Taylor play the rôle. Betterton's Hamlet was a vivacious, enterprising character in a version that had most of its poetry and philosophy cut. He and Garrick, a century later, stressed Hamlet's horror at the appearance of the ghost.

At the end of the eighteenth century, Kemble introduced the tradition of the gloomy, melancholic prince, a characterisation based on thorough intellectual study.

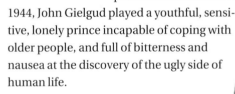

Edmund Kean first played Hamlet at Drury Lane in 1814 and he reduced the extreme physical horror of Hamlet meeting the ghost. He also introduced Hamlet's lasting love for Ophelia and a tameness in his confrontation with his mother. An agreeable, tender nature was characteristic of Macready's Hamlet, but he restored the character's wildness and excitement in the play-within-the-play and the graveyard scene.

The mid-nineteenth century saw the arrival of the completely sane Hamlet. Barry Sullivan played him as a keen-witted, bitter man. Edwin Booth extended this line, adding Hamlet's sense of being haunted to a many-faceted interpretation. While Henry Irving stressed the self-generated excitement sometimes verging on hysteria, Forbes-Robertson developed Booth's concept, turning Hamlet into a Renaissance courtier trapped in a barbarous Teutonic court. His production restored Fortinbras and ended the nineteenth century custom of lowering the curtain on 'The rest is silence'.

In 1925, Barry Jackson produced the first modern-dress *Hamlet* and freed the play of many of the stifling preconceptions of the past; notably, he rescued Polonius from being played as an old fool. In four productions between 1930 and 1944, John Gielgud played a youthful, sensitive, lonely prince incapable of coping with older people, and full of bitterness and nausea at the discovery of the ugly side of human life.

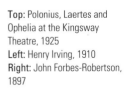

Top: Polonius, Laertes and Ophelia at the Kingsway Theatre, 1925
Left: Henry Irving, 1910
Right: John Forbes-Robertson, 1897

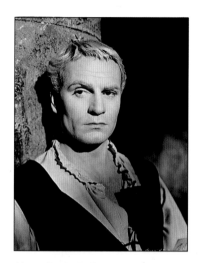

Above: *Hamlet the Dane*
Laurence Olivier, 1948

Above: *most sovereign reason*
Innokenti Smoktunovsky, 1964

Above: *a noble mind*
David Warner, 1965

Above: *desperate with imagination*
Alan Howard, 1970

Productions often use the first public scene to show Hamlet's isolation within the society of Denmark. Thus Olivier's Hamlet is seated at a distance from the court. The 'nighted colour' [I.2.68] of his clothes and his brooding mood further separate him from the other courtiers. Dressed in an overcoat with a suitcase by his side, Mark Rylance's very vulnerable and unstable Hamlet waited like a schoolboy for permission to leave the loathed court and go back to Wittenberg. However, Peter Hall emphasised Hamlet's isolation by placing a highly uncomfortable and intimidated Hamlet between Claudius and Polonius, two coolly efficient politicians who run the smoothly effective bureaucratic machine of the court. Kozintsev stresses Hamlet's isolation in the very midst of a busy diplomatic scene by presenting his first soliloquy as a voice-over while a deeply melancholic Hamlet moves among the courtiers like an alien.

The revelation of the true cause of his father's death upsets Hamlet's emotional balance. Derek Jacobi's passionate, repressed Hamlet weeps at the report of the murder, while Kenneth Branagh in the Renaissance Theatre production re-enacted the murder to the words of the disembodied voice and shaft of light representing his father's ghost. The

Above: *dangerous lunacy*
Mark Rylance, 1989

Above: *rose of the fair state*
Daniel Day-Lewis, 1989

Above: *the glass of fashion*
Mel Gibson, 1990

Above: *the mould of form*
Kenneth Branagh, 1992

'wild and whirling words' [I.5.133] Hamlet addresses to Horatio and the guards foreshadow the 'antic disposition' [172] which he will adopt to hide his true purpose. The exact nature of his madness differs considerably between productions. Branagh's interpretations of the rôle in both 1988 and 1992 suggested a sane Hamlet whose madness was always a pretence. In Daniel Day-Lewis' Hamlet, however, there lurked real hysteria behind his simulated madness. While his rational powers never left him, his hold on his emotions often slipped. The extreme vulnerability of Mark Rylance's Hamlet conveyed by his frequent foetal positions on the floor, developed into neurotic behaviour which could no longer be differentiated from genuine insanity. Characteristic of Alan Howard's Hamlet, for whom madness lay solely in the disturbing power of his thoughts, were the shifts between feigned and real madness of which the character himself was often unaware. Howard's frenzied stabbing of Polonius was just one point at which his madness overwhelmed him.

The first instance of Hamlet's madness is his appearance in Ophelia's closet. Instead of having Ophelia relate the incident to Polonius as in the text, Olivier and Kozintsev present it visually, thus focussing on Hamlet rather than Ophelia. Although Hamlet might want to use Ophelia to convince others of the genuineness of his madness, his visit can also be seen as a futile attempt to establish a difference between his mother and his beloved. Olivier's Hamlet doubts Ophelia's loyalty because she ignores his silent appeal. The camera reveals Polonius instructing her to follow him but from Hamlet's perspective down the long corridor it is an act of rejection. His visit to her closet is to test her. A puzzled Jean Simmons' lack of understanding deepens his disappointment at what he considers the general frailty of all women.

Hamlet's disgust at his mother's remarriage disrupts his relationship with Ophelia. His sense of betrayal turns to violent rejection in the nunnery scene when he discovers her complicity in Polonius' and Claudius' plan to spy on him. Torn between her loyalty to her father and her love for Hamlet, she is a pawn manipulated by the men in the politics of the court. In John Barton's production which stressed the relationship between art and real life, Ophelia could be glimpsed rehearsing her 'rich gifts' speech [III.1.101] according to Polonius' instructions. Although their personal relationship is overwhelmed by the moral and political corruption at the court, Hamlet's disgust at Ophelia's betrayal is mixed with his former love. Thus, Olivier tenderly kisses Ophelia's hair before he leaves her lying on the floor. Branagh took Joanne Pearce's Ophelia in his arms between hurling her to the floor, ripping up his love letters and

Above: *Confess yourself to heaven. Repent what's past. Avoid what is to come*
Judi Dench and Daniel Day-Lewis, 1989

spitting in her face. Lalla Ward's Ophelia weeps when she lies to Hamlet about the whereabouts of her father, because she realises that he knows she is lying. Again Hamlet's love for Ophelia is apparent when Derek Jacobi embraces her. Here his line 'it hath made me mad' [147-8] is an astonished realisation of the perverse situation in which he finds himself.

Ophelia's madness is due as much to Hamlet's rejection of her as to her father's sudden death. In Sophie Thompson's interpretation, the onset of insanity announced itself in her 'O what a noble mind is here o'erthrown' [151]. Having been the mute addressee of Hamlet's 'To be or not to be' [56] and a witness to most of the action as she hovered on the edges of the stage, this Ophelia's madness was due to her ample knowledge of the goings-on at Elsinore.

The atmosphere of moral corruption at the Danish court poisons most of Hamlet's personal relationships. Thus, his attitude to Polonius is characterised by an irrepressible urge to mock and insult him. While Felix Aylmer plays Polonius as a deferential busybody and thus partly justifies the aggressiveness of Olivier's Hamlet, Eric Porter's Polonius betrays signs of genuine concern for the demented prince, which makes Jacobi's impatient Hamlet appear particularly rude and cruel. In John Barton's production at Stratford, however, Hamlet's banter with Polonius was purely good-natured. Tony Church's Polonius was a truly benevolent man and he and his family were the only good things at Claudius' court.

Mark Rylance felt deep disappointment at the discovery that his old friends Rosencrantz and Guildenstern, whom he had greeted enthusiastically and unsuspectingly, were spying for Claudius. Jacobi, however, suspects Rosencrantz and Guildenstern from very early on and his questions are designed to test them. His suspicion turns to hatred and later to cold indifference when he tells Horatio how he sent them to England to be killed. Apart from Horatio, who remains the loyal friend and confidant to the end, the players are the only people who engage Hamlet's genuine interest and enthusiasm. For Alan Howard their feigned madness constituted an alternative to the real madness that loomed over him. In a production that presented the events at the Danish court as play acting, by means of, among other things, a stage-on-the-stage set and the carefully orchestrated entrances of the king and queen, Michael Pennington's Hamlet discovered real life in the players' acting. He relished his contact with their theatrical world and recognised himself in

Pyrrhus, finishing the First Player's line:

So as a painted tyrant Pyrrhus stood,
And like a neutral to his will and matter

[II.2.478–79]

with 'Did nothing' [80]. Smoktunovsky, however, presents a self-centred Hamlet using the players as mere means to an end. As his persistent beating on a tabor during the Pyrrhus speech expresses, Hamlet is preoccupied with his own thoughts; the players only function as instruments to establish Claudius' guilt.

Though furnished with a strong reason to kill Claudius, Hamlet never makes serious plans to effect his revenge. Under cover of his 'antic disposition', he, unlike Laertes and Fortinbras, who both turn their filial loyalty

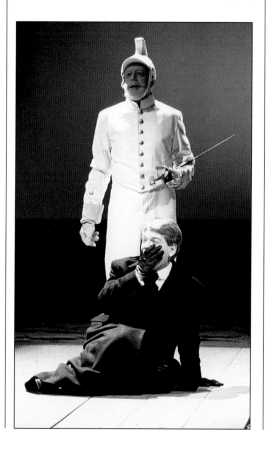

into immediate action, merely provokes and threatens the murderer of his father. The play-within-the-play serves at once, to establish Claudius' guilt and as a provocation and threat. Basil Sydney's Claudius is visibly shocked by a dumbshow resembling the flashback that had accompanied the ghost's report of the murder. Alarmed by the suspecting glances and whispers of the courtiers, he breaks off the play after the dumbshow and throws the court into utter confusion. Patrick Stewart's Claudius manages to retain his composure for much longer. He even reassuringly pats the hand of Claire Bloom's increasingly nervous Gertrude, until he realises that the scene enacted is that of his own crime and breaks off the show. However, when Branagh's impatient Hamlet took over the part of Lucianus in *The Murder of Gonzago*, John Shrapnel's Claudius left the theatre not because his guilt was awakened but because he felt insulted by his mad nephew.

Hamlet's inability to kill Claudius is dramatically linked to his confrontation with his mother, for it is on his way to her closet that he wastes the opportunity to revenge his father. In the closet scene, Hamlet most strongly expresses his idolisation of his dead father and his disgust at Gertrude's sexuality. The incestuous affection between mother and son which Olivier had established from the beginning of his film reaches its climax in this scene. Olivier displaces the action from the closet to Gertrude's bedchamber which is dominated by a huge, stage-like bed with curtains and steps. While the long, passionate kiss he exchanges with Gertrude at the end of the scene simply continues their earlier behaviour, the same gesture emerged as a

NOTABLE PRODUCTIONS OF *HAMLET*

	THEATRE	DIRECTOR	DESIGNER	PRINCIPALS
1948	Two Cities Film	Laurence Olivier	Roger Furse	Laurence Olivier ....*Hamlet* Basil Sydney ....*Claudius* Eileen Herlie.........................*Gertrude* Jean Simmons ....*Ophelia* Felix Aylmer ....*Polonius*
1964	Sovexportfilm	Grigori Kozintsev	Y. Yenei, G. Kropachev, S. Virsaladze	Innokenti Smoktunovsky ......*Hamlet* M. Nazvanov ....*Claudius* E. Radzin...............................*Gertrude* A. Vertinskaya ....*Ophelia* Y. Tolubeyev ....*Polonius*
1965	Royal Shakespeare Theatre, Stratford-upon-Avon	Peter Hall	John Bury	David Warner ....*Hamlet* Brewster Mason ....*Claudius* Elizabeth Spriggs ....*Gertrude* Glenda Jackson ....*Ophelia* Tony Church.........................*Polonius*
1970	Royal Shakespeare Theatre, Stratford-upon-Avon	Trevor Nunn	Christopher Morley	Alan Howard...........................*Hamlet* David Waller ....*Claudius* Brenda Bruce ....*Gertrude* Helen Mirren ....*Ophelia* Sebastian Shaw ....*Polonius*
1980	BBC-tv	Rodney Bennett	Don Homfray	Derek Jacobi ....*Hamlet* Patrick Stewart......................*Claudius* Claire Bloom..........................*Gertrude* Lalla Ward ....*Ophelia* Eric Porter.............................*Polonius*
1980	Royal Shakespeare Theatre, Stratford-upon-Avon	John Barton	Ralph Koltai	Michael Pennington ....*Hamlet* Derek Godfrey ....*Claudius* Barbara Leigh-Hunt..............*Gertrude* Carol Royle.............................*Ophelia* Tony Church.........................*Polonius*

sudden eruption of long repressed feelings in Daniels' and Eyre's productions, and was deeply disturbing to both mother and son. The revelation of Claudius' guilt and her son's admonitions change Gertrude's attitude towards her husband. Judi Dench was shattered by the experience of the closet scene and instinctively withdrew from Claudius. Eileen Herlie withdraws her hand from her husband's touch after the mad Ophelia has left them. Sydney's playing of:

> **O, Gertrude, Gertrude,**
> **When sorrows come, they come not single spies,**
> **But in battalions**
>
> [IV.5.78-80]

refers as much to his awareness of her new coldness as to Hamlet's murder of Polonius and Ophelia's madness.

It is also in the closet scene that, for the first time in the play, Hamlet takes impulsive action. His reaction to Polonius' death allows widely different interpretations. While Pennington cradled the dead Polonius in his arms and Derek Jacobi's Hamlet weeps over the death of this 'rash, intruding fool' [III.4.32], Rylance did not repent his deed, and his exit with his dagger clenched between his teeth while pulling Polonius out of his mother's room triggered uneasy laughter from the audience. In the BBC version, Rosencrantz and Guildenstern emerge as the next victims of Hamlet's new-found resolution. Following the Second Quarto rather than the First Folio, this version retains Hamlet's lines expressing his antipathy towards his former friends and his determination to catch them in their own trap [III.4.203-11]. His resolve is confirmed when Jacobi glances at them on 'my thoughts be bloody!' [IV.4.66]. With a text that gives no clear indications concerning the extent to which Rosencrantz and Guildenstern are informed of Claudius'

Above: – *But now, my cousin Hamlet, and my son –*
– A little more than kin, and less than kind!
– How is it that the clouds still hang on you?
Mark Rylance, Peter Wight and Clare Higgins, 1989

NOTABLE PRODUCTIONS OF *HAMLET*

	THEATRE	DIRECTOR	DESIGNER	PRINCIPALS
1988	Renaissance Theatre Company	Derek Jacobi	Jenny Tiramani	Kenneth Branagh ....*Hamlet* Richard Easton ....*Claudius* Dearbhla Molloy ....*Gertrude* Sophie Thompson ....*Ophelia* Edward Jewesbury ....*Polonius*
1989	Royal Shakespeare Theatre, Stratford-upon-Avon	Ron Daniels	Antony McDonald	Mark Rylance ....*Hamlet* Peter Wight ....*Claudius* Clare Higgins ....*Gertrude* Rebecca Saire.........................*Ophelia* Patrick Godfrey ....*Polonius*
1989	National Theatre London	Richard Eyre	John Gunter	Daniel Day-Lewis....................*Hamlet* John Castle ....*Claudius* Judi Dench ....*Gertrude* Stella Gonet ....*Ophelia* Michael Bryant......................*Polonius*
1990	Carolco International N.V.	Franco Zeffirelli	Dante Ferretti	Mel Gibson ....*Hamlet* Alan Bates.............................*Claudius* Glenn Close ....*Gertrude* Helena Bonham-Carter ....*Ophelia* Ian Holm...............................*Polonius*
1992	Riverside Studio London	Robert Sturua	Giorgi Meskhishvili	Alan Rickman ....*Hamlet* David Burke ....*Claudius* Geraldine McEwan ....*Gertrude* Julia Ford ....*Ophelia* Michael Byrne ....*Polonius*
1992	Barbican Theatre London	Adrian Noble	Bob Crowley	Kenneth Branagh ....*Hamlet* John Shrapnel ....*Claudius* Jane Lapotaire ....*Gertrude* Joanne Pearce ....*Ophelia* David Bradley.......................*Polonius*

true purpose, the grimness of Hamlet's punishment for these despicable, yet possibly innocent royal toadies is conveyed in Zeffirelli's film version through the interpolated scene of the terrified Rosencrantz and Guildenstern being rushed to their execution.

On his return to Denmark, Hamlet's violent mood swings between paralysing disgust and hyperactivity give way to a more detached and relaxed attitude. Still fully aware of the world's corruption, Hamlet no longer rants and raves at it, but contemplates it with humorous melancholy when faced with the levelling force of death in the graveyard scene. Yet, the news of Ophelia's death and Laertes' extravagant expressions of grief throw him once again into a 'towering passion' [V.2.80]. Olivier's melodramatic appearance, arms spread wide, as 'It is I,/Hamlet the Dane' [V.1.253-4] draws attention to the theatricality of their competitive display of mourning. The grief of Mel Gibson's Hamlet on the other hand, is truly felt and not tinged with the determination to outdo Laertes in his lamentations.

The impulsiveness which led to Polonius' death is the first sign of Hamlet's new resolution to take decisive action, which becomes fully apparent in his account of the sea voyage. No longer paralysed by courtly corruption, he uses his knowledge of it:

> **to have the enginer**
> **Hoist with his own petar.**
>
> [III.4.207- 8]

The man who, earlier in the play, had carefully weighed the pros and cons of action is now convinced that impulsiveness can be successful where detailed planning fails. He considers this a sure sign of 'a divinity that shapes our end' [V.2.10] and confidently submits his fate to the 'special providence' he perceives 'in the fall of a sparrow' [213-14]. Inaction now appears as damnable to him as unpremeditated action had earlier. Yet he needs Horatio's approval to 'quit [Claudius] with this arm' [68]. In the BBC production, Horatio expresses disapproval in 'So Guildenstern and Rosencrantz go to't' [56]. The evasiveness of his 'Why, what a king is this!' [62] as answer to Hamlet's justification for the deaths of his former friends is here converted to approval when, after a moment's hesitation, Robert Swann smilingly takes Jacobi's hand.

Despite his new-found determination, Hamlet is swept away by the rapid succession of events which leads to the multiple deaths of the final scene. Laertes is killed by his own poisoned weapon and Gertrude drinks the

Above: *O my dear Gertrude*
Glenn Close and Alan Bates, 1990

poison intended for Hamlet. Repeated shots of Eileen Herlie looking at the cup establish her suspicion that the drink is poisoned. When she finally drinks it, she does so to protect her son. Clare Higgins drank the poisoned cup to defy her husband and to escape the pointlessness of her life shattered in the closet scene. After her death, Peter Wight's besotted Claudius, who had killed his brother more for Gertrude's love than the crown, welcomed death. In contrast, Sydney's Claudius, grabbing the crown in his death throes, clings to his royal authority. Although Hamlet finally revenges his father, he only kills Claudius when faced with his own imminent death. Learning that his life is at an end, Olivier savagely stabs Claudius. Jacobi not only runs his rapier through his uncle, but forces the poisoned drink down his throat.

Hamlet's own death is characterised by his concern for his public image when he entreats Horatio to 'tell my story' [343]. The big, sloppy grin on the face of David Warner's Hamlet mocked such a concern and expressed his continuing contempt for the Danish court. In many productions, Hamlet's death is a return to his father. In Olivier's film, such a return remains symbolic as Hamlet is carried to the platform where he first met his father's ghost. Noble and Eyre, however, created stage images which vividly connected father and son. Day-Lewis' Hamlet, dying spread-eagled at the foot of a huge Commendatore-like statue of Old Hamlet, emerged as the victim of filial duty, while Branagh's Hamlet was greeted by the open arms of Clifford Rose's benign Old Hamlet waiting in the golden light of a sunset.

A new era begins in Elsinore with the arrival of Fortinbras. The character's ambiguity between Hamlet's 'delicate and tender prince' [IV.4.48] and Horatio's ruthless soldier 'Of unimprovèd mettle hot and full' [I.1.96] finds expression in different stage presentations. The BBC production and Kozintsev present a martial, yet not unsympathetic Fortinbras showing his respect for Hamlet in the military rites he orders for his burial. In most modern productions, however, Fortinbras emerges as an oppressive ruler worse than Claudius. In Sturua's production, his boorish behaviour and propensity to rape suggested a dim future indeed. Yet seldom has a director gone as far as Jacobi, who interpreted Fortinbras' final line as an order to execute Horatio and attendant lords:

> **Go, bid the soldiers shoot.**
>
> [V.2.397]

Romana Beyenburg

HENRY IV PARTS ONE AND TWO

*Valour and cynicism collide and loyalties are confused
as a young man apprehensively prepares for kingship.*

The relationship between the two parts of *Henry IV* is rather more architectural than chronological. Although the plays move forward towards both the reconciliation of father and son and the achievement of civil order with the coronation of Henry V, much of the action in *Part Two* repeats the pattern of *Part One*. The rebellion which is defeated in *Part One* at the battle of Shrewsbury revives and gains fresh impetus from the leadership of the Archbishop of York. The tension between Prince Hal and his father which is relieved at the close of the first play remains prevalent in the second, where Henry continues to voice his anxiety about Hal's future rôle, up to the intensely moving scene of reconciliation on the King's deathbed.

What differentiates the two plays is a metamorphosis of mood and tone: *Henry IV Part Two* is an altogether more sombre drama haunted by images of death, disease and national decline. In Michael Bogdanov's eclectic and sometimes brilliantly anacronistic production, the audience witnessed the evolution of England into a harsh, militaristic state. In the scene at Gaultree Forest, in which Prince John ruthlessly double-crosses the rebels, the King's army was represented as a band of assassins in terrorist hoods.

National decay in Adrian Noble's production was interpreted through extended character development. As the King, Julian Glover was, in the earlier play, possessed by a deep melancholy, a note struck in the play's opening lines 'So shaken as we are, so wan with care' [*Part One*, I.1.1]. This note deep-

ened later in the scene as he expresses the longing that Hotspur, and not Hal, were his son. In *Part Two*, Henry seems increasingly tormented by guilt as he views both the nobles' insurrection and Hal's apparent profligacy as retribution for his usurpation of Richard II. Julian Glover appeared unkempt, gaunt and ravaged. Instead of wearing the crown, he held it loosely by his side, as if he had forfeited the right to wear it. In his relationship with Hal, he changed from the embodiment of cold, distant paternal

Above: – *When wilt thou leave fighting a-days, and foining a-nights, and begin to patch up thine old body for heaven?*
   – *Peace, good Doll, do not speak, do not speak like a death's head, do not bid me remember mine end.*
Orson Welles, 1964

authority seen in *Part One*, to the sick and fearful father of *Part Two*. This air of mortality also pervaded the tavern scenes, so that as Doll Tearsheet was summoned by Falstaff, the sleepless, unshaven king wandered into the Eastcheap tavern and in a chair recently vacated by Falstaff, delivered his wracked

'BANISH PLUMP JACK, AND BANISH ALL THE WORLD'

The Early Production History of *Henry IV Parts One* and *Two*

The first production of *Henry IV Part One* was in about 1596 and that of its sequel shortly after. When both plays were performed in 1613 during the wedding celebrations of Princess Elizabeth, daughter of James I, they were referred to as *The Hotspurre* and *Sir John Falstaffe*, an early indication of the imaginative appeal these characters have continued to exert. The two parts were next abridged for a private production at the home of Sir Edward Dering. *Henry IV Part One* was among the first plays to be performed on the Restoration stage and it continued to be popular throughout the seventeenth century. In 1700, Thomas Betterton produced a heavily cut version of the play which prominently advertised Falstaff's part and classified the play as 'a Tragi-comedy'. The adaptation of the sequel, also attributed to Betterton, shortened rebellion scenes and included part of Act I of *Henry V*. It was performed at Drury Lane in 1720.

While *Henry IV Part Two* has been performed less frequently than *Part One*, the play's closure with the accession of Hal has made it especially popular on the occasion of a coronation. It was given an ostentatious performance for the coronation of George III in 1761, and again in 1821 with William Charles Macready and Charles Kemble, for the coronation of George IV.

Only in the twentieth century have the two parts been presented together largely unabridged, often on a single day. They were thus staged at the Birmingham Repertory Theatre in 1921, and again in Stratford on 23 April 1932 at the ceremonial opening of the rebuilt Memorial Theatre. At the New Theatre in 1945, the cast of the Old Vic production included Ralph Richardson as a mentally agile and drily spoken Falstaff, and Laurence Olivier doubling as Shallow and a stammering Hotspur. The two plays were part of the series of history plays mounted to critical acclaim in 1964 at Stratford by Peter Hall, John Barton and Clifford Williams.

Top: Laurence Olivier as Justice Shallow, 1945.
Left: Part of the engraved frontispiece to *The Wits, or Sport upon Sport*, reflecting the popularity of Shakespeare's play after the Restoration, 1662.
Right: The coronation procession of George IV, 1821

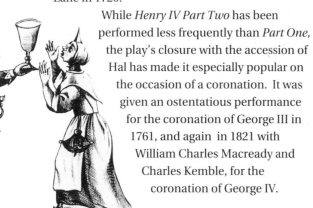

soliloquy on sleeplessness in the presence of the sleeping roisterers:

> Why rather, sleep, liest thou in smoky cribs,
> Upon uneasy pallets stretching thee,
> And hushed with buzzing night-flies to thy
>   slumber,
> Than in the perfumed chambers of the great,
> Under the canopies of costly state,
> And lulled with sound of sweetest melody?
>
> [*Part Two*, III.1.9-14]

The finely tuned scene at Justice Shallow's estate in Gloucester adds a dimension to *Part Two* absent from *Part One*. In this scene, age, memory and death are portrayed not only with humour but also with pathos and unsentimental realism. However, in *Chimes at Midnight*, such nostalgia is pervasive. Before the opening credits, the distant figures of two old men are seen walking through a snowy landscape. The figures are revealed as Falstaff and Shallow and in close-up they embark on maudlin reminiscences of *Part Two*. Falstaff's unfocused and introspective look as the credits appear gives the impression that the friendships of the tavern, the deeds of chivalry and heroism, and the acts of political scheming which we are about to witness represent the shared memory of Falstaff and Shallow. Age and decay were strongly evoked in the late afternoon sunlight of Trevor Nunn's Gloucestershire scenes, but Robert Eddison as Shallow retained his autocratic instincts and was worldly enough to register how he could advance his personal interests through an alliance with Falstaff.

The three contrasting worlds of court, rebel camp and tavern run throughout both plays; they interlock dramatically and offer a panoramic view of the state of the country. As a national epic, the plays link high and low life, and their engagement with the condition of England provides great scope for directors

Above: *clipped in with the sea*
That chides the banks of England, Scotland, Wales
John Napier's set, 1982

and designers. In 1982, the plays were treated almost novelistically as a portrait of society, with the daily life of the tavern and the stable represented in great detail. John Napier designed a massive timber construction of stairways, ramps, jetties and spinning wheels. It provided the base for an ever-changing superstructure of streets, tavern and court which was cleared for the crucial encounter between Hal and Hotspur. In the opening scene of *Henry IV Part One*, the King emerged from banked masses of candle-clutching pilgrims. London street life was strongly evoked as singing mendicants, monks and peasants wandered about asking for alms, and before the Gadshill robbery the stage bustled with ostlers and carriers. The Eastcheap scenes were alive with Hogarthian activity as the encounters between Hal and Falstaff were accompanied by the buzz of background chatter.

In contrast, the sparse set and eclectic costuming of Michael Bogdanov's production eschewed a coherent portrait of an historically based society. Instead, the iconography of the production suggested a divided nation. Henry and his urbane court were dressed in frock coats and battle-red military tunics. Hotspur and his supporters spoke with strong northern vowels and dressed in jerkins and military overcoats, marking them out as a clan and a region apart. Their anger was directed at a king who had dispossessed much of the provincial nobility of its power. Michael

Pennington's Hal, dressed in tattered jeans, moved between the Boar's Head, represented as a bikers' pub frequented by punks, and the court, maintaining a critical distance from both.

Against this acutely observed social background, the plays explore and juxtapose the claims of kingship and ties of kinship, whilst revealing a pattern of substitution and displacement among rival sons and fathers. The climax of *Henry IV Part One* is Hal's killing of Hotspur at the Battle of Shrewsbury after saving his father from the sword of Douglas. As Hotspur bitterly acknowledges, Hal's victory over him should bring the transference of 'those proud titles' possessed by Hotspur:

O Harry, thou hast robbed me of my youth!
I better brook the loss of brittle life
Than those proud titles thou hast won of me.
They wound my thoughts worse than thy sword my flesh.

[*Part One*, V.4.76-9]

Above: Away, you cutpurse rascal, you filthy bung, away. By this wine, I'll thrust my knife in your mouldy chops.
Jenny Quayle as Doll Tearsheet, June Watson as Mistress Quickly and John Price as Pistol in *Part Two*, 1986

But Hal's killing of Hotspur also represents the defeat of a rival whom the King had earlier wished could be proved to be his own son. In Bogdanov's production, the fatal thrust inflicted on Hotspur by Hal was a desperately ignominious one. On a bare stage the pair, dressed in tabards and chain mail, battled with broadswords until Hal lost his weapon. In an abject pose of defeat, Hal cowered in front of Hotspur until, after a significant pause, Hotspur returned his sword, for only then could Hal deliver the death blow. Pennington's Hal displayed intense grief and remorse over the corpse of his dead rival. Tearfully and tenderly, he covered Hotspur's face. When later the body was wheeled off stage, he viewed it with anguish intensified by the fact that Falstaff's deceitful claim to have killed Hotspur had robbed him of the 'titles' he sought to gain.

While the text of the play ends with the King's announcement of a continuing campaign to defeat the rebels, Bogdanov transposed to the end the previous scene in which Falstaff claims in the presence of the King to have killed Hotspur. In a fine psychological stroke, Pennington's Hal, incredulous at Falstaff's brazenness, suggested that by endorsing the lie he had lost the chance to win his father's love. He exited with swords crossed over his shoulders, discredited in the eyes of his father. Such a personal loss was also conveyed in the equivalent scene in *Chimes at Midnight*. Father and son face each other across the body of Hotspur while Falstaff flushes with pleasure, expecting a royal reward. Expressions of doubt, disappointment and betrayal are registered as the film links the three figures and their complex relationships.

The emotional climax of *Henry IV Part Two* is the turbulent reconciliation of father and son. Again it is a scene rich in symbolic stagecraft as Hal takes the crown from the pillow of his sleeping father, leaves the chamber and on his return is admonished by the King for his ambitious presumption:

O foolish youth!
Thou seek'st the greatness that will overwhelm thee.

[*Part Two*, IV.5 97-8]

Henry's anguished and bitter political confession enables Hal in self-justification to pierce his father's emotional defences. The impact of the reconciliation can vary substantially in performance. In the death-bed scene of Bogdanov's production there was a sense that Hal remained a disappointment to his father even to the end. In contrast, Julian Glover and Michael Maloney extracted great emotional reserves from the relationship as Henry slowly recognized that Hal's ambition was not incom-

impassioned self-defence with a blazing sincerity. The King, convinced by his son's words and energized by confessing his own deep sense of guilt, was able to move towards the long and tender embrace of father and son. As the two men held the crown together, the bonds of kingship and kinship were emotionally and symbolically cemented.

Hal's affirmation of his relationship with his real father makes inevitable his severance from Falstaff, his surrogate father. It is abun-

Below: *Ah, you sweet little rogue, you! Alas, poor ape, how thou sweatest! Come, let me wipe thy face. Come on, you whoreson chops! Ah, rogue, i'faith, I love thee. Thou art as valorous as Hector of Troy…*
Joanne Pearce as Doll Tearsheet and Robert Stephens, 1991

Above: *I have turned away my former self*
Michael Pennington in *Part Two*, 1986

patible with filial love. The playing of the scene was indicative of Hal's ambivalence towards his future rôle. As his father lay sleeping, Maloney approached the crown with wary dread, seized it and rammed it onto his head as if to rid himself of the impending ordeal. The earlier scene of the King's insomnia was recalled in Hal's apostrophe to the crown, fiercely delivered as if to an antagonist:

O polished perturbation! Golden care!
That keepest the ports of slumber open wide
To many a watchful night!

[*Part Two*, IV.5.24-6]

The mock coronation was repeated by the King, as with savage fury he turned on his son, pressing the crown down on his temples. In response to his father's accusations of wishing his death and imperilling the stability of the realm, Michael Maloney delivered Hal's

dantly clear throughout *Part One* that it is through his relationship with Falstaff that Hal finds his greatest emotional sustenance. Gerard Murphy's Hal enjoyed a rumbustious physicality with Falstaff, throwing himself across his chest and sitting on his knee, then later cowering awkwardly before the King when questioned about his profligate life. When Hal suggests that he and Falstaff enact the parts of King and Prince in preparation for the real encounter, Joss Ackland's 'Shall I? Content!' [*Part One*, II.4.371] suggested that such rôle-playing was not uncommon in the tavern. In a production which was strong on psychological detail, Murphy's immature Hal was seen as dependent on and under the influence of Falstaff, while Ackland's philosophical, but also brutally realistic Falstaff maintained a certain sardonic detachment from his protégé, even to the point of suggesting that his display of warmth towards the Prince was no more than a mask.

In contrast, Robert Stephens' Falstaff successfully conveyed the image of a man in search of a filial substitute. The final line of his eulogy to sack:

If I had a thousand sons, the first human principle I would teach them should be to forswear thin potations, and to addict themselves to sack

[*Part Two*, IV.3.120-2]

was given with great emphasis, as if he was obsessed with his own childlessness. In the 1982 production, this triangle of emotional relationships was symbolically projected during the scene in the royal camp before Shrewsbury, the only scene in which the King and Falstaff share the stage. Although no words are exchanged, Trevor Nunn capitalised on the dual presence to present Henry and Falstaff as competing father figures in relation to Hal. The usually austere, self-controlled King surveyed Falstaff with envy and contempt and then, from a distance, watched with an air of defeat as Hal and Falstaff resumed their affectionate bantering.

The comedy of *Part Two* is more muted than that of the first play. Hal is increasingly disenchanted with the life he clearly relished in *Part One* and Eastcheap has begun to exasperate rather than attract him. Nowhere is this more apparent than in the contrasting pair of tavern scenes (II.4 in each play). In the first, Hal and Poins enjoy tricking Falstaff as his account of the attack after the Gadshill robbery becomes more and more preposterous. Yet the rôle-playing which follows clearly demonstrates the social cohesion of the tavern and the warmth between Hal and Falstaff. In reply to Falstaff's assertion, 'Banish plump Jack, and banish all the world', Hal's 'I do, I will' [*Part One*, II.4.465-6], was in Noble's production a throwaway line greeted by the tavern audience as uproariously funny. In Noble's *Part Two* tavern scene, a sense of foreboding hung in the air despite the gaudiness of the red stage set. Falstaff was a man overshadowed by mortality. Robert Stephens delivered the admonition to Doll Tearsheet:

Peace, good Doll, do not speak like a death's head; do not bid me remember mine end

[*Part Two*, II.4.229-30]

with an agonised realisation that death is not far away. Hal's disenchantment with the life of the Boar's Head was conveyed in the urgency with which Michael Maloney delivered his departing lines:

Below: *What canst thou not forbear me half an hour?*
Then get thee gone, and dig my grave thyself,
And bid the merry bells ring to thine ear
That thou art crownèd, not that I am dead.
Michael Maloney and Julian Glover, 1991

Above: *Will Fortune never come with both hands full,*
But wet her fair words still in foulest terms?
Julian Glover, 1991

By heaven, Poins, I feel me much to blame,
So idly to profane the precious time
When tempest of commotion, like the south
Borne with black vapour, doth begin to melt
And drop upon our bare unarmèd heads.

[*Part Two*, II.4.356-60]

As Hal distances himself from the tavern and is reconciled with his father, the signs of Falstaff's rejection are there to be read. In consequence of Falstaff's opportunist

NOTABLE PRODUCTIONS OF *HENRY IV PARTS ONE AND TWO*

	THEATRE	DIRECTOR	DESIGNER	PRINCIPALS
1964	Internacional Films Española	Orson Welles	J. A. de la Guerra, M. Erdorza, Orson Welles	Orson Welles.........................*Falstaff* Keith Baxter ....*Hal* John Gielgud.........................*Henry IV* Norman Rodway ....*Hotspur*
1982	Royal Shakespeare Company, Barbican, London	Trevor Nunn	John Napier	Joss Ackland ....*Falstaff* Gerard Murphy ....*Hal* Patrick Stewart ....*Henry IV* Timothy Dalton.....................*Hotspur*
1986	English Shakespeare Company	Michael Bogdanov	Chris Dyer	John Woodvine.......................*Falstaff* Michael Pennington ....*Hal* Patrick O'Connell.................*Henry IV* John Price ....*Hotspur*
1991	Royal Shakespeare Theatre, Stratford-upon-Avon	Adrian Noble	Bob Crowley	Robert Stephens.....................*Falstaff* Michael Maloney ....*Hal* Julian Glover..........................*Henry IV* Owen Teale ....*Hotspur*

recruiting activities and the unleashing of his predatory instincts towards Shallow, the audience has in a sense been prepared for his inevitable rejection. Hal knows that the time to sever the bond is imminent but, because the relationship has been that of a spiritual father and son, he finds the decision a painful one. Michael Maloney eloquently conveyed his distress as Falstaff pushed his way through the crowds at the coronation, trying to attract his attention. The newly-crowned King Henry V could not bring himself to look at his old companion. He has earlier addressed the Lord Chief Justice as 'father to my youth' [V.2.118], and now appeals to him:

'My Lord Chief Justice, speak to that vain man' [V.5.45-6]. It was, for Maloney, not a peremptory command, but a desperate attempt to stave off the cruel moment which comes with:

I know thee not, old man. Fall to thy prayers...

[50]

Stephens' Falstaff took his leave with dignity and resignation, as if this was the fulfilment of his darkest expectations.

Janet Clare

'A LITTLE TOUCH OF HARRY IN THE NIGHT'

The Early Production History of *Henry V*

Henry V dates from 1599 and is mainly based on Holinshed's *Chronicles* and on the anonymous play *The Famous Victories of Henry the Fifth* which was entered in the Stationers' Register on 14th May 1594 and printed in 1598. The first recorded performance of Shakespeare's play was at Court in 1605. However, the existence of pirated editions dated 1600, 1602 and 1619 before the First Folio provided a more authoritative text suggests that the play was staged frequently. Henry was probably played by Richard Burbage, possibly with Shakespeare as the Chorus. After the English Civil War the play was not revived until 1735, but then it again became a favourite.

Elaborate processions and sets were a popular feature in the nineteenth century following John Kemble's 1789 Covent Garden production. The Chorus, omitted by Kemble, was restored as Time in Macready's spectacular 1839 revival. Moving dioramas showed the English fleet sailing to Harfleur, the English and French camps before Agincourt and the King's triumphal entry into London.

Lewis Waller and Frank Benson were both acclaimed Henrys. Benson played the part at Stratford almost every year from 1897 to 1916. Reviewers record his voice trembling on 'We few, we happy few...' at the Shaftesbury Theatre matinée on Boxing Day 1914. In the 1920s Sybil Thorndike performed the rôle of the Chorus, dressed as an Elizabethan page, and she also appeared as Katherine. Laurence Olivier first played Henry at the Old Vic in the Coronation year of 1937, and his film was made with an explicit propaganda purpose towards the end of World War II. Productions since then have been fewer but interestingly diverse, examining Henry not only as heroic king but as commander, politician and private man. Bernard Miles set the play against newsreels from World War I at the Mermaid in 1960, provoking considerable critical debate.

An outstanding feature of the past forty years has been the production of cycles of Shakespeare's English history plays. Richard Burton launched his career playing Hal and Henry V at Stratford in 1951, Peter Dews produced his brilliant *Age of Kings* for BBC-tv in 1960 and at Stratford Hal's journey from rebellious teenager to heroic King was explored in the full cycle of 1964.

Top: Frank Benson, who first played Henry V in 1897
Left: Richard Burton as Henry V, 1951
Right: Richard Burbage, c. 1567-1619

HENRY V

*The clarion call of stirring patriotism is set
against the uncompromising harshness of war.*

Above: *Then forth, dear countrymen! Let us deliver
Our puissance into the hand of God,
Putting it straight in expedition.*

A publicity photograph to herald the wartime release of a stirring, patriotic film, produced and directed by Laurence Olivier, 1944

Shakespeare's histories are about power: getting power, keeping power, using power. 'Warlike Harry' [Prologue 5] sets aside the roistering Hal of the earlier plays to become a model king and military leader, winning back his great grandfather's French lands. Performing the two *Henry IV* plays and *Henry V* in 1975 gave Alan Howard scope for an outstanding study of a complex man. His Henry toured America and Europe before returning to Stratford in 1977 and appearing again in London the following year. Michael Pennington took a similar journey with the English Shakespeare Company. Their remarkable sequence of the English history plays was launched in 1986 with the same trilogy and *The Henrys* also toured the world.

For Elizabethan audiences, Henry V's achievements were secure in history, yet rather than glorify heroic images of war Shakespeare juxtaposes them with an uncompromising sense of its reality. The audience is invited to enter a debate as scene is set against scene. The professional soldiers Fluellen, Williams and MacMorris discuss the rules of combat while Bardolph, Nym and Pistol, opportunist mercenaries, shirk and thieve. Whilst Henry himself embodies the qualities of leadership and courage that characterise a successful commander, he is also acutely aware of the human cost of war and of his responsibilities as King:

**For never two such kingdoms did contend
Without much fall of blood.**

[I.2.24-5]

Above: *A kingdom for a stage, princes to act …*
A publicity photograph showing Henry performing before a painted cloth in the Globe theatre, Laurence Olivier, 1944

Olivier's film begins with a clear reminder in the screen dedication of just such a harsh reality that prevailed when it was released:

To
THE COMMANDOS and AIRBORNE TROOPS
of
GREAT BRITAIN
the spirit of whose ancestors it has been humbly attempted to recapture
in some ensuing scenes

Fewer than half of Shakespeare's lines are performed and the emphasis is firmly upon the glory of a victory that is hard-won. It opens with aerial shots of a model of Elizabethan London, before a decision is made to visit the Globe playhouse. The film never quite forgets its theatrical frame and 45 years later Kenneth Branagh used a cinematic correlative. His film opens with the Chorus striking a light and strolling through an empty film studio to push open great doors and reveal the Bishops in secret conversation. The King, outlined against a shaft of light, enters. In Terry Hands' production the actors strolled onto the stage in casual modern dress, and gradually assumed costume.

To divert the King from sequestering Church lands, the Archbishop of Canterbury and the Bishop of Ely urge Henry to make war upon France, justifying his claim with complex genealogical argument, but the Council is interrupted by ambassadors bearing a gift from the Dauphin. In 1975 the opened casket revealed a hand, mockingly thrust up, tennis balls between the fingers. Alan Howard responded in a menacing crescendo:

> many a thousand widows
> Shall this his mock mock out of their dear
> husbands;
> Mock mothers from their sons, mock castles
> down…
> His jest will savour but of shallow wit
> When thousands weep more than did laugh
> at it.
>
> [I.2.285-7; 296-7]

The audience is not allowed to be caught up in the excitement for very long for the Chorus intervenes to prompt a shift in perspective:

> Now all the youth of England are on fire,
> And silken dalliance in the wardrobe lies.
>
> [II.1-2]

Detailed observation encourages a more reasoned, dispassionate assessment, as does the lurch from heroic words to squabbling jealousies as Nym, Pistol, Bardolph and the Boy prepare to join the army. Branagh's film catches the pathos beneath the comedy and we see that Hal's old companions are filthy, disease-ridden and decrepit. Judi Dench is a

Above: The expedition of the French and Genoese to Barbary, from the Harley MS. of Froissart's *Chronicles*, c. 1450

care-worn Mistress Quickly, tearfully bidding her menfolk goodbye.

The play employs abrupt transitions and sudden shifts of mood. After the intimacy of the stews, great banners billowed overhead as Alan Howard prepared to embark at Southampton. Immediately after showing regal clemency to a critical commoner he displayed an agonised ruthlessness in dealing with the nobles who had turned traitor. Scroop, Cambridge and Grey were dragged to the sides of the stage, knives at their throats. The ESC embarked to a nostalgic guitar rendering of 'My way'. Suddenly, as Mistress Quickly left, they burst into a raucous chorus of ''Ere we go, 'ere we go, 'ere we go…' and 'Jerusalem'. Football scarves and rattles were waved and a banner was unfurled, obscenely insulting the French. There was nervous recognition of a contemporary truth as the audience laughed at the disdainful comment of the French King at the very beginning of the next scene:

Thus come the English…

[II.4.1]

He and his nobles were leisured Edwardian gentlemen dressed in white.

Rallying his troops for the assault on Harfleur, Olivier, on a white horse, provided an heroic image for a nation at war:

Once more unto the breach, dear friends,
    once more…

[III.1.1]

On the Stratford stage Alan Howard and his troops struggled up scaling ladders against the enormous walls of the town, providing an impromptu vantage point for Henry to urge on his flagging army. Michael Pennington was an older, ostensibly more ruthless commander and his threats were chilling:

        look to see
The blind and bloody soldier with foul hand
Defile the locks of your shrill-shrieking
    daughters…

[III.3.33-4]

But when the portly Governor and his attendants in their black suits capitulated, Pennington, in commando camouflage, whistled and visibly sagged with relief.

Olivier also makes us aware of the deeper conflicts that need to be reconciled. As the soldiers discuss the art of war, Captain MacMorris almost weeps with frustration at losing the opportunity to demonstrate his professional skill by blowing up Harfleur. His dedication is thrown into relief by the way the citizens parley from fairy-tale battlements. The settings for the film are based on medieval illustrations to Froissart's *Chronicles* and to the Duc de Berri's *Les Très Riches Heures*. While the French nobles prepare confidently for battle Katherine and Alice

Above: *There is no bar*
To make against your highness' claim to France …
– May I with right and conscience make this claim?
Alan Howard takes advice, 1977
Right: Alan Howard, 1977

laugh over their English lesson, seriousness only intruding when Katherine looks out over the idyllic landscape of peaceful French towns and villages. In contrast the ESC Katherine was consistently serious and determined, preparing for a political union. Her struggles with the English language foreshadowed the fragility of the treaty.

Olivier cut the scene in which Bardolph is to be hanged for robbing a church. Fluellen and Gower reject Pistol's plea for intervention, and Henry's own refusal to reprieve Bardolph demonstrates his determination to put duty above personal friendship. Branagh extends this moment and shows Bardolph, riding on a cart to execution, meet Henry's eye with accusing reproach. There is an insertion from a previous play:

Do not thou when thou art King hang a thief

[Henry IV Part 1, I.2.60-1]

before the cart drives on and Bardolph is left hanging from a tree.

In the long night before Agincourt the French nobles are nervous but confident. Andrew Jarvis as the ESC Dauphin, was wonderfully manic in his flamboyant sonnets to his horse and his eagerness to eat the English. In contrast to the self-indulgent languor of the French noblemen, Henry goes in disguise amongst his men, receptive to their doubts and fears. His debates with the rank-and-file soldiers and his private reflections on the responsibilities of kingship are central to the play. While Henry and Williams can agree that the King is not responsible for the private consciences of his subjects, Henry knows the responsibility of a ruler, and the personal isolation that is the price of power:

What infinite heart's ease
Must kings neglect that private men enjoy!
And what have kings that privates have not too,
Save ceremony, save general ceremony?

[IV.1.229-32]

Branagh steals through the camp, his face half hidden in a cloak. The soldiers are receiving absolution, and debate the uncertain future. Surrounded by sleeping bodies, Henry reflects on the heavy, lonely responsibilities of kingship and begs God not to exact retribution now for his father's murder of Richard II and the usurpation of the crown.

In 1984 the Battle of Agincourt was staged in pouring rain. Branagh, exhausted, was uncertain of the outcome and the English were a ragged, desperate band. The French nobles provided a spectacular contrast, refulgent in

golden armour, as they were hoisted onto their horses. Both the 1944 and 1989 films present the hissing flights of swarms of arrows, the massed charging horses, the nervous anticipation of the pikemen, the confusion, blood, mud and exhaustion of battle. For Olivier the slaughter of the boys and camp-followers is the incentive which spurs Henry on to win the battle:

I was not angry since I came to France
Until this instant.

[IV.7.53-4]

Turning away to remount he leads the final attack, which becomes single combat on horseback against the Constable of France who wears black armour. The struggle culminates in the Frenchman crashing to the ground.

Henry's order 'Then every soldier kill his prisoners!' [IV.6.37] was cut from both films. In the ESC production, the soldiers took up the cry against the rattle of machine guns, shouting it across the stage. Pistol, wheeling his captive Frenchman on a shopping trolley, first attempted to hide him under a helmet, then reluctantly cut his throat. Immediately, Fluellen and Gower entered, pulling the bodies of the slaughtered boys piled on a luggage cart. Through their tears they sought to justify the killing of the French prisoners and debated the rules of war. In Branagh's film, Henry seizes the French herald by the throat and rolls him in the mud before hearing the French surrender. A single voice raises the hymn *Non Nobis*, slowly taken up by all the army as they make their way over the mud-churned, bloody carnage of the battlefield, with Branagh carrying the body of the Boy. Ian Holm's Fluellen reminds Henry with pride of his Welsh ancestry. The Welsh, Scots, Irish and English support for the King is constantly stressed. Alan Howard and the French herald paused to look back over the

Below: *We would not seek a battle as we are,*
Nor, as we are, we say we will not shun it
The English army, 1984

battlefield in shared sorrow, the soldiers sinking to their knees.

Olivier plays Henry's wooing of Katherine in the vein of light romantic comedy. When he claims a kiss from the French Princess it is easy to believe they will love each other. The camera closes on their entwined hands and shows rings bearing the crests of England and France. As they move to their thrones and turn, the audience is jolted back to the Globe theatre seeing again the heavy make-up of the actor playing the King and a boy in the costume of the French Princess. In Branagh's film Emma Thompson is reluctant to be wooed, but she is won over by Henry's forthright honesty. Her eyes widen in astonishment as he agrees that it is not possible for her to love the enemy of France. This Katherine and her Henry work their way towards an understanding, both showing their willingness to learn each other's language. Branagh's 'O Kate, nice customs curtsy to great kings' [V.2.265] as he kisses her, is the speech of an honest but powerful man. Jacobi's epilogue is a regretful coda to so promising a match.

The signing of the treaty and wooing of Katherine were sombrely treated by the ESC. The entire French court was in deep mourning, Katherine was veiled, and Henry and his officers wore scarlet uniforms. As Henry and Katherine were left together, Alice removed the veil as though displaying goods for sale. Henry's initial wooing sounded

Above right: *What a long night is this! I will not change my horse with any that treads but on four pasterns. Ça, ha! He bounds from the earth as if his entrails were hairs* – le cheval volant, *the Pegasus*, chez les narines de feu! *When I bestride him, I soar, I am a hawk.*
The French nobles on the eve of Agincourt, 1984

Far right: *… as I am a soldier*
Kenneth Branagh, 1989

Right: *And gentlemen in England now abed
Shall think themselves accursed they were not here,
And hold their manhoods cheap whiles any speaks
That fought with us upon Saint Crispin's day.*
Kenneth Branagh, 1989

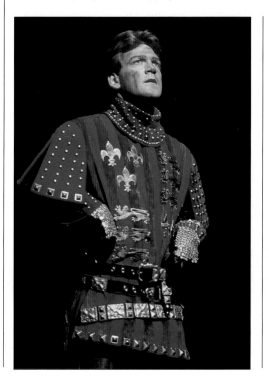

NOTABLE PRODUCTIONS OF *HENRY V*

	THEATRE	DIRECTOR	DESIGNER	PRINCIPALS
1944	Two Cities Film	Laurence Olivier	Paul Sheriff and Roger Furse	Laurence Olivier ....*Henry V* Leslie Banks.............................*Chorus* Renée Asherson ....*Katherine*
1975	Royal Shakespeare Theatre, Stratford-upon-Avon	Terry Hands	Farrah	Alan Howard ....*Henry V* Emrys James ....*Chorus* Ludmilla Mikael ....*Katherine*
1977	Royal Shakespeare Theatre, Stratford-upon-Avon	Terry Hands	Farrah	Alan Howard ....*Henry V* Alfred Lynch ....*Chorus* Barbara Kellermann...........*Katherine*
1984	Royal Shakespeare Theatre, Stratford-upon-Avon	Adrian Noble	Bob Crowley	Kenneth Branagh...................*Henry V* Ian McDiarmid ....*Chorus* Cécile Paoli ....*Katherine*
1986	English Shakespeare Company	Michael Bogdanov	Chris Dyer	Michael Pennington ....*Henry V* John Woodvine ....*Chorus* Jenny Quayle.......................*Katherine*
1989	English Shakespeare Company	Michael Bogdanov	Chris Dyer	Michael Pennington ....*Henry V* Barry Stanton ....*Chorus* Francesca Ryan ....*Katherine*

In the last week of its theatrical life the ESC cycle of history plays, *The Wars of the Roses*, was recorded and it has been released on video.

	THEATRE	DIRECTOR	DESIGNER	PRINCIPALS
1989	Renaissance Films	Kenneth Branagh	Phyllis Dalton and Tim Harvey	Kenneth Branagh...................*Henry V* Derek Jacobi ....*Chorus* Emma Thompson ....*Katherine*

Above: *By mine honour, in true English, I love thee, Kate: by which honour I dare not swear thou lovest me, yet my blood begins to flatter me that thou dost, notwithstanding the poor and untempering effect of my visage.*
Emma Thompson and Kenneth Branagh, 1989

unconvincing and awkward, Katherine's responses almost tearful. They sat upright on two distant chairs. Only when Henry attempted to express himself in French did Katherine smile with amusement and respond. As Henry sealed the treaty with his public kiss, the Dauphin stormed out. The ESC set this political marriage very firmly within the context of their entire *Wars of the Roses* cycle, emphasising the uncompromising ebb and flow of history known to Shakespeare's audience and foretold in the Epilogue:

Henry the Sixth, in infant bands crowned King
Of France and England, did this King succeed,
Whose state so many had the managing
That they lost France, and made his England
bleed:
Which oft our stage has shown.

[Epilogue 9 -13]

Niky Rathbone

HENRY VI PARTS ONE, TWO AND THREE

*The incessant struggle for power provides the context
for the development of a princess into a military leader.*

The overflowing narratives of *Henry VI Parts One, Two* and *Three* pack in decades of history, cover the Hundred Years War, the Wars of the Roses and the rise and fall of one aspiring hero or heroine after another. The plays focus on bad government, the horrors of war and political manoeuvring. This latter theme seems to have been the aspect which most attracted attention in the late 1980s.

For Shakespeare's audience however, one of the most urgent topics covered in these plays would have been that of succession. At the time of the first performances of *Henry VI* the succession in England was unsettled; by the 1590s it was clear that Elizabeth was not going to produce an heir as she was past child-bearing age and she did not name a successor until she was on her deathbed. The horrors of civil war, which are most memorably evoked in *Part Three* when a father finds he has killed his son and a son finds he has killed his father, were presented to an audience who feared they were facing the prospect of a contested succession.

Patriarchy's central relationship, that of father and son, constitutes a major concern in the three plays. Henry VI lives perpetually in the shadow of his glorious father but a father's legacy also deeply affects York, Clifford and many others. This relationship is dealt with particularly in *Part One* with the portrayal of the Talbots. Young John Talbot only exists dramatically in order to highlight the father-son relationship. The heinous crime of rejecting a father is committed by a woman,

Above: Julia Foster, 1982
Above right: *that devil's butcher*
Ron Cook in *Part Three*, 1982

Joan La Pucelle or Joan of Arc. The antipathetic characterisation of Joan towards the end of the play comes as a shock to those used to a more liberal, Shavian approach. There is a tendency now to offer compensation for Shakespeare's misogyny and chauvinism by rendering Joan's death as horrifying as possible; for example, the ESC had her 'necklaced' by a tyre that was set alight with petrol.

Joan's rejection of her father is in line with the presentation of insubordinate women in all three *Henry VI* plays. Women in these plays are often strong, active and formidable. Two women – Joan and the woman who acts as her successor in unruliness, Margaret – go to war, don armour and lead armies. As Joan's power fades, Margaret's grows, something that is stressed by the juxtaposition of Joan's final and Margaret's first appearance. Accusations of witchcraft also abound: Joan is burnt as a witch, Margaret is described as one and the 'good' Duke Humphrey's wife Eleanor

'LET OUR HEARTS AND EYES, LIKE CIVIL WAR, BE BLIND WITH TEARS'

The Early Production History of *Henry VI Parts One, Two* and *Three*

The three *Henry VI* plays were probably first performed around 1592 although they may have been written earlier. Since Shakespeare's day the plays have rarely been presented in their entirety; they are often retitled and the focus shifted from Henry to other characters. In 1681 John Crowne converted *Parts Two* and *Three* into two plays, one focusing on Humphrey, Duke of Gloucester and one entitled *The Misery of Civil War*. An adaptation by Theophilus Cibber appeared in 1723 and Richard Valpy's *The Roses*, was given in 1795. In 1817 Edmund Kean played the title role in J.H. Merivale's adaptation, *Richard Duke of York*.

F. R. Benson directed all three *Henry VI* plays at Stratford in 1906. Douglas Seale's production for Barry Jackson's Birmingham Repertory Theatre in 1951 revived interest in the plays. They transferred to the Old Vic in London in 1953 and were staged again in 1957 with *Parts One* and *Two* collapsed into one instalment. The BBC adapted the plays for television as part of *An Age of Kings* in 1960. The action was parcelled out into roughly one hour broadcasts entitled: *The Red Rose & the White, The Fall of a Protector, The Rabble From Kent, The Morning's War* and *The Sun in Splendour*.

John Barton's radical adaptation for Peter Hall's 1963 RSC *The Wars of the Roses* added passages from Holinshed's *Chronicles* and some material of Barton's own. The three plays became two, entitled *Henry VI* and *Edward IV*. Peggy Ashcroft's Margaret and David Warner's Henry were highly praised.

Terry Hands directed all three plays in 1977 in a season which featured an Alan Howard marathon. That season Howard played Henry VI and his Henry V was revived. In 1987 the plays were presented as part of the ESC *The Wars of the Roses* series in which *Henry VI* was split into two parts: *Henry VI: House of Lancaster* and *Henry VI: House of York*. 1988 saw the RSC adaptation *The Plantagenets* which again reduced the three plays to two, played alongside *Richard III*.

Top: Alan Howard as Henry VI, 1977
Left: Helen Mirren as Margaret and Alan Howard, 1977
Right: David Warner as Henry VI in the 1964 RSC *The Wars of the Roses*, as televised in 1965

stressing the episodic nature of the action, the emblematic quality of the scene construction and the political commitment of the plays, have made them seem hard hitting in their acute focus on instance after instance of political skulduggery by the ruling classes.

The ruled classes appear most in *Part Two*, which presents us with Saunder Simpcox who forges a miracle 'for pure need' [II.1.153]; Horner, a master armourer, duelling against his assistant; Margery Jourdain and her crew who are led off to execution while the aristocratic Duchess of Gloucester merely does penance; and Jack Cade's rebellion. Whether Shakespeare is being radical or snobbish in his creation of these incidents, there is no doubt that the working classes are a force to

Far left: Peter Benson, 1982
Left: Frank Middlemass as Winchester in *Part One*, 1982
Below: *These words will cost ten thousand lives this day* The forces of Lancaster take up their defensive positions in *Part Three*, 1982

consults one, Margery Jourdain.

Margaret is the only character who survives the whole of the tetralogy and we follow her from youth to experience in court machinations and war, bloodshed and torture. In the BBC-tv production, this maturing process is highlighted when Margaret spills blood for the first time; Julia Foster registers a rite of passage and loss of innocence as she stabs York. Her costume also becomes more militaristic as scene succeeds scene, paralleling her success in entering the traditionally masculine domain of war.

The three *Henry VI* plays have a huge dramatis personæ and sometimes hardly pause to do much more than sketch in characters. Audiences yearning for detailed character construction sometimes find these plays unsatisfactory. *Henry VI Part One* is the most extreme. However, modern productions which have adopted a Brechtian approach,

Above: Paul Brennen, 1987

Right: *Hung be the heavens with black, yield day to night!*
Comets, importing change of times and states,
Brandish your crystal tresses in the sky,
And with them scourge the bad revolting stars
That have consented unto Henry's death!
King Henry the Fifth, too famous to live long –
England ne'er lost a king of so much worth.
The funeral of Henry V in *Part One*, 1988

be reckoned with in *Part Two*. Most productions present Jack Cade's rebellion very unsympathetically; the ESC had a punk Cade dressed in a Union Jack vest, evoking the racist National Front party and skinhead culture. This Cade was a yob who led his followers in football chants and mindless violence. The BBC production includes a long book burning sequence interspersed with bloody violence by Cade's followers which is often shown in close-up.

Recent productions of *Henry VI* have taken various design approaches to the problem of whether they should be set in an accurate historical context, Shakespeare's time, the modern world or outside history. Bogdanov's production adopted an eclectic approach to costume, mixing visual quotations from World Wars I and II. More old-fashioned characters such as Talbot were dressed for battle in Victorian uniforms whereas Richard of Gloucester donned battle fatigues. This device

was very effective in commenting both on a character's attitude and chances of survival. Noble's RSC production on the other hand, had costumes from the period of Henry VI's reign.

In the BBC production, characters are generally dressed in costume appropriate to their historical period although in *Part One* the armour is reminiscent of American football equipment and later, some of the leather armour shows Asiatic influences. Even the authentic-looking costumes are, however, secured by the anti-illusionistic style adopted overall which is epitomised by the playing area. This roughly constructed arena, approximately circular in shape, made up of pieces of old wood and doors hammered together, suggests both a playground and an Elizabethan playhouse. The production also plays self-consciously with acting styles and the representation of battles varies enormously. In *Part One* horses are strapped on, hobby-horse style; many battles are fought in the manner of the Keystone cops with frantic chase sequences. For more serious moments slow motion is used. By contrast, the closing shots of *Part Two* and the opening shots of *Part Three* focus on the blood-stained bodies strewn on the floor after the battle of St Albans and so signal a far more serious approach to the violence. In *Part Three*, mirrors are used to create the appearance of battles being fought by long rows of identical robotic killing machines. The battle of Tewkesbury is rendered even more sombre by falling snow, howling wind and slow motion violence.

The production's overall commitment to anti-realism also reaps great benefits more generally. Characters talk easily to the camera and performers double energetically generating a strong sense of ensemble, energy and fun. A joke is created by the appearance of Ron Cook as a hunch-backed porter to the Countess of Auvergne; he later plays Richard III. Overall, Jane Howell's productions are remarkable for their clarity, their zest and their demonstration that the *Henry VI* plays are challenging, exuberantly theatrical and politically hard-hitting.

Elizabeth Schafer

Right: – *Presumptuous priest ...*
– *Gloucester, I do defy thee*
David Waller as Humphrey, Duke of Gloucester, and Antony Brown as the Bishop of Winchester confront each other before Ralph Fiennes in *Part One*, 1988

NOTABLE PRODUCTIONS OF *HENRY VI PARTS ONE, TWO & THREE*

	THEATRE	DIRECTOR	DESIGNER	PRINCIPALS
1982	BBC-tv	Jane Howell	Oliver Bayldon, John Peacock	Julia Foster .... *Margaret* Peter Benson .... *Henry VI* Bernard Hill .... *Richard, Duke of York* Ron Cook............................... *Richard, Duke of Gloucester*
1987	English Shakespeare Company	Michael Bogdanov	Chris Dyer, Stephanie Howard	June Watson.......................... *Margaret* Paul Brennen .... *Henry VI* John Castle .... *Richard, Duke of York* Andrew Jarvis .... *Richard, Duke of Gloucester*
1988	Royal Shakespeare Theatre, Stratford-upon-Avon	Adrian Noble	Bob Crowley	Penny Downie .... *Margaret* Ralph Fiennes .... *Henry VI* David Calder .... *Richard, Duke of York* Anton Lesser .... *Richard, Duke of Gloucester*

PEACE, PLENTY, LOVE, TRUTH, TERROR

The Early Production History of *Henry VIII*

Henry VIII's stage history started spectacularly: stage cannons fired during a performance on 29 June 1613 set the Globe theatre's roof on fire and the building burned to the ground within two hours. A contemporary report of this performance makes mention of 'many extraordinary circumstances of pomp and majesty', and it is this element of the play which has proved most alluring over the centuries.

There was a growing tendency in the eighteenth and nineteenth centuries for spectacle and pageantry. Anne's coronation procession in Garrick's 1762 production at Drury Lane required 137 participants including numerous musicians and attendants. Kean's 1855 production had Buckingham rowed off to execution in a barge with four oarsmen and Katherine's vision was staged as flights of angels in a shaft of light. For a production at the Lyceum in 1892, Henry Irving reconstructed entire Tudor street scenes complete with three-storeyed wooden-beamed houses and people on all three levels.

Characteristic of set and costume designs from the Restoration to the present is their fidelity to historical style. The first Restoration productions in the 1660s were, as John Downes, actor and book-keeper at Davenant's theatre, explained, 'all new Cloath'd in proper Habits'. A wave of antiquarianism in the stage design for *Henry VIII* was introduced by Kemble in his 1811 production at Covent Garden. A desire for elaborate pageantry prompted producers from Garrick (1762) via Kemble and Irving to Beerbohm Tree (1910) to cut large portions of Shakespeare's text. As a result, interest shifted to the antagonism between Wolsey and Katherine, and Henry became marginal.

The pageantry exalting royal power made the play a favourite for festive occasions. Thus productions of *Henry VIII* celebrated the coronations of George II in 1727 and of Elizabeth II in 1953 and inaugurated the open-air theatre at Regent's Park in 1936.

Top: William Terris as Henry VIII at the Lyceum Theatre, 1892
Left: The setting for Katherine's confrontation with Wolsey in Henry Irving's production at the Lyceum Theatre, 1892
Right: Henry Irving as Wolsey, 1892

HENRY VIII

*The process of myth-making is exposed in a play
which reaches beyond history to proclaim eternal truths.*

Beset by critical unease about its quality and doubts about authorship, *Henry VIII* occupies a precarious position within the canon of Shakespeare's plays. Critical and theatrical efforts to prove that *Henry VIII* is not a haphazard sequence of theatrical set pieces have resulted in a renewed interest in Henry as the play's central figure. *Henry VIII*'s curious generic nature halfway between Shakespeare's history plays and his romances has led to the centrality of Henry being understood as either the political coming of age of a monarch or the spiritual development of a husband and father. These approaches were adopted by the only two Royal Shakespeare Company productions to have reached the stage in the last 30 years. Trevor Nunn set his production in the context of the late plays and concentrated on Henry's maturation as a man and father. In contrast, Howard Davies saw *Henry VIII* as a political play dealing with the inexorable accretion of power to one man.

Whether the play is regarded as a history play or as a romance, it is suffused with ambivalence and contradictions usually ascribed to divided authorship. Yet they are so intricately woven into the fabric of the play that they rather seem to point a warning finger at the myth-making processes presented by the play itself. Thus, the Prologue's vague contention that:

> **Such as give**
> **Their money out of hope they may believe**
> **May here find truth too**
>
> [Prologue, 7-9]

Above: *Nothing but death*
Shall e'er divorce my dignities
Peggy Ashcroft, 1969

sheds an ironic light on the play's subtitle, *All Is True*. Henry's motives for discarding Katherine in favour of the young Anne Bullen are ambivalent. According to contemporary ecclesiastical doctrine, his marriage to his brother's widow is considered to be incestuous and the resulting 'issue's fail' [II.4.198] may well be a divine punishment. Yet, his dynastic anxieties are unwarranted as English succession laws allowed for female heirs. They appear even more so in view of the fact

Above: *thus hulling in*
The wild sea of my conscience
Donald Sinden, 1969

that the play ends with the celebration of the birth of another daughter – the future Queen Elizabeth. What in Henry's argument emerges as dynastic considerations urging the exchange of one unproductive royal mate for another appears to be of even lower moral value in the eyes of the Duke of Suffolk, who suspects that the King's 'conscience / Has crept too near another lady' [II.2.16-17].

Donald Sinden's Henry juxtaposed sincere moral conflict with a forceful attraction to

Anne, so that the ambivalence of the King's proceedings became obvious without reducing his moral stature. Richard Griffiths' angry reaction to papal protocol at the beginning of the trial suggested that he had reached a decision in favour of a divorce beforehand. Ian Judge's production accepted at face value Henry's reasons for discarding Katherine and expressed this through changes in the lighting. As Keith Michell delivered the lines concerning the workings of his conscience, a spot-light focused on him indicating that he was confiding his private thoughts to the audience.

The ambivalences and contradictions surrounding Henry's divorce extend beyond the question of his true motives. During the whole play, the nobles constantly adjust their views and behaviour to conform to the shifting conditions at Henry's court. In the case of Henry's change of queens, their opportunism becomes especially obvious. Norfolk and Suffolk, members of Katherine's entourage in the tax scene, become supporters of Anne and profit from this move by having honours heaped upon them at her

coronation. Howard Davies highlighted Norfolk's opportunism as the most explicit example of aristocratic selfishness. In the tax scene, Norfolk belonged to Katherine's court party which fought against the influence of Cardinal Wolsey's ecclesiastical party. But when Norfolk noticed Henry's infatuation with Anne, who as a result of textual changes had become his niece, he used her as a means to secure political influence for himself by pushing her into Henry's arms.

The object of Henry's amorous and dynastic quest, Anne Bullen, is indeed an object to be displayed rather than a fully developed dramatic character. The Chichester production revealed her status as an object of male gazes and lust by means of her plunging neck-line. The only scene which shows more of Anne than her physical beauty in a context of spectacle and pageantry, extends the ambivalences which pervade the play. Although appalled by the Queen's declining fortune, Anne claims to have no worldly ambition, the Old Lady's intimations of 'hypocrisy' and prostitution leave a vague, yet lasting, blemish on Anne's character. When Anne is presented as happily joining the bawdy conversation at Wolsey's banquet, as in the BBC-tv production, the sense of Anne exploiting, even unwittingly, the sexual politics at Henry's court is increased. In contrast, Davies chose to underline the victim status not just of Anne, but of the women at Henry's court in general. Sarah Berger's Anne detested Lord Sands' suggestive implications and tried to evade his repeated efforts to kiss her. Thrust unwillingly into Henry's arms, she and the other court ladies were hurled about the stage by the King and his followers. What is usually depicted as a courtly dance, became in this production, a humiliation of the male guests at Wolsey's party who had to watch helplessly while their ladies were brutalized by the King and his men.

The only unambiguous character in *Henry VIII* is Katherine. Throughout the play, she displays a strength based on strict moral uprightness and an uncompromising sense of

Top right: *Madam, you wander from the good we aim at.*
John Thaw, 1983
Right: *I stood not in the smile of heaven*
Richard Griffiths, 1983

justice. Beside Buckingham and Wolsey, she is the third character in the play whose fall from royal favour leads to a heightened spiritual awareness. Her vision of heavenly glory shortly before her death seems the culminative reward of her perfect patience in adversity. Yet her final resignation might not be as selfless as is often suggested. Most actresses playing Katherine grab the opportunity of disclosing those layers in Katherine's character which free her of the stereotypical traits of the patiently suffering heroine. Gemma

Jones' steely Katherine smiled viciously and Dorothy Tutin had to fight back malicious pleasure at the news of Wolsey's downfall and death. Even Peggy Ashcroft's more tender and feminine Katherine could hardly bring herself to forgive her enemy.

The culmination of Henry's maturation in the play is his intervention on behalf of Archbishop Cranmer. For the first time, he takes active political steps without the help or instigation of others. In the council scene, Henry's emergence as a strong king is linked

Above: *I love him not, nor fear him, there's my creed*
John Dicks as the Duke of Suffolk, Bruce Alexander as the Duke of Norfolk and Geoffrey Beevers as Lord Chamberlain, 1983

to the establishment of Protestantism as the true religion. Trevor Nunn presented the scene as the high point of Henry's spiritual development, with a father achieving reconciliation through the birth of his daughter. Davies viewed the same scene as the apex of Henry's political empowerment. In this disillusioned interpretation, Richard Griffiths'

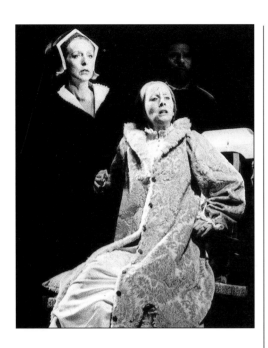

Above: *I was a chaste wife to my grave*
Eileen Page as Patience and Gemma Jones, 1983

NOTABLE PRODUCTIONS OF *HENRY VIII*

	THEATRE	DIRECTOR	DESIGNER	PRINCIPALS	
1969	Royal Shakespeare Theatre, Stratford-upon-Avon	Trevor Nunn	John Bury	Donald Sinden	*Henry VIII*
				Peggy Ashcroft	*Katherine*
				Brewster Mason......................	*Wolsey*
				Janet Key	*Anne Bullen*
1979	BBC-tv	Kevin Billington	Don Taylor	John Stride	*Henry VIII*
				Claire Bloom	*Katherine*
				Timothy West	*Wolsey*
				Barbara Kellermann........	*Anne Bullen*
1983	Royal Shakespeare Theatre, Stratford-upon-Avon	Howard Davies	Hayden Griffin	Richard Griffiths	*Henry VIII*
				Gemma Jones	*Katherine*
				John Thaw	*Wolsey*
				Sarah Berger	*Anne Bullen*
1991	Chichester Festival Theatre	Ian Judge	Russell Craig	Keith Michell	*Henry VIII*
				Dorothy Tutin.....................	*Katherine*
				Tony Britton	*Wolsey*
				Fiona Fullerton	*Anne Bullen*

Henry relished his new-found absolutist power when he led Cranmer, presented as the servile keeper of the King's conscience, to believe he was about to exchange Anne Bullen for yet another queen:

> **My lord of Canterbury,**
> **I have a suit which you must not deny me:**
> **That is, a fair young maid [*pause*] that yet wants**
> **baptism.**

[V.3.159-61]

Far from pointing to reconciliation, this production showed the mechanics of power fully intact with only the participants reshuffled.

The final scene celebrating the baptism of the newborn Elizabeth is often regarded as unabashed flattery on Shakespeare's part. However, read in the context of the play's other ambivalences and the fact that Elizabeth's birth meant the failure of Henry's dynastic plans, it is exactly the hyperbolic style of Cranmer's eulogy on Elizabeth and her successor James which should alert us to the speech's true aim, the construction of a myth designed to justify Henry's expedient use of unproductive mates. Nunn's production, with its emphasis on the patterns of romance, presented the baptism as the climax of Henry's personal development as a father, with Elizabeth cast as the regenerative daughter in the mould of Perdita in *The Winter's Tale* or Miranda in *The Tempest*. It is significant that Nunn, in order to bring the play firmly in line with his interpretation, had to cut the word 'terror' not only from Cranmer's prophecy, but also from the chant of 'peace, plenty, love, truth' which formed part of the white hippy mass ending the play. Davies extended the opportunism characteristic of Henry's court to Cranmer's speech, which emerged as a sycophant's effort to secure his monarch's favour by legitimizing royal wilfulness with ecclesiastical approval. Both directors had to cut aspects of the play as a whole to make their interpretations dramatically consistent. Nunn sacrificed the ambivalence of the last scene in particular, whereas Davies neglected the spiritual dimension of the play in favour of a disillusioning view of Tudor *realpolitik*.

Romana Beyenburg

'THE CHOICE AND MASTER SPIRITS OF THIS AGE'

The Early Production History of *Julius Caesar*

Julius Caesar was one of the first plays to be performed at the newly constructed Globe theatre in 1599. The earliest reference to its performance appears in the diary of a Swiss traveller, Thomas Platter, who refers to Shakespeare's play as being 'very well acted' and 'elaborately costumed'. It is likely that items of classical costume such as shaped breast plates, military skirts and plumed helmets were used.

The play was performed regularly at Court until the English Civil War. After the Restoration, various acting versions contained substantial textual alterations which simplified the central characters and accentuated the forceful plot. Little scenery was used. Between 1708 and 1728 Thomas Betterton, Barton Booth and James Quin established Brutus as stoical and dignified, and the play was presented as a contest between ambition and freedom. *Julius Caesar* was rarely staged during the second half of the eighteenth century.

In the early nineteenth century John Philip Kemble made strategic cuts to the text emphasising Brutus as strong and determined, but he balanced this carefully with an equally powerful Antony. Classical costumes,

sometimes stylised movements and realistic scenery suggested Roman grandeur. Another tradition also developed during the nineteenth century. William Macready and later Samuel Phelps, directed with such energy that the assassination becoming realistically bloody. Caesar was portrayed as ambitious and restless and Brutus as not only having great dignity but also possessing gentle sensitivity.

To varying degrees twentieth century productions have projected images of naturalism and contemporary dictatorships. In Orson Welles' 1937 New York production for example, Antony's strident delivery of the funeral oration – 'Friends, Romans, countrymen, lend me your ears...' [III.2.74] – was against a background of searchlights and blood-red walls suggestive of a Nazi rally.

Top: Joseph Holland as Caesar is assassinated by Orson Welles as Brutus and Martin Gabel as Cassius at the Mercury Theatre, 1937
Left: The Murder Scene with William Charles Macready as Cassius, Charles Mayne Young as Brutus and Charles Kemble as Mark Antony in John Philip Kemble's 1822 production at the Theatre Royal, Covent Garden, painted by George Clint, 1770-1854
Right: The conspirators, 1937

JULIUS CAESAR

Intrigue, political manoeuvring and an assassination
conspire against a rôle for moral integrity.

*J*ulius Caesar is principally about the threat which the titular hero presented to the commonwealth. Before and after his death, conflicts between the conspirators and the loyalists focus on Caesar's indomitable spirit. In view of this it is not surprising that the play is never more moving in performance than when Caesar's appearances show his ability to control, influence and evoke strong emotional reactions. This is also evident when the staging of the second half of the play reflects Plutarch's remark that the divine power which some thought he possessed during his life seemed to exist after his death.

The dictator's return to Rome has often been presented spectacularly. The MGM film introduced Caesar in a military procession being acclaimed by a crowd of epic proportions. His authority instantly silenced the rabble. In Glen Byam Shaw's production, several white fluted pillars, initially arranged in a triangular configuration were parted to reveal Caesar splendidly costumed in scarlet and gold, silhouetted against an imperial blue sky. It was as if Caesar controlled the movement of the pillars and the rich colour of the sky itself reflected his glory. Trevor Nunn's production also gave particular impact to Caesar's entrance. To an underscore of triumphant drums and horns and clad in black leather, Caesar strode along a red carpet which unrolled down the raked stage before him. Adopting an arrogant pose he demanded salutes from the grey-uniformed soldiers who lined the stage.

Using a contrasting though equally effective

Above: – *Yond Cassius has a lean and hungry look;*
He thinks too much; such men are dangerous.
– *Fear him not, Caesar; he's not dangerous.*
Louis Calhern and Marlon Brando, 1953

style David Thacker created an air of expectation by confronting the audience on arrival with large portraits of Caesar and crested banners adorning the interior of the acting area. The play was set in an eastern European dictatorship sometime in the 1980s to early 90s. The promenade production encouraged the audience to mingle with the actors. Initially this meant actors in the crowd began to address one another so the audience became eavesdroppers, viewing events from the perspective of the common people. This made Caesar's power seem intimidating. Heralded by a loud fanfare, the suave, silver-haired

dictator appeared from behind one of the corner podiums, paraded across the red-carpeted floor, smiled at the crowd and commanded attention. His movements were followed by a shoulder-held television camera, while suited security men mingled with the onlookers. This set the level of audience participation for the first half of the performance and put Caesar firmly at the centre of the play. It was obvious that such a figure would not be swayed by others and Calphurnia's attempts to dissuade her husband from going to the Capitol seemed futile.

Whatever laudable ideals motivate the conspirators, realistic staging of the assassination can create unforgettable images of Caesar. Watching a defenceless man being savagely slaughtered is deeply disturbing and engenders sympathy for the victim whatever his faults may be. Close-ups in the MGM film show the anxiety of the conspirators before Casca cautiously approaches Caesar from behind. After the vigorous thrust of knives, the weakened dictator, with a look of hope and outstretched arm, staggers across an expanse of floor towards Brutus. Caesar frowns as the

Right: *This was the most unkindest cut of all*
Marlon Brando, 1953
Below right: *I come to bury Caesar, not to praise him*
Marlon Brando, 1953
Below: Marlon Brando about to 'run his course', 1953

Above: *Fly not; stand still; ambition's debt is paid*
Donald Layne-Smith as Metellus Cimber, Alec Clunes, Cyril
Luckham, Mark Dignam as Casca, Geoffrey Keen, William
Elmshirst as Publius, Donald Eccles as Cicero, and James
Wellman as Cinna, 1957

final blow is struck. Antony's reference to Caesar's 'spirit' [III.1.270] is spoken beside the corpse lying at the foot of Pompey's statue. At the funeral Antony stills the crowd when he appears alone at the top of a large flight of steps bearing the body in his arms.

The BBC-tv production's presentation of Caesar's final moments is similar to the MGM version, focusing on the hopeless isolation of his final moments when everyone seems to have turned against him. The struggling dictator reaches towards Brutus who coldly inflicts the fatal wound. This is followed by ritualistic blood smearing.

Byam Shaw choreographed the assassination. In a sequence of moves, Caesar, who was standing, turned to each conspirator who swayed towards him before thrusting their swords. The action was underscored by clamorous music and sound effects. The funeral scene which followed was presented at twilight with a single star reminiscent of Caesar's ironic words that he was as 'constant as the northern star' [60].

Nunn also gave special prominence to the

murder. The scale of proceedings was indicated by Caesar entering as a Mussolini-type dictator borne on an eagle-backed chair emphasising his seemingly indomitable spirit. The staging exploited the white marble set and predominantly white costumes, particularly when the senators parted and turned, revealing blood-splattered togas and a naked, mutilated corpse. A statue of monolithic proportions which was moved onto stage right for the funeral remained there to the end of the play. It echoed Cassius' claim that Caesar was like 'a Colossus' [I.2.135] and gave the impression that even after his death Caesar's power and influence overshadowed the action of the murderers. Red spotlights focused on its features at relevant moments, signalling the demise of each of the assassins.

The urgent action of the play's first half was presented by the use of imposing theatrical pictures of Julius Caesar and culminated in the chilling murder of Cinna, whereas in the second half the centre of attention was on the intimacy of the relationships between the play's main characters, but with permanent visual reminders that the dead dictator's influence was inescapable. Dramatic tension was sustained in the proscription and reconciliation scenes by interplay between a Brutus who was a dignified, gentle idealist, clearly the 'noblest Roman of them all' [V.5.68], a proud, dangerous, resolute Antony and a Cassius who was an angry revolutionary. Ultimately the brooding presence of Caesar's spirit would prove inescapable.

David Thacker's presentation of the assassination scene made the audience feel uncomfortably close to the action. The conspirators ominously emerged from the audience one by one and in a trance-like series of moves advanced towards Caesar and stabbed him. Caesar who was reduced to his knees finally grabbed Brutus by the legs and looked into his eyes before uttering 'Et tu,

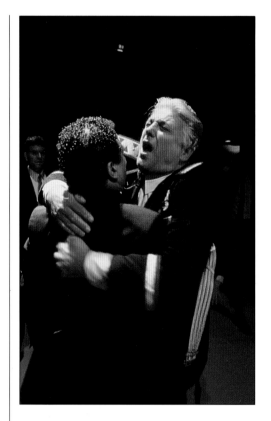

Above: – Et tu, Brute? – Then fall Caesar!
– Liberty! Freedom! Tyranny is dead!
Jeffery Kissoon and David Sumner, 1993

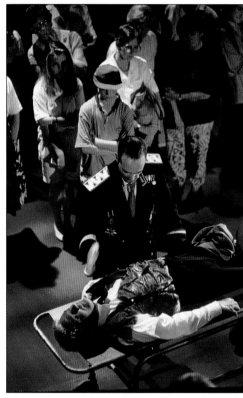

Above: Look you here,
Here is himself, marred as you see with traitors
Barry Lynch, 1993

Brute?' [III.1.77]. All of the conspirators avoided making eye contact with the audience in the moments after, as Caesar's body was wheeled out on an hospital trolley.

Antony's intense quietly spoken funeral oration evoked strong emotions: members of the cast mingled with the audience and led the responses. This was a particular strength of the production which served to highlight the importance of Caesar's power even after his death through the feelings which his memory evoked – the silver-haired man with whom the audience had stood shoulder-to-shoulder earlier in the play.

Shakespeare's plot during the remainder of the play follows the conflicts between the loyalists and conspirators over the morality of the assassination. After his death the dictator's irrepressible power to evoke both love and hate has been held in focus by a number of ingenious stage devices presenting visual reminders of Caesar. At the National Theatre in 1977, John Schlesinger represented Caesar's ghost above the plains of Philippi with four large masks. In Byam Shaw's production the star prominent during the funeral orations was seen again above the plains of Philippi, and together with a large statue of Caesar served as reminders of the titular hero. An omnipresent Caesar was suggested in Nunn's production by the imposing statue which turned towards the

Above:
but as he was ambitious, I slew him
Jeffery Kissoon, 1993

NOTABLE PRODUCTIONS OF *JULIUS CAESAR*

	THEATRE	DIRECTOR	DESIGNER	PRINCIPALS	
1953	Metro-Goldwyn-Mayer	Joseph L. Mankiewicz	Cedric Gibbons, Edward Carfagno	Louis Calhern	*Julius Caesar*
				James Mason	*Marcus Brutus*
				Marlon Brando	*Mark Antony*
				John Gielgud	*Caius Cassius*
1957	Royal Shakespeare Theatre, Stratford-upon-Avon	Glen Byam Shaw	Motley	Cyril Luckham	*Julius Caesar*
				Alec Clunes	*Marcus Brutus*
				Richard Johnson	*Mark Antony*
				Geoffrey Keen	*Caius Cassius*
1972	Royal Shakespeare Theatre, Stratford-upon-Avon	Trevor Nunn	Christopher Morley, Ann Curtis	Mark Dignam	*Julius Caesar*
				John Wood	*Marcus Brutus*
				Richard Johnson	*Mark Antony*
				Patrick Stewart	*Caius Cassius*
1978	BBC-tv	Herbert Wise	Tony Abbott	Charles Gray	*Julius Caesar*
				Richard Pasco	*Marcus Brutus*
				Keith Michell	*Mark Antony*
				David Collings	*Caius Cassius*
1993	The Other Place, Stratford-upon-Avon	David Thacker	Fran Thompson	David Sumner	*Julius Caesar*
				Jeffery Kissoon	*Marcus Brutus*
				Barry Lynch	*Mark Antony*
				Rob Edwards	*Caius Cassius*

ghost at Sardis.

By contrast David Thacker did not try to suggest Caesar's continued influence by introducing visual reminders of his presence, but simply let the initial images remain by concentrating on the psychological realism of the characters. Of all the characters, perhaps Cassius showed the greatest range of emotions and sustained credibility. He first appeared as a conscientious businessman whose hands-in-pockets stance suggested a degree of quiet assurance; in the storm scene he stood in the rain with resolve and later in the play he presented a light-hearted side to the character. There was obviously more to this Cassius than the 'lean and hungry look' [I.2.93] and potential for dangerous action noted earlier by Caesar. By comparison Brutus remained scowling and bombastic as during his strident delivery of:

Romans, countrymen, and lovers, hear me for my cause, and be silent, that you may hear. Believe me for mine honour, and have respect for mine honour, that you may believe.

[III.2.13-16]

By clearly presenting Shakespeare's interest in the irrepressible power of the titular hero, sustained expression can be given to Cassius' reference to 'immortal Caesar' [I.2.60]. Brutus' predicament, Cassius' frustration and Antony's loyalty when seen in this context seem all the more poignant.

Mike Paterson

'MODULE OF CONFOUNDED ROYALTY'

The Early Production History of *King John*

Although allusions to *King John* confirm that it was performed in the 1590s, there is no evidence to suggest that it was popular in Shakespeare's time. The first recorded production of the play was in 1737 at Covent Garden and it was firmly established there in 1745 when Colley Cibber's anti-Catholic adaptation, *Papal Tyranny in the Reign of King John*, played opposite David Garrick's revival of the original at Drury Lane. Thus began a period of popularity that lasted for 150 years. *King John* became a central work in the canon with such notables as John Philip Kemble, Charles Kean and Sarah Siddons seeing potential in the rôles of John, the Bastard and Constance.

King John particularly suited the vogue for elaborate, historically accurate sets much loved by audiences in the late nineteenth century; such productions were offered by Macready (1842) and Charles Kean (1852). The fashion for theatrical splendour faded at the turn of the century and Herbert Beerbohm Tree's spectacular production of 1899 can be viewed as a swan song for both the style of presentation and the play itself. Ironically, it contributed to an emerging style by becoming the first Shakespearean play to be filmed.

Twentieth century tastes have looked unkindly on the play as it became associated with outmoded forms of acting, staging and political presentation. When Peter Brook staged a relatively unsuccessful revival at the Birmingham Repertory Theatre in 1945, the play was virtually unknown and the rare revivals since, such as Buzz Goodbody's in 1970 and John Barton and Barry Kyle's in 1974, have quite radically adapted the text. The play's only known full text production was provided by Deborah Warner at The Other Place, Stratford-upon-Avon, in 1988. It gained critical accolades and demonstrated for the first time this century that the play can be a theatrical success.

Top: Herbert Beerbohm Tree as King John at Her Majesty's Theatre, 1899
Left: Julia Neilson as Constance, 1899
Right: The second Theatre Royal, Drury Lane, six years before it was demolished, 1785

KING JOHN

*Issues of legitimacy are debated in a raw and exciting play
in which the Bastard has the authoritative voice.*

The opening scene of *King John* introduces the principle themes of legitimacy and diplomacy which run throughout the play, as well as establishing the juxtaposition of the two main characters, King John and the Bastard. John's insecurity over his own legitimacy is apparent from the outset and throughout the play it becomes an obsession. In 1988 John clearly lacked the regal authority that his political situation demanded and that he so obviously craved. Woodeson's diminutive stature was emphasised by a trench coat which reached the ground and an outrageously large broad sword that dwarfed him. His temperament was subject to violent, childlike swings, at one moment pleased with himself and the next throwing a tantrum amidst diplomatic decorum. In the opening scene John commanded the French lord to 'depart in peace' [I.1.23] but when the French envoy began to leave too soon for his liking, John ran across the stage to bellow 'be thou the trumpet of our wrath' [27] looking up the French ambassador's nose whilst Eleanor chuckled at the churlish but harmless boy.

The Bastard brings energy and fresh vitality both physically and verbally. In 1988 David Morrissey took every entrance at a sprint and, on being knighted by John, sprang up with an almighty 'Yahoo!' and gave two fingers to his brother. Richard Pasco had been far more controlled: the country gentleman to David Morrissey's country bumpkin. The opposi-

Right: *But since you are a gentle convertite,
My tongue shall hush again this storm of war*
Jeffrey Dench as Cardinal Pandulph and Emrys James, 1975

commodity. Richard Pasco stepped forward to deliver the speech as cool observer. David Morrissey leapt from a ladder and landed with a two-footed stamp on 'Mad world! Mad kings! Mad composition!' [561]. The Bastard is still the outsider, able to pierce the hypocrisy of international politics, but the realisation that his motives are governed by the same commodity presages his later involvement in the political arena.

Pandulph, the papal legate, inspires renewed conflict between England and France and in the ensuing battle, the one true threat to John's legitimacy, Prince Arthur, is captured. King John's instruction for Hubert to kill the child is a chilling moment. In 1974,

tion of John and the Bastard is crucial to the shape of the play which, in simplistic terms, documents the rise of the Bastard and the fall of John. The Bastard ignores his claim for inheritance and takes a chance. This forward momentum is juxtaposed with John who, already defensive in the first scene, continues to retreat in order to protect what he has.

In Angiers, the English and French meet and present a scene of international diplomacy at its worst. In 1974 it was an elaborate set piece of political rhetoric. In 1988 arguments followed at tremendous speed, from King John and King Philip's international debate, to Constance and Eleanor's private grudge, to the Bastard's wilful scolding of Austria just for the sake of a good argument. Each took centre stage in turn, or hurled abuse from diagonals, and thus the inability of the citizens of Angiers to distinguish the true king was entirely understandable.

The Bastard argues that English and French

Above: David Suchet, Emrys James, Richard Pasco and Clement McCallin as King Philip of France, 1974
Right: *– Must you with hot irons burn out both mine eyes?*
   – Young boy, I must.
David Suchet and Benedict Taylor, 1974

should join to sack the town. Richard Pasco was calculating and commanding whereas David Morrissey's boorish attitude indicated that he was spoiling for a fight, causing 'Your royal presences, be ruled by me' [II.1.377] to receive a dismissive laugh. When this policy is agreed, Hubert, the citizens' representative, successfully suggests a marriage between John's niece Blanche and the French Dauphin: a peace that values expediency above principles.

As the nobles retreat to celebrate the marriage, the Bastard is left alone on stage. In one of the most celebrated speeches of the play, he accuses the nobles of changing principles according to the 'purpose-changer' [567] and 'all-changing word' [582] –

Above left: *Doth not the crown of England prove the King?*
Nicholas Woodeson, 1988
Above right: *This act is as an ancient tale new told,*
    And in the last repeating troublesome
Richard Bremmer as Pembroke and Nicholas Woodeson, 1988

evil and sensual pleasure combined as the order was issued while Hubert massaged John's back. In Deborah Warner's production, John removed his crown as if to speak off the record and began with a conversational 'I had a thing to say' – and then after a pause finished the line in a harsh whisper, 'but let it go' [III.3.33]. A slow build up ensued as John carefully drew the unsuspecting Hubert into his plan and then unleashed a sudden rapid exchange:

KING JOHN   **Death.**
HUBERT   **My lord.**
KING JOHN   **A grave.**
HUBERT   **He shall not live.**
KING JOHN   **Enough.**

[66]

Hubert was left in blinking bewilderment and John walked away pleased with his success only to scurry back and snatch up the forgotten crown.

The blinding scene reduces the political squabble between nations to an intense human moment: a boy has to be brutally murdered by a friend. Robert Demeger entered alone and began an appalling wait, loosening his tie and pacing the floor. With a keen craftsman's eye he perused a selection of tools to put out Arthur's eyes, relieved to have a distraction from the imminent crime, 'Heat me these irons hot' [IV.1.1]. Terrible torture is threatened but Arthur's pleading pierces Hubert's resolve. In 1988 the actor delivered:

Well, see to live.

[IV.1.121]

with kisses on both Arthur's eyes. For one brief moment human tenderness replaced political resolve.

After this scene of brutal intensity, John is left physically and emotionally alone to receive the news of his mother's death. His grief is translated into his brief and only soliloquy: 'My mother dead!' [IV.2.181]. Nicholas Woodeson's delivery was painfully slow, his voice deteriorating with every syllable. His one private moment is then interrupted by the entrance of Hubert. Arthur falls while attempting to escape, and meets an accidental and pathetic death.

John's stasis is in contrast to the Bastard, whose once boundless energy has now been channelled into the affairs of state and he displays a new maturity. Now addressed as 'Sir Richard' [IV.3.41] he has stopped rebellious accusations by the nobles with the carefully measured, 'Whate'er you think, good words, I think, were best' [28]. He is still self-

Above: *The Dauphin is preparing hitherward*
Richard Bremmer as Pembroke, David Morrissey,
Edward Harbour as Salisbury and Nicholas Woodeson, 1988

NOTABLE PRODUCTIONS OF *KING JOHN*

	THEATRE	DIRECTOR	DESIGNER	PRINCIPALS
1974	Royal Shakespeare Theatre, Stratford-upon-Avon	John Barton with Barry Kyle	John Napier with Martyn Bainbridge and Ann Curtis	Emrys James ....*King John* Hilda Braid ....*Queen Eleanor* Richard Pasco ....*Philip the Bastard* Benedict Taylor ....*Arthur* Sheila Allen ....*Constance* David Suchet ....*Hubert*
1988	The Other Place, Stratford-upon-Avon	Deborah Warner	Sue Blane	Nicholas Woodeson ....*King John* Cherry Morris ....*Queen Eleanor* David Morrissey ....*Philip the Bastard* Lyndon Davies ....*Arthur* Susan Engel ....*Constance* Robert Demeger ....*Hubert*

assured but his language is now tempered with collective needs. With this change comes the self-realisation that political responsibilities threaten personal identity:

I am amazed, methinks, and lose my way
Among the thorns and dangers of this world.

[140-1]

At this point, tender emotion crept into David Morrissey's voice for the first time, yet he emerged with renewed zeal to grapple with the 'thousand businesses' [158] at hand, as John's authority and kingdom near collapse.

The final scenes are anti-climactic: the French fleet is beaten by a storm; the warlike rhetoric of the Bastard is not fully tested in the field; and John is fatally poisoned offstage. His death is both lonely and pitiful. In 1974, Emrys James as King John descended into gibbering madness after physical and mental humiliation at the hands of Pandulph. A crudely symbolic enactment of the last supper was staged emphasising John's rôle. Deborah Warner showed that John's death shifts the focus to the Bastard and England's future. Nicholas Woodeson died without histrionics, still clutching the crown as the Bastard told him of the 'unexpected flood' [V.7.64] that has drowned his last army in the 'Lincoln Washes' [V.6.41]. The flood became tears in the Bastard's eyes and the transition from rustic to loyal knight was complete.

The much anthologised final speech by the Bastard has often been viewed as blindly patriotic:

Come the three corners of the world in arms
And we shall shock them! Naught shall make us
rue
If England to itself do rest but true!

[V.7.116-8]

John Barton reacted against this sentiment to produce a cynical ending but he needed to adapt the text heavily in the process. Deborah Warner, however, held faith with the text; the speech was directed at the rebellious lords as a reaction to the immediate needs of the affairs of state, not as a moral that simplified the complexities of the play. It was indicative of a production that ignored the theatrical reputation of *King John* and grappled with the text afresh to rediscover the potential of the play for modern audiences.

James Shaw

KING LEAR

The crass and bungling insensitivity of two old men precipitates
searing journeys towards understanding and reconciliation.

S ince World War II, *King Lear* has received
more productions than at any other
period in its history. The question of which
text to use has taken a new form in the wake of
scholarly debate about the differences
between the 1608 Quarto and the 1623 Folio
editions. Most directors have worked with a
conflated text, but Nicholas Hytner deliberately followed the Folio, enhancing the thrust
and clarity of the narrative in later scenes.
Particular controversy has surrounded the
practice of cutting for purposes of interpretation, most vehemently in response to Peter
Brook's excision not only of the Quarto
episode of the servants who tend the blinded
Gloucester, but also of Edmund's repentance
and attempt to avert the murder of Cordelia,
which have the authority of both Quarto and
Folio texts.

Even apart from such textual matters, *King
Lear* poses many problems in the theatre. The
main plot of an old king who subjects his
three daughters to a test of filial devotion
contains strong elements of folk tale, in which
chaos is let loose by an act that is inexplicable
in rational terms. The subplot of Gloucester
and his two sons, with its 'credulous father'
[I.2.175] and its villain (Edmund) motivated
by resentment at the stigma of illegitimacy
and determined to 'have lands by wit' [179], is
inherently more realistic. This mixture of
theatrical styles seems to invite resolution in

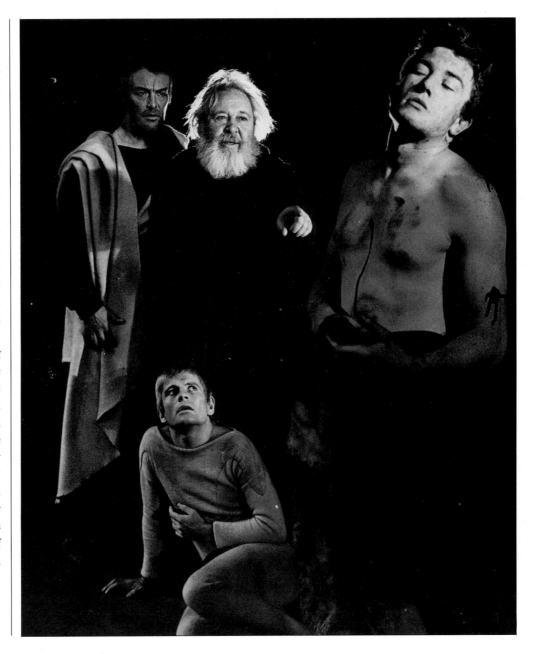

Right: *Didst thou give all to thy daughters?*
   And art thou come to this?
Anthony Nicholls as Kent, Charles Laughton, Ian Holm and
Albert Finney as Edgar, 1959

'I AM A MAN MORE SINNED AGAINST THAN SINNING'

The Early Production History of *King Lear*

Although the first recorded performance of *King Lear* was on 26 December 1606 at the court of James I, it was probably seen earlier at the Globe. Apart from a production by a provincial company in Yorkshire in 1610, the only other performances known in the seventeenth century were by Davenant's company in 1664 and 1675.

Following the appearance of an adaptation by Nahum Tate in 1681, a fully Shakespearean version of the text was not staged again until well into the nineteenth century. With a love interest between Cordelia and Edgar, no Fool and the survival of Lear, Gloucester and Cordelia, Tate's *King Lear* appealed to an age which demanded plausibility of motivation, tragic seriousness uncompromised by humour and the ultimate triumph of virtue over evil.

The play was less frequently performed than other Shakespearean tragedies in the early eighteenth century, but it rose in favour under David Garrick's management at Drury Lane. He kept the Edgar-Cordelia love story and the happy ending from Tate's adaptation and omitted the Fool, but by the time he retired in 1776 he had restored much of Shakespeare's language and

order of scenes. Although John Kemble reverted to Tate in 1809, the reinstatement of Shakespeare's text in the theatre came a step closer when Edmund Kean performed the tragic ending in 1823 and was finally accomplished in 1838 when William Macready brought back the Fool in a shortened and rearranged version of the original play. Victorian taste for spectacle and historical authenticity was indulged by the Anglo Saxon sets and costumes of Charles Kean in 1858 and by the ruined villas and temples of Henry Irving's late Roman Britain in 1892.

Early twentieth century reactions against such archaeological realism included an experimental Elizabethan staging by the Phoenix Society in 1924 and Komisarjevsky's symbolic set at Stratford in 1937.

Top: Charles King as Lear, 1858
Left: Joyce Bland as Gonerill and Clare Harris as Regan, 1937
Right: Mrs Poole as the Fool, 1863

performance. On the one hand, heightened psychological plausibility may be achieved at the expense of more universal implications, as with Charles Laughton's genial paterfamilias and Peter Ustinov's mischievous and difficult old man who played out his tragedy in a carefully constructed context of nineteenth century domesticity. On the other hand, the domestic tensions which may be used to root the drama in familiar experience were sacrificed by Peter Brook and Paul Scofield in their pursuit of a nihilistic vision of human isolation and cosmic indifference.

Another kind of problem is created by the narrative density of a play which not only follows the fortunes of Lear and Gloucester, but also disperses interest across a wide spectrum of subsidiary characters and stories. Audience attention may be more or less sharply focused on the sexual rivalry between Gonerill and Regan and their marital relationships with Albany and Cornwall, the political ambitions of Edmund, the antagonism between Oswald and Kent, and the spiritual journey that transforms Edgar, through his experiences as Poor Tom, from a gullible young aristocrat into a stoic philosopher and a champion of justice.

The difficulty lies in striking a balance between the competing claims of overall coherence and individual performances. Antony Sher's virtuosity as a red-nosed Fool gave his scenes such prominence that the status of Edmund as the play's chief mediator between stage and audience was diminished and the production lost much of its impetus once the Fool had been disposed of in Act III. By contrast, the steady growth in moral authority which distinguished Julian Glover's Albany was fully integrated into Glen Byam Shaw's conception of Lear's pilgrimage towards redemption, providing a strong and dignified centre for the emergence of opposition to the forces of evil.

Above: *You see me here, you gods, a poor old man,*
As full of grief as age, wretched in both
Charles Laughton, 1959

Above: – *Who is it that can tell me who I am?*
– *Lear's shadow.*
Paul Scofield and Alec McCowen, 1962

The particular emphases of a production are often clearly established at the start, when Lear commits the political and personal errors of dividing his kingdom and banishing his youngest child. Aloof on a primitive throne, Scofield's king conducted a joyless public ritual in which a large orb was placed in the hands of each daughter in turn as she repeated a formal expression of love to ratify the handing over of power. Charles Laughton's Lear, crownless and eschewing regal ceremony, settled himself complacently for a gratifying display of family affection planned to mark his retirement. Disposing of Cordelia's share to his sons-in-law, Ustinov

waved a hand indecisively over the symbol of power as if defeated by the task of giving political effect to his words, 'This coronet part between you' [I.1.139]. Robert Stephens' Lear enjoyed the reaction to his order, 'Give me the map there' [37], as a tense ring of courtiers looked about uneasily, until they caught sight of an outline of Britain crudely painted across the floor and, with evident relief, applauded the ingenuity of his conceit. He took a malicious delight in watching Gonerill and Regan improvise their responses to his unexpected demand, glancing quizzically towards Cordelia while they spoke and then forcing her to stand on the chair where they had been

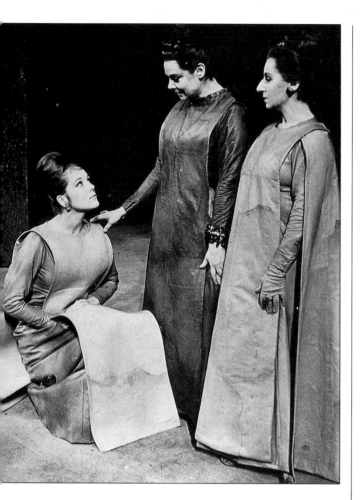

Left: *Prescribe us not our duty*
Diana Rigg as Cordelia, Irene Worth as Gonerill and Patience
Collier as Regan, 1962
Right: *Come not between the dragon and his wrath*
Paul Scofield, 1962

Nicholas Hytner sought an explanation for the later cruelty of the older daughters in their thwarted love for a self-centred man whose curses hurt them deeply. Sally Dexter's Regan, the more unstable of the two, diverted her affection towards Gloucester, wrapping him tenderly in a blanket when he was raised from his bed by Kent's altercation with Oswald and later trying to comfort him after her long pent-up frustrations had been exorcised by the blinding of this substitute father. As Gonerill, Estelle Kohler took a chillingly practical course in coping with the vagaries of a troublesome old man. Her arrival at Gloucester's castle with two uniformed nurses and an invalid chair drew from John Wood's Lear a cry of panic, 'I prithee, daughter, do not *make* me mad' [II.4.213].

In Michael Kahn's production there was even greater emphasis on the complex dynamics of Fritz Weaver's family. Emotional need had forged an alliance between the very different personalities of Kate Skinner's voluptuous and spoiled Regan and Mary Lou Rosato's pinched and discontented Gonerill, in response to a father whose abuse of power in the test imposed upon them was clearly not unprecedented. On the words, 'He always loved our sister most' [I.1.290], the catch in Gonerill's voice evoked sympathy for the pain inflicted by Lear's neglect. Their later descent into evil could not be condoned but it was understandable in the context of these early scenes, and their subsequent competition for Edmund's favour took on a tragic aspect as it broke a bond created by mutual suffering.

The opposition of good son and bad son in the subplot presents its own kind of challenge to performers. Owen Teale's Edmund used

seated, for the climax of this humiliating game.

Another interpretative decision that must be faced in the first two acts is whether to accept the moral polarity of Lear's daughters as a fact of the story or to suggest more naturalistic reasons for their behaviour. In Byam Shaw's family drama, Stephanie Bidmead's Gonerill was harassed by the inconveniences of housekeeping for her father's large retinue, Angela Baddeley's Regan was an aristocratic wanton accustomed to getting her own way, and Zoe Caldwell's Cordelia was a stubborn child who saw through her father's sentimentality but lacked her sisters' sophisticated ability to humour it.

his early soliloquies to enlist support for the schemes of an easy-going young rogue against David Bradley's tetchy and petulant Gloucester, and an Edgar who sat primly engrossed in a book during the opening scene. Later, this Edmund's attractive qualities were undermined by the flattering attentions of the king's daughters and a growing fascination with Cornwall's disdainful exercise of power. Much more dangerous from the outset was the cold-blooded cruelty evident behind the witty and sophisticated detachment of Robert Hardy's cynical opportunist.

The shape-changing Edgar is often reduced to a series of symbolic functions. In the BBC-tv production, for example, Anton Lesser wears a Christ-like crown of thorns during his monologue at the start of Act IV and appears for the duel in a white mask which recalls the white make-up of the Fool. Grigori Kozintsev, the Russian director, chose to integrate Edgar into the political vision of his 1970 film by having him join a procession of beggars when he assumes his disguise as Poor Tom. At Stratford-upon-Avon in 1993, Simon Russell Beale went for a more psychologically consistent and morally ambivalent reading of his development from effete scholar to desperate avenger, ignoring all rules of combat in the duel and making a vicious lunge for the wounded Edmund's eyes.

The nature of the Fool and his relationship with Lear have taxed the ingenuity of directors and actors since Macready cast the nineteen-year-old Priscilla Horton as a fragile half-wit and established a tradition in the Victorian theatre recently revived by the casting of Linda Kerr Scott as an almost spastic, doll-like creature, sniffing at Lear with the instinctive affection of a dog. Other Fools have been crippled in body if not in mind. Sher staggered with bent legs and in-turned toes, but during his prophecy in Act III miraculously straightened up and was able to dance, until a whistle blew and a malevolent universe reimposed his disability. Philip Goodwin, teetering on the edge of insanity and with only stumps of legs, propelled himself about the stage on a small trolley.

At the other extreme, Alec McCowen was alarmingly lucid; and Frank Middlemass, an old man like the king, is more conscience than companion to Michael Hordern, lecturing him relentlessly on the folly of his actions.

Above right: *You do me wrong to take me out o' the grave. Thou art a soul in bliss*
Yuri Yarvet and Valentina Chendrikova as Cordelia, 1970
Below right: *We two alone will sing like birds i' the cage*
Yuri Yarvet and Valentina Chendrikova as Cordelia, 1970

NOTABLE PRODUCTIONS OF *KING LEAR*

	THEATRE	DIRECTOR	DESIGNER	PRINCIPALS
1959	Royal Shakespeare Theatre, Stratford-upon-Avon	Glen Byam Shaw	Motley	Charles Laughton ....*Lear* Cyril Luckham ....*Gloucester* Ian Holm ....*Fool* Robert Hardy ....*Edmund*
1962	Royal Shakespeare Theatre, Stratford-upon-Avon	Peter Brook	Peter Brook	Paul Scofield ....*Lear* Alan Webb ....*Gloucester* Alec McCowen ....*Fool* James Booth ....*Edmund*
1970	Lenfilm	Grigori Kozintsev	Eugene Ene, S. Virsaladze	Yuri Yarvet ....*Lear* Karl Sebris ....*Gloucester* Oleg Dal ....*Fool* Regimastas Adomaitis ....*Edmund*
1979	The Shakespearean Festival Theatre Stratford, Ontario	Robin Phillips	Daphne Dare	Peter Ustinov ....*Lear* Douglas Rain ....*Gloucester* William Hutt ....*Fool* Richard Monette ....*Edmund*
1982	BBC-tv	Jonathan Miller	Colin Lowrey, Raymond Hughes	Michael Hordern ....*Lear* Norman Rodway ....*Gloucester* Frank Middlemass........................*Fool* Michael Kitchen ....*Edmund*

William Hutt's professional jester was a long-standing friend of Ustinov's Lear, who shared jokes and even a dance with him. Sher went further still in stressing the Fool's rôle as an entertainer and his relationship with Michael Gambon was conceived in theatrical terms, their first big scene together being played as ventriloquist and dummy and their second as a double-act routine. The Fool of Ian Hughes was also very much a professional clown, welcomed for his skills by Lear's knights and accompanying his songs on a mandolin, but his sensitive personality was agonised by its compulsion to tell the truths that would drive his master mad, and there was painful sincerity in his plea:

> **Prithee, nuncle, keep a schoolmaster that can teach thy fool to lie; I would fain learn to lie.**
>
> [I.4.175-6]

Act III moves through the mental frenzy of the storm on the heath and the crazy convocation of king, beggar, and fool to the physical atrocity perpetrated on Gloucester.

Ever since the complaint that Edmund Kean could scarcely be heard above the clamour of sound effects, there has been controversy over the extent to which 'this tempest in my mind' [III.4.12] during the storm scene should be represented by a tempest on the stage. For Robin Phillips, occasional thunder and flashes of lightning were a naturalistic background to Lear's rage, not an expression of it. Peter Brook rendered the uproar visible by lowering three rusty thundersheets from the flies and orchestrated Scofield's voice and loud bursts of thunder as a dialogue between the enraged king and 'the great gods/That keep this dreadful pudder o'er our heads' [III.2.49-50]. In 1982, Adrian Noble perched Lear and the Fool precariously in a crow's nest above swirling clouds of dry ice and made Gambon compete with blasts of music as well as thunder in a symbolic evocation of mind and universe in turmoil. Lear takes a faltering step on the path to wisdom as bodily deprivation forces him to recognise his kinship with the Fool:

> **Come on, my boy. How dost my boy? Art cold?**
> **I am cold myself. Where is this straw, my fellow?**
> **The art of our necessities is strange**
> **And can make vile things precious.**
>
> [68-71]

The sudden appearance of Edgar/Poor Tom, however, tips him into madness. His growing obsession with this emblem of 'unaccommodated man' [III.4.103] causes the displacement of the Fool, which was brilliantly visualised in the image of Ian Hughes clinging forlornly to Poor Tom's hand at the end of a human chain that Gloucester led across the stage in Noble's 1993 production.

Above: *Poor Tom's a-cold*.
Jonathan Hyde as Edgar in disguise, 1982

NOTABLE PRODUCTIONS OF *KING LEAR*

	THEATRE	DIRECTOR	DESIGNER	PRINCIPALS	
1982	Royal Shakespeare Theatre, Stratford-upon-Avon	Adrian Noble	Bob Crowley	Michael Gambon	Lear
				David Waller	Gloucester
				Antony Sher	Fool
				Clive Wood	Edmund
1990	Royal Shakespeare Theatre, Stratford-upon-Avon	Nicholas Hytner	David Fielding	John Wood	Lear
				Norman Rodway	Gloucester
				Linda Kerr Scott	Fool
				Ralph Fiennes	Edmund
1991	Shakespeare Theatre at the Folger, Washington DC	Michael Kahn	Thomas Lynch	Fritz Weaver	Lear
				Tedvan Griethuysen	Gloucester
				Philip Goodwin	Fool
				Daniel Southern	Edmund
1993	Royal Shakespeare Theatre, Stratford-upon-Avon	Adrian Noble	Anthony Ward	Robert Stephens	Lear
				David Bradley	Gloucester
				Ian Hughes	Fool
				Owen Teale	Edmund

The scene of Gloucester's torture often builds on earlier characterisation of Cornwall and Regan. In two RSC productions, the latent sadism of Cornwall was indicated by the light, impatient taps Tony Church gave to Kent's cheek with his riding whip in 1962 and by Simon Dormandy's vicious and erotic handling of the self-inflicted wound on Edmund's breast in 1993. Church went on to a literal execution of his threat, 'Upon these eyes of thine I'll set my foot' [III.7.67], while Dormandy extracted Gloucester's eye-balls with his fingers. More shocking, perhaps, was the intrusion of such savagery into the civilised comfort of Douglas Rain's Victorian study, where his eyes were put out with a paper knife. Kate Skinner's Regan at the Folger assisted Cornwall in removing Gloucester's second eye and their shared sexual excitement culminated in a passionate embrace. In Byam Shaw's production, Paul Hardwick was left to face death alone as his wife swept past him, disdainfully ignoring his terror-stricken appeal, 'Regan, I bleed apace' [96].

After the interval, usually taken at the close of Act III in the modern theatre, a change of mood is reflected in Edgar's advice to Gloucester: 'Bear free and patient thoughts' [IV.6.80] and 'Ripeness is all' [V.2.11]. In Act IV, there is a striking difference between the urgency with which the evil characters pursue the rivalries that will destroy them and the calm that settles over their victims. Many productions exploit the opportunities for pathos in the encounter between mad Lear and blind Gloucester, and in Lear's awakening in the presence of Cordelia. Alan Webb and David Bradley broke down and wept at the command, 'Pull off my boots' [IV.6.174], the former clumsily obeying and the latter overwhelmed by his failure to perform this simple service for his king. Rodway makes no

Above: *I know thee well enough; thy name is Gloucester.*
Thou must be patient; we came crying hither.
Thou knowest the first time that we smell the air
We wawl and cry.
Jonathan Hyde as Edgar, David Waller and Michael Gambon, 1982

attempt to respond at this point, since Hordern's Lear, in a clinically convincing portrayal of lunatic behaviour, is too far gone for any rapport to develop between them.

Sitting up in bed for the later reunion with his daughter, Hordern is like a patient who has recovered from an illness, in sharp contrast to Laughton, who spoke the words, 'I think this lady/To be my child Cordelia' [IV.7.69-70], with the quiet wonder of a man reborn.

The overall impact of a production is often dependent upon the extent to which Lear makes progress towards greater insight and

humanity. Earlier in Act IV, drenched in the rich light of late summer and enthroned on a harvest-cart which seemed to validate the optimism of Cordelia's allusion to 'our sustaining corn' (IV.4.6), Laughton had achieved a serene dignity even in madness, and his redemption was later affirmed in the tableau of father and daughter kneeling to receive each other's blessing. Gambon conveyed little sense of such spiritual development, however, revealing a flash of his old selfish authority in the line, 'I am mightily abused' [IV.7.53]; and Ustinov, playing some of the mad speeches of Act IV for comedy, stressed senility rather than transcendence at the end.

The end itself offers no easy answers to the human and metaphysical problems raised by this harrowing tragedy. Once various narrative situations have been resolved in the course of Act V – the battle, the fate of Gloucester, the showdown between Edgar and Edmund, the jealous contest which leaves both Gonerill and Regan dead – the audience is confronted with the powerfully ambiguous images of Lear bearing the body of Cordelia in his arms and dying over it in moral outrage or deluded hope. Ustinov's heart broke in pain not joy, but he fell back into the arms of attendants who surrounded his last moments with love. Similar devotion from David Calder's Kent accompanied the departure of Robert Stephens, who died pointing excitedly towards some vision of a life to come: 'Look there! look there!' [V.3.309]. The bleakness of Brook's absurdist vision precluded any hint of affirmation and his final stage picture was not that of the exhausted representatives of resurgent goodness mourning over Lear and Cordelia, but of a lonely Edgar dragging away the corpse of his brother to the rumble of distant thunder.

Robert Wilcher

LOVE'S LABOUR'S LOST

*The academic posturing of four young men crumbles
with the arrival of four beautiful and intelligent women.*

In the style of Peter Brook's ground-breaking production, recent stagings of *Love's Labour's Lost* have also been designed pictorially with exquisite visual effects. John Barton's autumnal park suggested the richness of a Millais painting. In 1984, Bob Crowley created an ash-white parkland strewn with flower petals and decorative puddles evocative of Parisian parks of the *Belle Epoque.* Above the park was a canopy of towering white parasols which opened and floated when the ladies entered. In the 1990 production hand-painted multi-coloured leaves were strewn across the French garden landscape so that the lighting created an effect similar to that of the pointillist art of Henri Cross. The opening scene – when the men took their oaths against a background of green and russet – presented an image reminiscent of Manet's *Le Déjeuner sur l'herbe.* When the French ladies arrived, the stage was bathed in the shimmering light of a late afternoon sun. In contrast, Ian Judge's production departed from French impressionism to trade on a somewhat sentimental view of late Edwardian England. Here the pedantic dialogue of Holofernes and Sir Nathaniel was exchanged while watching a cricket match, and Costard misdelivered his letters as a butcher's boy. The very English setting made more of the potential pathos of Don Armado's rôle as a cultural misfit and social oddity.

As comedy, *Love's Labour's Lost* displays a fascination with language as the tool of wit, learning and persuasion at all social levels. From their first encounter with the preten-tious lords, the ladies respond with witty rejoinders, and the lords are no match for such verbal dexterity. In Terry Hands' production, Carol Royle's cool and worldly Princess contrasted with Amanda Root's sprightly, sparky Rosaline. Boyet's affectionate address to them and to the retinue ' My mad wenches' [II.2.243] beautifully capped a scene of nimble, witty exchange. Such scenes as the conversations between Don Armado and Mote are apparently constructed principally to enable characters to indulge in verbal display. In Terry Hands' production, John Wood as Don Armado bantered eagerly and

Above: *The words of Mercury are harsh after the songs of Apollo. You that way; we this way.*
Daniel Massey as Don Armado, 1993

earnestly with Mote, attaching supreme importance to argument and definition. In 1993, a more precocious Mote, appearing as a bespectacled chorister, handled language with rigour and delighted in outwitting a slower, more lugubrious Don Armado. Above all, Berowne possesses the rhetorical brilliance to present a case with authority. Roger Rees argued passionately in the opening scene against the lords' renunciation of

'TH'ANOINTED SOVEREIGN OF SIGHS AND GROANS'

The Early Production History of *Love's Labour's Lost*

As the sophistication of the rhetoric and poetic language suggests, *Love's Labour's Lost* was a court play, performed before Elizabeth I in 1597 and again during the Christmas revels of 1604-5. The play was not performed again until 1839 at the reopening of the Theatre Royal, Covent Garden under the management of Elizabeth Vestris, who also took the part of Rosaline. Critical concentration on the lavishness of the production suggests that difficulties with the play's verbal abstruseness found compensation in the visual element. The dominant critical response was that *Love's Labour's Lost* with its 'gentility of poetic romance' was Shakespeare's least theatrical play.

In Stratford, *Love's Labour's Lost* was first performed as part of the birthday celebrations in 1885 and then not again until 1907 when Frank Benson played Berowne. Peter Brook's production at the Shakespeare Memorial Theatre in 1946,

however, helped to change critical attitudes to the play. Brook's version was pictorially inspired with costume and set executed in the *fêtes galantes* style of the early eighteenth century artist Antoine Watteau, and in particular, his *Voyage à Cythéré*. Watteau's park-like settings, his displays of elegant society and representations of comedy actors provided appropriate images for the play. The Princess and her retinue were arrayed in dresses of billowing satin and an additional character – the zany – was introduced. The subtle poetic mood of fleeting happiness encapsulated in Watteau's scenes was remarkably consonant with the loss and unfulfilled expectation of the final act, or with what Brook described as 'the play's essential sweet-sad mood'. David King-Wood's Berowne sustained an opposition to love, expressing the bitter passion of Shakespeare's *Sonnets*, although such an interpretation has not featured in more recent productions. When the news of the death of the Princess's father was brought to the park, the company stood stricken and still; following the songs of the owl and the cuckoo, the play's closing words, 'You that way; we this way' were spoken by the Princess rather than by Armado.

Top: Queen Elizabeth I dancing with Robert Dudley, Earl of Leicester
Left: An early print of the present theatre in Covent Garden, which opened in 1858
Right: Elizabeth Vestris, 1797-1856

sensual delight before calling their bluff with a bray of laughter and taking the pledge. Jeremy Northam, however, appeared more as a lawyer savouring his own advocacy before an appreciative audience.

But the comedy is also concerned with the intrusion of love and death into the artificially constructed world of the King's little 'academe'. In one of the turning points of the play, the men painlessly reject the ascetic life to become men of arms intent on courtship. Navarre's short-lived academy has been variously evoked. In the 1984 production the men were votaries taking their vows with solemnity. This rigour was registered in the set on which four desks were positioned across the stage, each supporting a green shaded reading lamp and an ostentatious skull as *memento mori*. The gowned lords were intent upon their life of seclusion and study while apprehensively waiting for Berowne to take the pledge. In contrast, the lords' commitment to study and celibacy appeared absurd from the start of Terry Hands' production. The men took their oaths lounging on cushions, surrounded by food and wine, in the midst of a luxuriant park. The silence which followed the signing of the pact was punctured by the lethargic swotting of a fly. That the park is out of bounds to women was signified in the comically juvenile gesture of a notice, 'interdit aux femmes', prominently displayed at the entry to the privileged space. The Academy again had a recreational air in the 1993 production in which the King's court was the wisteria-covered courtyard of an Oxford college; the men, as Edwardian dandies, listened nonchalantly while the King enthusiastically projected the subjugation of their senses. Berowne's impassioned attempt to set experience against dry scholarship:

Above right: The women arrive at the Court of Navarre only to find that the park is out of bounds to them, 1990
Right: Roger Rees, 1984

'Now step I forth to whip hypocrisy' [IV.3.149]. At this juncture, the King collapsed in a dead faint at the humiliation of his exposure. Comic embarrassment is intensified but short-lived, as first Dumaine retrieves Berowne's letter to Rosaline and, as the play's tempo quickens, Berowne eloquently exhorts the men to pursue their desires. Ralph Fiennes was driven by an ardent celebration of love already communicated in the soliloquy, 'And I, forsooth, in love!' [III.1.170]. For Roger Rees, the moment was one of delighted impulsiveness, whilst Jeremy Northam used both wit and sentiment to persuade. In Kyle's production, following Navarre's rallying cry, 'Saint Cupid, then! And soldiers to the field!' [IV.3.342] the courtiers tore off their academic

Left: *We are wise girls to mock our lovers so.*
Caroline Loncq as Katharine, Carol Royle as the Princess, Amanda Root and Katrina Levon as Maria, 1990
Below: *Now, at the latest minute of the hour*
                    Grant us your loves.
The women as above, Griffith Jones as Marcade, Simon Russell Beale, Ralph Fiennes, Bernard Wright as Longaville and Paterson Joseph as Dumaine, 1990

> So, ere you find where light in darkness lies,
> Your light grows dark by losing of your eyes.
>
> [I.1.78-9]

had dramatic power, but appeared as no more than polished rhetoric when he then sprang forward to subscribe and join the brotherhood.

The scene in which one by one the lords renege on their vows and reveal their passions for the ladies is another pivotal point and one rich in comic embarrassment. Barry Kyle's production departed from common stage practice by positioning Berowne behind a headless statue of Eros whose bow appeared targeted at the King and courtiers. More usually he perches in a tree to overhear the lords' declarations of love. With mocking relish, Roger Rees made his presence known:

gowns and pursued their quarry into the open. In Judge's production the men departed in a mood of urgent almost predatory exuberance, a spirit driven by Berowne's injunction:

**Advance your standards and upon them lords!
Pell mell down with them!**

[343]

What impresses in the latter part of *Love's Labour's Lost* is its visual symmetry. The four lords court the four ladies first as Muscovites, in which guise they are mockingly dismissed, and later in their own persons. Their emotional immaturity and the fact that they are essentially still acting parts are communicated by the ridiculously comic disguise. In Hands' production one was in a bear's costume; in 1993 the men appeared as dancing Cossacks. They return to the game of courtship as themselves where Berowne is chastened into plain speech:

**Henceforth my wooing mind shall be expressed
In russet yeas and honest kersey noes.**

[V.2.412-13]

Nothing differentiates the female embassy from the male Navarre court so much as their responses to the play of the Nine Worthies. The Princess' courteous and encouraging remarks to the actors appear the more so in contrast to Berowne's derisory interruptions of the performance. Owen Teale's King was edgy, registering discomfort at the mocking response of the Court. Gazing intently at the Princess, he sat apart, downstage, attempting physically and morally to distance himself from his courtiers.

The world of the Academy, artfully constructed to keep time, love and death at bay, is dealt its final blow in the midst of the lords' cruel laughter at Armado's revelation that he has no shirt, when Marcade arrives to announce the death of the Princess' father. In 1990, Griffith Jones was a memorable messenger, appearing from a darkening wood as a sombre undertaker. The couples meet and the ladies impose on the men their conditions of marriage and a year long delay before their hasty return to France. Jenny Quayle in Judge's production announced her departure with heavy emotion, making the King's attempt to return the conversation to matters of love all the more inappropriate. In 1990 there was an affecting vignette of female solidarity as the women grouped to console the Princess. Six years earlier the four lords were left standing at the front of the stage, positioned as they had been at the beginning of the play but without the emblematic desks. The women had left them; uncertain learning lay before them. Ian Judge halted his production after the departure of the French party. The backdrop of Oxford changed to one of the Western Front. Dusk had fallen, and in the distance, sounds were heard of shells and artillery. The intimation of the battlefields of the Somme and the likely fates of the men before the close of a year introduced a further, poignant note of uncertainty into this open-ended comedy.

Janet Clare

NOTABLE PRODUCTIONS OF *LOVE'S LABOUR'S LOST*

	THEATRE	DIRECTOR	DESIGNER	PRINCIPALS
1978	Royal Shakespeare Theatre, Stratford-upon-Avon	John Barton	Ralph Koltai	Richard Griffiths ....*King of Navarre* Carmen Du Sautoy ....*Princess* Michael Pennington ....*Berowne* Jane Lapotaire.......................*Rosaline*
1984	Royal Shakespeare Theatre, Stratford-upon-Avon	Barry Kyle	Bob Crowley	Kenneth Branagh ......*King of Navarre* Emily Richard ....*Princess of France* Roger Rees ....*Berowne* Josette Simon ....*Rosaline*
1990	Royal Shakespeare Theatre, Stratford-upon-Avon	Terry Hands	Timothy O'Brien	Simon Russell Beale ....*King* Carol Royle ....*Princess of France* Ralph Fiennes.......................*Berowne* Amanda Root ....*Rosaline*
1993	Royal Shakespeare Theatre, Stratford-upon-Avon	Ian Judge	John Gunter	Owen Teale ....*King of Navarre* Jenny Quayle ....*Princess of France* Jeremy Northam...................*Berowne* Abigail McKern ....*Rosaline*

'BY THE PRICKING OF MY THUMBS, SOMETHING WICKED THIS WAY COMES'

The Early Production History of *Macbeth*

Macbeth was almost certainly written in 1606, the year after the gunpowder plot, and was based on the *Chronicle of Scotland* by Holinshed. However the play did not appear in print until the First Folio of 1623. A very popular play, it is thought that one of its earliest performances was at Court for James I and the King of Denmark. It was performed in the Globe Theatre in daylight, but was also staged indoors at the Blackfriars Theatre – a setting well-suited to this darkest of plays. Simon Forman's eye-witness account of a performance in 1611 describes one of the most frightening scenes: 'the ghost of Banquo came and sat down ... behind him. And he (Macbeth) turning about to sit down again saw the ghost which fronted him so that he fell in a great passion of fear and fury...'.

The popularity of the play continued after the Restoration. A version by Davenant, performed from 1674-1744 treated the witches as rather comic characters, and Samuel Pepys reported how much he had enjoyed the singing and dancing! The porter scene, with its complicated and sophisticated word-play was often cut or replaced with a 'turn' of popular current jokes. David Garrick started a gradual move away from the Davenant version of the play, although he still performed in the powdered wig and high fashion of the times.

The continued success of *Macbeth* owed much to the performances of eighteenth and nineteenth century actresses. One of the most famous was Sarah Siddons. Sheridan Knowles wrote of her sleepwalking scene: 'I smelt blood! I swear that I smelt blood!' It was not until Irving's production of 1888 that the play was restored as a serious and dark drama. Ellen Terry gave a performance which revealed the erotic power Lady Macbeth has over her husband.

The popularity of *Macbeth* has not waned. It has provided inspiration for painters such as Fuseli and Zuccarelli, film-makers as diverse as Orson Welles and Akira Kurosawa (in his 1957 film *Throne of Blood*) and it still offers fresh material for twentieth century interpretations – Macbeth has been played as a survivor of World War I, as Adolf Hitler and as a present-day fascist.

Top: Sarah Siddons first played Lady Macbeth in 1774 at the age of 20
Left: *Macbeth and the Witches*, a painting by Henry Fuseli, 1741–1825
Right: Sir William Davenant

MACBETH

*Witchcraft frames a story of vaulting ambition
in which prediction and prophecy are confused.*

Above: *There's no art*
                              To find the mind's construction in the face
Erskine Sandford as Duncan and Roddy McDowall as Malcolm
watch the execution of Cawdor, 1948

Macbeth is a powerful play; its subject matter and the speaking of spells have even led some people to believe that it is cursed. It is a play of contrasts and oppositions: good and evil, darkness and light, guilt and innocence, masculine and feminine. The basic question posed by the play – that of Macbeth's guilt – is one which must be addressed by the director and actors of each new production: did the witches suborn Macbeth, or recognise him as an agent for their own plans?

The play opens with the three witches making plans to meet Macbeth. In Roman Polanski's film, this scene comes before the opening credits. On a deserted beach the witches dig a hole in the wet sand and bury a severed arm holding a dagger. Orson Welles also establishes the witches before the opening credits, as if they are outside the film. His witches make a clay doll of Macbeth, showing that they control him totally. Welles' Macbeth is a victim, entirely at the witches' mercy, while Polanski sees him as a willing acolyte. Laurence Olivier was convinced that the ambitious Macbeth had wanted to kill Duncan, even before the witches persuade him to it, and his guilt stemmed from this as much as from the murder. In 1994, the witches spoke their opening lines on a huge platform which slowly rose high above the stage. They remained there while the next scene took place, watching the action from their vantage point.

The opening of the English Shakespeare Company's production revealed how readily

Macbeth lends itself to new interpretations. The scene was a deserted battlefield, heaped with the dead and the dying. Moving among the bodies were three 1990s 'bag-ladies' who removed items of clothing and jewellery. Here were the three witches, doing what had to be done to survive. This production constantly alluded to present day economic and social issues. From its opening scene to the closing anthems, Michael Bogdanov showed a society breaking up, with Macbeth a product and a victim of that society. Trevor Nunn used the opening scene to illustrate the powerful sense apparent throughout the play of the forces of evil ranged against goodness. While Duncan and his court were at prayer, the three witches

moved into the centre of the acting circle and began to groan and howl. Their voices became louder, until they drowned out the pious Duncan.

When Lady Macbeth makes her first appearance, she is reading Macbeth's description of his meeting with the witches and, as she is alone, she is able to reveal her fears about Macbeth. He is 'too full o'the milk of human-kindness' to succeed [I.5.15]. Judi Dench chilled the audience when she called on spirits to:

> unsex me here
> And fill me from the crown to the toe top-full
> Of direst cruelty. Make thick my blood;
> Stop up the access and passage to remorse
> That no compunctious visitings of nature
> Shake my fell purpose.
>
> [39-44]

At the end of the speech, she drew back, as though horrified at her own evil. Francesca Annis is seen high on the battlements, with the approaching Duncan a tiny figure in the distance; there is no doubt that she is the raven 'That croaks the fatal entrance of Duncan under my battlements' [37-38] circling round, waiting to strike.

Polanski shows us Duncan's murder in gory detail; the king awakens while Macbeth is in the chamber and a bloody fight ensues. Throughout the film Polanski offers potent symbols, beginning with the arm and the dagger in the sand. In the murder scene Duncan's crown falls off in the struggle and rolls onto the ground; the crown represents Macbeth's reason for the bloody crime and his reward. Shakespeare, however, does not attempt to portray the event; the murder of a king would have been a shocking thing to see on stage in 1606, when King James had recently survived an attempt on his life. The horror is amply conveyed by Macbeth's reappearance, soaked in guilt and blood. When Ian McKellen came out of Duncan's chamber, his hands shook so violently that the daggers knocked together in a chilling anticipation of the knocking at the castle gate which interrupts the Macbeths at their hand-washing.

The Porter makes several references to himself as the gate-keeper of hell, and the man he lets in – Macduff – will later refer to Macbeth as a 'hell-hound'. This is one point when stage-time and plot-time coincide. While the Porter stumbles drunkenly towards the gate, the actor playing Macbeth is washing

Above: *Strange things I have in head, that will to hand, Which must be acted ere they may be scanned*
Laurence Olivier and Vivien Leigh, 1955

his hands and changing into his night clothes with the same urgency as the character. We must wait for the Porter to open the gate so that the King's body can be discovered and the play proceed. The ESC production heightened the tension by presenting a scene of domesticity. The thanes assembled outside Duncan's chamber in their dressing gowns, sleepy house-guests whose lives were about to be thrown into chaos.

Macbeth survives the entry of Macduff and the discovery of the murder, but again he relies on his wife. She distracts everyone by fainting when the bodies are discovered, giving Macbeth time to recover. Banquo and Macduff, the greatest dangers to Macbeth, both say 'Look to the lady!' [II.3.116,122], perhaps suggesting that she is deliberately attracting their attention. Francesca Annis faints at the sight of the dead grooms, and is almost unnoticed by the rest of the thanes but Judi Dench's Lady Macbeth was clearly thinking quickly and was prepared to play the weak woman from a position of strength. Cheryl Campbell seemed to faint in genuine shock as the horror percolated through her ambitious mind.

Macbeth must kill again to maintain his position, and he arranges for Banquo and Fleance to be murdered. When the murderers report that Fleance has escaped, the tide begins to turn for Macbeth:

> But now I am cabined, cribbed, confined,
>   bound in
> To saucy doubts and fears.
>
> [III.4.23-4]

Ian McKellen spoke to the murderers in tense whispers, circling the seated banquet guests, who looked curious and embarrassed at his behaviour. In Polanski's film, the horror of Banquo's ghost is made explicit; first we see a grey and bloodless figure at the table, then his wounds start to bleed. In contrast Ian McKellen stared intently into space. We had no doubt that Macbeth saw Banquo. The ESC presented an elegant house-party with women in lovely gowns and the men in evening dress. Banquo towered above the table on the kind of crane-cum-ladder more usually used for working on stage lights. This piece of equipment was central to the production: it could be wheeled quickly into position and could move horizontally and vertically; it was used to display dead bodies, crowned monarchs and here, the murdered Banquo.

Above: *More shall they speak*
The Witches and Ian McKellen, 1976
Left: *I bear a charmed life which must not yield*
   To one of woman born
Jon Finch, 1971

The bonds between Macbeth and his wife begin to fray and he must seek reassurance from another source. For his return to the weird sisters, the ESC used a giant vessel, big enough to hold the three witches. A huge mirror overhead reflected their heads and arms and Macbeth hung over the lip of the cauldron. The staging spoke of lost wealth and industrial might, of a Scottish past which unified this production. At The Other Place, the witches showed Macbeth a series of dolls, looking rather like stuffed and shrunken heads, and he retained them until the end. Laurence Olivier was faced with his own head

on a spike, and he spoke the first apparition's lines himself. Jon Finch meets not just the three witches, but a coven of naked women. His Macbeth drinks the witches' brew from the goblet used by his wife to drug the grooms; later, when Lady Macbeth performs her sleepwalking scene naked, her similarity to the young witch is evident. In 1994, Derek Jacobi discovered the witches in the heart of his home. The banqueting table was turned into an altar for a black mass, with the ingredients of the spell a sinister parody of the Macbeths' hospitality.

Macbeth's next move is against Macduff. On hearing of his escape to England, Macbeth resolves to wipe out any threat by murdering Macduff's children, his wife and all his household. In Polanski's film, Lady Macduff is lovingly bathing her son when she is startled by screams from the courtyard as the women of the household are raped and murdered.

In exile, Malcolm and Macduff raise an army, helped by the King of England and are heartened by news of the revulsion felt in Scotland for Macbeth's rule. Macduff exclaims:

> **Each new morn**
> **New widows howl, new orphans cry.**
>
> [IV.3.4-5]

The ESC continued to make political points here. Macduff wore a kilt in the English scenes, marking him out as a foreigner and a representative of a Scotland which Malcolm wishes to change. Adrian Noble also made explicit the connection between England and the final victory. England was illustrated by a

Above left: *My hands are of your colour*
Derek Jacobi and Cheryl Campbell, 1994
Centre left: *Out damned spot! Out, I say!*
Cheryl Campbell, 1994
Below left: *Hail King of Scotland!*
Macduff and his soldiers profess allegiance to Malcolm, 1994

simple backcloth painted with vivid green slashes, and this backcloth was used again to represent Birnan Wood.

Lady Macbeth, unable to absorb any more guilt, walks in her sleep, revealing her complicity in Macbeth's bloody deeds. Judi Dench, with her hair drawn back under a scarf, had only her face to suggest distraction. In the intimacy of a small theatre she was able to whisper her words, and her final terrible scream was a thin thread of sound. We know that she is aware of the death of Lady Macduff: the chilling 'The Thane of Fife had a wife' [V.1.41], with its nursery-rhyme tones, reminds us of the murdered children and reminds us too, that this was a step the decidedly unmaternal Lady Macbeth had claimed she was prepared to take:

> **I have given suck, and know**
> **How tender 'tis to love the babe that milks me;**
> **I would while it was smiling in my face**
> **Have plucked my nipple from his boneless**
> **   gums**
> **And dashed the brains out...**
>
> [I.7.54-8]

This is the last appearance of Lady Macbeth. Her unexplained death is reported to us and to Macbeth. By cutting to the spiky battlements, Orson Welles suggests that Lady Macbeth has impaled herself there, while Polanski shows us her broken body in the courtyard.

Although he mourns his wife, Macbeth has by now accepted death as inevitable; he is at bay and friendless. The play proceeds in a series of short, tense scenes, increasing the sense of claustrophobia and panic. Ian McKellen built himself a castle with orange-box seats, and hid there wearing his elaborate coronation robes with only his witch-dolls for comfort. Michael Pennington also built ramparts of props, but they were easily defeated by the arrival of the crane-cum-

Above: *Help me hence, ho!*
Cheryl Campbell comforted by her women, 1994

ladder, carrying troops into the castle.

Malcolm's troops approach Dunsinane carrying branches and leaves, and Welles reminds us of the larger battle. The branches appear at first to be a forest of crosses, a wave of Christianity attempting to overwhelm the evil within the castle. When Macbeth sees that 'a wood/Comes toward Dunsinane' [V.5.45-6], the audience knows this is a military device, but Macbeth is now so far removed from reality that he sees it as a sign of the witches' power. He takes refuge in their prophecy that 'none of women born' should harm him [IV.1.79] but it proves to be his undoing. Macbeth is destroyed by Macduff, a baby:

> **from his mother's womb**
> **Untimely ripped.**

[V.6.54-5]

The final scenes of Shakespeare's darkest play leave us with disturbing questions. In

NOTABLE PRODUCTIONS OF *MACBETH*

	THEATRE	DIRECTOR	DESIGNER	PRINCIPALS
1948	Mercury Films	Orson Welles	Fred Ritter	Orson Welles..........................*Macbeth* Jeanette Nolan ....*Lady Macbeth*
1955	Royal Shakespeare Theatre, Stratford-upon-Avon	Glen Byam Shaw	Roger Furse	Laurence Olivier....................*Macbeth* Vivien Leigh ....*Lady Macbeth*
1971	Playboy Productions	Roman Polanski	Fred Carter	Jon Finch...............................*Macbeth* Francesca Annis ....*Lady Macbeth*
1976	The Other Place, Stratford-upon-Avon	Trevor Nunn	John Napier	Ian McKellen ....*Macbeth* Judi Dench ....*Lady Macbeth*

This production was restaged in the main house the following year, was filmed for television in 1978 and released on video in 1979

	THEATRE	DIRECTOR	DESIGNER	PRINCIPALS
1992	English Shakespeare Company	Michael Bogdanov	Claire Lyth	Michael Pennington ....*Macbeth* Jenny Quayle ....*Lady Macbeth*
1994	Royal Shakespeare Theatre, Stratford-upon-Avon	Adrian Noble	Ian MacNeil	Derek Jacobi ....*Macbeth* Cheryl Campbell ....*Lady Macbeth*

Polanski's bloody and explicit climax, the thanes celebrate the public beheading of Macbeth while Donalbain slips away to find the witches; the process of evil may begin again. The quiet Malcolm and the war-weary Macduff at The Other Place simply sat, shocked and silent. The ESC suggested that troubles would continue to haunt Scotland after Macbeth's death. Malcolm makes his loyal thanes earls:

> **the first that ever Scotland**
> **In such an honour named.**

[102-3]

As Malcolm was crowned, pipers began to play *Oh Flower of Scotland* but they were soon drowned out by a more conventional band playing *God Save the King*. The new King did not wear the yellow and red robes of his Scottish predecessors but the velvet and ermine of his new English friends. This ending is faithful to the historical and theatrical context of the play – that *Macbeth* was first performed when a Scottish Protestant sat on the English throne, uniting the nations, but not in amity.

Suzanne Harris

'I HAD RATHER GIVE MY BODY THAN MY SOUL'

The Early Production History of *Measure for Measure*

The first record of the play in performance is an entry in the Revels Accounts for 1604-5 which indicates that *Measure for Measure* was presented by the King's Men at Whitehall on 26 December 1604. There would seem to have been very few performances during the seventeenth century, although an adaptation of the play by Sir William Davenant entitled *The Law Against Lovers*, was presented on 15 February 1662. This play follows the plot of *Measure for Measure* until half way through and includes Beatrice, Benedick and Balthazar from *Much Ado About Nothing*. At the end of Davenant's play, the impression is given that the Duke will enter a monastery and that Isabella and Angelo, Beatrice and Benedick will marry.

Performed in early 1700, Charles Gildon's play *Beauty the Best Advocate* was an adaptation of the First Folio text which omitted the bawdy characters and included musical interludes. The first known performance of Shakespeare's text since 1604 took place in 1720. The acting version of 1722, like others published during the period, records removal of the play's sexual humour and an attempt at rewriting the ending. Interest in the play towards the end of the century was prompted by

Sarah Siddons' fervent Isabella and her brother John Philip Kemble's spirited Duke.

Nineteenth century dissatisfaction with the play's explicit sexuality was reflected in the substantial cuts made to the text. Words such as 'fornicator' and 'virgin violator' were removed by William Poel for his productions in 1893 and 1908 which were notable for their Elizabethan theatre settings.

Tyrone Guthrie's production in 1933 drew attention to the relatively unknown work, and *Measure for Measure* was little performed until Peter Brook's watershed production at Stratford in 1950.

Act 5. MEASURE for MEASURE. *Scene I*

M.ᵣˢ SIDDONS in ISABELLA.
Justice, O royal Duke! vail your regard
Upon a wrong'd, I would fain have said, a Maid!

Measure for Measure,
OR
BEAUTY
THE
Best Advocate.
As it is ACTED
At the THEATRE in Lincolns-Inn-Fields.

VVritten *Originally* by Mr. *Shakespear* :
And now very much Alter'd ; VVith *Additions* of several *Entertainments* of MUSICK.

LONDON:
Printed for D. Brown, at the Black Swan without ... and R. Parker at the 'Unicorn Under the Royal ... in Cornhill. 1700.

Top: Sarah Siddons as Isabella at the Theatre Royal, Drury Lane, 1784
Left: Title page of Gildon's adaptation, 1700
Right: Peter Brook

MEASURE FOR MEASURE

Issues of legal and sexual morality inform
a disturbing exploration of the uses and abuses of power.

I n performance *Measure for Measure* can be not only outrageously funny but also deeply disturbing when the conflicts left unresolved by Shakespeare are kept in equal balance throughout. When the Duke of Vienna temporarily leaves office, his deputy Angelo is confronted with the unenviable task of trying to control the city's lawless sexuality. Strict enforcement of disregarded laws, religious idealism and irrepressible sexual desires ensnare all the citizens of Vienna in a series of dilemmas. Shakespeare creates psychologically credible characters in the first half of the play and then moves them through a series of implausible events.

Measure for Measure demands a strong, consistent directorial point of view which retains the play's deliberate ambiguities and the balance of opposites implied by the title. The departing Duke in the play's opening scene never says exactly what he is going to do during his absence from office, but it is soon obvious that his purpose is some kind of measurement of government. Several directors have added a prologue which establishes their particular interpretation of what might be part of that motivation.

The wordless prologue to Adrian Noble's production not only projected a possible reason for the Duke's imminent departure but also firmly established the world of the play. The production was set in an elegant though decaying Mozartian Vienna; the stage

Right: *Tomorrow? O, that's sudden; spare him, spare him.*
He's not prepared for death.
John Gielgud and Barbara Jefford, 1950

was draped with loops of black fabric in the background, with a Babel-style campanile positioned prominently stage left. During the opening moments, the Duke replaced his regal scarlet robe for more humble attire in front of a pier glass into which he gazed, suggesting that he was about to engage in some self-examination.

Nicholas Hytner also sought to establish the character of the Duke before a word was spoken in his production. Roger Allam was a man suffering from nervous exhaustion, in danger of losing both his self-control and control of the state. To the accompaniment of a discordant underscore, the Duke, with his shaking hands and distant stare communicated the tension of his Vienna. In the early dialogue his hesitant delivery of 'My haste may ... fare you well' [I.1.62-72] reinforced the sense of the Duke's insecurity.

An even more elaborate prologue was created by Trevor Nunn in 1991. Two press cuttings, an oval portrait of Mariana and an open book were placed on a Freudian couch. As the house lights faded, three couples emerged from the shadows and briefly danced to the *Kaizerwaltz*, thus establishing the *fin-de-siècle* setting. The Duke then read from the book some of the gnomic couplets which Shakespeare gives him later in the play:

He who the sword of heaven will bear
Should be as holy as severe.

[III.2.249-50]

This implied that the Duke's motivation in leaving office was to redress Angelo's past wrongs by making everyone including himself undergo self-examination. The three pieces of paper then enclosed in the book were retrieved by the Duke when he introduced the bed-trick to Isabella.

Above left: *Which had you rather, that the most just law*
Now took your brother's life, or to redeem him
Give up your body to such sweet uncleanness
As she that he hath stained?
Estelle Kohler and Ian Richardson, 1970
Above: *What dost thou? Or what art thou, Angelo?*
Michael Pennington, 1978

The strong contrast between the intimacy of the duologues and the extroversion of the scenes in which Vienna's ordinary citizens engage in bawdy repartee needs to be fully represented on the stage to establish the play's competing forces. Several productions have successfully exploited the play's rich texture by making the comic minor characters lawless yet engaging, and by clearly projecting the inner turmoil of the Duke, Isabella and Angelo through strongly pointed deliveries and aspects of visual interpretation.

Peter Brook's 1950 Stratford production gave equal emphasis to what he called the play's 'holy' and 'rough' elements. In performance this meant that the minor characters were invested with much life and energy. Brook even added a procession of prisoners. Isabella, the Duke and Angelo were projected as complex characters wrestling with religious and earthly demands. Another of Brook's innovations was Isabella's pause before pleading for Angelo's life, which Barbara Jefford was asked to hold for as long as she thought the audience could bear it. This exploited the ambiguity Shakespeare invests in the character's silences.

Extravagant costumes for the minor characters in Adrian Noble's production suggested a likeable anarchic populace. All the characters were aggrandized by their clothes, with Mistress Overdone in an outsize colourful dress suggesting a lamp-shade, Lucio extravagantly foppish and Froth sporting a large plume in his hat. Such a presentation gave substance to the calls for restraint by the Duke, Angelo and Isabella. Mark Thompson's 1987 settings focused on the conflict between irrepressible sexual desires and the need for order in society. The spaciousness of the executive office setting of the first scene hinted at remoteness and formality, and made the Duke seem isolated. By way of bold contrast, the seething backstreet scenes suggested barely suppressed anarchy on a set enriched by clashing colours, flashing off-stage lights, an abundance of service pipes and steam seeping through the cracks in the pavement. Exuberant inhabitants in knee breeches and Doc Martens boots could be seen snorting cocaine, making deals, disappearing and reappearing from around corners, all engaging in lawless behaviour of one kind or another.

The background of subversion reflected the dilemmas facing the central characters in their private lives and public rôles. Cuts made to the text shaped the part of the Duke so that he seemed spontaneous and inventive rather than manipulative. He used his nervous breakdown constructively to test both himself and Angelo:

> **Hence shall we see,**
> **If power change purpose, what our seemers be.**
> [I.3.53-4]

Throughout he was portrayed as a fallible human being. His 'Be absolute for death' [III.1.5] was delivered with heartfelt sincerity, and when confronted with Lucio's slanders that the absent Duke had 'some feeling for the sport' [III.2.113] he looked deeply offended.

The Duke's relationship with Isabella was established in the prison scene, when an embrace to comfort her over the supposed death of her brother was deliberately sustained, registering the Duke's awakening sexual awareness. However, it was made clear that they would be unlikely marriage partners; Isabella maintained a simple natural dignity for the character throughout and seemed too committed to her spiritual values to form a romantic attachment or even partnership with another person. The innate simplicity of Isabella was established on her first appearance, by her stark blue calf-length nun's robe and crucifix on a leather cord, her calm delivery and erect bearing.

In Hytner's production, Isabella provided a credible trigger for Angelo's emotional release at the end of their first encounter when he ran amok, overturning chairs. With his closely cropped hair, pin-striped suit, clipped delivery and twitchy mannerisms, he seemed on the verge of a nervous breakdown. He symbolically stripped Isabella by tearing away her veil demanding that she '...show it now/By putting on the destined livery' [II.4.137-8]; then slapped her face before throwing her to the floor and straddling her.

Trevor Nunn's approach to the contrast between the play's competing forces exploited the individuality of every character

Below: *If I must die*
I will encounter darkness as a bride,
And hug it in my arms.
Juliet Stevenson and Paul Mooney as Claudio, 1983

in a quasi-Freudian psychoanalysis of motivation. Designed for intimate theatre and staged in The Other Place, the production put the play under close scrutiny. All of the characters were presented sympathetically. Escalus took the dishevelled Master Froth kindly by the shoulder when advising him to keep away from the brothels, Lucio took Isabella's hand and broke down in tears when he told her that he 'loved' her brother, and Mistress Overdone, barely able to remain upright with the aid of her walking stick, kissed the Duke's hand in the final scene.

Angelo, Isabella and the Duke also revealed their unconscious feelings. Isabella often took hold of hands and initiated embraces. She bowed her head close to Angelo's chest in an unwittingly sensuous manner on her line 'Go to your bosom' [II.2.136], and she took his hand when she remarked 'Hark how I'll bribe you' [145]. Angelo delivered the soliloquy which follows in a hunched position suggestive of sexual arousal. Such frankness was repeated at the beginning of the second interview when in an erotic daydream his hands traced the imaginary curves of Isabella on top of him. Later in the same scene when he gave his 'sensual race the rein' [II.4.160] he sat astride Isabella in a pose evocative of rape, before holding her from behind with hands cupped over her breasts.

Later the Duke's comforting of Isabella for the supposed execution of her brother became a prolonged embrace. The Duke's subtle eye movement indicated that he was aware of the position of his hand on Isabella's back. After lifting it slightly he replaced it as if to acknowledge that he would accept that his own sexual interest had been awakened.

Above left: Claire Skinner kneels with Jason Durr as Claudio and Teresa Banham as Juliet, watched by Philip Madoc, 1991
Below left: Josette Simon, 1988
Below right: *Sweet sister, let me live.*
Jason Durr as Claudio and Clare Skinner, 1991

There is neither stage direction nor dialogue to indicate how Isabella responds to the Duke's proposals made at the end of the play. Therefore whatever reaction is played reflects an interpretation of the play as a whole. It is possible to suggest that she accepts or rejects his offer, or that she does not reach any conclusion. John Barton's staging suggested that she was contemplating the idea as she stood motionless. Sebastian Shaw's amiable, stumble-footed Duke had been out of his depth for most of the play and the proposal was made very publicly across the full width of the stage, at a crassly inopportune time, acutely embarrassing the stage-audience. For Isabella, the proposal was completely unexpected and it seemed unlikely that she would consider marrying this old man. In contrast, the discarding of a robe by the Duke and a veil by Isabella in Barry Kyle's production was followed by the two characters leaving the stage side by side in a manner suggestive of a practical partnership.

Nicholas Hytner staged an inconclusive ending, haunting for the way in which it reflected the equal energy of the play's competing spiritual and sexual forces. Isabella paused before responding to Mariana's plea for assistance to have Angelo's life spared by the Duke, and so reinforced the character's independence. In a series of choreographed moves, Isabella was shown to be overcome by emotion when she was reunited with her brother, thus making the absence of a response to the Duke's two proposals credible. The production's final moments were played before a brightly lit backdrop of an avenue of four flat-green poplar trees silhouetted against a pink-blue sky suggesting an inviting world there and beyond. In a wordless coda, Isabella stood stage centre and turned back towards the Duke who looked out nervously from the

NOTABLE PRODUCTIONS OF *MEASURE FOR MEASURE*

	THEATRE	DIRECTOR	DESIGNER	PRINCIPALS
1950	Royal Shakespeare Theatre, Stratford-upon-Avon	Peter Brook	Peter Brook	Harry Andrews ....*The Duke* John Gielgud ....*Angelo* Barbara Jefford ....*Isabella*
1970	Royal Shakespeare Theatre, Stratford-upon-Avon	John Barton	Timothy O'Brien	Sebastian Shaw ....*The Duke* Ian Richardson ....*Angelo* Estelle Kohler ....*Isabella*
1978	Royal Shakespeare Theatre, Stratford-upon-Avon	Barry Kyle	Christopher Morley	Michael Pennington ....*The Duke* Jonathan Pryce ....*Angelo* Paola Dionisotti ....*Isabella*
1983	Royal Shakespeare Theatre, Stratford-upon-Avon	Adrian Noble	Bob Crowley	Daniel Massey ....*The Duke* David Schofield ....*Angelo* Juliet Stevenson ....*Isabella*
1987	Royal Shakespeare Theatre, Stratford-upon-Avon	Nicholas Hytner	Mark Thompson	Roger Allam ....*The Duke* Sean Baker ....*Angelo* Josette Simon ....*Isabella*
1991	The Other Place, Stratford-upon-Avon	Trevor Nunn	Maria Bjørnson	Philip Madoc ....*The Duke* David Haig ....*Angelo* Claire Skinner........................*Isabella*

downstage shadows towards her. Trevor Nunn's production concluded with sensitive images of harmony which suggested that sexual impulses and spirituality are complementary. Therefore when Isabella accepted the Duke's second proposal, it seemed a natural conclusion in spite of the thirty year age difference. Everywhere on stage there was a show of unity, with Lucio sandwiched between an enormous Kate Keepdown and an equally enormous whore friend; Pompey and Mistress Overdone embraced; and even Barnadine found security by linking arms with the kindly Provost. Claudio and Juliet, who with Isabella had formed a three-person embrace when re-united, mirrored Angelo and Mariana who stood opposite. The characters had engaged the sympathy of the audience from the beginning. Warm acceptance of human frailty projected by the conclusion gave wonderfully moving expression to the play's fascinatingly irreconcilable opposites.

Mike Paterson

'THOU SHALT HAVE JUSTICE MORE THAN THOU DESIR'ST'

The Early Production History of *The Merchant of Venice*

The Merchant of Venice was probably written between 1596 and 1597. It was seen twice at court in 1605, but after that time there is no further record of a performance until 1741. In the intervening period the play's memory was kept alive by George Granville's adaptation, *The Jew of Venice* (1701). Despite the title, the rôle of Shylock was lightened and the romantic element expanded to make Bassanio a vehicle for Thomas Betterton.

In 1741 Charles Macklin restaged Shakespeare's original play at Drury Lane, choosing to play Shylock not as a comical figure but as a villain. To avoid peer objections Macklin kept his radical interpretation secret until the well-received first night. Edmund Kean achieved similar acclaim in 1814 with an equally fierce but sympathetic Shylock.

The theatrical vogue for elaborate staging in the nineteenth century brought detailed recreations of the Rialto best demonstrated by Henry Irving's success at the Lyceum in 1879. The production was notable for Irving's noble Shylock and Ellen Terry, whose seemingly natural performance as Portia was universally applauded.

In 1898 William Poel staged a fast-paced production and, in a defiant challenge to a sentimental reading of Shylock, reinstated the traditional red wig and false nose. The production was a harbinger of subsequent productions which have grappled with balancing the romantic and tragic elements in the play.

In the twentieth century the contrasts of romance, tragedy and racial issues have made *The Merchant of Venice* both problematic and popular worldwide. In 1955 at Stratford, Ontario, Tyrone Guthrie elevated the rôle of Antonio to provide the balance between Venice and Belmont. Katharine Hepburn played Portia as intelligent and sharp-witted in Jack Landau's 1957 production at Stratford, Connecticut. In 1962 the play was chosen by Joseph Papp as the inaugural production at the New York Shakespeare Festival with George C. Scott as Shylock and Nan Martin as Portia.

In Britain in 1932, Theodore Komisarjevsky stressed the comedy in a production notable for using a virtually uncut text. Boisterous comedy and a radical topsy-turvy design created a carnival atmosphere. Michael Langham's 1960 production restored a tragic interpretation by casting a youthful Peter O'Toole as Shylock.

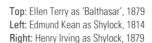

Top: Ellen Terry as 'Balthasar', 1879
Left: Edmund Kean as Shylock, 1814
Right: Henry Irving as Shylock, 1879

THE MERCHANT OF VENICE

*The strengths of love and friendship are formally tested
in the quest for an enduring basis of contract and commitment.*

The opening scene of *The Merchant of Venice* confronts issues of friendship and commerce as Antonio, the rich yet melancholic merchant, is called upon to finance Bassanio's romantic quest to Belmont. In 1970 Antonio listened with rapt enthusiasm as violins accompanied Bassanio's romantic recollection 'In Belmont is a lady richly left' [I.1.161]. His journey was generously funded. During the same recollection, John Carlisle's Antonio became agitated as Portia became a threat to his homoerotic love for Bassanio. Carlisle remained on stage as the scene changed to Belmont and fixed Portia with a confrontational glare. In 1978, the relationship between the men was based solely on money. Bassanio sat back at the lunch table with an emphatic 'That I should questionless be fortunate' [176]. There followed a long silence broken by Antonio discreetly signing the cheque.

Jonathan Miller filled Belmont with tasteless opulence, introducing a languid Joan Plowright, posing supine on a chaise-longue. She recalled Bassanio with a revealingly eager 'Yes, yes, it was Bassanio' and immediately checked herself and followed the slip with a nonchalant 'as I *think*, so was he called' [I.2.110].

Marjorie Bland was dressed in black, mourning both her father and her own plight. She was introduced staring intently at the three caskets, contemplating their significance for her future. The casket plot, expressing the conflict between outward show and inner truth, represents a life-

changing challenge both for Portia and her suitors. Portia's isolation was similarly suggested by the black dress Penny Downie wore. Her full-skirted gown denied her close physical contact with Nerissa or her suitors. The restrictions would be relieved later with the liberating experience of donning male attire and visiting Venice.

Shylock is first seen at the height of his powers, financially secure and enjoying the

Above: *You call me misbeliever, cut-throat dog,
And spit upon my Jewish gaberdine,
And all for use of that which is mine own.*
Antony Sher, 1987

imploring visit of the Christians who are at best his trading rivals and at worst his bitter enemies. Laurence Olivier was the fully assimilated Rothschild banker equipped with top hat and cane. Patrick Stewart was shabbily dressed and sat focused in front of a

Above: *Out upon it, old carrion*
Michael Cadman as Salerio and Gregory Doran as Solanio
taunt Antony Sher, 1987

ledger book and scales. Dustin Hoffman was an unremarkable figure, neatly dressed, whereas Antony Sher had a wild appearance, sitting defiantly cross-legged.

Olivier's Shylock entertained the Christian visitors, comfortable in home advantage and financial security. He established the full meaning of the visitation by dully repeating Bassanio's opening phrases, and then he began to enjoy himself. A self-indulgent chortle could be heard on the punning of 'land rats', 'water rats', and 'pirates' [I.3.22-3]. Dustin Hoffman offered the same pun to ingratiate himself with such important visitors, and their uncomprehending silence was greeted with a cross-eyed stare of frustration.

From this superficially pleasant opening exchange the bond plot is generated, indicating that conversational niceties disguise

very real differences. Olivier's arrogance enabled him to dictate the most outrageous terms. Patrick Stewart had a more practical motive, sensing an opportunity to sweep away a commercial rival. Both Hoffman and Sher were inspired by immediate causes. Hoffman received a spit in the face after offering a hand of friendship and Antony Sher, already covered in spittle, was physically throttled by John Carlisle.

In 1970, Portia's first two suitors were wholly inappropriate; Morocco crudely foreign and Arragon a doddering octogenarian. The concept of marriage with either was comically absurd and Portia showed no

trepidation. Bassanio went briskly through the business as if it were a merry jape, giggling as two chambermaids rattled through 'Tell me where is fancy bred' [III.2.63] at break neck speed. The result was a continuation of the Venetian scenes, full of jolly laughs and without threat of failure. In 1978 Marjorie Bland remained in the pose of her opening scene. The first two suitors approached her from behind, avoiding eye contact, whereas Bassanio knelt in front and addressed her directly over the caskets, giving full attention to the person not appearance, creating a silent moment of human contact. Portia sang 'Tell me where is fancy bred' and the servants joined in as John Nettles approached a decision. The exchange of lovers' rings occurred underneath a central spotlight emphasising the importance of the exchange and creating a strong image that would later prove significant.

As the marriage bond is established in Belmont, simultaneously a family disintegrates in Venice when Shylock's daughter elopes with Lorenzo. Olivier paused in deep despair and a solitary bell triggered the memory of Antonio's bond which then became a convenient outlet for his fury. This transfer of energy was skilfully heard during the 'Hath not a Jew eyes?' [III.1.53] speech. Starting gently, Olivier increased in pace with the repetition of each 'revenge' and ended on the determined resolve of:

The villainy you teach me I will execute, *and it shall go hard* but I will better the instruction.

[65-6]

Dustin Hoffman simply sat on a park bench imploring the heavens. His restrained manner broke on remembrance of his wife's ring and 'I had it of Leah when I was a bachelor' [111] became the emotional high point of the production. In contrast, Patrick Stewart

Above left: *A halter gratis! Nothing else, for God's sake!*
Nicholas Farrell, Antony Sher and Geoffrey Freshwater, 1987
Above: Arnold Yarrow as Old Gobbo and Phil Daniels as
Launcelot Gobbo, 1987
Below: John Carlisle and Antony Sher, 1987

remained cold and resilient throughout, his emotions never ruling his financial acumen. As Tubal handed him a bill for expenses in the midst of emotional recollection, Stewart immediately pocketed it without examination and scrupulously paid the exact amount.

Olivier displayed his private grief by carrying Jessica's dress, an emotional bandage and sign of bereavement. As the lights dimmed, the dress was replaced by a prayer shawl drawn menacingly over Shylock's head. A conspiratorial 'meet me at our synagogue' [119] signalled a retreat into revenge and established a dramatic tension neatly presaging the courtroom scene.

At the trial, the major characters come together for the first time. Shylock has set himself against both Antonio and the laws of Venice. In 1970 the scene opened quietly in a

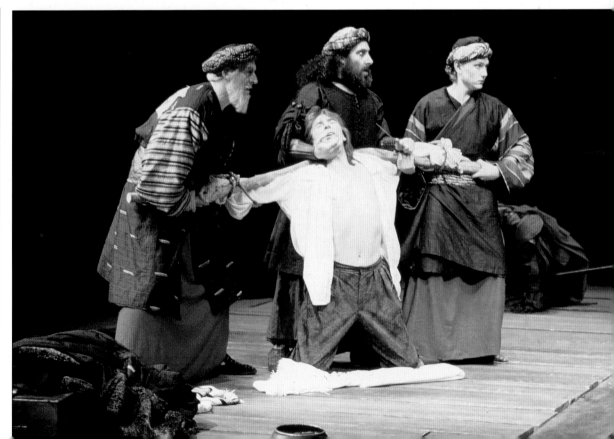

Above: Dustin Hoffman, 1989
Left: – *And you must cut this flesh from off his breast,*
The law allows it, and the court awards it.
– *Most learned judge! A sentence! Come, prepare!*
Geraldine James, Leigh Lawson and Dustin Hoffman, 1989

darkened room, an appropriate location to settle an embarrassing dispute and a potential threat to buoyant trading confidence. Olivier recaptured the supreme confidence of his opening scene, accepting abuse with complete indifference and not deigning to look at his inquisitors. In contrast Dustin Hoffman was still the little man in unfamiliar surroundings, full of nervous energy and flashing excited smiles. On entering he claimed grandiosely 'I stand for judgement' [IV.1.103] and immediately sat on his suitcase. The joke simultaneously confirmed his desire to belong and also his status as outsider.

As Geraldine James entered the court her

'Which is the merchant here? And which the Jew' [171] was brusque and authoritative and she took control thereafter. On the same line Penny Downie fumbled with her glasses, betraying understandable nerves. Previously she had been closeted in Belmont cherishing a belief in an ideal love. In Venice she saw Bassanio as vulnerable and reliant on her help. This insight destroyed an illusion but replaced it with something stronger, a greater appreciation of the human rather than the ideal.

The dramatic tension increases as Shylock closes in to claim his pound of flesh. Antony Sher lustfully licked the knife and the tension became almost unbearable before Portia's last gasp interjection: 'Tarry a little, there is something else' [302]. Fortunes now turn as Portia, having implored Shylock to mercy, now invokes ancient Venetian laws against aliens to disinherit Shylock.

The pronouncement of the word 'alien' physically shook Olivier who managed to draw enough energy to rise stiffly and bark 'I am content' [391]. He gave vent to his frustration by unleashing a chilling wail offstage leaving a stunned silence. The Duke's 'Sir, I entreat you home with me to dinner' [398] was a blatant attempt to change the subject from an unbearable reality. Dustin Hoffman's wry knowing smile suggested that he knew it was all too good to be true. Bundled unceremoniously out of court, Hoffman was returned to the anonymity from whence he came. Patrick Stewart, sensing defeat, threw himself to the floor with cringing apologies and willingly removed his yarmulka. All his energies focused on receiving a merciful decision and his purpose became transparent

Above right: *Have by some surgeon, Shylock*
Christopher Robbie as the Duke, Penny Downie, David Calder, Debra Gillett, 1993
Right: Penny Downie and Owen Teale, 1993
Far right: David Calder, 1993

NOTABLE PRODUCTIONS OF *THE MERCHANT OF VENICE*

	THEATRE	DIRECTOR	DESIGNER	PRINCIPALS	
1970	National Theatre, London	Jonathan Miller	Julia Trevelyan Oman	Antony Nicholls	*Antonio*
				Jeremy Brett	*Bassanio*
				Derek Jacobi	*Gratiano*
				Joan Plowright	*Portia*
				Anna Carteret	*Nerissa*
				Laurence Olivier	*Shylock*
				Jane Lapotaire	*Jessica*
1978	The Other Place, Stratford-upon-Avon	John Barton	Christopher Morley	David Bradley	*Antonio*
				John Nettles	*Bassanio*
				John Bowe	*Gratiano*
				Marjorie Bland	*Portia*
				Diana Berriman	*Nerissa*
				Patrick Stewart	*Shylock*
				Avril Carson	*Jessica*
1987	Royal Shakespeare Theatre, Stratford-upon-Avon	Bill Alexander	Kit Surrey	John Carlisle	*Antonio*
				Nicholas Farrell	*Bassanio*
				Geoffrey Freshwater	*Gratiano*
				Deborah Findlay	*Portia*
				Pippa Guard	*Nerissa*
				Antony Sher	*Shylock*
				Deborah Goodman	*Jessica*
1989	Phoenix Theatre, London	Peter Hall	Chris Dyer	Leigh Lawson	*Antonio*
				Nathaniel Parker	*Bassanio*
				Michael Siberry	*Gratiano*
				Geraldine James	*Portia*
				Abigail McKern	*Nerissa*
				Dustin Hoffman	*Shylock*
				Francesca Buller	*Jessica*
1993	Royal Shakespeare Theatre, Stratford-upon-Avon	David Thacker	Shelagh Keegan	Clifford Rose	*Antonio*
				Owen Teale	*Bassanio*
				Mark Lockyer	*Gratiano*
				Penny Downie	*Portia*
				Debra Gillett	*Nerissa*
				David Calder	*Shylock*
				Kate Duchêne	*Jessica*

with 'You take my life / When you do take the means whereby I live' [373-4]. His previously unpleasant behaviour made the judgement not excessively harsh and, even as he left, the audience had no doubt he would survive.

In 1970, the memory of Shylock made the lovers' exchange of rings and the last scene in Belmont unpalatable and inconsequential baggage to what was Shylock's production. The final image was not of newly married lovers but of Antonio and Jessica staring, not in recognition of future happiness, but in melancholy memories of Shylock. Faith in Venetian law had been irretrievably shaken. The final image in 1987 confirmed the brutality that had informed the production, as John Carlisle's Antonio stooped to pick up Jessica's crucifix, potentially a rare moment of tenderness. Instead, he cruelly held it tantalisingly out of her reach, condemning her to be forever on the periphery of a closed society. There was to be no progression, only a cyclical dread that the prejudice expressed at court would continue indefinitely.

In 1978 John Barton conjured a scene of genuine warmth, recognition and romance, a clear thematic progression carried through from the sombre opening scene in Belmont. The exchange of rings became not a trivial exercise but an important learning process. Marjorie Bland's original calm meditation resulted in an improvised test to reinforce the importance of marriage vows. Antonio rejoined the lovers' hands, reconciling the worlds of Belmont and Venice, and the rings were once again held in the central light used during the betrothal scene. This was evidence of a greater understanding gained through experience, and as Portia pronounced 'It is almost morning' [V.1.295] it promised an understanding that would develop and mature in the future.

James Shaw

THE MERRY WIVES OF WINDSOR

*A jealous husband and a would-be seducer are out-witted
by resourceful women in a comedy of social manners.*

The *Merry Wives of Windsor* has long been marginalised in Shakespeare criticism; the play is seen to be too broadly comic, too farcical to fit many critics' formulations of Shakespearean comedy and consequently most omit it from their discussions. The play's base in farce also makes it far more difficult to read in the study than to enjoy in performance. For example, in reading, the ramblings of the opening scene supplemented by endless earnest footnotes seem tedious in the extreme. However, in performance the senile delinquent Shallow, the asinine Slender and the Welsh-accented Evans can be very funny; their endeavours to impress each other only succeed in convincing the audience that these characters are fools. Generally, the language jokes in the play – malapropisms, French and Welsh accents, catchphrases and bombast – are much funnier when heard than when read.

However, *Merry Wives* goes beyond farce in many ways, as it glances at pathological jealousy, the breakdown of communication and the materialistic workings of Shakespeare's own bourgeois class. The presentation of women can also be read as complex – Mistress Quickly, the quean or bawd, startlingly becomes the fairy queen in the last act, a title usually associated with the virgin queen Elizabeth I. This action challengingly collapses the divisions between the traditional female rôles of patriarchal virgin and whore. Mistress Quickly also plays a comic proto-feminist by refusing to take seriously the male academic discourse on Latin

Above: *I warrant he hath a thousand of these letters, writ with blank space for different names*
Brenda Bruce and Elizabeth Spriggs compare their letters from Falstaff, 1968

grammar in the lesson scene. Here she refuses to accept the authority of the male teacher Evans and she punctures the pretensions of academic discourse, which in the sixteenth century was predominantly the preserve of men. From talk of 'genitive case' [IV.I.53] she creates an insubordinate female character 'Jenny' whose case – or genitalia – Quickly feels should not be discussed by young William Page. The heady combination of bawdiness, slyness and prudery which are called for in this character are well conveyed in the BBC-tv production by close-ups of

Elizabeth Spriggs' expressive face.

Unusually for Shakespeare, *Merry Wives* features sympathetically portrayed, but extremely dynamic women characters. The audience is encouraged to laugh as foolish men are outmanœuvred and ridiculed by the cleverness of the wives. The only character the wives cannot control is Anne Page who uses the same tactics as her mother to obtain

'ADMIRABLE PLEASURES AND FERY HONEST KNAVERIES'

The Early Production History of *The Merry Wives of Windsor*

The 1602 Quarto of *The Merry Wives of Windsor*, the first published text, tells us that the play 'hath been divers times acted by the Right honourable my Lord Chamberlain's Servants, both before her majesty and elsewhere'. This text is probably a memorial reconstruction by the performer who played the Host of a production cut and adapted for touring.

A tradition exists, based on little real evidence, that *The Merry Wives of Windsor* was written in fourteen days, because Queen Elizabeth I wanted to see Falstaff, the character from *Henry IV Part One*, 'in love'. Falstaff is not in love in *Merry Wives* but many critics have accepted this story and suggested that the first performance was by royal command, for a celebration associated with the Order of the Garter,

which is referred to in the final scene of the Folio text. The story of a royal command is first recorded by John Dennis who adapted the play under the title *The Comical Gallant* (1702). Dennis is not a reliable source since he was trying to sell the text of his play which had failed in the theatre, and the royal command story may well have been a publicity stunt.

There are several operas based on *Merry Wives* including *Falstaff* by Verdi (1893) and *Die Lustigen Weiber von Windsor* by Nicolai (1849).

In the twentieth century, the play has proved popular in the theatre. Indeed, Terry Hands' 1968 production was so popular that it was revived in 1969 and 1975 at Stratford and in 1970 in Tokyo.

Top: Anthony Quayle as Falstaff, 1955
Left: Alice Ford, Nannetta, Meg and Mistress Quickly in the English National Opera production of Verdi's *Falstaff*, 1989
Right: Beerbohm Tree as Falstaff painted by J. Collier, 1904

what she wants; she deploys a traditional 'feminine' deceitful appearance of acquiescence and willingness to please. There is little approaching feminism in the play; the wives act in conformity with patriarchal values regarding property and female chastity when they react with the same question to the discovery that Falstaff has sent them the same love letters, 'How shall I be revenged on him?' [II.1.27-8&61]. The wives are also cushioned by class and they have, like many a liberal feminist, learned to play the men's games so extremely ably that they have little reason to demand real change. Mistress Quickly describes Mistress Page's life style:

Never a wife in Windsor leads a better life than she does. Do what she will, say what she will, take all, pay all, go to bed when she list, rise when she list, all is as she will.

[II.2.113-16]

Although Mistress Quickly talks about wife-beating, 'Mistress Ford, good heart, is beaten black and blue, that you cannot see a white spot about her' [IV.5.102-4], the play presents the wives as women functioning very effectively in a system designed to disable them. Even Ford finally concedes publicly his wife's right to autonomy and independent judgement when he tells her 'Henceforth do what thou wilt' [IV.4.5]. Ironically, while the title *The Merry Wives of Windsor* makes the absolute centrality of the wives clear, theatre history tends to give star billing to the performers playing Ford and Falstaff. Ian Richardson and Ben Kingsley were both Fords who were deservedly memorable for their comic and also very seriously manic explo-

Above right: Elizabeth Spriggs, Brenda Bruce and Brewster Mason, 1968
Right: *I rather will suspect the sun with cold*
   Than thee with wantonness.
Elizabeth Spriggs and Ian Richardson, 1968

Above: *Why, this is the very same: the very hand, the very words. What doth he think of us?*
Janet Dale and Lindsay Duncan, 1985

sions of jealousy, but their performances are usually remembered at the expense of their productions' merry wives.

Ford is a wonderful comic rôle and his greatest moments come when he is disguised as Brook and forced to listen to Falstaff unwittingly abusing him to his face. Ford cannot respond or he will give away his disguise and his attempts to suppress his fury in order to gain the information he needs can be very funny. Nicky Henson and Ben Kingsley both milked this joke extremely successfully – mainly by appearing constantly in danger of bursting blood vessels in their desperate attempts to control their jealous fury. Ford's discomfort however, seems appropriate because what he is doing is so vile – procuring a man to seduce Ford's own wife. Similarly, critical sensitivity to Falstaff's physical suffering should be alleviated by remembering that it is only Falstaff's determination to play the gigolo which exposes him to such treatment.

The punishments of Falstaff are directed by the wives and constitute the funniest moments in the play. Falstaff's misadventures with the buck basket create a spectacularly comic theatrical moment at the same time as carefully preparing for an even funnier comic climax when Ford, in his second attempt to detect his wife *in flagrante*, meets John and Robert taking out the buck basket for the second time. A moment of superb broad comedy can be produced by the line 'Well, he's not here I seek for' [IV.2.148] after Ford

Left: *... as I am a man, there was one conveyed out of my house yesterday in this basket. Why may not he be there again? In my house I am sure he is. My intelligence is true. My jealousy is reasonable.*
Lindsay Duncan, Paul Webster as Page, Nicky Henson and David Bradley as Dr. Caius, 1985

has tipped every item from the buck basket, has desperately thrown dirty linen (especially underwear) around the room and even climbed inside the basket to ensure that Falstaff really is not in there.

Falstaff's second punishment, to be beaten in the clothes of a woman, 'the fat woman of Brainford' [70-1] usually involves the classic farce routine of the violent chase. This routine highlighted the inadequacies of the BBC-tv production. With an extremely low energy Falstaff, the production was doomed despite Ben Kingsley's reprise of his successful Ford from the RSC production of 1979. *Merry Wives* needs energy, verve and fast pacing, as was demonstrated in the successful Terry Hands' production, which used flown scenery to effect extremely fast scene changes to help keep the pace frenetic, and in Bill Alexander's production which used a revolve to similar effect.

Falstaff's final punishment is to be horned and disguised as Herne the Hunter and mocked at midnight in Windsor Forest. The horns evoke the Elizabethan joke of the cuckold, the state Ford so fears, of being unable to control a woman's sexuality by the institution of marriage. Falstaff's horns have also been interpreted on a mystical level, representing a fertility spirit, the horned man, the green man or the scapegoat for the community. The final scene certainly shifts in theatrical mode, away from the bourgeois

Left: *Since I plucked geese, played truant and whipped top, I knew not what 'twas to be beaten till lately. Follow me. I'll tell you strange things of this knave Ford, on whom tonight I will be revenged. And I will deliver his wife into your hand.*
Peter Jeffrey and Nicky Henson as 'Master Brook', 1985

NOTABLE PRODUCTIONS OF *THE MERRY WIVES OF WINDSOR*

	THEATRE	DIRECTOR	DESIGNER	PRINCIPALS
1968	Royal Shakespeare Theatre, Stratford-upon-Avon	Terry Hands	Timothy O'Brien	Brenda Bruce ....*Mistress Page* Elizabeth Spriggs ....*Mistress Ford* Brewster Mason ....*Falstaff* Ian Richardson ....*Ford*
1982	BBC-tv	David Jones	Don Homfray	Prunella Scales ....*Mistress Page* Judi Davis ....*Mistress Ford* Richard Griffiths.....................*Falstaff* Ben Kingsley ....*Ford*
1985	Royal Shakespeare Theatre, Stratford-upon-Avon	Bill Alexander	William Dudley	Janet Dale ....*Mistress Page* Lindsay Duncan ....*Mistress Ford* Peter Jeffrey ....*Falstaff* Nicky Henson ....*Ford*
1987	Royal Queensland Theatre, Brisbane	Geoffrey Rush	William Dudley	Hazel Phillips ....*Mistress Page* Justine Anderson ....*Mistress Ford* Bille Brown ....*Falstaff* Mark Owen-Taylor ....*Ford*

farce of the rest of the play. This shift, signalled by the move to patterned verse, is often a problem in modern productions because the model of the court masque, which possibly prevailed in the original performances of the Folio text, is not available to audiences now.

Alexander's 1985 production radically rewrote this scene to try to deal with the 'problem' of this shift. Sheila Steafel's Mistress Quickly never became fairy queen because she got drunk, was lost in the forest and kept wandering round and round the revolve which just kept up with her walking pace so that she never got anywhere. The entire cast also assembled onstage at the end to give an energetic and celebratory display of jive dancing. Other strategies for dealing with the final scene have included a sort of *Pyramus and Thisbe*-style poor quality piece of amateur dramatics (as in the 1993 Northern Broadsides production directed by Barry Rutter) or, more successfully, evoking Hallowe'en, mystery and a hint of the witches' coven as in Terry Hands' production.

Merry Wives has often inspired nostalgia in its designers. Terry Hands' production was remarkable for its nostalgic recreation of the Elizabethan golden age, with great attention paid to details such as schoolboys playing conkers. Nostalgia also featured in Bill Alexander's supposedly iconoclastic production, which relocated *Merry Wives* from the 1590s to the 1950s, producing a conservative period piece. Geoffrey Rush's 1987 production lovingly created a 1947 Brisbane suburb of Windsor: extras included the iceman and the dunny man, and Falstaff made one exit on a passing tram.

Elizabeth Schafer

Left: Ian Talbot as Slender, Paul Webster as Page, Nicky Henson, Trevor Martin as the Host of the Garter, Bruce Alexander as Sir Hugh and David Bradley as Dr Caius, 1985

A MIDSUMMER NIGHT'S DREAM

*A nightmare pursuit, magical transformation and theatrical enterprise
prepare the way for relationships of enduring worth.*

At the beginning of *A Midsummer Night's Dream* Theseus and Hippolyta are scarcely allowed a quiet moment to relish the prospect of their wedding in four days' time. Their opening speeches are patterned and delivered within a public context. Whilst his driving urgency modulates into petty impatience, she is more susceptible to romantic love and the image of the moon, like Cupid's bow 'New-bent in heaven' [I.1.10] suggests both her warrior power and a potential for love. Philostrate is dispatched on a vague pretext, but Theseus has just four lines to express his personal commitment with no opportunity for Hippolyta to reply before their public responsibilities intrude. The exclusive and repeated intimacy of 'I' and 'thee' [16 & 18] is shattered by the entrance of four individuals, each exhibiting different degrees of enthusiasm and impatient to establish their very different motives for being there.

In seeking to deal with the conflict between Hermia and her father fairly and efficiently, Theseus tries to temper reason with reasonableness:

Take time to pause, and by the next new moon –
The sealing day betwixt my love and me
For everlasting bond of fellowship –

[83-5]

We are prompted to register Hippolyta's non-verbal reaction and Theseus is evidently disconcerted. His parenthesis drifts into conventional rhetoric and his easy assurance

Above: *Fetch me that flower – the herb I showed thee once.*
The juice of it on sleeping eyelids laid
Will make or man or woman madly dote
Upon the next live creature that it sees.
Alan Howard and John Kane as Puck, 1970

is gone. He stutters and stumbles his way through the rest of the scene and is oddly silent for some twenty lines whilst Lysander and Demetrius brawl. His clear invitation to her to speak, 'What cheer, my love?' [122] goes unanswered.

In 1986 Hippolyta reacted to the way Hermia was treated by crushing the rose that her boringly conventional Theseus had given her. She threw it to the ground as she moved to leave the stage. She passed Bottom in the doorway and the exchanged glance was held just long enough for him to feature in what became the imaginative escape of her dream. She slipped through the centre of a huge spider's web to become Titania in a fairy world peopled with figures from childhood

'COME, NOW A ROUNDEL AND A FAIRY SONG'

The Early Production History of A Midsummer Night's Dream

A *Midsummer Night's Dream* may have been written for a private occasion, possibly to celebrate Elizabeth Carey's wedding in February 1596. What is certain is that it was given public performances before 1598 and that when it was published in 1600 the title page claimed that it had been 'sundry times publickely acted'. No principal source for the plot is known, though Shakespeare makes use of his reading of Ovid and Chaucer. When Samuel Pepys saw *A Midsummer Night's Dream* on 29 September 1662 he was determined never to see it again 'for it is the most insipid ridiculous play that ever I saw in my life'.

Betterton's lavishly expensive production of Purcell's *The Fairy Queen* in 1692 created a fashion for operatic versions of the play that would culminate in Frederick Reynolds' 1816 presentation of *A Midsummer Night's Dream* with seascapes and fairies singing in clouds. At Covent Garden in 1840 Madame Vestris restored Shakespeare's text, introduced Mendelssohn's incidental music and played Oberon herself. Samuel Phelps cast himself as Bottom in 1853 at Sadler's Wells in a production which freed the play from meretricious glitter and muslin fairies, achieving an appropriately magical effect. Ellen

Terry, aged nine, played Puck in 1856 for Charles Kean and when Beerbohm Tree mounted a sumptuous production in January 1900 it was with the customary troops of children as fairies and Oberon and Puck played by actresses. He provided a carpet of thyme and wild flowers, brakes and thickets full of blossom. Live rabbits were added for revivals in 1905 and 1911.

Harley Granville-Barker cut through such accretions at the Savoy in 1914 . His production was revolutionary. He presented the play using an apron stage with different levels and slate-grey canvas flats. Palace and woodland scenes were simply contrasted with drop-curtains, silken suggestions of trees and gauze. A row of futuristic columns complemented the outlandishness of fairies dressed and painted in gold, whose movements were perceived as oddly mechanical or vaguely oriental. The uncertainty liberated the imagination.

Top: *Bottom Asleep*, a painting by Sir Hubert von Herkomer, 1891
Left: Mr Duruset as Oberon in Frederick Reynolds' production, 1816
Right: Titania, Queen of the Fairies, a costume design by C. Wilhelm

Above: *Thou runnest before me, shifting every place,
And darest not stand nor look me in the face.*
John Kane as Puck and Ben Kingsley as Demetrius, 1970
Far right: *Love takes the meaning in love's conference*
Mary Rutherford as Hermia and Christopher Gable as
Lysander, 1970

Above: *To dance our ringlets to the whistling wind*
The Royal Ballet's 1964 production remains in the repertoire.
Viviana Durante as Titania, 1994

tales. Though Janet McTeer played both parts, Gerard Murphy's near-naked, virile Oberon was a very different figure from the stuffed-shirt, cigar-smoking, middle-aged businessman that was Richard Easton's Theseus. The rôles of Theseus/Oberon and Hippolyta/Titania had been sensationally doubled in Peter Brook's 1970 production, when the tensions between the mortal couple were worked out in a white-box fairyland of the imagination. Previously, as under Peter Hall's direction in 1959/62 it had been customary to take Titania's sneering description of 'the bouncing Amazon' [II.1.70] and contrast a 'buskined mistress and…warrior love' [71] with a gossamer fairy queen. Such was the impact of Brook's insight that it has become theatrically imperative to interrogate Hippolyta's silence in the first scene.

In 1989, the doubling of rôles took the audience from a marquee hired for the wedding reception to a scrap-yard in which the fairies wore clip-on wings, tutus, big boots and big ears. The young lovers were callow and gauche and eloped wearing pyjamas and dressing-gowns; but adolescent infatuation was part of fairyland too and the First Fairy almost swooned as she asked Puck for his autograph. The production was anarchic: Puck soon threw away his copy of the *New*

Penguin Shakespeare, Titania's request for a roundel and a fairy song brought groans of dissent and there was the problem of where to put the chewing gum.

The mechanicals consistently delight with their warmth, humanity and sincerity. Our presence in the theatre implicates us and is evidence of our indulgence for their essential purpose. They meet to put on a play and we may be tempted to contrast their corporate commitment and earnest creativity with the selfish, destructive impulses that motivate other characters – be they mortal or fairy – in the early scenes. Quince and company share a desire to make a success of the whole enterprise and that is displayed in the way in which the group tackles the problems that arise during the rehearsal process. Their vital energy carries them through undaunted and the solutions they find reflect an ability to improvise of which any experimental theatre group might be proud. In 1986 the earnestness of the amateur actors had led them to study Brechtian theory. The sensitivity as to how their performance will be received:

Will not the ladies be afeard of the lion?

[III.1.25]

would be contrasted with the crass insensitivity of their social superiors.

In Ashton's ballet movement derived from Morris dancing and clowning expresses the camaraderie of the mechanicals. Their mood is boisterous, happy and energetic. Puck joins the 'hempen homespuns' [70], invisibly inspiring them to a coordinated sequence of movement. Upstage, unnoticed, Bottom is 'translated' [112]. As the line clears to disclose

Above left: *I know a bank where the wild thyme blows,*
Where oxlips and the nodding violet grows,
Quite overcanopied with luscious woodbine ...
Sue Blane's scrapyard set design, 1989
Left: Sally Jacobs' model of her white-box set, 1970

Right: *Some war with reremice for their leathern wings*
To make my small elves coats
The fairies and Janet McTeer, 1986
Below right: *Through the house give glimmering light*
Janet McTeer and Gerard Murphy, 1986

Bottom with the ass's head, he is immediately seen on pointe. There is a spindly tentativeness in the Covent Garden production which suggests his aspiration and indicates his absorption into the fairy world. However, the hoof-like leggings used in the touring company's production still permit him to move with the delicacy of pointe shoes, yet they are more expressive of the essential contradiction between his aspirations and the inevitability of his earth-bound existence. The ass's head, however, is uncompromising in its denial of the human form and the contrast establishes a powerful dynamic. Bottom's decision to walk up and down provides the opportunity for him to explore cautiously his newly acquired grace. He ends flat-footed and takes a bow. This is the first time the audience has been acknowledged as part of the performance and for a moment there is something of the self-conscious theatricality of Shakespeare's text as we consider a complexity of rôle play: the dancer as Bottom and Bottom as ass.

Titania wakes and Ashton has her express through gesture and mime 'What angel wakes me from my flowery bed?' [122] and 'Out of this wood do not desire to go' [143]. At first Bottom seems more beast than man, scratching his back on a tree stump and remaining hunched after bowing to Titania. However, as she moves to him he is sensitive to her ethereal grace and as they take hands both rise on pointe:

And I will purge thy mortal grossness so
That thou shalt like an airy spirit go.

[151-2]

Titania takes the initiative in their *pas de deux* and there is a powerful sense of her capacity to release a tender lyricism. Bottom nudges her away and she responds by leaping onto his back and riding him. Brook gave full value to the sexuality of the encounter, but with Ashton the sexuality is combined with the child-like simplicity of a game. The fairies' reactions are variously shocked, surprised and amused.

It is during this scene that Bottom's surprise, even embarrassment, at Titania's love for him is expressed:

Methinks, mistress, you should have little reason for that. And yet, to say the truth, reason and love keep little company together nowadays – the more the pity that some honest neighbours will not make them friends.

[135-8]

We have seen how Theseus had failed to harness 'reason' and 'love' initially and how Oberon and Titania have moved from the entrenched positions they took up during their first debate and dissension. The lovers' extravagant posturing is presented in rhymed couplets which make their protestations ring trite and jingly and their experience in the forest is essentially educative. Their quest to establish truthful, trusting relationships requires redefinition of a 'love' that has merely been infatuation, for it must be tempered with 'reason'. Though Helena had asserted 'Love looks not with the eyes but with the mind' [I.1.234] it takes time for her to learn the lesson, but when she does the couplets give way to a flexible, emotionally committed blank verse. In 1970, the chase was fiercely physical; the lovers fought, cannoned off each other and off the hard walls of the set and became enmeshed in the coils of wire which the fairies dangled from above.

As Demetrius wakes and instantly falls in love with Helena, the stage is set for a scene of conflict, confusion and turmoil which relies heavily upon any director's choreographic skills. Ashton has the four weave patterns of comedy and pathos. The *pas de quatre* resolutely resists its desired pairings. Lysander and Demetrius compete to partner Helena whilst Hermia is treated as an object in the way she is repeatedly lifted and jumped aside. She can only spin, hold her head in dismay, walk, run, stand, as she seeks to disentangle the other three. In echoes of the first scene of the play there is masculine claim and counter claim, accusation and derision. Ashton makes the men square up in a ridiculous fashion, fists bobbing, feet tapping and bodies swaying. As the girls wrangle, the men have to pull them apart and although the tableau has a comic symmetry the girls threaten and hit each other in replication of the men's behaviour. There is a darker side which is not wholly dissipated by the humour.

When we next see Titania and Bottom there are signs that her 'love' for him is being tacitly tempered with 'reason'. Having offered him music she prefers not to accede to his request for 'the tongs and the bones' [IV.1.29], but seeks to divert him with an alternative:

Or say, sweet love, what thou desirest to eat.

[30]

Even then she seeks to modify and improve upon his request for a bottle of hay suggesting the more fashionable health food: 'new nuts' [35]. Her reawakening is the first of several and once Oberon has proclaimed their reunion as 'new in amity' [86] we return to the relationship between Theseus and Hippolyta which has prospered in our absence. The waking of the lovers takes us onto another

Below: Jimmy Gardner as Snug, Graham Turner as Flute, Paul Webster as Quince, Dhobi Oparei as Starveling, David Troughton and David Shaw-Parker as Snout, 1989

plane of experience. Self is submerged as they piece together tentatively their shared experience, drawing and giving reassurance:

DEMETRIUS
These things seem small and undistinguishable,
Like far-off mountains turnèd into clouds.

HERMIA
Methinks I see these things with parted eye,
Where everything seems double.

HELENA   **So methinks:**
And I have found Demetrius, like a jewel,
Mine own and not mine own.

DEMETRIUS   **Are you sure**
That we are awake? It seems to me
That yet we sleep, we dream.

[186–93]

The stillness of the stage picture in Brook's *Dream* was remarkable and the lovers held the precious moments in which they were at one with themselves and their environment.

The mechanicals have their reunion too and the enthusiasm with which Bottom is welcomed back reflects much more than the rescue of *Pyramus and Thisbe*. The court audience's comments upon the performance may suggest that Lysander and Demetrius have learned little from their experience, but the silence of Hermia and Helena can be eloquent. Hippolyta's words are worth weighing and the doubling of rôles can give particular resonance to her:

Beshrew my heart but I pity the man.

[V.1.282]

Whether the motivation for Theseus' line: 'With the help of a surgeon he might yet recover, and prove an ass' [303] is thoughtful or thoughtless, tender or savage and whether

NOTABLE PRODUCTIONS OF *A MIDSUMMER NIGHT'S DREAM*

	THEATRE	DIRECTOR	DESIGNER	PRINCIPALS
1959	Royal Shakespeare Theatre, Stratford-upon-Avon	Peter Hall	Lila de Nobili	Robert Hardy ....*Oberon* Mary Ure ....*Titania* Charles Laughton ....*Bottom*
1962	Royal Shakespeare Theatre, Stratford-upon-Avon	Peter Hall	Lila de Nobili	Ian Richardson ....*Oberon* Judi Dench ....*Titania* Paul Hardwick ....*Bottom*

This production (with Paul Rogers as Bottom*) was filmed in 1969*

	THEATRE	DIRECTOR	DESIGNER	PRINCIPALS
1964	Royal Opera House, Covent Garden	Choreography by Frederick Ashton	Henry Bardon, David Walker	Anthony Dowell ....*Oberon* Antoinette Sibley ....*Titania* Alexander Grant ....*Bottom*

A touring version with designs by Peter Farmer was mounted in 1966 – it is now in the repertory of The Birmingham Royal Ballet. The present Royal Ballet production has scenery and costumes by David Walker. It had its first performance in 1986.

	THEATRE	DIRECTOR	DESIGNER	PRINCIPALS
1970	Royal Shakespeare Theatre, Stratford-upon-Avon	Peter Brook	Sally Jacobs	Alan Howard ....*Oberon* Sara Kestelman ....*Titania* David Waller ....*Bottom*
1986	Royal Shakespeare Theatre, Stratford-upon-Avon	Bill Alexander	William Dudley	Gerard Murphy.......................*Oberon* Janet McTeer ....*Titania* Pete Postlethwaite ....*Bottom*
1989	Royal Shakespeare Theatre, Stratford-upon-Avon	John Caird	Sue Blane	John Carlisle ....*Oberon* Clare Higgins ....*Titania* David Troughton ....*Bottom*

Hippolyta or Bottom react to what he says has implications for our response to the whole dream-experience. In 1986 as the three couples took their positions for the formal wedding photograph, Hippolyta slipped her hand from under Theseus' proprietorial arm without him noticing and moved upstage to be reunited with Oberon.

Keith Parsons

'I DO SPY SOME MARKS OF LOVE IN HER'

The Early Production History of *Much Ado About Nothing*

Much Ado About Nothing was probably written between late 1598 and early 1599. It was popular from the first: audiences delighted not so much in the traditional romantic plot of Hero and Claudio but in the 'merry war' [I.1.57] between Beatrice and Benedick. *Much Ado* gained royal approval and formed part of the celebrations for the marriage of James I's daughter. It was much liked by Charles I who noted the title of this play as 'Benedicte and Betteris' in his copy of Shakespeare's plays.

During the seventeenth century *Much Ado* was adapted and augmented: Davenant's company put on a hybridised version called *The Law Against Lovers*, which combined *Much Ado* with *Measure for Measure*. In 1662 Pepys noted his pleasure at the singing and dancing of a 'little girl' who played the baby sister of Beatrice.

The eighteenth century saw productions at Lincoln's Inn Fields and Covent Garden with Garrick giving his first performance at Drury Lane in 1748. Benedick remained one of his most animated and admired comic parts until he retired twenty-eight

years later. In the following century, Ellen Terry made Beatrice one of her most popular rôles, first seen in a production with Henry Irving in 1882. She played with vivacity, tenderness, dignity and deep feeling; it seems that her Beatrice was especially good-natured.

In the twentieth century, the play has had numerous successful productions in London, Stratford-upon-Avon, the provinces and abroad. John Gielgud directed Anthony Quayle and Diana Wynyard as Benedick and Beatrice in 1949 and himself played opposite Peggy Ashcroft in later revivals. Ashcroft gave a sense of naturalness and spontaneity to her interpretation of Beatrice and her wit seemed very much the inspiration of the moment.

Gielgud strove for a credible character underneath the glorious costumes and comic hats.

Top: Sir Anthony Van Dyck's portrait of King Charles I
Left: Ellen Terry as Beatrice and Henry Irving as Benedick, 1882
Right: David Garrick as Benedick, 1748

MUCH ADO ABOUT NOTHING

*The shallowness of a society which puts a premium upon posturing,
verbal dexterity and fine clothes is exposed by honesty and integrity.*

The events of *Much Ado About Nothing* are generated by the impact of the military on the small Italian township of Messina. Production sets have been both evocative and diverse. The opening of Kenneth Branagh's 1993 film gives vigorous energy to the encounter between army and community. Deliberately evoking *The Magnificent Seven*, it shows a line of virile, glowing young men on horseback galloping exultantly towards a small Tuscan estate where the women are thrown into a frantic and revealing toilette – all to the thunder of hooves and rousing music. In Franco Zeffirelli's *Much Ado* the soldiers were given a rumbustious welcome by a gaudy and festive town band. Audiences engaged in a sparkling, hot-blooded entertainment with darker undertones of Sicilian vendetta.

The play has taken on guises other than the Italianate. The 1982 production in Stratford began with a plaintive melody from a solitary woman playing the cello before an ethereal set of semi-translucent screens and mirrors. It was costumed in predominantly white Cavalier costumes, and evoked a rather narcissistic society. In John Barton's 1976 production set in the Indian Raj, soldiers settled into privileged leisure to the occasional off-stage clunk of leather against willow. Judi Dench, who played Beatrice wonderfully in this production, directed the play eleven years later for the Renaissance Theatre Company. The production began its tour in the Birmingham Repertory Theatre studio, where audiences were drawn into

great intimacy with the actors. Stage business before the start of the play established warm family relationships – a character passing Leonato would affectionately assist with the jigsaw he was puzzling over and there was a closeness between Beatrice and her cousin, Hero. With a clever anticipation of Margaret's later contribution to the catastrophe of mistaken identity, the director showed her in, but not of, the family group: she was distinguished by her noisy and enthusiastic consumption of an apple.

Don Pedro, Prince of Arragon, Claudio, Benedick and the Prince's brother, Don John, are welcomed by Leonato, the governor of

Above: *Prince, thou art sad; get thee a wife, get thee a wife.*
Ian McKellen as Claudio, Caroline John as Hero, Maggie Smith, Robert Stephens and Albert Finney, 1965

Messina. The men set war behind them and Leonato soon finds himself embracing Claudio as a future son-in-law. For Benedick, however, skirmishes are not over. He and Beatrice, in compulsive mutual antagonism, swiftly take up again the 'merry war' of words that always enlivens their encounters and entertains their friends. Beatrice has been played at a range of ages – as an altruistic and briskly resigned middle-aged spinster by Elizabeth Spriggs and as a musically-voiced

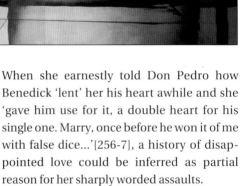

Above left: Ralph Koltai's set with its lone cellist, 1982
Above: *This can be no trick. The conference was sadly borne. They have the truth of this from Hero. They seem to pity the lady*
Derek Jacobi, 1982

and sensitive young woman with a touch of pathos by Samantha Bond. The subtlest of characterisations was Judi Dench's. With delicacy of gesture, magical inflexion of voice and perfect timing – in humour or pathos – she created a complex woman, losing none of Beatrice's brilliant wit whilst indicating depths of emotion that stirred the audience's empathy and won their love. Suggesting someone assuaging her spinsterhood with activity, she also refined the emotions in moments of great stillness or pause. A strain of sadness surfaced at times such as that when Beatrice talks of her mother crying in childbirth: from the slight pause and crack in Judi Dench's voice we might infer that her mother died then:

No, sure, my lord, my mother cried; but then there was a star danced, and under that was I born.

[II.1.309-10]

When she earnestly told Don Pedro how Benedick 'lent' her his heart awhile and she 'gave him use for it, a double heart for his single one. Marry, once before he won it of me with false dice...'[256-7], a history of disappointed love could be inferred as partial reason for her sharply worded assaults.

Having witnessed the swift and cutting verbal battles of Beatrice and Benedick, the audience gains immense pleasure from seeing them brought into love with each other in the comic climax of the play. For the other characters, the tricking of the two is a sport to pass the time before Hero's wedding to Claudio. In the first of a pair of 'overhearing' scenes, Benedick is hidden in an arbour and Don Pedro, Claudio and Leonato weave a plaintive tale of Beatrice's languishing love for him. In the sequence that follows it, Hero and Ursula practise a similar deception on her. Branagh's film shows the gentry playing this game of deception against a lush landscape

peopled with those who sustain the estate. Against the olives, ochres and russets of the Tuscan countryside and under a warm sky, we see maids carrying and folding washing, and men tending the gardens. The scene is a wonderful opportunity for comic business. Much humour was generated in the 1982 production from Benedick's command to his boy to fetch a book from his chamber-window. During the gulling of Benedick that follows, the boy made repeated attempts to pass the book to Benedick, who was desperate to remain, as he thought, concealed. Several times frustrated, the boy finally flung the book at his master and made an angry exit. Zeffirelli's production added the 'Inanimates' (living statues) to the cast. For Benedick's soliloquy which opens this first overhearing scene, two mermaids and a Triton took up poses as a fountain behind him, giving an opportunity for some apt and delightful upstaging. When Benedick moved in very close to listen to the conversation, comedy was added by Don Pedro nonchalantly flicking ash from his cigar onto Benedick's head.

In his soliloquy Benedick considers these revelations of Beatrice's passion for him, instantly concluding:

This can be no trick.

[II.3.215]

He decides Beatrice's love has to be reciprocated for:

the world must be peopled. When I said I would die a bachelor, I did not think I should live till I were married.

[234-6]

Donald Sinden had a marvellous time with this speech, fully exploiting his rapport with the audience and relishing the flavour of the words like a wine-tasting. Beatrice is sent by the others, against her will, to call Benedick in to dinner. Her words are delivered peremptorily and Judi Dench punctuated their delivery by violent blows on a gong brought to emphasise the summons and, incidentally, her own irritation. After her departure, and with an extraordinarily liberal display of lateral thinking, Sinden made hilarious capital from his reasoning:

Ha! 'Against my will I am sent to bid you come in to dinner' – there's a double meaning in that.

[249-50]

Beatrice is similarly beguiled by Hero and Ursula who, in Zeffirelli's production, were hanging out washing. Maggie Smith was

easily deceived. She was covered with a nightshirt and overheard the conversation whilst draped on the line. The two women indict Beatrice for her scorning of Benedick and after their departure, it is clear she has taken their criticisms to heart. After the mirth of Benedick's prose scene and the merriment at the start of this parallel one in verse, Judi Dench effected a rapid change of mood. She had hidden behind a semi-opaque muslin blind to overhear Hero and Ursula. After their exit, she lifted it tentatively, dipped underneath it and paused. Her response was solemn and reflective. When she spoke, the joy of being loved only risked manifesting itself in one or two lines. She seemed taken aback by her own surfacing emotion.

The emotions released bring Beatrice and Benedick closer to an increasingly deep commitment to each other. Verbal wit cedes to emotional truth, underlining the more self-regarding elements in their society. This was

Above: *My visor is Philemon's roof; within the house is Jove* Joanna Foster as Hero, John Carlisle as Don John, Derek Godfrey and Edward Jewesbury, 1982.
Below: *... for which of my bad parts didst thou first fall in love with me?* Samantha Bond and Kenneth Branagh, 1988

Above left: *Don Pedro is approached*
The army arrives in Messina, 1993.
Above: *Silence is the perfectest herald of joy*
Kate Beckinsale as Hero and Robert Sean Leonard
as Claudio, 1993

most effectively pointed by the setting and costumes of Terry Hands' production. The society's valuing of verbal acumen and sleight of tongue came to seem a gloss over an emotional paucity and emptiness at its heart, which Ralph Koltai's set elegantly emphasised. The screens and mirrors gave a beautiful but ambivalent context for their rather self-regarding games. Like his fellow officers, Don John regards deception as an amusement. His project, however, is destructive and results in a dramatic climax at the wedding of Hero and Claudio – the play is thrust suddenly into the tragic mode.

Much Ado remains a comedy because of the Watch, a simple and peace-loving band of householders in the command of 'Master Constable' Dogberry. He provides a garrulous and posturing parody of the word-centred world of wit of those who consider themselves his betters. Giving instructions to his men is complicated by the fact that in Dogberry's mouth, language becomes an unreliable and obscure assembly of parts in which malapropisms are legion. In 1965, Frank Finlay played him as a passionately Italian small-town autocrat, animated and volatile. In John Barton's Raj setting, John Woodvine was a mild and turbaned Indian Dogberry, whose errors in speech were ambitious and quaint attempts to acquire the language of the sahibs. Watching events played out on a hot, languid evening in colonial India, we laughed but may also have sensed the irony in this gentle Dogberry's aspirations to the language of those who have colonised his country. The

Watch does not only provide opportunities for comedy and slapstick humour: their presence is also salutary. Through their anxieties, unsophisticated reactions and mistakings, Shakespeare underlines the faults of the fashion-loving class from which they are excluded. They enter the play as Benedick and Beatrice are beginning to detach themselves from the habits of those who set a premium on wit at the expense of emotion.

The Watch outdoes its masters in exposing Don John's villainy and the play ends as such a comedy should in celebration, merry-

Above: *You have been always called a merciful man, partner*
Michael Keaton and Ben Elton as Verges, 1993

making and a dance. Only Don Pedro is left in conspicuous military bachelordom. Barton's production had Benedick enthusiastically directing the dancers while Beatrice stood by slightly bemused, holding his sword. When the capture of Don John is announced, discord intrudes momentarily but the villain is not allowed to mar the mirth and does not reappear until the curtain call. Barton's production was an exception. Having suggested earlier that the character's actions came from faults within the group, rather than the individual, Barton returned Don John to the action, partnering him in the final dance with Ursula. Zeffirelli's was a festival *Much Ado*, bubbling with invention, with bright strings of lights, tumbling colours, fluctuating moods and moments, the dances among the most ebullient. It ended magically, a blend of delight and poignancy. The line of characters disappeared, exuberantly dancing off-stage into a party elsewhere. We were held by Don Pedro's isolation. As the stage lights dimmed, cigar between his teeth, he looked up at the one remaining light, and, blowing it out with a slight puff, excluded us from the magic for a time.

Susan L. Powell

NOTABLE PRODUCTIONS OF *MUCH ADO ABOUT NOTHING*

	THEATRE	DIRECTOR	DESIGNER	PRINCIPALS	
1965	National Theatre, The Old Vic	Franco Zeffirelli	Franco Zeffirelli, Peter J. Hall	Maggie Smith	*Beatrice*
				Robert Stephens	*Benedick*
				Gerald James	*Leonato*
				Albert Finney	*Don Pedro*
				Frank Finlay	*Dogberry*
1971	Royal Shakespeare Theatre, Stratford-upon-Avon	Ronald Eyre	Voytek	Elizabeth Spriggs	*Beatrice*
				Derek Godfrey	*Benedick*
				Tony Church	*Leonato*
				Jeffrey Dench	*Don Pedro*
				Peter Woodthorpe	*Dogberry*
1976	Royal Shakespeare Theatre, Stratford-upon-Avon	John Barton	John Napier	Judi Dench	*Beatrice*
				Donald Sinden	*Benedick*
				Ivan Beavis	*Leonato*
				Robin Ellis	*Don Pedro*
				John Woodvine	*Dogberry*
1982	Royal Shakespeare Theatre, Stratford-upon-Avon	Terry Hands	Ralph Koltai	Sinead Cusack	*Beatrice*
				Derek Jacobi	*Benedick*
				Edward Jewesbury	*Leonato*
				Derek Godfrey	*Don Pedro*
				Terry Wood	*Dogberry*
1988	Renaissance Theatre Company, Birmingham Repertory Theatre	Judi Dench	Jenny Tiramani	Samantha Bond	*Beatrice*
				Kenneth Branagh	*Benedick*
				Richard Easton	*Leonato*
				Richard Clifford	*Don Pedro*
				David Lloyd Meredith	*Dogberry*
1993	Renaissance Films	Kenneth Branagh	Phyllis Dalton, Tim Harvey	Emma Thompson	*Beatrice*
				Kenneth Branagh	*Benedick*
				Richard Briers	*Leonato*
				Denzel Washington	*Don Pedro*
				Michael Keaton	*Dogberry*

'OF ONE THAT LOVED NOT WISELY, BUT TOO WELL'

The Early Production History of *Othello*

Shakespeare's main source for *Othello* was a story by Giraldi Cinthio published in 1565. The first recorded performance of the play was in 1604: 'By the Kings Maiesties plaiers…A Play in the Bankettinge House at Whit Hall Called the Moor of Venis'. The play was published in a Quarto edition in 1622, but the Folio of 1623 prints a fuller text. Its early popularity continued despite heavy cutting to suit Restoration tastes. It is generally believed that the first appearance of an actress on the English stage was as Desdemona in November 1660.

In 1683 Thomas Betterton conveyed powerfully his emotional pain as he questioned Desdemona about the handkerchief. David Garrick succeeded as Iago but failed as Othello though he added a turban to Othello's customary British Army uniform and restored the epileptic scene. Throughout the eighteenth century there were just seven years in which there was no London performance. At the beginning of the nineteenth century, John Philip Kemble was a dignified Othello with his sister, Sarah Siddons, a sweet and tender Desdemona. However, the performance that had the greatest impact upon its audience was that of Edmund Kean. Contemporary accounts testify to an astonishing emotional range which instilled pity and fear. Moments of primitive violence were juxtaposed with elegiac lyricism. The night after his initial success as Othello on 5 May 1814 he gave an almost equally brilliant interpretation of Iago and alternated the parts for several seasons.

From the time of Kean there has been a general reluctance to believe English actors capable of the part though Irving, Forbes-Robertson, Ralph Richardson and John Gielgud have all tried. In 1875 Thomaso Salvini (acting in Italian amidst an English-speaking cast) was the first Othello to strike his Desdemona. The vocal range and physical power of both Frederick Valk in 1947 and Paul Robeson at Stratford in 1959 won praise, but Laurence Olivier in 1964 was the first to challenge the legendary supremacy of Kean's performance.

Top: Paul Robeson as Othello at the Shakespeare Memorial Theatre, 1959
Left: Edmund Kean as Othello at the Theatre Royal, Drury Lane, 1814
Right: Laurence Olivier as Othello at the Old Vic, 1964

OTHELLO

Obsessive sexual jealousy, enmeshed with issues of race,
gender and political policy, precipitates a tragedy of inexorable power.

The opening of *Othello* plunges its audience into a conversation in which the more likeable character will only later be suspected to be the villain. Iago's resentment seems eminently reasonable and David Suchet recounted in a straightforward way the unfairness of background and education being preferred to experience and proven merit in the matter of promotion. He showed no hint of self-pity or bitterness, seeming sensibly resigned to the way of the world:

Why, there's no remedy. 'Tis the curse of service.
[I.1.35]

In his stage performance Frank Finlay was earnest and self-effacing, and when the production was filmed he retained every impression of openness and integrity even in close-up. However, Bob Hoskins exploits the intimacy of the television camera to suggest an instability that flutters just beneath the surface, masked from those around him by a bluff, jocular exterior. Orson Welles forestalls the likelihood of an audience being taken in (as Roderigo and everyone else is) by beginning his film with Othello and Desdemona's funeral procession. Iago watches, suspended in a cage.

Initially, an audience may well accept Iago's evaluation of Othello. For two hundred lines he is referred to simply as 'he' or 'the Moor' or

Right: *Yet I'll not shed her blood,*
        Nor scar that whiter skin of hers than snow,
        And smooth as monumental alabaster
Orson Welles and Suzanne Cloutier, 1952

163

else he is spoken of in racially derogatory terms: 'thick lips', 'old black ram', 'Barbary horse' and 'lascivious Moor'. It is only when he enters accompanied by Iago that we might realise something of the latter's chameleon nature. Ben Kingsley's Othello was an Eastern Moor. In flowing white robes and elegantly turbanned, he seemed to glide downstage, his eyes fixed on some distant fixed point, conveying powerfully the sense of a meditative man untouchable by humdrum reality, almost godlike in his grace and bearing. Laurence Olivier played Othello as a Negro in a performance of remarkable physical detail. He entered relaxed, strolling onto the stage bare-foot, holding a long-stemmed red rose between his fingers, sniffing it now and then. It hinted at both his acquired sophistication and his sensuous nature. He projected an air of racial confidence and rejected the concerns for his safety expressed by Iago or Cassio. He countered Brabantio's display of force with a gently patronising amusement:

> Keep up your bright swords, for the dew will
>   rust them.
> Good signor, you shall more command with
>   years
> Than with your weapons.

[I.2.59-61]

Othello's position in Venetian society is secured by his military prowess and the Duke is the first to greet him by name. Calling him 'Valiant Othello' [I.3.48] proclaims his worth to Venice and prepares us for the Duke's pragmatic response to Brabantio's complaint. In 1990 Clive Swift avoided caricature and presented a convincing portrait of a father who could not accept his daughter's marriage to a foreigner. He alerted us to the platitudes that the Duke expresses in rhyming couplets. We could understand Brabantio's feelings without condoning his bigotry. At the end of

Above: *What noise is this? Not dead? Not yet quite dead?*
I, that am cruel, am yet merciful:
I would not have thee linger in thy pain.
Orson Welles and Suzanne Cloutier, 1952

the scene there was the sadness of a deeply hurt and lonely father and it was possible to appreciate the cost to Desdemona as Imogen Stubbs tried vainly to re-establish some physical contact.

In this production the isolation of Desdemona was made evident since Zoë Wanamaker's Emilia had no previous relationship with her but merely became a companion on the journey to Cyprus as a result of Othello's order to Iago:

> I prithee let thy wife attend on her,
> And bring them after in the best advantage.

[I.3.293-4]

Emilia seemed to be jealous of a relationship which made her acutely aware of the inadequacy of her own marriage. Her Iago was a meticulous army man with a brutal briskness towards his wife. In contrast, Joyce Redman played Emilia as a surrogate mother providing kindly support and the comfort of experience.

By shifting the focus to the military outpost of Cyprus, Shakespeare puts pressure on Othello. The storm-tossed journey that separates the ships prefigures the tumult to come, but more practically deals with the threat of the Turkish invasion so the islanders celebrate even before their hero arrives. While Othello and Desdemona enjoy their postponed wedding night Cassio is to keep the watch. In 1964 Derek Jacobi was an elegant, educated man while Sean Baker at The Other Place seemed tense and insecure from the start. When Othello is summoned from his bed to witness the drunken brawl, his treatment of Cassio is complicated by the intertwining of

his public and private rôles. As Ben Kingsley stood cradling his scimitar, his Desdemona appeared framed in the doorway and seemed unaware of the transparency of her pale blue robe or of her own sensuality. Ben Kingsley's dismissal of Cassio was informed by both public anger and private uncertainty. He loses not only his lieutenant but also the man whom both he and Desdemona had trusted during their surreptitious courtship: Othello tells Iago that Cassio 'went between us very oft' [III.3.99] and it is natural that Desdemona should wish to intercede on Cassio's behalf.

Iago successfully exploits his public image of 'honesty and trust' [I.3.281] to cause division and disquiet. Actors have been keen to find motives where Shakespeare is elusive. Bob Hoskins plays him as psychopath, David Suchet had a repressed homoerotic desire, and Richard Haddon Haines was motivated by ugly, racial hatred. Ian McKellen suffered from 'the green-eyed monster' that was a wide-spread infection in Trevor Nunn's production. Early in the play Iago tells Roderigo that: 'My cause is hearted' [361], which succinctly suggests both an emotional imperative and a desire to strike at the core of feeling and emotion.

At the play's centre lies the temptation scene in which Othello moves from the loving assurance to Desdemona:

I will deny thee nothing

[III.3.76]

to the violent commitment of hatred: 'I'll tear her all to pieces!' [428]. Willard White began calmly, absorbed in paper-work, hardly paying attention to Ian McKellen's insidious suggestions. As the scene developed there was

Left: *The royal banner and all quality,*
Pride, pomp and circumstance of glorious war!
Sergei Bondarchuk and V. Soshalsky as Cassio, 1955

Above left: *Valiant Othello*
Anthony Hopkins, 1981
Above: *I hate the Moor*
Bob Hoskins, 1981

the sense of the man becoming disorientated, powerless against the skilful manipulation of a practised, professional liar. Olivier had played Iago himself in 1938 and was well aware of the theatrical power of the rôle and was determined that his Othello should not be an easy victim. He shunned notions of the noble Moor, preferring to present a man prone to self-dramatisation and delusion, a man who had acquired a veneer of sophistication and whose claim of being 'not easily jealous' [V.2.341] was ingenuous. For him, Frank Finlay's low-key observation: 'Ha! I like not that' [III.3.35] was enough to start the inexorable process. He became confused and uncertain, out of his depth in matters of the morality of Venetian wives. Anxious to be alone, he dismissed Iago peremptorily when he seemed reluctant to leave. 'Why did I marry?' [240] was quietly spoken, but with the stress directed to 'I'. But his vigorous self-dramatisation returned and he moved onto the offensive. He grabbed Iago by the throat

and hurled him to the ground on:

Villain, be sure thou prove my love a whore

[356]

and threatened him with a stiletto blade concealed in his bracelet, establishing the weapon with which he would later take his own life. Olivier revealed the irrationality of a man whose demand for 'ocular proof' will be satisfied with the flimsiest of evidence and his Othello retreated into primitive ritual and atavism. He tore the crucifix from his neck as he severed his links with a civilisation he now derided and condemned.

Film enables Othello's metaphor; 'Like to the Pontic sea…' [450] to be visually realised. Sergei Bondarchuk seeks the stability provided by a huge beached anchor while Iago drowns his sense in a flood of innuendo. As the tide comes in inexorably Othello's sense of disorientation and dependence upon Iago is absolute. Welles' frame of reference

exploits cramped arches, low ceilings and claustrophobic interiors. Patterns of latticed windows create an environment which exemplifies Iago's:

net
That shall enmesh them all.

[II.3.351-2]

A handkerchief spotted with strawberries not only serves Iago's purpose but it draws together the three women in the play allowing an audience to appreciate their common cause and tragic patterns. It was Othello's first gift to Desdemona and solicitous for the headache of which he complains:

I have a pain upon my forehead here

[III.3.281]

she seeks to use her napkin to 'bind it'. He pushes it away and Emilia picks it up. She knows its importance to her mistress and yet gives it to Iago in an attempt to please 'his fantasy' [296]. When Emilia denies to Desdemona any knowledge of what has happened to the handkerchief, it can be an uncomfortable moment inconsistent with loyal friendship, but for Zoë Wanamaker it read powerfully as a moment in which she was prepared to have Desdemona suffer a little of the marital disharmony that for Emilia was habitual. When Cassio finds the handker-chief in his room he gives it to Bianca who assumes it is indeed evidence of infidelity. She flings it back at him, determined not to be taken for granted or humiliated, for like

Right: *I'll tear her all to pieces*
David Suchet and Ben Kingsley, 1985
Below: Ben Kingsley and Janet Dale, 1985

Above left: *If thou dost love me*
Show me thy thought.
Willard White and Ian McKellen, 1990
Above: *What did thy song bode, lady?*
Imogen Stubbs and Zoë Wanamaker, 1990

Desdemona and Emilia she loves a man who treats her badly and her love makes her vulnerable:

If you'll come to supper tonight, you may. If you will not, come when you are next prepared for.

[IV.1.159-60]

Such is the play's emphasis upon the blackness of Othello and the purity of Desdemona that the black/white opposition becomes emblematic. The play's structure swings from night to day and back again. Shakespeare operates a double-time scheme to allow both a naturalistic expansiveness and a dramatic compression. On the play's third night Desdemona lies in bed waiting for her husband and Othello debates what is for him a judicial killing in the language of the play's central metaphor: 'Put out the light' [V.2.7]. As Orson Welles' majestic and statuesque Othello makes his way towards the bedroom, we see a frightened Desdemona pretending to sleep. Olivier was calm, convinced of the moral imperative to carry out what he was sure is an honourable murder. There was solemnity and dignity in:

It is the cause, it is the cause, my soul:
Let me not name it to you, you chaste stars!

[1-2]

spoken away from her sleeping figure and as he parted the curtains and bent to kiss her there was an overwhelming sense of the pain of his resurgent love. The BBC-tv version is committed to a small scale, domestic setting throughout. Anthony Hopkins sits on the edge of the bed and speaks quietly lest she wake. In the intimacy of The Other Place, Imogen Stubbs determinedly rejected the passivity of a sacrificial victim and desperately, frenetically tried to escape from the room.

On discovering Desdemona's body Emilia takes control. She berates Othello and as her own culpability is revealed she displays remarkable courage and moral strength. For Zoë Wanamaker, this was all the more

powerful because of the absence of any easy sentimentality in her earlier relationship with Desdemona. Not only was her attack upon Othello scathingly contemptuous but there was a searing sense of self-castigation. As Iago sought to silence her by invoking the traditional subservience of wife to husband, 'I charge you get you home' [193], her refusal revealed an impressive clarity of moral purpose:

> 'Tis proper I obey him, but not now.
> Perchance, Iago, I will ne'er go home.
>
> [195-6]

Her epitaph for Desdemona, 'so good a wife' [232], could powerfully apply to herself.

Willard White delivered Othello's final speech with understated dignity and sincerity, whereas Olivier began imperiously, 'Soft you...' [334]. He was unashamedly firm and confident in his reminder that:

> I have done the state some service and they know't.
>
> [335]

In talking of the 'unlucky deeds' he gave particular point to the descriptive word. His delusion gave his lines a gloss of self-pity:

> then must you speak
> Of one that loved not wisely, but too well;
> Of one, not easily jealous but, being wrought,
> Perplexed in the extreme; of one whose hand
> Like the base Indian threw a pearl away
> Richer than all his tribe...
>
> [339-44]

He gathered Desdemona in his arms and with a final assertion of authority, 'Set you down this...' [347], he cut his jugular vein with his concealed stiletto.

NOTABLE PRODUCTIONS OF *OTHELLO*

	THEATRE	DIRECTOR	DESIGNER	PRINCIPALS
1952	Films Marceau/ Mercury Productions/ Mogador Films	Orson Welles	Alexandre Trauner	Orson Welles ....*Othello* Suzanne Cloutier ....*Desdemona* Micheál MacLiammóir ....*Iago* Fay Compton ....*Emilia*
1955	Mosfilm	Sergei Yutkevich	A. Weisfeld, V. Dorrer	Sergei Bondarchuk ....*Othello* I. Skobtseva ....*Desdemona* A. Popov ....*Iago* A. Maximova ....*Emilia*
1964	National Theatre at the Old Vic, London	John Dexter	Jocelyn Herbert	Laurence Olivier ....*Othello* Maggie Smith ....*Desdemona* Frank Finlay ....*Iago* Joyce Redman ....*Emilia*
This production was filmed in 1965 under the direction of Stuart Burge				
1981	BBC-tv	Jonathan Miller	Colin Lowrey	Anthony Hopkins ....*Othello* Penelope Wilton ....*Desdemona* Bob Hoskins.................................*Iago* Rosemary Leach ....*Emilia*
1985	Royal Shakespeare Theatre, Stratford-upon-Avon	Terry Hands	Ralph Koltai	Ben Kingsley ....*Othello* Niamh Cusack.................*Desdemona* David Suchet ....*Iago* Janet Dale...............................*Emilia*
1988	Market Theatre of Johannesburg	Janet Suzman	Johan Engels	John Kani.................................*Othello* Joanna Weinberg ....*Desdemona* Richard Haddon Haines ....*Iago* Dorothy Gould.........................*Emilia*
1990	The Other Place, Stratford-upon-Avon	Trevor Nunn	Bob Crowley	Willard White ....*Othello* Imogen Stubbs ....*Desdemona* Ian McKellen ....*Iago* Zoë Wanamaker......................*Emilia*

'LED ON BY HEAVEN, AND CROWNED WITH JOY AT LAST'

The Early Production History of *Pericles*

Pericles was written between 1606 and 1608 and is the first of Shakespeare's late plays. It was an immediate success and, after the Restoration, was one of the first plays performed. The play was not included in the First Folio and, although a very 'bad' Quarto was produced in 1609, it was only in 1664, in the second edition of the Third Folio, that it appeared with the rest of the plays under Shakespeare's name. There is now general agreement that the first two acts are by another writer, possibly George Wilkins.

The popular old story on which the play is based – *Confessio Amantis* – was recorded by John Gower, a fourteenth century poet. Shakespeare capitalised on this by writing Gower into the play as a chorus figure: 'To sing a song that old was sung, From ashes ancient Gower is come.' Scenes of incest and prostitution meant that the play lost favour in the more decorous eighteenth century theatres, although an entertainment called *Marina*, loosely based on *Pericles*, was first performed in 1738.

The play did not receive a full revival in the nineteenth century, but the opportunity for lavish spectacle was seen in Samuel Phelps' production at Covent Garden in 1854. There were plenty of effects: a storm-tossed ship, a glittering banquet, a rolling panorama to augment Pericles' voyaging, but the text of the play still presented a problem. Phelps cut the play so vigorously that Henry Morley remarked that: 'There remained not a syllable at which true delicacy could have conceived offence.' In the twentieth century the whole text has generally been used in performance as directors see the uneven quality of the play and the subject matter not as a fault, but as a challenge.

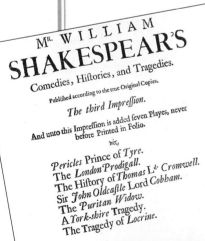

Top: Samuel Phelps, actor-manager at Sadler's Wells from 1844
Left: Title page of the Third Folio, 1664
Right: John Gower, 1325-1408

PERICLES

*A father's unremitting quest for his daughter leads him
across the Mediterranean to a magical, miraculous reunion.*

The play presents the story of Pericles, the Prince of Tyre, and with the aid of dumb-show and Gower's narrative, we follow his trials. Gower opens the play by speaking directly to the audience. In 1969, Emrys James was a powerful figure, almost a puppet-master, calling on the actors to perform his story in a large, neutral-coloured box. He had no need of scenery or special effects: the words and the emblematic costumes provided the locations. In the BBC-tv production, Gower is also the studio manager,

dimming the lights when he is ready for the action to begin. In 1989, Rudolph Walker carried a book and read from it, setting the scene but also reminding us that he would illustrate an old story. Gower remained on stage throughout the play, sometimes sitting in an armchair while the action continued around him.

Pericles solves the riddle set by King Antiochus for the hand of his daughter and thereby discovers the King's incest. Realising the knowledge endangers his life, he flees to

Above: *A man whom both the waters and the wind,
In that vast tennis-court, hath made the ball
For them to play upon entreats you pity him.
He asks of you that never used to beg.*
Ian Richardson sitting amidst the Fishermen, 1969

Tarsus. As in the best fables, he goes straight into another adventure. He relieves a famine in Tarsus: here the resources of the BBC showed us bodies being carried away and starving citizens but the words are so powerful that we need the minimum of staging:

Those mothers who to nuzzle up their babes
Thought naught too curious are ready now
To eat those little darlings whom they loved.
So sharp are hunger's teeth that man and wife
Draw lots who first shall die to lengthen life.

[I.4.42-6]

In 1969, tattered clothes were all that Dionyza and Cleon needed to suggest the disintegration of their kingdom. Pericles leaves Tarsus and again is seized by events beyond his control. He is shipwrecked and washed up in tatters on a seashore. He is found by three fishermen who offer him help:

Come, thou shalt go home, and we'll have flesh for holidays, fish for fasting-days, and moreo'er puddings and flapjacks, and thou shalt be welcome.

[II.1.80-3]

Left: *Now, by the gods, he could not please me better.*
Ian Richardson and Susan Fleetwood, 1969
Above: Rudolph Walker, 1989

Above: *I am the daughter to King Pericles*
Suzan Sylvester, 1989
Above right: *Where am I? Where's my lord? What world is this?* Sally Edwards, 1989
Right: The starving people of Tarsus, 1989

Pericles is a symmetrical play with its pairs of fathers and daughters and the fishermen are part of this formal pattern. They are as good, noble and honest as the inhabitants of the brothel are ignoble and wicked. In 1969 the spare style of the setting conveyed the sea-shore with a simple wave of fishing net across the stage.

Pericles can enter a tournament for the hand of the King's daughter, Thaisa, but he needs the armour which the fishermen find washed up in their nets. The Oxford Stage Company gave Pericles little more than a breastplate and the rest of his costume was fashioned from nets and items found on the beach. He even wore an upturned basket on his head, but his amusing appearance served a purpose. The courteous and dignified reception he receives from Simonides and Thaisa shows just what warm and honest characters they are. Pericles gains his wife – Thaisa, a daughter loved honourably by her father in contrast to his first proposed bride. Thaisa dies in childbirth on board ship in a terrible storm and she is thrown overboard in a coffin. Here the BBC eschewed lavish effects, simply showing us Gower's face with film of a raging sea behind it. The actors in Terry Hands' production mimed the storm scene. Shakespeare provides all the effects we need:

> Thou god of this great vast rebuke these surges,
> Which wash both heaven and hell. And thou that hast
> Upon the winds command, bind them in brass,
> Having called them from the deep!
>
> [III.1.1-4]

In the Swan the huge crow's nest, the percussive storm sounds and the almost balletic movements of the sailors gave way to calm and silence as Cerimon, the healer, brings the dead Thaisa back to life. Believing Pericles dead, she becomes a votaress at the temple of Diana.

After Pericles returns to Tarsus to leave his baby daughter in the care of Cleon and Dionyza, the action leaps forward to the adulthood of Marina. In Terry Hands' production Marina was played by Susan Fleetwood, who was also playing Thaisa. Such doubling embodied two halves of a single experience. Thaisa, loved by her father and husband, dies young, while Marina, friendless and alone, struggles to find a husband and father. She is in danger from Dionyza, who is jealous for the marriage chances of her own daughter. Dionyza arranges that Marina shall be

Right: *'Tis but a blow, which never shall be known.*
Grant Parsons as Leonine and Susan Colverd as Dionyza, 1992
Far right: Leader Hawkins, 1992

murdered by the aptly named Leonine. Just when we think things could not get any worse for Marina, she is carried off by pirates. In the Swan they made their appearance SAS style, down long ropes suspended from the roof. It was an unexpected device, making us acutely aware of Marina's vulnerability.

Marina is sold to a brothel in Myteline and

Leonine reports that she was killed. The brothel scenes in the Swan were revoltingly explicit. Poxy whores vomited copiously, and the scenes between Marina, the Bawd and

Below: *– Search the market narrowly. Mytilene is full of gallants. We lost too much money this mart by being wenchless. – We were never so much out of creatures.*
Del Henney as Pander and Eliza Hunt as the Bawd, 1992

Boult created a claustrophobic sense of oppression and evil. David Thacker reminded modern audiences just what is at stake for Marina here – physical ruin and death, and immortal ruin too. Marina's salvation lies in her fluency and expressive language. Boult complains when Marina refuses to satisfy a customer:

The nobleman would have dealt with her like a nobleman, and she sent him away as cold as a snowball, saying his prayers too.

[IV.6.136-8]

In John Retallack's production, Marina wore a pure white gown of timeless design while the denizens of the brothel were 1950s spivs and tarts in leopardskin and diamanté. Through reasoning and virtue, Marina converts Lysimachus (the governor of Myteline and an important client at the brothel) and eventually Boult to her plan to earn an honest living. Meanwhile, Pericles, believing Dionyza's story of Marina's death, is desolate and will not speak. His ship arrives at Myteline. When Lysimachus hears of this, he is insistent Marina's 'sweet harmony' [V.1.42] can cure the mourning man. In the Swan, Marina in her azure gown shone amongst the grey and beige of the other characters as she approached Pericles, who was hiding under a tarpaulin, cowering like a wild and shaggy animal. Father and daughter, each having believed the other dead, are reunited. Here, the physical likeness of the two actors playing Thaisa and Marina can move the audience as we watch Pericles recognising his daughter, and seeing his dead wife through her:

O, stop there a little!
This is the rarest dream
That e'er dull sleep did mock sad fools withal.
This cannot be my daughter, buried!
...

	THEATRE	DIRECTOR	DESIGNER	PRINCIPALS
1969	Royal Shakespeare Theatre, Stratford-upon-Avon	Terry Hands	Timothy O'Brien	Ian Richardson ....*Pericles* Susan Fleetwood ....*Thaisa & Marina* Emrys James ....*Gower*
1983	BBC-tv	David Jones	Don Taylor	Mike Gwilym ....*Pericles* Juliet Stevenson ....*Thaisa* Amanda Redman ....*Marina* Edward Petherbridge...............*Gower*
1989	Swan Theatre, Stratford-upon-Avon	David Thacker	Fran Thompson	Nigel Terry ....*Pericles* Sally Edwards...........................*Thaisa* Suzan Sylvester.......................*Marina* Rudolph Walker ....*Gower*
1992	Oxford Stage Company	John Retallack	Julian McGowan	Philip Bowen ....*Pericles* Ginny Holder ....*Thaisa* Catherine Prendergast...........*Marina* Leader Hawkins ....*Gower*

NOTABLE PRODUCTIONS OF *PERICLES*

Down on thy knees, thank the holy gods as loud
As thunder threatens us. This is Marina.

[160-3; 199-200]

After their reunion, Pericles sleeps and sees a vision of the Goddess Diana who tells him to go to her temple and relate what has happened to him, his wife and child. In the television production, the temple is on the beach where the play began. The action has taken place on and around these featureless dunes, as if to remind us that the sea laps at the edges of this play. The parents and their child are reunited – with the help of a 'double' in 1969 – and Marina and Lysimachus are given a kingdom of their own.

Pericles is a play which tantalises. It contains many of the elements of mature and finely developed drama which we find in the best of Shakespeare's plays, yet it is in form and subject a much older play, almost a medieval morality play. Somewhat static perhaps in its treatment of character, but dealing with the most elemental and powerful themes, the play, above all, reveals:

Virtue preserved from fell destruction's blast.

[Epilogue 5]

Suzanne Harris

'A STRANGE BROOCH IN AN ALL-HATING WORLD'

The Early Production History of Richard II

Shakespeare's elegant and poised *Richard II*, entirely in verse, was probably written around 1595, with Raphael Holinshed's *Chronicles* as its main source. Elizabeth I, still unmarried and heirless, had been Queen for nearly forty years when the play was first published in 1597. During Elizabeth's lifetime, there was a significant omission – the scene of Richard's deposition was considered too politically sensitive to be included in editions. On 7 February 1600, the eve of the Earl of Essex's attempted rebellion, the play was put on for his followers at the Globe theatre. The Essex rebellion failed and before the end of the month the Earl had been beheaded. *Richard II* lost none of its political force after the Restoration: Nahum Tate's attempts to put the play on in an adapted form as *The Sicilian Usurper* failed and his theatre was closed.

The play seems to have been of little interest to eighteenth century audiences and producers; it lost favour for portraying a bad king. However, in the nineteenth century, it became a focus of historical rather than political interest and Richard's character was seized upon as a star vehicle. Edmund Kean reintroduced the play to Londoners in 1815 and Macready and Charles Kean also played Richard. Kean's popular, mediaeval production boasted an added scene of Richard's arrival in London with nearly 600 extras, including a young Ellen Terry, who swarmed up a lamp-post! F. R. Benson's many performances at the end of the nineteenth and the beginning of the twentieth century furthered the play's popularity, and in 1929, the Old Vic saw John Gielgud perform Richard – perhaps the greatest interpretation of the rôle this century.

Top: After the portrait in Westminster Abbey of Richard II, 1367–1400
Left: John Gielgud as Richard II at the Queen's Theatre, 1937
Right: Robert Deveraux, 2nd Earl of Essex, 1566–1601

RICHARD II

Regal complacency must yield to political expediency
and the deposition of the king will reverberate though the ages.

A young man rests on the English earth in a pool of light, kingly in robes of gorgeous blue pointed with stars. He stares into a darkened theatre; King Richard awaiting his court, an actor contemplating his audience. Thus sat Jeremy Irons at the opening of Barry Kyle's

1986 production. As the evening progressed, we watched the waning fortunes of this king and the rise of the next. By the end of the play, Richard is dead, brutally murdered and his cousin, Henry Bolingbroke is king.

Thirteen years before Kyle's fastidious and

Above: Wrath-kindled gentlemen, be ruled by me:
Let's purge this choler without letting blood.
Richard Moore, Jeremy Irons and Michael Kitchen, 1986

visually sumptuous version, the story of the parallel and inextricably linked fall and rise of the two kings was told in John Barton's

Above: *This blessèd plot, this earth, this realm, this England*
William Dudley's model of the set, 1986
Above right: The illustration for September from the Duc de Berri's *Les Très Riches Heures*, 15th century MS

immensely creative production with its running metaphor of king as actor and rule as rôle. A troupe of actors clad in brown breeches and jerkins negotiated the start of a play. The playwright himself ('WS' in the prompt copy), consulted his Folio, considered two actors – Ian Richardson and Richard Pasco – and chose one of them to play the king, as if spontaneously. The play leapt into life, and throughout the season, these actors alternated the two major parts, exploring areas of coincidence and complementary elements.

The metaphors of kingly ascent and decline were made literal on stage by devices such as two parallel 'escalators' or stairs, one on either side of the stage. A bridge between the two

raised and lowered the actors and we saw them literally rise and fall. Barton realised the patterns and rhythms of the play in strong visual images.

The early scenes push the action forward swiftly. Henry Bolingbroke challenges the Duke of Norfolk and, indirectly, the King, accusing him of plotting the death of Richard's uncle, Gloucester. Unable to reconcile them, the King orders a jousting at Coventry – a scene in which the pageantry, ritual and patterning so abundant in the play can have vivid scope. Trumpets ring out, combatants announce their honour and heralds pronounce challenge and riposte. Kyle's production revelled in spectacle, and heraldic colour with actors sporting bright costumes and glittering coats of arms. Barton's actors reined in unruly hobby horses as they waited in the lists. The encounter is

halted by the King, in an action that may be played as premeditated or petulant. The banishment of both men follows, Norfolk for ever and Bolingbroke for ten years, whimsically reduced to six by Richard, when he observes the sorrow of John of Gaunt, Bolingbroke's father.

Hardly has Bolingbroke departed than Gaunt falls fatally ill. In a speech famous for its vigorous patriotism, he elaborates the central metaphor of England as a garden:

**This blessed plot, this earth, this realm, this
England.**

[II.1.50]

Richard's bad 'husbandry' of his country is vehemently indicted: he is accused of being 'Landlord of England ... not king' [113].

Throughout John Barton's production, this

notion of the precious English earth was made manifest in a symbolic pot of soil at the front of the stage, which actors touched at salient points, the characters literally taking their native soil in their hands. In the BBC-tv version of this scene, Gaunt's rousing poetry flows eloquently from the tongue of John Gielgud, fifty years after he first played the king, and the camera signposts the emotional movements of the play.

During the drama, the Duke of York acts as a kind of weather vane. His dilemma lies in conflicting loyalties to his two nephews: to Richard, his anointed king, he owes absolute fidelity; to Bolingbroke, he owes allegiance as to a man treated unjustly by a frivolous, irresponsible monarch. In the BBC production York often occupies a position at the front and right of the television frame. Located thus he becomes, by word or expression, a kind of chorus on the action.

When Gaunt dies, Richard instantly seizes his estate, and the seed of Bolingbroke's usurping return is planted. At this moment in the Kyle production, Jeremy Irons sat unconsciously plucking the petals from a red rose: an intimation of drops of blood shed later.

Conspiracy is already afoot: in Barton's production, the rebel lords, Northumberland, Ross and Willoughby reared up on high *cothurni* or stilts, like sinister black crows. While Richard is at war in Ireland, Bolingbroke returns, making allies wherever he marches. York, left as Lord Governor during Richard's absence, is absorbed into Bolingbroke's forces. A Welsh captain announces that his soldiers, loyal to Richard but believing him dead, have dispersed and fled; the portents they witnessed 'forerun the death or fall of kings' [II.4.15]. In Barton's production, the captain's lines were spoken by eight actors, backs to the audience, a mysterious and prophesying chorus. It was as if the 'body politic' rose and spoke with a single voice, unanimous and impressive:

'Tis thought the King is dead. We will not stay.
The bay trees in our country are all withered,
And meteors fright the fixèd stars of heaven.
The pale-faced moon looks bloody on the earth,
And lean-looked prophets whisper fearful
    change.

[7-11]

There is a rapid shift from the evocative and mysterious to the pragmatic and peremptory. Propelled by the ambitious Northumberland in particular, Bolingbroke consolidates his position with the summary execution of Richard's favourites. His justification for these sudden and autocratic killings includes the claim that:

You have in manner with your sinful hours
Made a divorce betwixt his [Richard's] Queen
    and him.

[III.1.11-12]

Above and right: Jeremy Irons, 1986

This suggestion has little support in the rest of the play and the BBC-tv production showed astonishment on York's face. In the 1973 version, the accusations were read from a paper with growing disbelief. Bolingbroke was patently embarrassed by the propaganda his civil servants had prepared for him.

Richard returns, greeting his native earth with reverence. At the news of defection and disaster, he is three times thrown into defeatist thoughts and rallies three times. In despondency, he begins an aria about the death of kings:

For within the hollow crown
That rounds the mortal temples of a king
Keeps death his court; and there the antic sits,
Scoffing his state and grinning at his pomp.

[III.2.160-3]

Richard realises he has no power now except the power of words. Speaking from the high

walls of Flint Castle to Bolingbroke below, he must acknowledge the triumph of military force. Abdication is the subtext. In a superb moment where poetry and stage image fuse brilliantly, Richard descends:

Down, down I come like glistering Phaethon,
Wanting the manage of unruly jades.

[III.3.178-9]

In Barton's inventive production this was the gorgeous moment when Richard, wearing a refulgent, pleated gold robe, spread his arms as he descended, light flashing from him as if he were indeed a sun god. Nevertheless, he must submit to Bolingbroke's political will.

In a short scene in the garden, Richard's Queen and her women overhear his fate from the gardeners; Shakespeare's horticultural metaphor is here at its most intense. For Kyle's production, William Dudley contrived an elegant set design evoking the Duc de Berry's *Les Très Riches Heures*, which, for this scene, provided a bright and graceful context. Ironically, the delicate gazebo was later to become the cage in Richard's gloomy prison.

The narrative moves inexorably towards the point where Richard 'undoes' himself. In his last grand performance, he completely steals the scene. Bolingbroke must watch and listen to the virtuoso display – Michael Kitchen's Henry became increasingly impatient. Richard identifies those betraying him as Judases, Pilates, and this analogy was fully exploited by Jeremy Irons in his strong,

Below: – *Here standeth Thomas Mowbray, Duke of Norfolk …*
Attending but the signal to begin.
– Sound, trumpets; and set forward combatants!
Denis Holmes and, at this performance, Richard Pasco as the King and Ian Richardson as Bolingbroke, 1973

poignant, narcissistic identification with Christ. Richard ritually and rhythmically deposes himself:

With mine own tears I wash away my balm,
With mine own hands I give away my crown,
With mine own tongue deny my sacred state,
With mine own breath release all duteous oaths.

[IV.1.206-9]

Richard calls for a 'glass', a mirror to see what inroads sorrow has made upon his face. He finds it a flatterer – his face shows few signs of his tragedy – and smashes it into pieces. In Barton's production, Bolingbroke placed the empty frame over Richard's head, creating for Richard a Christ-like halo, crown and halter. The attendant lords, picking up Bolingbroke's words and Richard's own musing repetition of them, chanted:

The shadow of your sorrow hath destroy'd
The shadow of your face.

[291-2]

Having made his touching farewell to his queen on his way to imprisonment, Richard finds himself incarcerated in Pomfret Castle. Passing long hours alone, he philosophises, achieving new wisdom in an extended and moving soliloquy with a strong biblical frame of reference. Typical of the style of the play, it has elegance, and rich figurative language:

I wasted time, and now doth time waste me;
For now hath time made me his numbering
    clock.
My thoughts are minutes, and with sighs
    they jar
Their watches on to mine eyes, the outward
    watch
Whereto my finger, like a dial's point,
Is pointing still in cleansing them from tears.

[V.5.49-54]

Through this deeply personal and dignified monologue, Richard manifests resilience and fortitude, and the maturity he has until now sadly lacked. In this still, sombre place, Richard makes his final journey to self-knowledge. His last visitor is a gentle groom who remembers him from happier days. Barton, extending his exploration of two characters as aspects of one kingly being, cast the groom as Bolingbroke; thus Richard's last exchange is with his other self. Although he defends himself royally, Richard is slaughtered by Exton and his men.

The Kyle production ended with a strongly proleptic image. Henry was enthroned above Richard's coffin, attended by two grim reapers. The gazebo turned and sprouted warring roses, red and white, symbols of the civil factions to come. Barton's, however, was the most brilliant *coup de théâtre*. Amidst climaxing drums, Bolingbroke was crowned, a single hooded courtier standing on each side of him. The King turned as the sound crescendoed, and the two attendants threw back their hoods to reveal Pasco and Richardson. So whose face then stared out at us from beneath the hollow crown? It was the unequivocal face of Death.

Susan L. Powell

NOTABLE PRODUCTIONS OF *RICHARD II*

	THEATRE	DIRECTOR	DESIGNER	PRINCIPALS
1973	Royal Shakespeare Theatre, Stratford-upon-Avon	John Barton	Timothy O'Brien, Tazeena Firth	Richard Pasco/Ian Richardson played *Richard II* and *Bolingbroke* at alternate performances Tony Church...*Gaunt* Denis Holmes...*Mowbray* Sebastian Shaw...*York* Lisa Harrow...*Queen Isabel* Clement McCallin...*Northumberland* Ian Richardson/Richard Pasco...*Groom*
1978	BBC-tv	David Giles	Tony Abbott	Derek Jacobi...*Richard II* Jon Finch...*Bolingbroke* John Gielgud...*Gaunt* Richard Owens...*Mowbray* Charles Gray...*York* Janet Maw...*Queen Isabel* David Swift...*Northumberland* Joe Ritchie...*Groom*
1986	Royal Shakespeare Theatre, Stratford-upon-Avon	Barry Kyle	William Dudley	Jeremy Irons...*Richard II* Michael Kitchen...*Bolingbroke* Brewster Mason...*Gaunt* Richard Moore...*Mowbray* Bernard Horsfall...*York* Imogen Stubbs...*Queen Isabel* Richard Easton...*Northumberland* Roger Moss...*Groom*

'DREAM ON, DREAM ON, OF BLOODY DEEDS AND DEATH'

The Early Production History of *Richard III*

The early stage history of *Richard III* is dominated by Colley Cibber's adaptation of 1700 which held the stage for nearly 200 years. Cibber cut all distractions from the central character, thus turning the play into Richard's show. Few productions are recorded before then, although some evidence suggests the play was popular in Shakespeare's time, and that it was possibly written for the most famous of all Elizabethan tragedians, Richard Burbage.

David Garrick played Richard almost continuously at Drury Lane between 1742–76. His new brand of naturalistic acting made him an overnight sensation and Richard his best remembered rôle. In 1817 Edmund Kean found similar success with an electrifying performance, dominating as Cibber had intended. When Junius Brutus Booth sought to compete with

Kean, the latter's supporters shouted his performance down. Booth later found success by taking *Richard III* to America where, in 1837,

Edwin Forrest presented a savage Richard, strongly influenced by his interest in indigenous Indian culture.

In 1821 William Charles Macready attempted an unsuccessful restaging of Shakespeare's original. But the deciding factor in the restoration of the original was to be the emergence of the Victorian actress. In 1845 Samuel Phelps discarded Cibber and in doing so Margaret was heralded as a new character suited to the Victorian taste for strong women.

The blatant theatricality of Richard did not suit early twentieth century audiences and Margaret continued to demand attention, particularly in the performances of Genevieve Ward and Edith Evans, who overshadowed their respective Richards. In 1937 Tyrone Guthrie attempted a more complex reading of Richard presenting a Freudian vision of maternal influence and sibling rivalry, but neither the text nor the audience endorsed such a reading. In 1942 Donald Wolfit restored Richard to a one-dimensional villain by basing the character on Hitler, a fascist interpretation echoed 48 years later by Ian McKellen at the National Theatre.

Top: David Garrick as Richard III, c. 1741
Left: Staffordshire figurines representing Richard III
Right: Genevieve Ward as Queen Margaret at the Lyceum Theatre, 1896

RICHARD III

*An opportunist wit and brilliant improvisation ensure that
a tyrant's accession is witnessed with compulsive fascination.*

Richard's appeal is established in his opening monologue. Initially the speech is full of joy and happiness, seemingly at odds with Richard's character, but he soon reveals the darkness that lurks within as he continues with 'I am determined to prove a villain' [I.1.30]. Laurence Olivier's film opens at the coronation of Edward IV to emphasise the contrast. Michael Bogdanov used a prologue to establish a Brechtian framework and the sense of actors playing parts. The characters mingled on stage at a tired cocktail party complete with sleazy lounge band. The production was set in the yuppified atmosphere of the late 1980s complete with pinstriped suits, champagne and computer screens. As a compère introduced each character in turn, it became clear the 'merry meetings' [7] were joyless for all the characters.

In 1992, a tapping walking stick and black shadow spreading across the stage heralded Simon Russell Beale's eerie entrance. His speech was lifeless until all his frustration and anger went into the bitter pronunciation of the final word in:

**He capers nimbly in a lady's chamber
To the lascivious pleasing of a *lute*.**

[12-13]

Antony Sher chose the same moment to indicate his character by using physical, not verbal technique. He began in mild tones in the shadow of a huge Gothic cathedral set. Then the speech and his performance sprang into life as he raised previously hidden

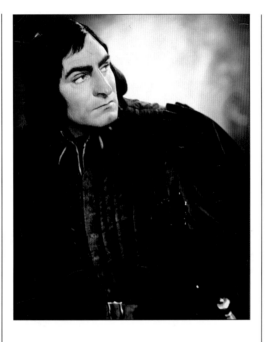

Above: *I, that am curtailed of this fair proportion,
Cheated of feature by dissembling Nature
Deformed, unfinished, sent before my time …*
Laurence Olivier, 1955

crutches and traversed the stage at lightning speed. The audience were captivated as Sher allowed a privileged insight into his twisted psyche. His villainous intentions were plotted, after which he took great delight in using the audience as his confidant in his terrible progression to the throne.

The implausibility of Lady Anne being wooed by Richard, the killer of both her husband and father-in-law, makes it a theatrical challenge and a test of Richard's powers. Olivier softens the scene by cutting it into two, and his persuasive voice hypnotises

the vulnerable Anne. Her 'Thou dost infect mine eyes' [I.2.148] is spoken looking away from Richard, the infection referring to her own temptation not Richard's appearance. Antony Sher's approach was more brutal as bullying, self-pity and disgust combined to create a scene of dark ambivalence. Deformity and sexuality were disturbingly expressed as he slipped his crutch underneath Penny Downie's skirt. Left alone, Sher addressed the audience with pride, pleasure and surprise: 'Was ever woman in this humour won – hmmmm?' [228]. The laughter generated was welcome relief after the intensity of the previous scene. Ian Holm denied the audience such relief by punctuating his speech with self-satisfying chuckles. Here was a psychotic and dangerous Richard.

The death of Clarence is the first scene without Richard, and it proves the most violent. Richard's foul plans create a scene of confusion where tender and violent gestures combine. In 1988 a tearful Clarence was dashed to the ground and one murderer, pricked by conscience, held out a hand to help him up while the other dealt the mortal blow. Clarence's death is the first challenge to the audience's engagement with Richard, as the brutal villainy behind his impressive shows of rhetoric is graphically exposed. Until the death of Clarence, Richard's control has been absolute. Two characters are then introduced who dilute Richard's command over the action: Margaret and Buckingham. The former reminds Richard of his murderous past and the latter assumes responsibilities in

Left: *A thousand hearts are great within my bosom!*
Advance our standards, set upon our foes.
Laurence Olivier, 1955
Right: *Can curses pierce the clouds and enter heaven?*
Peggy Ashcroft, 1963

curse came true, Margaret appeared in silhouette to repeat the words. She became a potent force recalling the spiritual misery of the past to temper Richard's temporal power.

Buckingham has a guiding influence on Richard's advancement. Michael Pennington was an experienced, grey-haired politician, pulling the strings behind the scenes, sponsoring the new upstart Richard in hope of self-advancement. As Buckingham and Richard conspire to destroy the unwitting Hastings, Andrew Jarvis spoke his words like a bad actor, struggling with lines scripted by Buckingham. Fittingly, Pennington remained on stage with Hastings and flashed a rueful smile before lifting the telephone off the hook and quietly leaving. In contrast, Simon Russell Beale injected terror as he accused Mistress Shore of witchcraft. Hastings' measured reply 'If they have done this deed, my noble lord –' was met with a thunderous 'If?'[III.4.73-4] behind which lay the full force of Richard's evil nature. This was the moment Richard's ambitions became apparent and the nobles had to chose between conformity or persecution. Olivier exits leaving a sinister silence during which, one by one, the nobles leave Hastings isolated. The normally optimistic, 'His grace looks cheerfully and smooth this morning' [48], is betrayed by the fear in Hastings' voice and the understanding that his fate is decided.

Having swayed the nobility, Richard's last hurdle to the crown is to gain popular support and convince the citizens. This is done by masquerading as a devout Christian and delegating the role of mediator to Buckingham. For Olivier, the lack of control proves too much. As Ralph Richardson claims, 'But we will plant some other in the throne' [III.7.215], Olivier

risks exposing the whole sham by dropping his prayer book. In this lack of self-control Olivier cleverly presages Richard's weakness in performing regal duties on a larger stage. As the citizens leave, Richard swings athletically down the church bell rope and thrusts his hand for Buckingham to kiss, defining the boundaries of their relationship and asserting his dominance by forcing him to kneel.

Richard's ascension to the throne marks the summit of his ambitions and the turning point for his fortunes. In the tradition of Victorian theatre, Bill Alexander devised a coronation scene full of pomp and ceremony. Before the throne, Sher was stripped to the waist, revealing his deformity in stark contrast to the beauty of Anne. After faltering for a moment he slithered into the chair like a snake, his weakness exposed at his moment of triumph. Olivier's Richard, by contrast, eases into the throne and allowed himself a brief but pleasurable lift of the feet before resuming normal duties. In 1992 Annabelle Apison sat next to an empty throne paralysed in fear as first Richard's shadow, then his body lumbered towards the throne.

helping Richard achieve the crown.

Peggy Ashcroft broke with theatrical tradition by presenting Margaret as haggard and bedraggled, the mad woman in the attic. Her 'Can curses pierce the clouds and enter heaven?' [I.3.194] was directed to the heavens and she clearly expected an answer. In 1992 Cherry Morris poured a ritualistic circle of dust before pronouncing her prophesies. During the course of the play, as each awful

Richard's decline begins as he realizes that possession of the crown cannot satiate his desire for security, and the immediate attempts to secure his position only expose his limitations. Simon Russell Beale's Richard used Anne's presence to great effect. Leaning across her, he instructed Buckingham to 'give out / That Anne, my Queen, is sick and like to die' [IV.2.55-6]; in effect issuing her death warrant. Then, in the most brutal moment of the production, his next line was spoken to her as if calming a confused child, 'I must be married to my brother's daughter' [59]. Buckingham is the next to be dismissed. After pestering Richard for his promised reward, Richard rejects him with a blunt 'I am not in the giving vein today' [115]. For Michael Pennington, this realisation was no great surprise, understanding that both players were involved in a corrupt political game and

Right: *Shall I be tempted of the devil thus?*
Frances Tomelty and Antony Sher, 1984
Below right: Set design by William Dudley, 1984. **Below:**
Christopher Ravenscroft as Richmond and Antony Sher, 1984

that a loser was inevitable. Buckingham had been outwitted by his own creation.

Having destroyed marriage and friendship, Richard then turns to the most heinous of crimes, the murder of the two princes. Olivier draws Tyrrel to the throne and issues the order behind a cushion. This both shields the audience from the horror and pre-figures the smothering. Having isolated himself from the other characters, by murdering the princes, Richard begins to strain the bond he has created with the audience.

Before meeting the invading army of the Earl of Richmond at Bosworth, Richard seeks to arrange another expedient marriage, this time with Elizabeth's daughter. In 1992 Kate Duchêne was Richard's intellectual match. The honesty of her emotions and desperation of her plight made Richard's harsh insult,

'shallow, changing woman!' [IV.4.431] quite patently untrue. The scene mirrored the wooing of Anne but the energy and seductive improvisation had disappeared. All that remained was an ugly desperation for self-survival.

When Olivier learns that Richmond intends to possess the throne a dart of panic crosses his face. On screaming 'Is the chair empty?' [469] he rushes to sit in the vacant throne, like a child claiming security in a game of musical chairs. As he leaves to prepare for battle, the camera focuses on the empty throne, which remains cold and unconcerned with the forthcoming bloodshed.

The scene preceding Bosworth contains Richard's first moment of self-doubt as he wakes in panic from being visited by the ghosts of his previous victims. The confidence

and determination of the play's opening soliloquy are replaced by self-doubt and insecurity. Antony Sher spoke hesitantly, trying to retain some logic in his confused state:

What do I fear? Myself? There's none else by.
Richard loves Richard: that is, I am I.
Is there a murderer here? No. Yes, I am.

[V.3.183-5]

The broken confidence was continued in the oration to his troops. Richard faltered on 'What shall I say' [315] as if it were a genuine question, not a rhetorical device. When he finally generated some momentum, his words sounded hollow and unconvincing. Olivier

Below left: Simon Russell Beale and Annabelle Apsion, 1992
Below: Kate Duchêne as Prince Edward, Simon Russell Beale and Annabelle Apsion as the young Duke of York, 1992

delivers the final oration as a man who knows defeat is imminent but has decided to defy the odds with stirring resolve:

...let us to't pell mell
If not to heaven, then hand in hand to hell.

[313-14]

In the ensuing battle Richard once again proves that, for all his faults, he remains a skilled soldier. Sam Mendes included Margaret in the battle scenes, causing Richard to freeze during the final struggle with Richmond. Margaret's presence gave a voice to past miseries and enabled Richmond to administer the death blow. In 1984, the battle became a symbolic struggle of good against evil as Sher, troubled by conscience, paused in the midst of the duel. During the pause Richmond stabbed him in the back, leaving a final image of Richard kneeling at prayer, the hilt of the sword suggesting a crucifix. The effect was the triumph of good over evil, a providential reading whereby the sins of the country were purged in the death of the tyrant.

Michael Bogdanov demonstrated in 1989 that Richard's death is not necessarily cathartic. On Richard's famous last line, 'A horse! A horse! My kingdom for a horse! [V.4.13], the stage was plunged into darkness. There followed a stylized battle between two knights with Richmond, dressed in gold armour, triumphing in what appeared to be a heroic contest. This apparent heroism was undermined by setting Richmond's final speech as a political broadcast in a television studio. Richard's conspicuous evil had been replaced by a more insidious evil couched in a pleasant visage. True evil lay in cyclical political tyranny, not the individual.

James Shaw

NOTABLE PRODUCTIONS OF *RICHARD III*

	THEATRE	DIRECTOR	DESIGNER	PRINCIPALS
1955	London Film Productions	Laurence Olivier	Roger Furse	Laurence Olivier ....*Richard* John Gielgud.........................*Clarence* Claire Bloom ....*Lady Anne* The rôle of *Margaret* was cut Ralph Richardson ....*Buckingham* Mary Kerridge ....*Elizabeth*
1963	Royal Shakespeare Theatre, Stratford-upon-Avon	Peter Hall	John Bury	Ian Holm ....*Richard* Charles Kay ....*Clarence* Janet Suzman......................*Lady Anne* Peggy Ashcroft ....*Margaret* Tom Fleming ....*Buckingham* Susan Engel ....*Elizabeth*
1984	Royal Shakespeare Theatre, Stratford-upon-Avon	Bill Alexander	William Dudley	Antony Sher ....*Richard* Roger Allam ....*Clarence* Penny Downie ....*Lady Anne* Patricia Routledge ....*Margaret* Malcolm Storry ....*Buckingham* Frances Tomelty ....*Elizabeth*
1987	English Shakespeare Company	Michael Bogdanov	Chris Dyer	Andrew Jarvis.........................*Richard* John Dougall.........................*Clarence* Mary Rutherford ....*Lady Anne* June Watson.........................*Margaret* Michael Pennington ......*Buckingham* Lynette Davies.....................*Elizabeth*
1992	The Other Place, Stratford-upon-Avon	Sam Mendes	Tim Hatley	Simon Russell Beale ....*Richard* Simon Dormandy.................*Clarence* Annabelle Apsion ....*Lady Anne* Cherry Morris ....*Margaret* Stephen Boxer ....*Buckingham* Kate Duchêne ....*Elizabeth*

'THE FEARFUL PASSAGE OF THEIR DEATH-MARKED LOVE'

The Early Production History of *Romeo and Juliet*

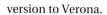

Romeo and Juliet was probably written in 1594 or 1595. Its main source was Arthur Brooke's poem of 1562, *The Tragical History of Romeus and Juliet*. There is no precise date for any early performance but the play was undoubtedly popular, because in 1597 a pirated text was published with a title page which boasts that it is 'An excellent conceited tragedie…often (with great applause) plaied publiquely.' Two years later the second Quarto was published assuring its readers that it was,.'Newly corrected, augmented and amended'. The first recorded performance was on 1 March 1662 of which Pepys wrote: '…it is the play of itself the worst that ever I heard in my life, and the worst acted…'. German versions were performed in Europe during the later sixteenth and early seventeenth centuries. In England, performances were alternated with a tragi-comical adaptation by James Howard. In 1679 Thomas Otway transferred the setting to Rome and changed the title to *The History and Fall of Caius Marius*. The play proved a popular and repeated success. Otway allowed his Lavinia (Juliet) to wake before the death of Marius Junior and this was imitated by Theophilus Cibber who returned his 1744

version to Verona.

Four years later Garrick aimed to 'clear the original as much as possible' from the 'Jingle and Quibble' and his production of 1748 (with some later modification by John Philip Kemble) was acted until the middle of the nineteenth century. Each of these adaptations still felt the need to allow Juliet to wake before Romeo died. Charlotte Cushman restored Shakespeare's text in a production at the Haymarket Theatre in 1845 in which she played Romeo to her sister's Juliet. At the New Theatre in 1935, John Gielgud and Laurence Olivier exchanged the rôles of Romeo and Mercutio which drew attention to the play's stark opposition of lyricism and direct and colloquial passion.

Top: Peggy Ashcroft as Juliet, painted by Ethel Gabain, 1935
Left: A drawing of Henry Irving as Romeo, 1882
Right: Fanny Kemble as Juliet, 1829

ROMEO AND JULIET

The uncompromising hostility of two families forbids
the natural growth of a youthful, committed love.

Romeo and Juliet begins at the end. In form and content the Prologue encapsulates what is to come. Its fourteen lines of tightly patterned verse are written in almost wholly regular iambic pentameter and in just two lines the regular rhythm is broken, allowing 'grudge' and 'break', 'death' and 'bury' to clash against each other. The disruption of social order and stability is signalled but there is no easy target for blame.

Franco Zeffirelli's film begins authoritatively with Olivier delivering the Prologue, but Bill Alexander dispensed with it. He propelled his American audience straight onto the streets of Verona. Two young men were seated at the back of the stage on a low wall which was flanked by ruins of Roman columns and a fountain. One of the men laid his dagger on the stone between them and each was poised to beat the other at laying a hand on the dagger. Their honing of reaction time was necessary in this anarchic world where the Prince was only one man amongst the crowd, unable to exercise any authority. In the Swan Theatre in 1989, the heat of Verona was suggested by the indolence of the young men, but a spark of opposition rapidly ignited. The conflict spreads through all levels of society and the tableau which ends the first scene of MacMillan's ballet shows the Capulets and Montagues confronting each other defiantly on either side of the Prince whilst, in front of him centre stage, there is a pile of bodies: the human cost of such intransigence.

The social hierarchy within Verona exerts a pressure upon attitudes and behaviour. Juliet is first seen with her Nurse and her mother. Bogdanov's modern Italian setting presented Lady Capulet as a sophisticated socialite who had little time to invest any interest in her daughter's development. As the Nurse recounted with pride and love her memories of Juliet's childhood, she implied that Lady Capulet had abdicated her responsibility:

My lord and you were then at Mantua.

[I.3.29]

In the New York production Lady Capulet was also glamorous and she seemed too young to be Juliet's mother. As she talked to Juliet about marriage she displayed a vicarious excitement which served to indicate a personal unhappiness that she was locked into a marriage with a man old enough to be her father. On the Swan stage, Linda Spurrier resented her daughter and excluded any possibility of physical contact; she was a deeply repressed and unhappy woman. In that same production Georgia Slowe's Juliet was convincingly naïve and her Nurse relaxed and good-humoured, whereas in New York, Miriam Healey-Louie showed her spirited independence unusually early. A middle-aged Nurse offered no physical affection to a vulnerable Juliet who was simply dressed in a white sheet.

Both Romeo and Juliet are provided with alternative partners. Romeo initially thinks that he is in love with Rosaline and MacMillan's ballet makes that the first relationship we witness. Romeo goes to the

Above: *The measure done, I'll watch her place of stand*
And touching hers, make blessèd my rude hand.
The Royal Ballet's 1965 version is still in the repertoire today.
Gelsey Kirkland as Juliet and Anthony Dowell as Romeo, 1986

Capulet ball to see her. Juliet is there to meet Paris. Her caution gives way to a fresh, engaging enthusiasm to dance and she and Romeo are also distinguished from the older, stately guests by their youthful good looks in Zeffirelli's opulent setting. At Stratford in 1986, a rock band played and Juliet was a debutante who failed to achieve the level of poise and sophistication her mother so clearly expected. Lady Capulet found Tybalt attractive and this interpretation intensified the emotional commitment of her grief at his

Above: *In fair Manhattan, where we lay our scene*
Richard Beymer as Tony (Romeo) is confronted by George
Chakiris as Bernardo (Tybalt) during the 'rumble' in the film
of Leonard Bernstein's *West Side Story*, 1961

death. In New York the Capulet ball combined ancient and modern motifs; the music and choreography were decorously Elizabethan while Romeo grabbed Juliet and held onto her with an urgency which an audience prepared to be cynical found convincing.

Juliet's despairing lament that Romeo comes from the wrong family:

O Romeo, Romeo! – wherefore art thou Romeo?

[II.2.33]

reflects the powerful force of the 'ancient grudge' which is tearing apart the society of Verona. The fate of the lovers is determined by stubborn, inflexible, flawed humanity and the timelessness of the theme is demon-

strated by the translation of the two households into Jets and Sharks in *West Side Story*. Bill Alexander's production sought to re-invent the balcony scene for its new audience and vigorously eschewed any hint of senti-mentality or poetic self-consciousness. One of the theatre's boxes provided the balcony. Juliet was unromantic to the point of appearing pedantic in her reasoning. Romeo's excited, even melodramatic:

I take thee at thy word...

[49]

brought an excited scream from Juliet. He was prepared to be inept to point her strength and pragmatism here. She called him back with a piercing 'pssst'.

Friar Laurence functions as a surrogate father to Romeo in parallel to the rôle of the Nurse in her relationship with Juliet. His spiri-tuality is infused with an empathy with the natural world and he is first seen as a creature of the night collecting 'baleful weeds' and 'precious juiced flowers' [II.3.4]. His solemn metaphor:

The earth that's nature's mother is her tomb.
What is her burying grave, that is her womb

[5-6]

brings us down to earth. His rôle does not always translate well to contemporary settings but Bill Alexander re-defined him as an urban priest. He was engagingly young with gold-rimmed glasses and an endearing habit of drawing out his religious exclama-tions: 'Holy Saint Francis' [61]. The audience was allowed to see his vulnerability and there was no sense that the spiritual world could provide easy solutions. His words were inef-fectual when confronted by the passionate urgency of the lovers' mutual desire, and his hope that their relationship might lead to a social harmony lacked conviction. They knelt at the low wall facing upstage then both turned at the same time to look for the Friar, who could only stare from downstage at their eager faces caught in a corridor of light. An interval followed, leaving the audience with the sense of a momentary stillness in the turbulent world.

There is an inevitability about the return to the tension on the streets. Benvolio character-istically urges caution and seeks to get Mercutio to 'retire' [III.1.1]. Michael Kitchen was at ease sipping his drink at a café table and Tybalt in black leather arrived in his

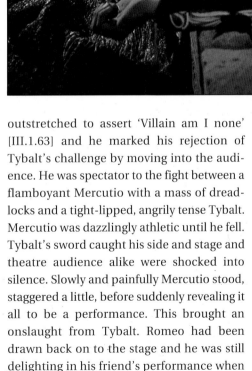

gleaming red Alfa Romeo sports car. Bogdanov explored the group dynamic and desire to impress which operate here. The fight began when the aerial was snapped from Tybalt's car to become an improvised sword. The fighting rapidly became vicious with chains and flick knives. When Romeo enters he is at odds with his peer group. Against the poetic lyricism of his words: 'love', 'greeting', 'tender', 'dearly', 'gentle', resounds the technical jargon of combat: 'Alla stoccata', 'passado' as Mercutio jars at Romeo's 'submission' [72]. The men on the streets of Verona are wedded to the imperative expressed at the beginning of the play: 'draw, if you be men' [I.1.61].

Mark Niebuhr's Romeo stood with hands outstretched to assert 'Villain am I none' [III.1.63] and he marked his rejection of Tybalt's challenge by moving into the audience. He was spectator to the fight between a flamboyant Mercutio with a mass of dreadlocks and a tight-lipped, angrily tense Tybalt. Mercutio was dazzlingly athletic until he fell. Tybalt's sword caught his side and stage and theatre audience alike were shocked into silence. Slowly and painfully Mercutio stood, staggered a little, before suddenly revealing it all to be a performance. This brought an onslaught from Tybalt. Romeo had been drawn back on to the stage and he was still delighting in his friend's performance when Mercutio was wounded. Romeo continued to laugh: 'Courage, man. The hurt cannot be

Above left: *what envious streaks / Do lace the severing clouds in yonder East.* Leonard Whiting and Olivia Hussey, 1968
Above: *This is thy sheath; there rust, and let me die.* Olivia Hussey and Leonard Whiting, 1968

much.' [95] Mercutio's underplaying of his injury came as a response to Romeo's mood and 'I thought all for the best' [104] was exposed for its inadequacy. Romeo's change of heart was sudden and determined. He fought Tybalt passionately, but Tybalt was better. Disarmed by Tybalt's superior skill, Romeo fled downstage where, desperate and frightened, he picked up a gun, turned and shot him. There was silence. Crouched downstage Romeo looked aghast at the gun. His actions were instinctive, convincingly derived from fear and self-preservation.

Once again the Prince surveys a scene of violent death born of familial hostility. Despite Benvolio's objective account, the Prince banishes Romeo. His judgment is clearly affected by the way in which Mercutio's death has drawn his own family into the conflict between the Capulets and the Montagues:

My blood for your rude brawls doth lie a-bleeding.

[189]

MacMillan dispenses with the Prince's entrance here, focusing instead upon Lady Capulet's grief at Tybalt's death. Her violent grief makes Romeo's attempts to explain futile and Benvolio rushes him away leaving a tableau of agonised loss which Lord Capulet

Right: Hugh Quarshie as Tybalt, Michael Kitchen as Mercutio and Martin Jacobs as Benvolio, 1986. **Below right:** Sean Bean, Hugh Quarshie and Michael Kitchen, 1986. **Below:** Sean Bean, Martin Jacobs as Benvolio and Donald McBride as Peter, 1986

Left: *Thou wast the prettiest babe that e'er I nursed*
Anna Nygh as Lady Capulet, Dilys Laye as the Nurse and
Niamh Cusack, 1986
Right: *O, thinkest thou we shall ever meet again?*
Georgia Slowe and Mark Rylance, 1989

can do nothing to assuage. He stands on the upper level looking down at his wife rocking Tybalt's corpse. Also looking down is a bedraggled, maimed beggar. He symbolises the world's frailty generally but more precisely the particular cruelty and inadequacy of Verona.

Not knowing what has happened, Juliet thinks about her wedding night. Georgia Slowe was the impatient child who wants to wear her new clothes and yet intuitively her metaphor:

> O I have bought the mansion of a love,
> But not possessed it
>
> [III.2.26]

conveys deep sexual longing. Zeffirelli sets the second balcony scene in Juliet's bedroom, dwelling on the immediacy of the lovers' sexual awakening and stage productions frequently give prominence to a bed. In New York the emphasis was less on the physical consummation that had taken place than on an easy intimacy, which was given a contemporary emblem with Juliet wearing Romeo's

jacket round her shoulders. When she rushed to her mother on: 'Madam, I am not well' [III.5.68] expressing a spontaneous need for maternal affection, Lady Capulet was angered by her daughter's statement, 'I will not marry yet' [121] and hit her shockingly hard on:

> Here comes your father. Tell him so yourself
> And see how he will take it at your hands.
>
> [124-5]

Linda Spurrier's Lady Capulet could not cope with her daughter's emotions and an audience was more inclined to pity than condemn her coolness as Juliet begged: 'O sweet my mother, cast me not away!' [199].

Capulet moves swiftly from concerned father to violent tyrant. His instinct is to resort to physical violence when he cannot get his own way: 'My fingers itch' [164]. Olivia Hussey is an emotional Juliet who cries and screams almost hysterically as her parents intimidate her. MacMillan's choreography clearly crafts Juliet's isolation in this scene as her pleas to her father, mother and the Nurse fail and she is left crouched, sobbing on the floor. As she clutches her shawl we see something of the child with her comfort blanket but then she moves to sit on the edge of the bed, absolutely still. For sixteen bars of stillness we share her thoughts and the tableau reflects a control and determination in Juliet which contrasts strongly with her darting, agonised searching for support in the previous scene. After this mental journey the decision to take the Friar's potion and feign her own death will be relatively easy. As Anna Nygh knelt beside what she took to be her daughter's corpse, she paused to ease up her skirt. Even at this

moment her concern for appearance took precedence. Friar Laurence pointed out in an uncompromisingly critical way his awareness of the Capulets' motives behind their arrangements for their daughter's marriage:

> The most you sought was her promotion.
>
> [IV.5.71]

Zeffirelli's film offers a far more traditional interpretation without social commentary. The swelling music and the visual beauty give

NOTABLE PRODUCTIONS OF *ROMEO AND JULIET*

	THEATRE	DIRECTOR	DESIGNER	PRINCIPALS
1965	The Royal Ballet at The Royal Opera House, Covent Garden	Choreog. Kenneth MacMillan	Nicholas Georgiadis	Margot Fonteyn ....*Juliet* Rudolf Nureyev ....*Romeo*

A film of Fonteyn and Nureyev was released in 1966 and a video recording was made in 1984 with Alessandra Ferri and Wayne Eagling

	THEATRE	DIRECTOR	DESIGNER	PRINCIPALS
1968	Paramount	Franco Zeffirelli		Leonard Whiting ....*Romeo* Olivia Hussey ....*Juliet*
1986	Royal Shakespeare Theatre, Stratford-upon-Avon	Michael Bogdanov	Chris Dyer	Sean Bean ....*Romeo* Niamh Cusack ....*Juliet*
1989	Swan Theatre, Stratford-upon-Avon	Terry Hands	Farrah	Mark Rylance ....*Romeo* Georgia Slowe.............................*Juliet*
1991	Victory Theatre, New York	Bill Alexander	Fotini Dimou	Mark Niebuhr ....*Romeo* Miriam Healy-Louie ....*Juliet*
1992	The Birmingham Royal Ballet at the Birmingham Hippodrome	Choreog. Kenneth MacMillan	Paul Andrews	Nina Ananiashvili ....*Juliet* Kevin O'Hare ....*Romeo*

Above: *I have more care to stay than will to go.*
Come, death, and welcome! Juliet wills it so.
Mark Rylance and Georgia Slowe, 1989

the closing sequence a powerfully emotional impact. In New York, as Romeo drank the poison, Juliet moved her hand. Then as he turned to reach her, he saw her hand reach out to him in a moment which recalled earlier moments at the ball and in the balcony scene. It made the ending excruciatingly painful, drawing attention to the tragic mis-timings of their love. Romeo died in agony with his realisation that Juliet lived and her death was as carefully grounded in reality. It hurt to push in the dagger.

Consistent with Bogdanov's indictment of contemporary society, Romeo used a hypodermic syringe to kill himself. The end of the play was cut so that in the blackout which immediately followed the lovers' suicide, Romeo and Juliet in golden cloaks became the 'statue(s) in pure gold' [V.3.299] that their fathers promise at the end of the play. Reporters and photographers rushed down the aisles of the theatre to capture the story and Lord Capulet read a prepared statement: the play's Prologue re-cast in the past tense. Bogdanov took the Prince's words 'All are punished' [295] and applied them disconcertingly to us all. In the capitalist, competitive world of this Verona, the priorities remained wealth, status and power. There was no room for gentleness or fellow-feeling. The story of the star-crossed lovers was being exploited by the families and the media for its commercial possibilities.

Pamela Mason

THE TAMING OF THE SHREW

A theatrical frame complicates an audience's response
to the definition of the rôles people play within marriage.

The *Taming of the Shrew* deals with the subjugation of a female character reviled as a 'shrew' because she is aggressive, vocal in her unhappiness and occasionally violent. The taming is demonstrated in public when the formerly obstreperous Katherina acts as the demure wife and argues for the total submission of all wives to their husbands. Thus one of the major challenges for a modern performer playing Katherina is how to play this submission. Seriously? Ironically? As if in a playful partnership with Petruchio? As a lobotomised or bashed wife?

Any decision made about the playing of this speech is further complicated by the question of whether or not the production should include the full Sly framework, which generates an alienation effect. As Katherina's submission is read simplistically by the unsophisticated Sly, the framework effectively encourages the audience not to fall into the trap of reading the taming of Katherina as simply as he does. The Sly framework undercuts the inner play further by offering an emblem for Katherina as a male construction of femaleness; 'Kate' is not a 'real' woman and in the Elizabethan playhouse 'she' would have been played by a boy; the Sly framework points to this by showing the page Bartholomew acting as Sly's wife. When the full Sly framework is used, this image of male constructed femininity is kept before the audience for most of the play, not just the opening scenes. As Sly is particularly active when Katherina submits over the issue of what constitutes the sun and what the moon,

and before and after her more public submission in the final scene, it seems that the successful conclusion of the taming process originally came equipped with a comic alienation effect.

This was certainly the effect generated by Peter Dews' production for the Stratford, Ontario, festival of 1982 which used the full framework and emphasised the metatheatricality of *The Shrew*. This production not only had Sly, Bartholomew and the Lord always on

Above: – *Good morrow, Kate – for that's your name I hear.*
– *Well, have you heard, but something hard of hearing;*
They call me Katherine that do talk of me.
Elizabeth Taylor, 1966

display on the upper stage area, but also had the players of the Katherina and Petruchio story constantly acknowledging their onstage audience's presence. They bowed and curtseyed to the Lord, Sly and to the audience on the main stage level. This audience also took small rôles, such as Petruchio's servants, and

'I AM PEREMPTORY AS SHE IS PROUD-MINDED'

The Early Production History of *The Taming of the Shrew*

The *Taming of the Shrew* may represent a cut version of what Shakespeare originally wrote. The evidence for this is provided by the existence of *The Taming of A Shrew* (1594), a text generally believed to be either a 'bad' quarto or a source for *The Shrew*. *The Taming of A Shrew* has a framework which expands on *The Shrew*'s induction scenes where the tinker Christopher Sly is tricked into believing he is a lord. In *A Shrew* Sly stays onstage for most of the play, commenting on the action. At the end he 'wakes up' believing he has dreamt how to tame his wife. Original performances of *The Shrew* may have included a full framework like that of *A Shrew* with the Sly scenes cut later for pragmatic reasons.

John Fletcher wrote a sequel around 1611 entitled *The Woman's Prize, or The Tamer Tamed*. In this play Katherina has died and Petruchio marries again but his second wife tames him. A Restoration adaptation of *The Taming of the Shrew* appeared in John Lacey's *Sauny the Scot* where Katherina is threatened with such violence as having

her teeth pulled out. In the eighteenth century James Worsdale adapted *The Taming of the Shrew* as *A Cure for a Scold*. This was superseded by Garrick's *Catharine and Petruchio* in 1754 which simply presented the shrew taming plot.

The Shrew continues to be very popular in the theatre, and despite feminist critiques of the play's 'jokes', it is still often presented as a jolly romp. Recently it has become increasingly common for the whole Sly framework from *A Shrew* to be performed. *The Taming of the Shrew* has also inspired the musical, *Kiss Me Kate*, where the husband and wife team playing Katherina and Petruchio fight as much as the characters they are playing but end up reconciled. Charles Marowitz adapted the play in 1975, stressing the obnoxiousness of Petruchio's actions, and in his version Kate is raped.

A CURE FOR A SCOLD. A Ballad FARCE OF TWO ACTS.

(*Founded upon* SHAKESPEAR'S *taming of a Shrew*)

As it is Acted by his Majesty's Company of Comedians at the Theatre Royal in *Drury-Lane*.

By J. WORSDALE, Portrait-Painter.

LONDON:
Printed for L. GILLIVER, at *Homer's* Head, *Fleetstreet.*
(Price One Shilling.)

Top: John Fletcher, 1579–1625
Left: James Worsdale's adaptation included an abundance of sentimental songs, 1735
Right: Charles Marowitz

moved furniture and played music when needed. The video of this production provides an extremely useful contrast with the more readily available videos of the Zeffirelli film and the BBC production which completely omit the Sly framework, not even playing the induction scenes which are present in the First Folio text.

Bill Alexander's production expanded the Sly framework considerably and had a cast list which featured such characters as Rupert Llewellyn and Lady Sarah Ormsby. These were part of a group of hooray Henries who replaced the Lord's party in the Induction of *The Shrew*. Sometimes this framework was very effective: although Sly and his tormentors were all in modern dress, as were the actors when they first arrived, the inner play was performed in Elizabethan dress in Lord Simon's ancestral home, which was an Elizabethan mansion. The implication was that Lord Simon and his cronies, by choosing to watch such a piece of 'entertainment', were more in tune with Elizabethan than twentieth-century gender politics. When Katherina submitted at the end of the inner play, Lord Simon's girlfriend, Lady Sarah, seemed to realise that she was risking a not dissimilar fate, and she clearly disengaged herself from Lord Simon. The submission was a sixteenth-century event and the twentieth-century woman would not accept it.

However, Alexander's primary focus was on the class hostility between the actors and their patrons. This was made clear when the aristocrats were co-opted into performing in the inner play as Petruchio's servants; they were handed scripts and treated roughly – Lady Sarah in particular got kicked around by Petruchio when she was taking off his boots,

Above right *For I am he am born to tame you, Kate,*
and right: *And bring you from a wild Kate to a Kate*
Conformable as other household Kates.
Elizabeth Taylor and Richard Burton, 1966

Above and right: Elizabeth Taylor and Richard Burton, 1966
Below right: Paul Jones as Fred Graham (Petruchio) and
Nichola McAuliffe as Lilli Vanessi (Katherina) in the RSC revival
of Cole Porter's 1948 musical adaptation, *Kiss Me Kate*, 1987

again underlining the risk she was running in associating with Lord Simon, the modern Petruchio. The main problem with all this inventiveness was that Katherina's submission speech was almost sidelined – as indeed was the whole inner play – by the business of the expanded Sly framework.

Alexander's production frankly acknowledged *The Shrew*'s potential for misogyny, but many other directors and critics have been keen to rescue Shakespeare from the fate of being cast as a misogynist. In criticism, for example, it has sometimes been claimed that Shakespeare deserves credit because *The Taming of the Shrew* is not as offensive as other shrew taming texts of the Middle Ages and Renaissance. In the theatre, directors such as Michael Bogdanov have claimed Shakespeare as a feminist for portraying his own culture's gender politics and confronting his contemporaries with an unpalatable

vision of their own misogyny. Bogdanov's own production was in modern dress and included a sensational entrance by Petruchio on a motorbike. This was actually the second sensational entrance by the actor Jonathan Pryce who doubled Petruchio and Sly, or at least Sly metamorphosed into a drunken tramp. Before the audience realised the play had begun, he erupted on stage and wrecked the scenery despite the apparent efforts of an usherette (Paola Dionisotti) to stop him. On some nights members of the audience tried to help to eject the trouble maker. This meta-theatrical prologue substituted for the Sly induction scenes. The production was notable for stressing the appalling way that Petruchio behaves towards Katherina, and the modern dress confronted contemporary audiences with the idea that such oppression still exists and is not confined to sixteenth-century plays.

A more common approach to rescuing Shakespeare from being labelled a misogynist is to stress how much Katherina is actually gaining from her experience; for example, she

Above right: Sir Simon's friends and Anton Lesser, 1992
Right: Amanda Harris and Rebecca Saire as Bianca, 1992
Below right: Amanda Harris, 1992

Above: – *Now pray thee, love, stay.*
– *Is not this well? Come, my sweet Kate,*
Better once than never, for never too late.
Anton Lesser and Amanda Harris, 1992

learns to play, to jest, or to be at peace. Petruchio becomes Katherina's psychotherapist, liberating her from the psychological trap of her anger and shrewishness. This was Jonathan Miller's approach in the BBC production. He abandoned the Sly framework entirely, claiming it was essentially a theatrical device (although he still did not use Sly when he directed the play in the theatre in 1987). Miller directed the BBC *Shrew* as a piece of realistic social drama. Many shots are convincing realisations of Vermeer interiors. The emphasis on realistic and understated characterisation is pronounced, particularly in John Cleese's playing of Petruchio. Cleese was once very much associated with his television rôles in *Monty Python* and his creation of Basil Fawlty. He evokes something of the

manic quality of these rôles in his Petruchio, but speaks softly and earnestly to Katherina whenever he is really serious about what he is saying. The whole production's earnestness about domestic harmony culminates in the final moments when all the characters gather together to sing a hymn on the subject which serves to validate Petruchio's campaign. Stripped of the Sly framework, the production offers Katherina's submission as a simple *desideratum*.

Fortunately Bianca and the widow offer alternative views to onstage and offstage male approbation towards Katherina's submission;

Bianca comments 'Fie, what a foolish duty call you this?' [V.2.124]. However, the sub-plot of Bianca and her wooers is often cut back or given scant attention compared with the Katherina and Petruchio story. Alexander's production was again remarkable in making Bianca a much more challenging character, more interested in pursuing a relationship with Tranio than with her husband, Lucentio. A strong Bianca also complicates the portrait of sisterhood in the play; Katherina beats Bianca and Bianca knows how to make Katherina suffer because of the danger of Katherina graduating from one patriarchal stereotype (shrew) to another (old maid). A strong Bianca renders this portrait of distorted sisterhood serious and provocative; by contrast, the popular spoilt schoolgirl version of Bianca gets only easy laughs.

The Taming of the Shrew is one of the few plays Shakespeare wrote dealing with his own class, the bourgeoisie. The economics of bourgeois marriage and in particular, the dowry system are clearly in focus, as is the objectification of women that such a system entails. This is exacerbated by Baptista's decision to withhold his attractive goods (Bianca) until he has disposed of his unattractive goods (Katherina). Economics are also crucial in the betting at the end of the play when Katherina wins a second dowry for Petruchio.

The economic basis of Katherina's and Petruchio's marriage is very much emphasised in Zeffirelli's film version of *The Shrew*, a production which mirrored the offscreen turbulence of the love affair between its stars, Elizabeth Taylor and Richard Burton. Settings are very lush, realistic and romantic, with beautifully Italianate backgrounds, gorgeous palaces and clothes, and convincingly realistic social detail. It is also a very crowded production and the thousands of extras all help to create a vivid sense of a bustling community.

Given the commitment to film realism it is not surprising that there is no alienating Sly framework; however, the detailed realism helps create an emphasis on the acquisitive materialism of the society depicted and on the importance of money in negotiating marriages. Katherina is made very aware of the fact that money is involved in marrying her off – she surreptitiously watches the money changing hands. During one of the many wild chases in this production which involves Katherina running along the roof top, Burton makes it clear that his Petruchio is worried primarily about the possible loss of his money if Katherina were to fall. This obsession with money is something the film suggests needs to be cured in Petruchio, as does his heavy drinking, which owes more to Burton's real life notorious indulgence than it does to Shakespeare's text. It is Katherina's disapproving gaze which finally stops Petruchio on the road to alcoholism and as this gaze is juxtaposed with Katherina gazing fondly on some adorable children it is clear that Zeffirelli signals the approach of conventional domestic bliss. This is anticipated when Katherina, after her first night in Petruchio's home, starts spring cleaning and home improvements.

Zeffirelli cut the text radically and very little is left except for what is needed to make sense of the story and carry the narrative at a galloping speed. The pacing is also affected by the recurrent chase motif; even at the end of the play, after the submission speech, Petruchio has to chase after Katherina who disappears through the crowd of guests. Overall Zeffirelli's film is too much of a jolly romp, but at least it also suggests that some taming of Petruchio is in order.

One performance possibility which is uncommon in the twentieth century is to have a man play Katherina, stressing that 'she' is a male construction, created by a male author for a boy player to perform. The Mediaeval Players explored this idea in 1985 in a gender-bending production which not only had Katherina and Bianca played by men but also used the full Sly framework and had Mark Heap double Katherina and the Lord, while Mark Saban played Petruchio and Sly. Several male rôles were played by women. The production was played in *commedia* style and this, coupled with the fact that a male performer was playing Kate, seemed to give the audience permission to laugh more than is usual in modern productions of *The Taming of the Shrew*.

Elizabeth Schafer

NOTABLE PRODUCTIONS OF *THE TAMING OF THE SHREW*

	THEATRE	DIRECTOR	DESIGNER	PRINCIPALS
1966	Royal Films, FAI	Franco Zeffirelli	Renzo Mongiardino, Danilo Donati	Elizabeth Taylor ....*Katherina* Richard Burton ....*Petruchio*
1978	Royal Shakespeare Theatre, Stratford-upon-Avon	Michael Bogdanov	Chris Dyer	Paolo Dionisotti ....*Katherina* Jonathan Pryce ....*Petruchio*
1980	BBC-tv	Jonathan Miller	Colin Lowrey, Alun Hughes	Sarah Badel.....................*Katherina* Jonathan Cleese ....*Petruchio*
1982	The Shakespearean Festival Theatre, Stratford, Ontario	Peter Dews	Susan Benson	Sharry Flett ....*Katherina* Len Cariou.....................*Petruchio*
1992	Royal Shakespeare Theatre, Stratford-upon-Avon	Bill Alexander	Tim Goodchild	Amanda Harris.................*Katherina* Anton Lesser ....*Petruchio*

'BY MY SO POTENT ART'

The Early Production History of *The Tempest*

The only two performances of *The Tempest* recorded during Shakespeare's lifetime were at court: on Hallowmass night 1611, and during the wedding festivities for James' daughter, Elizabeth, to the Elector Palatine. No records exist of performances at the Globe or at Blackfriars, although in the preface to his adaptation of the play, William Davenant claimed that *The Tempest* had been performed successfully at Blackfriars.

The stage history of *The Tempest* was shaped to a considerable degree by Davenant's adaptation of 1667. Catering to Restoration tastes, *The Enchanted Island* increased the play's scenic spectacle and love interest. Davenant introduced a companion for Ariel and sisters for Caliban and Miranda, calling them Sycorax and Dorinda. Dorinda also served as mate for Hippolito, a young man who, mirroring Miranda, had never seen a woman before. In 1674, Thomas Shadwell modelled an opera on Davenant's version. Both adaptations enjoyed tremendous popularity holding the stage for the next 150 years.

Although eighteenth century scholars showed an increasing interest in Shakespeare's play, the stage preferred Davenant's and Shadwell's adaptations. Only two attempts were made at restoring the original; a 1746 Drury Lane production was followed by David Garrick's more successful attempt eleven years later. In 1838, Macready returned to Shakespeare's own text but this did not mean the reduction of the lavish sets which were the hallmark of nineteenth century performances. In Charles Kean's 1857 production at the Princess' Theatre, the elaborate stage machinery considerably reduced the acting space and increased the running time to five hours. Not until the early twentieth century did stagings of *The Tempest* turn to simpler, more flexible sets reducing the spectacular visual effects to a bare minimum.

Top: Elizabeth of Bohemia (1596–1662) was married in 1613
Left: An engraving of the last scene at the Princess's Theatre, 1857
Right: Killing crocodiles, an illustration from Theodore de Bry's *Historia Americae*, 1590

THE TEMPEST

*A remote island is the testing ground for a reflective debate
upon the influence of nature and nurture.*

At the centre of *The Tempest* is the figure Prospero who controls the play's action. In performance, his age and the nature of his magic influence the conception of the character. In Charles Laughton's serene, majestic octogenarian whose 'Every third thought' was indeed his grave [V.1.312], Prospero's desire to regain his dukedom was less immediate and disturbing than in Derek Jacobi's vigorous middle-aged portrayal. While Prospero's magic is often interpreted as wholly benevolent, it had strong elements of necromancy in both Jacobi's and Michael Bryant's interpretations. But whereas the attempts at playing God weighed heavy on Bryant and made him yearn for God's forgiveness, Jacobi found it hard to exchange the rôle of omnipotent magus for that of a mortal duke.

The creation of the storm which opens *The Tempest* is the first example of magical powers. Although it surprises the audience ignorant of Prospero's involvement, a production can establish the sense of an omnipotent stage manager by showing him producing the storm, as did Tom Fleming's furious Prospero. Cheek by Jowl presented the storm as the result of an improvisation exercise whipped up by Timothy Walker's tyrannical actor-director. Derek Jarman presented the storm as Prospero's dream, thus giving his subconscious feelings as much power as his conscious thoughts. But the storm scene can also establish the powers of someone other than Prospero. Sam Mendes had his Ariel stand on top of a skip swinging a lantern and

Above: *If thou more murmur'st, I will rend an oak,
And peg thee in his knotty entrails, till
Thou hast howled away twelve winters.*
Derek Jacobi and Mark Rylance, 1982

thereby initiate the storm. Not until halfway through the scene did Prospero appear behind a transparent gauze on top of a stepladder supervising his servant's actions. The production's first images introduced a collision of the master's will with that of the servant by presenting an Ariel powerful in his own right, who made it necessary for Prospero to check up on him.

In the long scene following the storm, Prospero is confronted with the passionate, concerned reproaches of his daughter Miranda. Neglecting the ambivalences apparent in her impetuosity, inquisitiveness and independence of mind, most productions stress her innocence and obedience as well as her function as a catalyst. She brings out Prospero's potential for tenderness, but also reveals his hidden obsessions. Thus, John Wood's and Michael Bryant's repeated requests for Miranda's attention during the description of the usurpation signalled their absorption in the past and the intense pain with which Prospero relived the past injustice suffered at the hands of his brother, Antonio.

Prospero's servants, Ariel and Caliban, are often described as symbolising two opposing forces in Prospero and in man in general. Ariel represents art, imagination and the supremacy of the mind, whereas Caliban stands for the gratification of man's animal impulses. Peter Hall substituted the Freudian concepts of sublimation and libido for the more general contrast between art and nature through his use of an asexual Ariel and a naked Caliban whose genitals were muzzled by a male version of a chastity belt. Nicholas Hytner contrasted air and earth in his presentation of Prospero's two servants by juxtaposing a deformed, mud-caked, heavy Caliban with an Ariel whose white wig and trousers decorated with little feathers not only suggested the airy element to which he belonged, but together with his habit of ascending the sides of the proscenium arch

Above: *How fine my master is! I am afraid He will chastise me.*
Bob Peck as Caliban and Derek Jacobi, 1982
Right: *They are both in either's powers*
James Purefoy as Ferdinand, Melanie Thaw as Miranda, Duncan Bell as Ariel and John Wood, 1988

made him seem almost to disappear into the blue and white of the cyclorama.

Characteristic of Prospero's relationship with his servants is the rigid control he achieves over them by depriving them of their liberty. Caliban is styed in 'this hard rock' [I.2.343] and Ariel is warned that Prospero:

> **will rend an oak,**
> **And peg thee in his knotty entrails, till**
> **Thou hast howled away twelve winters**
>
> [294-6]

thereby threatening to aggravate the punishment Ariel had suffered at the hands of the witch Sycorax, who had imprisoned him within 'a cloven pine' [277]. The horror of this threat was visualised when Alec McCowen presented a cone to Ariel, who seemed to realise with terror that it came from the very pine in which he had been imprisoned. Yet, the play counterbalances the dictatorial

control over Ariel with hints of affection, notably in Ariel's question, 'Do you love me, master? No?', to which Prospero answers, 'Dearly, my delicate Ariel' [IV.1.48-9]. It is the first time Prospero turns to another creature in unselfish affection, apart from his love for Miranda, and the line marks the beginning of the end of his desire for revenge, a development which reaches its climax in his assertion that:

> **Yet with my nobler reason 'gainst my fury**
> **Do I take part**

because he finally finds that:

> **The rarer action is**
> **In virtue than in vengeance.**
>
> [V.1.26-8]

However, directed not to one of his fellow human beings but to a spirit he is about to

Above: *This island's mine, by Sycorax my mother*
John Kane as Caliban at the Royal Shakespeare Theatre, 1988

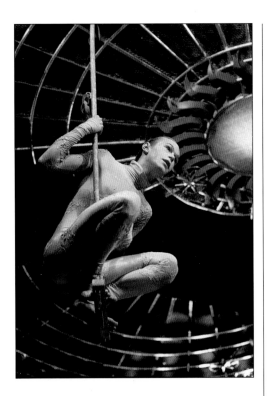

release, these lines highlight Prospero's isolation due to his basic inability to communicate. Thus Ian Richardson emerged as a deeply lonely figure, who, stretching out his hand to reach for Ben Kingsley's completely unmoved Ariel, only grasped the air.

To interpret Caliban as representing the dark side of humanity with its unchecked animal impulses, especially unbridled sexual desire, is, as are most assumptions about *The Tempest*, only half the story. He also speaks some of the most beautiful lines in the play. Regarding Caliban's claim to the island 'by Sycorax my mother' [I.2.331] as valid and Prospero's contention that he was:

> **got by the devil himself**
> **Upon thy wicked dam**
>
> [319-20]

as prejudiced, has served as a starting point for interpretations sympathetic to Caliban.

Above left: Steven Mackintosh as Ariel at the National Theatre, 1988.
Above: Michael Bryant, 1988
Above right: Timothy Walker, 1988
Right: Max von Sydow and Cyril Nri as Ariel, 1988
Below right: Johanna Benyon as Ceres, 1993

The most striking examples of such an approach were Jonathan Miller's productions at the Mermaid Theatre in 1970 and at the Old Vic in 1988, where the play emerged as a parable for colonisation. Rudolph Walker's enslaved black Caliban exchanged the white master Prospero for the black master Ariel, who at the end of the play reassembled Prospero's discarded staff and held it threateningly over Caliban and his fellow-islanders. In *La Tempête*, Peter Brook turned Miller's concept on its head. David Bennent's dwarfish, white Caliban was an intruder into the serene primitive culture of a black Prospero and Ariel.

The past looms large in *The Tempest*, as

NOTABLE PRODUCTIONS OF *THE TEMPEST*

	THEATRE	DIRECTOR	DESIGNER	PRINCIPALS
1934	The Old Vic, London	Tyrone Guthrie	Tyrone Guthrie	Charles Laughton..................*Prospero* Elsa Lanchester ....*Ariel*
1963	Royal Shakespeare Theatre, Stratford-upon-Avon	Clifford Williams with Peter Brook	Abd'Elkader Farrah	Tom Fleming ....*Prospero*
1970	Royal Shakespeare Theatre, Stratford-upon-Avon	John Barton	Christopher Morley with Ann Curtis	Ian Richardson ....*Prospero* Ben Kingsley ....*Caliban*
1979	BBC-tv	John Gorrie	Paul Joel	Michael Hordern ....*Prospero*
1982	Royal Shakespeare Theatre, Stratford-upon-Avon	Ron Daniels	Maria Bjørnson	Derek Jacobi ....*Prospero* Mark Rylance...............................*Ariel*
1988	National Theatre, London	Peter Hall	Alison Chitty	Michael Bryant ....*Prospero*

Above: *I am your wife, if you will marry me.*
If not, I'll die your maid.
Sarah Woodward as Miranda and Mark Lewis Jones as
Ferdinand, 1993

Prospero's extensive reminiscence in his first scene with Miranda suggests. The play's action is a controlled re-enactment of the past with the purpose of avoiding earlier mistakes. Instead of 'neglecting worldly ends' [89] as in Milan twelve years before, Prospero now has to act on a tight schedule, for, as he says himself:

> **my zenith doth depend upon**
> **A most auspicious star, whose influence**
> **If now I court not, but omit, my fortunes**
> **Will ever after droop.**
>
> [181-4]

Recovering his kingdom is tied to the reformation of his enemies, notably his brother

and Alonso, the King of Naples. The text leaves open the precise extent to which Prospero has set up the opportunity for Antonio and Sebastian to plan the murder of Alonso. With the help of his spirits, Sotigui Konyaté induced Alonso's and his courtiers' 'strange drowsiness' [II.1.202] and so allowed the opportunity for Antonio's second conspiracy, which echoed the past usurpation and provided Prospero with further proof of his brother's evil nature. Alec McCowen reinforced the sense of Prospero's control over this usurpation by appearing again behind the gauze backdrop.

The plot involving Caliban, Stephano and Trinculo comically mirrors past and present conspiracies. The ridiculous failure of the

plans of these three characters, who end up in a stinking puddle smelling of 'all horse-piss' [IV.1.199], indicates the ultimate harmlessness of their pretensions. Yet there is a streak of nastiness in Stephano and the fact that the thought of Caliban and his conspiracy disrupts the betrothal masque for Ferdinand and Miranda hints at the potential threat these three characters pose to Prospero. David Troughton's Caliban appeared disguised as one of the reapers in the masque, which dispersed when he revealed himself.

Prospero inflicts punishment for past and present rebellion upon most characters in the play. The punishment can result from his desire for revenge or his wish to reform his enemies. Caliban's imprisonment has a didactic function, albeit initially ineffectual. His ordeal, however, finally makes him 'seek for grace' [V.1.296]. Slaving as a 'patient logman' [III.1.67], Ferdinand learns to appreciate Miranda, 'the prize' of his labour [I.2.453]. Alonso's supposed loss of his son generates repentance for his part in the usurpation. Productions have tackled the question of Prospero's motivation for punishing his enemies in different ways. While Michael Hordern and Alec McCowen emerged as rather avuncular, schoolmasterly figures pursuing forgiveness rather than revenge from the beginning, Michael Bryant and Derek Jacobi did not consider forgiveness until Ariel told them that his 'affections/ Would become tender [...] were [he] human' [V.1.17–19].

Seeking to reconcile himself with his enemies and to recover his lost dukedom, Prospero assembles all the characters on stage in the final scene. The extent of his success, however, is open to question. Whereas Alonso is truly penitent, Sebastian's and Antonio's reactions to their experience on the island allow for opposing interpretations. Antonio's silence can be a sign of his shame and express contrition. Sebastian's words commenting on the appearance of Ferdinand and Miranda, 'A most high miracle' [177], may indicate his amazement and acceptance of a benign providence. Both appear to be ready for the final reconciliation. Stressing the personal liberation of all characters on Prospero's island, *La Tempête* included the two wicked brothers in the final mood of reconciliation. Most modern productions, however, make Sebastian's lines ironic and present Antonio's silence as evidence of his unwillingness to return the

Right: *Yea, yea, my lord, I'll yield him thee asleep,*
Where thou mayest knock a nail into his head.
Mark Lockyer as Stephano and David Troughton, 1993

NOTABLE PRODUCTIONS OF *THE TEMPEST*

	THEATRE	DIRECTOR	DESIGNER	PRINCIPALS
1988	Cheek by Jowl	Declan Donnellan	Nick Ormerod	Timothy Walker ....*Prospero*
1988	Royal Shakespeare Theatre, Stratford-upon-Avon	Nicholas Hytner	David Fielding	John Wood ....*Prospero* Richard Haddon Haines ....*Antonio*
1988	The Old Vic, London	Jonathan Miller	Richard Hudson	Max von Sydow ....*Prospero* Rudolph Walker....................*Caliban*
1990	Théâtre des Bouffes du Nord, Paris, *La Tempête*	Peter Brook	Chloe Obolensky	Sotigui Konyaté ....*Prospero* David Bennent......................*Caliban*
1993	Royal Shakespeare Theatre, Stratford-upon-Avon	Sam Mendes	Anthony Ward	Alec McCowen ....*Prospero* David Troughton...................*Caliban* James Hayes...........................*Antonio*

207

Above: *Go, charge my goblins that they grind their joints*
With dry convulsions, shorten up their sinews …
David Bradley as Trinculo, Mark Lockyer as Stephano, David
Troughton and Simon Russell Beale as Ariel, 1993

dukedom and accept Prospero's forgiveness. James Hayes and Richard Haddon Haines remained stubbornly outside the reconciliatory circle. Cheek by Jowl went as far as presenting an unrepentant Queen of Naples – Alonso became a Margaret Thatcher look-alike, Alonsa. Such an interpretation, however, went against the text and necessitated significant cuts. Other productions have stressed not so much Antonio's unwillingness to accept forgiveness, as Prospero's difficulty in forgiving, an interpretation warranted by his ambivalent wording:

For you, most wicked sir, whom to call brother
Would even infect my mouth, I do forgive
Thy rankest fault – all of them.

[130-3]

In a production interpreting the play as a journey of self-discovery, Michael Bryant emphasized the hard-won quality of Prospero's forgiveness of his brother. Max von Sydow was even tempted to smash Antonio's face with his staff before he decided to forgive him. Prospero's recognition of Caliban as his own, 'This thing of darkness I/Acknowledge mine' [275-6], is often interpreted as an acceptance of his darker self. Sam Mendes, however, presented the line as the master's reaction towards a creature who will always need rigid control. In his production Prospero imprisoned David Troughton's repentant Caliban in the skip. As with Cheek by Jowl's unrepentant Alonsa, this staging necessitated rewriting Shakespeare's text: the pronoun in Prospero's line, 'Go, sirrah, to my cell' [292], was changed to 'thy'.

Prospero's last action is the release of Ariel. This moment can express a close, friendly relationship between master and servant as in *La Tempête*, where Ariel almost preferred staying with Prospero to regaining his freedom. But it can also convey Ariel's impatience at the prospect of his liberty. Thus, Mark Rylance's Ariel had already gone when Prospero spoke the words which were supposed to release him. Sam Mendes offered a startling revision of the entire relationship between Prospero and Ariel. The previously unemotional, efficient servant turned to Prospero and, spitting in his face, released the hatred and disgust accumulated during the twelve years of his servitude. The subsequent epilogue for Alec McCowen became the painful, weary recognition of his project's failure and a true prayer for pardon and relief from the 'good hands' of the audience [10]. John Wood turned the Epilogue into the desperate plea of an insecure man for attention and affection. Both interpretations exemplify modern productions' efforts to avoid presenting Prospero as the retiring Shakespeare's double saying his serene farewell to the stage.

Romana Beyenburg

TIMON OF ATHENS

*Openness and generosity cede to a bitter cynicism as
a man turns his back upon a materialistic society.*

In the late twentieth century, *Timon of Athens*' ruthless exposure of society's materialism has commended the play to directors as an image of our times. Peter Brook's 1974 Paris version used a modern prose translation and deliberately exploited the gaping holes of its derelict theatre-space as an image of Western decadence and decay. The 1980 production created a Japanese setting of graceful formality, with merchants, artists, warriors and noblemen gathering to enjoy the hospitality of Timon's feast. In 1988 the play was presented by only seven actors in modern dress, with simple staging and striking lighting effects. Timon's final exit was an escape through prison bars, thrown in shadow on the stage floor.

The movement of the play is simple: from riches and prodigality, Timon falls to penury and bitter misanthropy. When the friends on whom he has showered gifts refuse to help him, Timon retires to a desert place, heaping curses on the ungrateful city of Athens. The dizzying swings of Timon's fortunes are made explicit:

**The middle of humanity thou never knewest,
but the extremity of both ends. When thou
wast in thy gilt and thy perfume, they mocked
thee for too much curiosity. In thy rags thou
knowest none, but art despised for the contrary.**

[IV.3.302-5]

At the beginning of the play, Timon is surrounded by men eager to feed fat at his table. Only Apemantus, a professional cynic,

Above: *Thou singly honest man,
Here, take. The gods, out of my misery,
Ha' sent thee treasure.*
Arthur Kohn as Flavius and Richard Pasco, 1980

protests against this getting and spending. At the Young Vic, Apemantus was a filthy, woolly-hatted tramp, dogging Timon's footsteps but resolutely refusing any of his handouts. This production seized on the ambiguity of the opening scene in its presentation of the 'Masque of the Amazons'. A stately group of ladies, decorous in eighteenth century white wigs and hooped gowns, at first presented a courtly dance only to strip off their skirts to reveal black stockings, frilly knickers and a whole new style of dancing. Their invitation to join the dance was embraced with enthu-

siasm by Timon's guests. In 1963 Duke Ellington's original jazz music enhanced the party, which also had a bevy of call-girls. Apemantus, a shabby Hollywood reporter, with a cigarette permanently attached to his lower lip, had his photographer ready to record it all for the next day's gossip columns. The Masque in the BBC-tv production retains its dignity, but shows Timon distracted from

'WHAT IS AMISS, PLAGUE AND INFECTION MEND!'

The Early Production History of *Timon of Athens*

imon of Athens is one of Shakespeare's most rarely performed plays. Plutarch's *Lives* provides the primary source, with 1607-8 as the most likely date of composition; various loose ends and uncertainties of lineation suggest that it is an unrevised draft. As a result of the textual problems, adaptation of some kind has been the approach of most productions.

There is no record of performance before that of Thomas Shadwell's adaptation in 1678. Shadwell boasted that, although Shakespeare had 'never made more masterly strokes... I can truly say, I have made it into a Play'. His version was a satire of contemporary life, with an admixture of fashionable sentimentality and romantic intrigue which sought to remedy the original play's lack of important female characters. Timon's Steward becomes a grasping schemer and Timon is loved by the constant Evandra. Melissa is betrothed to Timon, but she abandons him for Alcibiades. Evandra dies by her own hand at Timon's side.

Shadwell's version formed the basis of similar adaptations in the eighteenth century. In 1816 George Lamb presented a fuller text, but with considerable omissions 'such as the

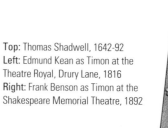

refinement of manners has rendered necessary'. Edmund Kean scored a great success as Timon. Throughout the nineteenth century, the play was performed in similarly sanitised versions. Samuel Phelps, at Sadler's Wells, and Frank Benson, at Stratford-upon-Avon, capitalised on the opportunity to display magnificent 'panoramas' of ancient Greece.

The play's bleakness appealed to the post-war atmosphere of the 1940s and 1950s. In 1947, at the Birmingham Repertory Theatre, a bomb crater overlooked by a howitzer provided Timon with a cave. Ralph Richardson played the rôle at the Old Vic in 1956, under the direction of Michael Benthall, who cut and transposed text so that Alcibiades' mercy towards Athens resulted from his reading of Timon's bitter epitaph.

Top: Thomas Shadwell, 1642-92
Left: Edmund Kean as Timon at the Theatre Royal, Drury Lane, 1816
Right: Frank Benson as Timon at the Shakespeare Memorial Theatre, 1892

the dance as he bestows jewels on everyone in sight. The camera lingers on the sensual appetite of the feasters as they tear apart succulent chicken legs and sink their teeth into greasy joints. Timon, played with a hectic intensity by Jonathan Pryce, eats nothing; it is satisfaction enough for him to watch excitedly as his goods are consumed.

Doubt was cast upon the nature of Timon's bounty at the very opening of the 1965 production, when he walked along a busy street, surrounded by friends but indifferent to the leprous beggars crouched by the walls. Such ambiguity is present when Ventidius offers the return of double the sum paid by Timon to release him from prison. Timon refuses repayment, declaring that:

> **there's none**
> **Can truly say he gives, if he receives.**
>
> [I.2.9-10]

Despite his question 'what need we have of any friends, if we should ne'er have need of 'em?' [93-4], Timon appears to hold himself exempt from the reciprocal obligations of human society, unique in his power to give and need no one. There is an inevitability in his discovery that his friends behave as though they owe him nothing when it is he who needs their help.

Digging for roots in the lonely woods, Timon finds gold. Trevor Nunn invented the business of a thief hastily burying this booty immediately before Timon arrived at the place. The woods themselves, in this fiercely contemporary show, were an urban waste-land of abandoned cars and man-made rubbish. This was a significant departure from the text's emphasis on the natural world, in which the earth, the 'common whore of mankind' [IV.3.43] yields nourishing roots as indifferently as the gold:

Above left: *I am sick of this false world and will love nought*
Richard Pasco, 1980
Above: *'Tis yours because you liked it.*
Julian Curry as the Senator, Rudolph Walker as Flavius and David Suchet handing over his car keys, 1991

> **That makes the wappened widow wed again –**
> **She, whom the spital-house and ulcerous sores**
> **Would cast the gorge at.**
>
> [39-41]

These corrosive speeches were delivered with a passionate intensity by Paul Scofield in 1965. As the play progressed, his voice broke down from the rich tones of elegance and noble innocence to inconsolable cries, erupting into incandescent curses. The opulent marble and mosaic walls of his palace yielded to the starkness of a pit of earth in which his mud-stained figure grovelled for food. This desert place was relieved by one blasted tree. There had been a stronger allu-

sion to the bleak world of Samuel Beckett's *Happy Days* in 1963, when Timon was half-buried in his sandy pit. The bleached-out landscape in the BBC production is haunted by the surge of the sea. Pryce's meagre frame is covered only with festering sores and a loin-cloth, rather than the rich velvets and ruffs of his earlier Jacobean dress.

As word of his new wealth reaches Athens, Timon again entertains gold-diggers. In this parodic replay of the first half, he gives gold with the explicit intention of bringing its recipients to ruin. The audience was reminded of Beckett's tramps as the Young Vic's Apemantus sat down with his carrot to

Above: *Painting is welcome.*
The painting is almost the natural man
David Suchet, 1991

swap insults with Timon. David Suchet's relish in biting off the top of his root was both funny and moving as his Timon imagined so consuming the whole of mankind. His Steward's devotion makes Timon grudgingly admit that there is 'One honest man' [500], but his misanthropy persists unshaken, as undiscriminating and excessive as his earlier prodigality. He gives his faithful Steward gold with the instruction to live apart from the world:

Hate all, curse all, show charity to none,
But let the famished flesh slide from the bone
Ere thou relieve the beggar.

[530-2]

Timon gives gold to Alcibiades to fund his war on Athens. Like Timon, Alcibiades seeks revenge upon the city for its ingratitude. The 1963 production was politically alert with an Alcibiades resembling Castro in his uniform and beard. The techniques of urban guerrilla warfare were deployed at the Young Vic, where Alcibiades and his khaki-clad whores terrorised the Athenians from the metal gantries surrounding the stage. Alcibiades finally listens to the entreaties of his countrymen and returns to the city, but Timon remains alone, wishing that even language might end. He prepares his tomb, comforting himself that he may:

Lie where the light foam of the sea may beat
Thy grave-stone daily.

[380-1]

In Nunn's adaptation at the Young Vic, Timon shot himself in the abandoned transit van he had adopted as his cave. The production's final image was of Timon's dead body cradled in the arms of his weeping Steward. This mixture of bitterness and pathos was

Above: *Here's that which is too weak to be a sinner,*
Honest water, which ne'er left man i'th' mire.
Barry Foster as Apemantus, 1991

NOTABLE PRODUCTIONS OF *TIMON OF ATHENS*

	THEATRE	DIRECTOR	DESIGNER	PRINCIPALS
1963	The Shakespearean Festival Theatre, Stratford, Ontario	Michael Langham & Peter Coe	Brian Jackson	John Colicos ....*Timon*
1965	Royal Shakespeare Theatre, Stratford-upon-Avon	John Schlesinger	Ralph Koltai	Paul Scofield............................*Timon*
1974	Théâtre des Bouffes-du-Nord, Paris	Peter Brook	Michel Launay	François Marthouret ....*Timon*
1980	The Other Place, Stratford-upon-Avon	Ron Daniels	Chris Dyer	Richard Pasco ....*Timon*
1981	BBC-tv	Jonathan Miller	Tony Abbott	Jonathan Pryce ....*Timon*
1988	Haymarket Studio Theatre, Leicester	Simon Usher	Jocelyn Herbert	Guy Williams ....*Timon*
1991	Young Vic, London	Trevor Nunn	John Gunter	David Suchet ....*Timon*

powerful, but the 1980 production followed the text in not explaining how Timon dies: Richard Pasco pulled the skein of a fishing net over his head and remained motionless on stage for the rest of the play. This death was an imaginative response to the sense of disintegration into the elements which marks Timon's retreat from life:

Hearing the surges threat. We must all part
Into a sea of air.

[IV.2.21-2]

Rebecca Flynn

'WELCOME, DREAD FURY TO MY WOEFUL HOUSE'

The Early Production History of *Titus Andronicus*

Although *Titus Andronicus* is set in fourth-century Rome, the details of its plot are unhistorical. Shakespeare certainly used Ovid's *Metamorphoses* as a source, indeed a copy is brought onto the stage. Henslowe records a performance in January 1594 (probably at the Rose Theatre) and the play was entered in the Stationers' Register in February of the same year. Its remarkable popularity with Elizabethan and Jacobean audiences is reflected in contemporary references and in the fact that there were three Quarto editions in 1594, 1600 and 1611. The fuller Folio text of 1623 may indicate that Shakespeare revised the text after its early performances. The earliest surviving drawing of any Shakespearean scene is of *Titus Andronicus*, attributed to Henry Peacham and dating from about 1595.

There were a few performances after the Restoration but in the autumn of 1678 Thomas Ravenscroft suggested that the original text 'seems rather a heap of rubbish than a structure'. He modified the play and increased its horrors. The assumption that adaptation of the text was necessary persisted until 1923 when Robert Atkins directed the play at the Old Vic. Influenced by William Poel, Atkins sought to restore

principles of Elizabethan staging and textual integrity.

Productions since 1951 have sought either to minimise or to maximise the play's atrocities. At the Old Vic in 1957 and at Stratford in 1981 audiences were comfortably distanced by stages set with costume skips and non-illusionistic props such as hobby-horses. Groups of Elizabethan actors self-consciously displayed their craft in tragedy and comedy. On both occasions the play was heavily cut to form half of a double-bill being paired with first *The Comedy of Errors* and then *The Two Gentlemen of Verona*. A production in New York in 1972 offered a plethora of gore and severed limbs whilst at the Bristol Old Vic in 1978 the action was set in a bear-pit.

Top: Keith Michell as Aaron and Barbara Jefford as Tamora at the Old Vic, 1957
Left: Henry Peacham's drawing shows Aaron watching Tamora plead with Titus for her sons, 1595
Right: George Hayes as Aaron and Wilfred Walter as Titus at the Old Vic, 1923

TITUS ANDRONICUS

*Rape, murder, mutilation and cannibalism are
the ingredients in a savage analysis of a disintegrating society.*

The world of *Titus Andronicus* is one in which actions speak most powerfully. Allegiance to Rome must be exhibited through deeds of heroic valour. From his first entrance Olivier was an old and battered soldier. He seemed aware of the hollowness of his rhetoric and there was no elation in his voice. In the Swan production 32 years later Titus was first seen perched in military triumph on a ladder born aloft by his sons. Chained to the ladder were the defeated Tamora and her sons. Brian Cox was simultaneously hero and a kind of Humpty Dumpty figure. It was only when he stood on the stage that an audience was aware of how tired he looked. However, it was with pride that he opened the tomb to bury those of his sons who had not survived the battle:

There greet in silence, as the dead are wont...

[I.1.90]

Obsequies in the harsh world of the play are not lyrical litanies but require human sacrifice and Titus orders the lopping of Alarbus' limbs in a brutal ritual which denies Tamora's plea for mitigation or mercy. Titus' words to her can suggest not so much an inherent viciousness but rather that he is the desensitised product of his society and Brian Cox was able to be almost disingenuously reasonable here:

Patient yourself, madam, and pardon me...

[121]

Although Lavinia asserts a similar allegiance to Rome, to her father and to her husband

Bassianus, she is viewed by Tamora's sons, Chiron and Demetrius, simply as an object of sexual desire. They murder her husband and her appeal to Tamora seeks sympathy from another woman. Tamora is determined to follow Titus' precedent and she 'will not hear her speak' [II.3.137] as Lavinia pleads to be saved from 'worse than killing lust' [175]. In the Swan Theatre this scene had an unbearable tension. The audience willed Lavinia to keep speaking in a recognition of the theatrical convention that words sustain a scene. In a terrible foreshadowing of the rape and mutilation to follow, Chiron announces

*Above: – So now go tell and if thy tongue can speak
Who 'twas that cut thy tongue and ravish'd thee.
– Write down thy mind, bewray thy meaning so ...*
Kevin Miles as Chiron, Vivien Leigh and Lee Montague as Demetrius, 1955

'I'll stop your mouth' [185] and he and Demetrius take her offstage.

The full stage direction in the First Quarto edition describes the moment of her reappearance:

Enter the Empress' sons, with Lavinia, her hands cut off, and her tongue cut out, and ravished.

[II.4]

215

Left: *dost thou not perceive*
That Rome is but a wilderness of tigers?
Laurence Olivier, 1955
Above: Vivien Leigh, 1955
Right: Anthony Quayle, 1955

In 1955 Peter Brook presented Lavinia here in a stylised tableau. Vivian Leigh stood with one hand to her mouth, the other arm stretched downwards. White chiffon from her dress bound her arms and from both stumps and from her mouth hung trailing red ribbons. Chiron and Demetrius uttered their speeches, numbed with a growing realisation of what they had done, as they both backed away in parallel movements. At the end of the scene Lavinia was enclosed in a tomb-like column from which she was later revealed to Titus.

In contrast, Deborah Warner allowed no stylisation to ease the emotional distress of this scene. Chiron and Demetrius crawled onto the stage, laughing as they clumsily pulled themselves forward using their fore-arms. Their movement was an appallingly callous parody of Lavinia's entrance which followed. As she struggled to her feet in an attempt to regain a human dignity she was seen to be covered with clay-like mud which served as a naturalistic means of stopping her wounds, yet also expressed her defilement and degradation. She was able to stand only briefly before tottering to the ground. The men laughed and waggled her arms 'see how with signs and tokens she can scrawl' [II.4.5]. Chiron fondled her breasts with distaste, spitting on her on 'I would go hang myself' [9]. Demetrius' joke 'if thou hadst hands to help thee knit the cord' [10] was pointed with loud, echoing laughter and their exit through the auditorium had uneasy implications for the audience.

Marcus' reaction to the maimed Lavinia has been judged an inappropriate piece of poetic narrative, cited as evidence of the young Shakespeare in his Ovidian period and condemned as unactable. It was simply cut in Peter Brook's production. In 1987 Donald Sumpter made the speech work. Seeing at first only a back view of Lavinia he was quite naturally unaware that anything might be wrong. His desire for 'a word' and his question 'where is your husband?' [12] opened up a silence as Lavinia turned and he stood stunned by what he saw. 'If I do dream' [13] enunciated precisely the audience's desire to believe that this was not real. Gently and credibly he assumed her silence to be born of shock and physical pain and he encouraged her again to confide 'Speak, gentle niece' [16] desperately anxious to assure her of his care 'Why dost not speak to me?' [21]. His words drew from Lavinia the physical effort to try. Sonia Ritter strained head, neck and throat and parted her lips. The way his words: 'Alas a crimson river of warm blood' [22] welded with the flow from her mouth drew a gasp from an audience completely held by the moment-by-moment truthfulness of the encounter. His speech provided a bridge of words which enabled an audience to come to terms step-by-step with the enormity of Lavinia's suffering. Only eventually could he move to offer her physical comfort. In performance it seemed perfectly natural for Marcus to take time before suggesting: 'let us go and make thy father blind' [52]. The mention of the family and the anticipation of Titus' 'months of tears' [55] effects a transition to the domestic

Right: *Alas, a crimson river of warm blood …*
Sonia Ritter, 1987
Below: *Good Aaron give his Majesty my hand …*
Brian Cox and Peter Polycarpou, 1987

and released tears from those watching. The audience was movingly included in Marcus' shift from 'I' to 'we':

> **for we will mourn with thee;**
> **O, could our mourning ease thy misery.**
>
> [56-7]

When Titus cuts off his own hand in vain ransom for his sons, 'jewels purchas'd at an easy price' [III.1.197], Olivier infused 'easy' with paternal love and fierce courage. He did not feel the pain until after Aaron's departure and there was intense truthfulness in the stunned silence before the onset of physical agony. Brian Cox allowed the absurdist comedy of the competing claims by Marcus and Lucius for self-mutilation to distract the others as he bustled Aaron to the corner of the stage and unceremoniously used a cheese-wire to slice off his own hand over a bucket. Titus' affinity with Lavinia is held in a natural metaphor in which she also finds a voice:

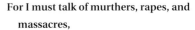

Above: *Eating the flesh that she herself hath bred*
Brian Cox and Estelle Kohler, 1987
Below: *Captive to thee, and to thy Roman yoke*
Estelle Kohler, 1987

I am the sea. Hark how her sighs doth flow!
She is the sleeping welkin, I the earth;
Then must my sea be moved with her sighs…

[224-6]

For Olivier's Titus this was a cry which revealed a man on the brink of insanity; for Brian Cox it was a moment of gentle affinity between father and daughter before the desperate simplicity of:

When will this fearful slumber have an end?

[251]

The members of Titus' family find solidarity in their commitment to revenge Lavinia's mutilation and they now reject allegiance to a corrupt Rome.

Aaron revels in his anarchic evil:

For I must talk of murthers, rapes, and
   massacres,
Acts of black night, abominable deeds,
Complots of mischief, treason, villanies,
Ruthful to hear, yet piteously perform'd.

[V.1.63-6]

Anthony Quayle had a statuesque dignity while Peter Polycarpou was disconcertingly colloquial and familiar with his audience. Initially Aaron's amorality is opposed to the patriotic fervour displayed by the Andronici but events in the play force another family tableau with Aaron cradling his son. The child, the symbol of his illicit union with Tamora, releases in him a capacity for paternal pride and encourages comparison with Titus. There is also Tamora's savage, maternal protectiveness. Before her death she will choke on her sons' flesh and both she and Aaron will be left to the pitiless destruction of the natural world.

In Deborah Warner's production Lucius kept his promise to save Aaron's child. Marcus' announcement 'Behold the child' [V.3.118] was given full rhetorical effect. In 1955 these final speeches had been heavily cut, but in 1987, far from being regarded as unnecessary recapitulation they offered a perspective upon preceding events enabling an audience to temper raw emotion and set it within a structured framework of experience. Donald Sumpter's Marcus was a gentle, good man who had earned our respect. He stood with Lucius on a stage bridge in the Swan and the house lights were brought up as he asked for support:

Now have you heard the truth, what say you
   Romans?
Have we done aught amiss? …
Speak Romans speak, and if you say we shall,
Lo hand in hand Lucius and I will fall.

[127-8; 134-5]

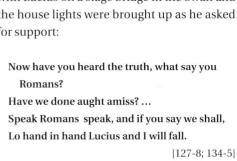

Above: *Tell on thy mind, I say thy child shall live*
Peter Polycarpou, Aaron's child and Derek Hutchinson as
Lucius, 1987

NOTABLE PRODUCTIONS OF *TITUS ANDRONICUS*

	THEATRE	DIRECTOR	DESIGNER	PRINCIPALS	
1955	Royal Shakespeare Theatre, Stratford-upon-Avon	Peter Brook	Peter Brook	Laurence Olivier	*Titus*
				Vivien Leigh	*Lavinia*
				Maxine Audley	*Tamora*
				Alan Webb	*Marcus*
				Anthony Quayle	*Aaron*
1985	BBC-tv	Jane Howell	Tony Burrough	Trevor Peacock	*Titus*
				Anna Calder-Marshall	*Lavinia*
				Eileen Atkins	*Tamora*
				Edward Hardwicke	*Marcus*
				Hugh Quarshie	*Aaron*
1987	Swan Theatre, Stratford-upon-Avon	Deborah Warner	Isabella Bywater	Brian Cox	*Titus*
				Sonia Ritter	*Lavinia*
				Estelle Kohler	*Tamora*
				Donald Sumpter	*Marcus*
				Peter Polycarpou	*Aaron*

The taut silence of the audience provided the answer before Emillius moved to respond more formally and affirm the compliance of both Roman citizens and the theatre audience. Marcus stood hand-in-hand with Lucius and cradled the child. There was a sense of catharsis and of hope for a future that would include both Young Lucius and Aaron's child.

Support for a harsher view of the conclusion of *Titus Andronicus* and a bleaker future for its society is provided by director Jane Howell in her BBC-tv production. As a unifying device she developed the rôle of Young Lucius. The realisation that a boy is witness to the horrors and hears the line 'How if that fly had a father and mother?' [III.2.60] prompted the director to add the frequent stage direction '*Young Lucius watches*'. His metal-framed glasses lend something of a modern dimension, bridging the gulf between the play and its television audience. The play's horrors are not only filtered by his perspective but there is also the sense of the action being the boy's dream or nightmare.

The BBC production reveals an integrity in its Aaron which challenges the ethos of Rome.

Here the older Lucius is a repressed sadist, as ruthless as Titus and yet more astute politically. It is entirely predictable that he will break his promise. On 'Behold the child' [V.3.118] Marcus opens a small black coffin to reveal the body of Aaron's son. When Aaron is brought on stage he is not surprised to see the coffin, but the audience's attention is directed to Young Lucius. He sees the coffin and then gazes straight ahead. The decision to kill the baby presents an indictment of the society and renders it beyond any immediate hope. In this production the faint possibility of salvation is transferred to the timeless figure of Young Lucius, who as the audience's representative, can only stare in horror.

Pamela Mason

'THE FEVER WHEREOF ALL OUR POWER IS SICK'

The Early Production History of *Troilus and Cressida*

There is no recorded evidence that *Troilus and Cressida* was presented on a public stage during Shakespeare's lifetime; however this does not mean that it was never performed. The 1609 Quarto claims the play was 'neuer clapper-clawd with the palmes of the vulgar,' leading many critics to conclude the play was written for private performance. Although this is a neat proposition, the lack of performance evidence is not peculiar to this play.

Before the twentieth century the only recorded production of the play on the English stage was John Dryden's adaptation, *Troilus and Cressida, or Truth Found Too Late* (1709). Dryden applied neoclassical rules to create a romantic tragedy where Cressida kills herself to protect her honour. The adaptation enjoyed some success but caused no renewed interest in the original text.

On 10 December 1912, William Poel, the great Elizabethan revivalist, staged the first recorded professional production at Covent Garden. The production leaned heavily on references to pre-war Europe and topicality became the cornerstone of productions in the first half of the century, notably Tyrone Guthrie's 1956 Old Vic production.

John Barton and Peter Hall's landmark production in 1960 enjoyed universal acclaim and helped to establish the play firmly. *Troilus and Cressida* has since enjoyed five subsequent revivals in Stratford alone.

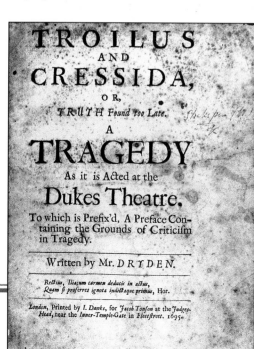

Top: John Dryden, 1631-1700
Left: Playbill for Dryden's adaptation, 1695
Right: Tyrone Guthrie, 1900-71

TROILUS AND CRESSIDA

*Against the backdrop of the Trojan War,
Shakespeare explores moral and military ethics.*

Troilus and Cressida is a satirical examination of the Trojan wars where heroic figures passed down from classical literature are systematically deflated; legendary characters are found wanting or reduced to minor players. Ideals of honour, courage, fidelity, love and war are treated equally, drained of meaning and shown to be insignificant against the Trojan conflict. The play is a broad mix of opposites – rhetoric and abuse, philosophy and violence, love and hate, high drama and low comedy – all linked by the decaying force of time. The Prologue describes the action as 'Beginning in the middle' [28] and the play offers no tragic catharsis nor comic resolution as an ending that would be recognisably Shakespearean.

This sounds an unattractive proposition but the play should not be judged by the criteria of conventional tragic or comic drama. It possesses a remarkable depth of tone and characterisation, containing genuinely poignant moments as well as humour, and it offers the rare opportunity for a number of virtuoso performances. The structure of the play is the key element that draws an ensemble of characters and themes into a clear progression from order to chaos. As modern post-war stage successes have demonstrated, a production that rises to the challenges of the text can provide powerful theatrical images and memorable characterisations.

Right: *Lechery, lechery, still wars and lechery; nothing else holds fashion! A burning devil take them!*
Peter O'Toole, 1960

Above: – *May I, sweet lady, beg a kiss of you?*
– *You may.*
Sebastian Shaw as Ulysses and Helen Mirren, 1968

The first five scenes establish the foundation of order whilst introducing a remarkable breadth of tone; five separate character groups present quite distinct perspectives. Characters and themes demand attention without being linked by plot. The opening scene is anticlimactic, with the eponymous hero presented in physical and mental limbo. Michael Williams was memorably vulnerable, dressed in white to suggest the hero and the innocent. Attention is placed not on the battlefield but on a disillusioned hero arguing against the merit of the war and impatiently nagging Pandarus to bring him to Cressida. At the end of the scene Troilus returns to the battlefield, a startling *volte face* which immediately raises questions about his strength of character.

Cressida is the classical symbol of infidelity but Shakespeare draws a subtler, more ambiguous character, allowing scope for interpretation. At various times the text presents her as both virgin and whore, contradictions that need to be resolved on stage. Cressida's reaction to the jibes of Pandarus and the procession of Trojan heroes require choices to be made that will reverberate throughout any production.

Dorothy Tutin played Cressida as a lewd minx, letting sand slide tantalisingly through her fingers like a Cleopatra. Tutin was the inconstant man-eater of Homeric legend, draped over the front of the stage as the Trojan procession of returning heroes became a parade of possible conquests. In contrast, Helen Mirren was an excitable teenager, gazing admiringly at her teen idols. In 1985, the Trojan procession was offstage and the focus was placed on the verbal parley between Cressida and Pandarus as they watched through binoculars. Juliet Stevenson appeared a self-assured, level-headed young woman, displaying intelligence, acute wit and a confidence in her desire for Troilus.

The following scenes widen the perspective from the private to the public and include long, rhetorical debates from both camps on the motives of the conflict. Ulysses is the supreme orator delivering the much anthologised speech on the need for order [I.3.75-137], impressive rhetoric that is immediately contradicted at the end of the scene. The unplanned interruption of a Trojan challenge is used to hatch an underhand plot and manipulate his countrymen. In 1990, Ulysses was the skilful observer of men, carefully singling out the man who would be receptive to his plot and with an intriguing 'Nestor...' drew him aside. The night-time location was a dark shroud to cover the manipulations. The sentiments on order are subtly undermined, revealing flaws in the concept, flaws that will eventually lead to the chaos of the final act. The Trojan scene is similarly interrupted, initially by the grim foreboding of Cassandra, and then by Hector, previously a powerful speaker against the war, who suddenly contradicts his argument publicly.

The rhetorical speeches in these two scenes are static and often considered difficult on stage, but they are far from dry speeches divorced from the rest of the play. A tension exists between private agenda and public personae, a tension that qualifies the rhetoric. The actions of Ulysses and Hector demonstrate that order is being maintained only in the skilful rhetoric of politicians.

Sandwiching the two debates is Thersites, who drags every ideal and character into a hurling invective of abuse. In 1990, Simon Russell Beale introduced himself by dropping a huge line of spittle into Ajax's dinner, a fact not lost on the audience when Thersites later had his face pushed into the same. The scene, set in Achilles' tent, swings from violence to abuse with Thersites dragging up the full range of abusive terms. Later, pausing for a few philosophical seconds, Russell Beale received the biggest laugh of the evening by dragging up the perfect insult – 'finch egg' [V.1.33] – from his eccentric vocabulary. At one moment, Thersites is the jester on the lowest rung of the social hierarchy, scurrying to retrieve Achilles' discarded apple core; at another, he becomes a choric figure revealing

Above left: *They are in action*
David Burke and Clive Russell as Ajax, 1985
Above: *Are you aweary of me?*
Anton Lesser and Juliet Stevenson, 1985

the underbelly of the war, where love and politics are mere 'juggling' acts of deception [II.3.70, V.2.25]. The interplay between Thersites, Ajax, Patroclus and Achilles is fast and blunt, and contains some of the darkest and funniest humour in Shakespeare. Achilles beats Ajax, who beats Thersites, who in turn insults everyone and we are led to believe this is an everyday scene of cosy domesticity.

The five opening scenes represent five distinct and separate perspectives amounting to the broadest opening in all Shakespeare. Each scene is static and each possesses a notion of order which is undermined, thus foreshadowing the chaos of the final scenes. The structure challenges directors to achieve a consistency that will maintain the audience's interest in each perspective and enable the increasing pace of the second half to be effective. Set and costume play a crucial rôle, often being the element which can make the traditionally difficult play intelligible.

In 1960, John Barton and Peter Hall empha-

sised the mythological framework, employing a bare sand pit and authentic Greek costumes, a radically simplistic departure from conventional staging. In the imagination of the audience, the sand would become a circus ring, children's play pen, gladiator's stage or Riviera beach. Simultaneously, the set maintained modern associations, a no-man's-land reminiscent of Samuel Beckett and T.S. Eliot. The Swan production in 1990 also drew on a simplistic set, using the bare thrust stage with a statue of Apollo as a symbol of time, one side immaculate, the other deteriorated. Characters wore an eclectic mix of costumes, from medieval armour, boating blazers, army boots, and woolly cardigans, thus providing a thread from the mythological to the modern. In both 1960 and 1990, the ravages of 'calumniating time' [III.3.174] became the main protagonist, consuming all values and characters.

The relationship between Troilus and Cressida is affirmed with the lovers

pronouncing an oath of fidelity before spending the night together. Juliet Stevenson was guarded but honest, carefully weighing her own desires with the dilemma of a woman trying to survive in a male-dominated environment. By contrast, Helen Mirren was blissfully unaware of coquettish etiquette, throwing herself at Troilus in a passionate kiss that dragged both to the floor. She displayed an irresistible appetite for excitement that could not be satiated by Troilus. The pronunciation of the fidelity oath sets the action self-consciously against time, attempting to ensure a permanency that the time will not allow. The characterisation of Cressida can make the scene ironic or provide an honest moment in a play of cynicism. The strength of Juliet Stevenson's conviction was confirmed when her protestations at being taken from

Above: *I have a woman's longing*
Hilton McRae as Patroclus and Alan Rickman, 1985

Above left: Amanda Root, 1990
Above: *O Cressid! O false Cressid! False, false, false!*
Ralph Fiennes, 1990

Troy had to be subdued by a harsh slap, a controlling male hand which presaged her treatment in the Greek camp.

At the Greek camp, public and private worlds collide, combining a formal welcome with an undercurrent of sexual threat or invitation, as Cressida is 'kissed in general' [IV.5.21] by the Greeks. In production, the scene determines whether Cressida's action to take Diomedes is a weakness of character or a necessary choice to ensure survival. Dorothy Tutin settled with the former, both inspiring and reacting favourably to the male laughter. Helen Mirren visibly grew in confidence as kisses on the hand developed to the lips, delighted with the apparent power she had over the legendary warriors. Juliet Stevenson responded to a brooding atmosphere of sexual threat, even rape. Her intelligence could be seen working as she nervously weighed up the situation, piercing the niceties of formal welcome to reveal a hidden agenda of sexual aggression that could destroy her. When Ulysses begs a kiss, Cressida replies 'Why, beg then' [48]. Helen Mirren curtsied alluringly. Juliet Stevenson snapped her fingers for him to kneel, offering a challenge. Ulysses' lines, 'Her wanton spirits look out/At every joint of her body' [56-7], were truthful in 1960. In 1985 his words were the reaction of a bitter man who had been out-manoeuvred by an equal and yet, in a male value system, an equal he had the ability to destroy.

Troilus' visit to the Greek camp is one of the most finely structured scenes in all Shakespeare. Four separate perspectives are presented: the sexual negotiations of Cressida, the pain of Troilus, the cold observation of Ulysses and the vitriol of Thersites. The tight stichomythic verse embraces philosophy, abuse, threats, tenderness, intimate whispers and booming invective. The audience is pulled relentlessly between them all. The perspectives of the opening scenes are brought together on one stage and yet each remains separate, thus mirroring the unconventional opening structure. The tragedy of the scene lies not in any one character, but in the balance of all the protagonists set against 'envious and calumniating time' [III.3.174] which denies all honest motives. Juliet Stevenson's performance was so sympathetic that it upset the balance, and, as a result, the plight of Troilus and power of the final battle scenes were diminished. The play is an ensemble piece and an understanding of each character is essential to a successful staging. Sam Mendes achieved a more balanced approach in 1990. At the end of the scene, Thersites swooped down to snatch Cressida's discarded love token. Holding it up to examine it in the light, he unleashed 'Lechery, lechery, still wars and lechery; nothing else holds fashion!' [V.2.197–8], not in anger but in anguish, an elegy for the failure of love at the moment when chaos escalates.

The war plot centres around the physical and ideological clash between Hector and Achilles. The former represents the classical ideal of honour, the latter the exercise of power for selfish and devious ends. Hector's honourable intentions are undermined as the duel with the oafish Ajax turns into farce, a pathetic shadow of the vicious and deadly duel to come. Hector, the great Trojan hope of the opening scenes, has become an anachronism believing in fair play when the rules have changed.

Achilles, like Cressida, is a character open to a number of interpretations. In 1960 he was a man of steel, clearly the warrior of legend. In 1968 he was dressed in a fur coat, sporting a fan and leaving no doubt as to his sexual orientation as he greeted Hector in gold wig and drag: 'I am Achilles...Behold thy fill.' [IV.5.235, 237]. In 1990, Ciaran Hinds clearly lacked humour and his sexuality was subversive rather than laughable. Dressed in black leather and chainmail, he was a panther enunciating in a slow drawl, leaping from the wall bars to meet Hector after several minutes' cold observation. The feline guile of Achilles confronts the canine honesty of Hector. The two great warriors come face to

face for the first time and every courteous line of formal welcome is punctuated with tension and the menace of the forthcoming battle.

The final battle scenes have proved difficult to stage and can serve as a gauge of the success of a production. The nine short scenes can appear messy and unresolved but they make perfect sense when set in the context of the play's overall structure. The ending signals the completion of the structural decline from order to chaos and has provided powerful, chilling moments in the theatre.

Above: *So be it, either to the uttermost*
Or else a breath. The combatants being kin
Half stints their strife before their strokes begin.
David Troughton and Richard Ridings as Ajax, 1990

In 1960 the scenes were conducted amidst dry ice with echoed shouts, stylized movements, and fractured lighting. The fog became the amorphous mass of time which stripped identity, engulfing both great and small. The scenes had an apocalyptic quality, self-conscious of the symbolic battle between order and chaos. Achilles' henchmen closed

NOTABLE PRODUCTIONS OF *TROILUS AND CRESSIDA*

	THEATRE	DIRECTOR	DESIGNER	PRINCIPALS
1960	Royal Shakespeare Theatre, Stratford-upon-Avon	Peter Hall and John Barton	Leslie Hurry	Dorothy Tutin .... *Cressida* Denholm Elliot .... *Troilus* Max Adrian .... *Pandarus* Eric Porter .... *Ulysses* Derek Godfrey .... *Hector* Partick Allen .... *Achilles* Peter O'Toole .... *Thersites*
1968	Royal Shakespeare Theatre, Stratford-upon-Avon	John Barton	Timothy O'Brien	Helen Mirren........................ *Cressida* Michael Williams .... *Troilus* David Waller .... *Pandarus* Sebastian Shaw .... *Ulysses* Patrick Stewart .... *Hector* Alan Howard .... *Achilles* Norman Rodway .... *Thersites*
1985	Royal Shakespeare Theatre, Stratford-upon-Avon	Howard Davies	Ralph Koltai	Juliet Stevenson .... *Cressida* Anton Lesser .... *Troilus* Clive Merrison .... *Pandarus* Peter Jeffrey .... *Ulysses* David Burke .... *Hector* Alan Rickman .... *Achilles* Alun Armstrong .... *Thersites*
1990	Swan Theatre, Stratford-upon-Avon	Sam Mendes	Anthony Ward	Amanda Root .... *Cressida* Ralph Fiennes .... *Troilus* Norman Rodway................. *Pandarus* Paul Jesson .... *Ulysses* David Troughton .... *Hector* Ciaran Hinds .... *Achilles* Simon Russell Beale .... *Thersites*

Above: – *... you ruinous butt, you whoreson indistinguishable cur.*
`– ... thou idle immaterial skein of sleave-silk.*
Paterson Joseph as Patroclus and Simon Russell Beale, 1990

on Hector on the portentous 'Look, Hector, how the sun begins to set' [V.8.5] and with three choreographed thrusts, stabbed Hector who fell on his face in the sand like a felled oak. In 1990, Achilles closed in to administer the *coup de grâce* by stabbing Hector through the eye, after asking Hector to see the sun setting on his honourable age. Hector's death is the one clear moment in battle scenes surrounded by confusion, a stark moment that can speak directly to a twentieth century audience.

The final scenes fade in comparison to the intensity of Hector's brutal slaughter. The retreating Trojans are seen in disarray and Troilus, who at the beginning of the play paced impatiently for Cressida, now roams the battlefield unable to achieve the satisfaction of death or revenge. There are no monuments to be erected to love or honour. It is left to a dishevelled Pandarus to proclaim that the oblivion witnessed on stage is left to future generations as he bequeaths the audience his diseases.

James Shaw

TWELFTH NIGHT

Illyria is a golden world, but one in which
the cost of present pleasure must be reckoned.

Twelfth Night is often seen nowadays as a melancholic comedy and the disturbing elements of the play are stressed at the expense of laughter. Maria's trick on Malvolio has often been transformed from a practical joke in revenge for a telling off, into what amounts to torture and the withholding of basic human rights. Donald Sinden was clear in his mind that the character exits in order to commit suicide. Anthony Sher, in 1987, transformed the play into *The Tragedy of Malvolio*. Having initially presented Malvolio as a figure of broad comedy, Sher then showed the character degenerating through appalling suffering into real madness. At the end of the production it was difficult to feel permitted to laugh at all. Richard Briers also suffered painful degradation and conveyed heart-rending anguish in his final line, 'I'll be revenged on the whole pack of you!' [V.1.375]. Briers' performance was coloured for the British audience by his high profile as a player of likeable characters in situation comedies – these associations somehow rendered his suffering as Malvolio more terrible. By contrast the English Shakespeare Company chose not to generate much sympathy for Malvolio. He returned onstage after Feste's final song and started supervising the striking of the set, the dismantling of the world of the play and the lovers, thus looking forward to the closing of the theatres which Malvolio's party, the Puritans, were to effect some forty years after *Twelfth Night* was written.

The character of Feste is rarely played as genuinely funny now and, prompted by the

Above: *Alas, Malvolio, this is not my writing,*
Though, I confess, much like in character.
Paul Spence as Sebastian, Antony Sher, Deborah Findlay,
Donald Sumpter as Orsino and Harriet Walter, 1987

remarkably gloomy content of his songs, he is often melancholic, visibly ageing and dependent on charity. In the BBC production Trevor Peacock's gruff-voiced Feste is clearly avoiding beggary only because of the soft heart of Sinead Cusack's Olivia. Anton Lesser was often quite manic, seemingly driven to the edge by unrequited love for Olivia. The final moments of the production had him gazing in sadly from outside the closed gate of Olivia's garden. His backpack suggested he was leaving the household for good. Kerry Walker's Feste was ambiguously androgynous, sang beautiful calypso songs in a very sexy voice and spoke mockingly in a dry or ironic tone. Real menace was projected through the sexual indeterminacy which Walker brought to the rôle.

A controversially uncomic reading of the ending of *Twelfth Night* appeared in Denise

'IF MUSIC BE THE FOOD OF LOVE, PLAY ON'

The Early Production History of *Twelfth Night*

The first performance of *Twelfth Night* may have been on 6 January, the day of the annual Twelfth Night festival associated with misrule and the end of Christmas celebrations. The first documented performance, however, is recorded in the diary of a barrister, John Manningham, for 2 February 1602. The production was in the Middle Temple Hall at the Inns of Court in London, and Manningham was particularly impressed by the Malvolio plot.

Davenant adapted the play for the Restoration stage but Shakespeare's text was revived, very frequently, from the mid-eighteenth century. Charles Macklin cast himself as Malvolio in 1741 and was followed by a long line of star performers in this role. Although his 1884 production at the Lyceum failed, Henry Irving set the tone for many modern Malvolios by stressing

the rôle's tragic potential. In 1895 William Poel broke with the tradition of scenically elaborate productions by emulating Elizabethan playhouse style with very little scenery.

Harley Granville-Barker's acclaimed production of 1912 featured a Feste whose melancholy and age were conspicuous. In 1958 Peter Hall's first production of *Twelfth Night* gave a new reading of Olivia, who was played as a young and rather silly girl. Hall also hinted at where Malvolio's puritanism was leading by using Cavalier costumes, thereby looking forward to the English Civil War and to the closing of the theatres. This production was revived in 1960 at Stratford with Eric Porter playing Malvolio – a rôle which he repeated for Hall in 1991.

Top: C. Hayden Coffin as Feste at the Savoy Theatre, 1912
Left: *The Lord of Misrule*, from a late nineteenth century drawing by Charles Green
Right: The duel between Aguecheek and Viola, 1788

Coffey's 1930s palm court production. An elegiac tone was evoked by Feste who sang a lamenting jazz alto; however, it was Antonio's fate which skewed the production finally away from comedy. It has become increasingly common to make Antonio's love for Sebastian explicitly homosexual. Antonio is then logically unenthusiastic and sometimes miserable amongst the outbreak of marriages at the end of the play. Coffey emphasised the fact that there are no lines actually ordering the freeing of Antonio, and the lovers were so wrapped in themselves that they forgot to have him released. Antonio was led on in a way which suggested he was en route to execution, and the fact that no counter-order was given was played as meaning that he would exit to his death. By contrast, in 1987, Declan Donnellan's production with the Cheek by Jowl company gave Antonio a much happier ending by having him pair off with Feste.

Homosexuality also surfaces in the predicament of Viola. Orsino's marriage proposal to her is often prepared for by showing great closeness and physical contact between the characters. Neil Armfield's production had Orsino and Viola sharing a large swing hammock, with other courtiers exchanging surprised looks at the physical intimacy that resulted. The fact that Viola spends nearly all of the play in male attire is also remarkable. She may talk of returning to women's clothes but she does not do so. When, as in the Renaissance Company's production, Viola, still dressed as Cesario, and Orsino kiss tenderly at the end of the play, an image of homosexual love is readily available, an image which would have been even more accessible in Shakespeare's playhouse, where Viola would have been played by a boy. Something of the sexual force of this is perhaps evoked in the video of Armfield's production, in which, unlike the original stage version, Gillian Jones

plays both Viola and Sebastian. When this Sebastian and Olivia kiss long and tenderly, part of the dynamic of the scene is clearly homosexual.

Viola can be a problematic heroine. She expects fate to sort things out for her; when presented with evidence that her twin brother is alive, she is too tentative to believe that such good fortune can possibly be hers. Her altruism in wooing Olivia on behalf of Orsino can be read as mildly masochistic and possibly callous towards Olivia; and in the duel with Sir Andrew Aguecheek she is often quite feeble. However, Frances Barber stressed the anguish Viola suffers here. In tears as she attempted to extricate herself from the duel, Barber's Viola collapsed to the floor abjectly howling in terror. The disturbing element in Viola's occasionally extreme passivity is compounded by the fact

Above: Stephen Lewis, 1983
Below: *Good beauties, let me sustain no scorn*
Harriet Walter, Deborah Findlay and Pippa Guard as Maria, 1987

Above left: Jim Hooper as Fabian, Roger Allam as Sir Toby and David Bradley as Sir Andrew, 1987
Above: Harriet Walter, 1987. Left: Antony Sher, 1987

that she has several lines which decry women, and one of her most famous speeches romanticises the idea of a suffering, disturbingly inactive woman, sitting 'like Patience on a monument,/Smiling at grief.' [II.4.113-14] Her love for Orsino can also seem unhealthy. For the Renaissance production, Christopher Ravenscroft was clearly so ill from his obses-

sion with Olivia that his whole world had become distorted – something that was underscored in the video by filming all of the Orsino sections in black and white. Yet Viola is so in love with this deeply neurotic character that she would die 'a thousand deaths' to do him 'rest' [V.1.131].

Olivia's relationship with Viola hints at lesbianism, something which is laughed at by Sebastian: 'You would have been contracted to a maid' [258]. Having fallen in love with the feminised male, 'Cesario', Olivia marries someone who looks like Cesario but has a capacity for violence Cesario never displayed. However, comic possibilities in Olivia's ending were suggested in Peter Gill's 1974 RSC production where Olivia seemed extremely excited by the prospect of access to two Cesarios, one male and one female.

Illyria has been located by directors and

designers in many different worlds. Peter Hall's Illyria was Caroline England. Similarly, the BBC evoked the pictures of Van Dyck for its setting. John Barton presented *Twelfth Night* in a willow cabin: a box of wattle with a slatted floor, with the recurring sound of the sea in the background. Kenneth Branagh's production was set in winter around Twelfth Night but in a slightly absurd Victorian world where the main feature of the dominant garden setting was a grandfather clock, emphasising the theme of 'Youth's a stuff will not endure' [II.3.50]. Branagh also used a device popular in nineteenth century productions, of opening the play at the second scene with its wave-like verbal repetition and play on the name Illyria:

VIOLA   **What country, friends, is this?**
CAPTAIN **This is Illyria, lady.**
VIOLA   **And what should I do in Illyria?**
         My brother, he is in Elysium…

[I.2.1-4]

Illyria in Alexander's RSC production was a Greek village with bright white buildings and a strong blue sky. Armfield set Illyria on a sundowner holiday isle with exquisite tourist brochure seascapes in the background. This was Illyria as a calypso version of Australia with John Wood's Toby as the stereotypical drunken, leering Aussie and Geoffrey Rush's Sir Andrew as a poseur, perpetually and desperately aspiring to appear cool but never succeeding. Aguecheek often receives a great deal of audience sympathy because of his comical hopelessness and ineptitude. His line 'I was adored once, too' [II.3.174] epitomises this forlorn quality, especially when it is played to suggest that Aguecheek's timing is always going to be wrong in love. A frequent piece of stage business which stresses his ineptitude is to have him dressed in yellow so that when he hears Maria's comment that this is a colour Olivia abhors, his dismay is total.

There is much broad comedy in *Twelfth Night* which resists directorial attempts to mute it. Such moments include the initial gulling of Malvolio, the eavesdropping by Toby, Andrew and Fabian, Malvolio's appearance in yellow stockings and the aborted duel between Cesario and Aguecheek. These are all classic comic set pieces and it is sometimes difficult to resist the temptation to exploit them. Donald Sinden's Malvolio reacted to Olivia's command 'Run after that same peevish messenger' [I.5.290] with utter horror that he was being asked to risk his dignity by running in public. At some performances Sinden would actually go further and repeat the word 'run' in disbelief. By contrast an unusual Toby who did not work for many laughs was Roger Allam. Whereas most Tobys are old and fairly cheerful, Allam was a young, virile and often unpleasantly sadistic Toby.

The apparent age of the characters in *Twelfth Night* can be crucial. Sebastian and Viola are often played as adolescents and if Olivia and Orsino are similarly youthful, the various love tangles seem the result of foolishness and immaturity. However, if, as was the custom until Hall's 1958 production, Olivia is a mature woman and Orsino even older, then there is a confrontational disparity in age between these characters and the twins they finally marry. Maria's age is similarly open to question but her class is not; Maria is a companion to Olivia, not a servant. However, some productions dress her as a maid and create class tensions which are not in the text when she marries Sir Toby.

A major dramatic highlight of *Twelfth Night* is the reunion of Viola and Sebastian. This

Above right: *By my life, this is my lady's hand*
Richard Briers, James Simmons as Sir Andrew, Shaun Prendergast as Fabian and James Saxon as Sir Toby, 1988
Right: Abigail McKern as Maria, Richard Briers, Caroline Langrishe and Frances Barber as 'Cesario', 1988

NOTABLE PRODUCTIONS OF *TWELFTH NIGHT*

	THEATRE	DIRECTOR	DESIGNER	PRINCIPALS	
1958	Shakespeare Memorial Theatre, Stratford-upon-Avon	Peter Hall	Lila de Nobili	Dorothy Tutin	*Viola*
				Geraldine McEwan	*Olivia*
				Mark Dignam	*Malvolio*
				Cyril Luckham	*Feste*
1969	Royal Shakespeare Theatre, Stratford-upon-Avon	John Barton	Christopher Morley, Stephanie Howard	Judi Dench	*Viola*
				Lisa Harrow	*Olivia*
				Donald Sinden	*Malvolio*
				Emrys James	*Feste*
1979	BBC-tv	John Gorrie	Don Taylor	Felicity Kendal	*Viola*
				Sinead Cusack	*Olivia*
				Alec McCowen	*Malvolio*
				Trevor Peacock	*Feste*
1983	Young Vic, London	Denise Coffey	Mark Wheeler, Christine Rowland, Lynn Clarke	Deborah Poplett	*Viola*
				Christina Nagy	*Olivia*
				Stephen Lewis	*Malvolio*
				James Bowman	*Feste*
1986	Film based on 1983 Lighthouse prod., Playhouse, Adelaide	Neil Armfield	Stephen Curtis	Gillian Jones	*Viola*
				Jacqy Phillips	*Olivia*
				Peter Cummins	*Malvolio*
				Kerry Walker	*Feste*
1987	Royal Shakespeare Theatre, Stratford-upon-Avon	Bill Alexander	Kit Surrey, Deirdre Clancy	Harriet Walter	*Viola*
				Deborah Findlay	*Olivia*
				Antony Sher	*Malvolio*
				Bruce Alexander	*Feste*
1988	Renaissance Theatre Company	Kenneth Branagh	Lyn Harvey, Robert Ide	Frances Barber	*Viola*
				Caroline Langrishe	*Olivia*
				Richard Briers	*Malvolio*
				Anton Lesser	*Feste*
1991	English Shakespeare Company	Michael Pennington	Claire Lyth	Jenny Quayle	*Viola*
				Allie Byrne	*Olivia*
				Timothy Davies	*Malvolio*
				Colin Farrell	*Feste*

Above: Anton Lesser and Richard Briers, 1988

moment confronts the audience with the non-realism of the play, even in a production which attempts maximum realism. Armfield has Gillian Jones play both twins with the only difference between them physically being Sebastian's hint of a beard. At the moment of the reunion Jones' sister steps in as a double. However, this improbable moment is so breathtaking that it overwhelms the sorting out of the various love tangles. The wonder of the moment is made more other-worldly by the bizarre tokens by which the twins formally recognise each other:

VIOLA **My father had a mole upon his brow.**
SEBASTIAN **And so had mine.**

[V.1.239-40]

This moment is heightened and unrealistic but the magic is such – even in very melancholic productions – that the price of believing the unbelievable seems a small price to pay. By contrast in his own life, Shakespeare could not arrange such a happy ending. His son Hamnet, twin brother to Judith, died in 1596.

Elizabeth Schafer

THE TWO GENTLEMEN OF VERONA

*The anguish of adolescent love and the agonies
of society's self-image are set against the virtues of dogged devotion.*

Left: *I remember the trick you served me when I took my leave
of Madam Silvia. Did not I bid thee still mark me and do as I do?*
Robert Helpmann with Duff as Crab, 1957

The song *Who is Silvia?* lies at the heart of the play. It brings pain to both its female listeners. Silvia has lost her true lover, banished through the treachery of his dearest friend, the man now offering this serenade. The singer's own faithlessness in love as well as in friendship is plucking at the heartstrings of his first love, the hidden audience of this bitter-sweet praise. Music was most thoroughly used as a potent language of desire in the 1991 production when a 1930s palm court orchestra and silver-voiced chanteuse were a permanent part of the set. As Proteus arrived in Milan, *I'm in the Mood for Love* prepared for his sudden inconstancy. The plot intensified to the insistent rhythms of *Night and Day* and the lovers entered the forest's shadows as the orchestra played *In the Still of the Night*. In 1971 the play was transformed into a hit musical by a cosmopolitan cast, which sang the gamut of musical styles from Caribbean to Motown and Country and Western.

The lovers' youth is often stressed in the play's casting, excusing their confusion over their own identities and those of their lovers and friends. This was clear in 1970, when Milan was a modern, *al fresco* university, allowing students plenty of time to play on the beach. Sunglasses were an apt image of love's blindness and provocative bathing suits pressed upon the eye the impact of outward show. Both Valentine and Thurio proudly displayed their long limbs and rippling

'THEN TO SILVIA LET US SING'

The Early Production History of *The Two Gentlemen of Verona*.

The Two Gentlemen of Verona is one of Shakespeare's earliest plays, probably written around 1593. Its exploration of love and friendship is a familiar one in the period: sources can be found in writings such as *Diana Enamorada*, a popular Spanish pastoral romance, and in Elyot's *The Book Named the Governor*.

The first recorded performance was presented by David Garrick in 1762 in an adaptation by Benjamin Victor which attempted to make the characters' swings of behaviour less startling. Despite the addition of new scenes at the end of the play focussing on the two comic servants, this version enjoyed only six performances.

John Philip Kemble had no more success in 1790 and 1808, and it was not until 1821 that the play, in an operatic version, attracted enthusiastic audiences. This was at Covent Garden, where Frederick Reynolds introduced a 'Carnival in the Great Square of Milan', displaying, among other marvels, the four seasons,

Cleopatra in her barge and an exploding mountain with Apollo's temple inside it.

There were occasional revivals in the nineteenth and early twentieth century. In 1895, in New York and later in London, Augustin Daly followed Victor's example in altering the text and the show's popularity was helped by Ada Rehan's performance of Julia and the presence of much singing and dancing. One year later William Poel produced the play at the Merchant Taylors' Hall in London. The intimacy of this venue was recreated for its transfer to His Majesty's Theatre, London in 1910, by the introduction of an apron stage over the orchestra pit and front lighting on the balconies. In 1896, the audience became part of the action as the outlaws entered through the aisles with flag and drum and ambushed their victims in the vestibule. In an intriguing reversal of Elizabethan stage-practice, female actors were cast as Valentine and Panthino.

Top: Ada Rehan as Julia, 1895
Left: Title page of Sir Thomas Elyot's *The Book Named the Governor*, 1565
Right: Mr Vernon as Thurio at the Theatre Royal, Drury Lane, 1763

muscles, to the chagrin of Proteus, whose own slighter frame caused him obvious distress. It was this sense of inadequacy which drove him into rivalry with Valentine. After his first sight of Silvia in the BBC-tv production, the very young Proteus turns back to the camera, his face changed from smiles to shock. An involuntary switch of allegiance has happened, as unpredictable as the wind which has just blown up a sudden storm, darkening the sky with:

The uncertain glory of an April day.

[I.3.85]

Youthful intemperance and the elemental power of the passions motivated the action in 1957, when the play was set in the early nineteenth century. The women were stylish in riding habits and sumptuous ballgowns, the men flamboyant in swirling cloaks and dark curls. The implicit evocation of Byron and

Shelley added a particular dimension to the friendship of the two passionate men. Their behaviour was characterized by an extreme Romantic self-consciousness so that the audience was prepared to accept the wildest reversals of fortune and desire. Indulgent laughter greeted Proteus' desperate cry:

were man
But constant, he were perfect!

[V.4.111-12]

In 1991, Proteus and Valentine struggled to express their affection for one another as Valentine prepared to depart on his travels. Their attempts to embrace resulted only in the

Above left: Terence Taplin as Thurio, 1970
Above: *Leave off discourse of disability;*
Sweet lady, entertain him for your servant.
Ian Richardson, Peter Egan, Estelle Kohler and Terence Taplin as Thurio, 1970

mock wrestle of schoolboys. The 1930s society of leisure and privilege, combined with that period's distinctive music, evoked the brittle gaiety of Noel Coward's comedies. The intense introspection of Lynch's Proteus contrasted strongly with Valentine's naive generosity. In 1970, Proteus was unable to express his emotions easily. Julia cannot speak for weeping when her lover departs for Milan, but it was insuperable inhibition rather than tears preventing this Proteus from full engagement:

Here is my hand for my true constancy

[II.2.8]

was spoken as he offered a brisk handshake rather than the fond kiss for which Julia had hoped.

The pattern of farewells is completed by Launce and Crab. Crab's indifference in parting is recounted with gusto by his master, as the offending cur stands by, impenetrable to pity. In 1991, there was an uncanny physical resemblance between man and dog: a lean and hungry look marked both. Launce's face expressed a lugubrious melancholy while Crab yawned on cue, eyeing his master with a lofty contempt. Patrick Stewart's Launce was a menacing, watchful presence. This dour northerner remained aloof even in the curtain

Above left: Leonie Mellinger as Ursula and Diana Hardcastle, 1981. Above: Peter Land and Peter Chelsom, 1981
Right: Clare Holman and Barry Lynch, 1991

call, framed in a panel at the rear of the stage. Despite his textual absence in the final scene, he had looked on at his superiors' apparent happiness, a silent reminder of a permanently unrecompensed love.

Earlier, silhouettes appeared on the panels matching the onstage action and focussing attention on the play's preoccupation with shadow and substance. The swimming pool, in which Proteus' father floated as he discussed his son's future, provided a shifting surface for Julia to muse on her changing image. The 'shadow' [IV.4.194] of Silvia which must satisfy Proteus was a photograph ripped disdainfully by its subject from a glossy magazine. In the revival of this production in 1975 Silvia was played as a manipulative egotist, exploiting her wealthy and pampered posi-

tion. She cartwheeled onto the stage for her first entrance and, from that moment on, demanded everyone's full attention. She maintained a peevish silence on being rescued from Proteus in the final scene since that rescue had removed her from the centre of the stage.

Both Ian Richardson and Barry Lynch skilfully expressed surprise at their own baseness as Proteus proceeds to cheat his friend and betray his lady. Lynch paused intriguingly before:

Well, give her that ring

[IV.4.82]

as he sent his new page on an embassy to Silvia. As he uttered the 'Well' it was impossible to guess whether or not Julia's protest might be successful. In 1970, Proteus received a slap on the face from Valentine as he described to him how the unhappy Silvia has

been imprisoned by her father. The memory of this slap remained a stinging rebuke, causing him to wince as Thurio pinched his cheek in thanks for his help in wooing Silvia. It was only when Valentine kissed his cheek in forgiveness at his final transformation that the shame was removed.

The comedy of the exodus, as Silvia follows Valentine to the forest and everyone follows Silvia, was exploited in 1970 when her escort, Sir Eglamour, was an enthusiastic but ageing boy scout, equipped with an ordnance survey map of the countryside around Milan. The outlaws lurking in these wilds were led, in 1981, by a lascivious female captain, salivating over the captive Valentine's good looks, only to be disappointed by his 'honourable mind' [V.3.13].

The extravagance and intensity of the relationships in 1957 prepared the audience for the extreme events of the final scene. In the style of Gothic romance, Proteus despairingly waved a pistol at his head after Valentine intervened in his attempt to rape Silvia. In contrast, Lynch held a suspenseful silence until his smug smile cracked into bitter self-awareness and he fell to his knees to beg forgiveness. The heedless spontaneity of Valentine's response was consistent with that character's behaviour throughout. Escaping from a graphically depicted rape attempt in 1970, Silvia took refuge in the arms of the disguised Julia and she, as well as Julia, swooned as she heard Valentine's:

All that was mine in Silvia I give thee.

[V.4.83]

The 'mutual happiness' [174] of all is secured by the revelation of Julia's identity and love's transforming power is, at the last, shown in its best light.

Rebecca Flynn

NOTABLE PRODUCTIONS OF *THE TWO GENTLEMEN OF VERONA*

	THEATRE	DIRECTOR	DESIGNER	PRINCIPALS
1957	The Old Vic, London	Michael Langham	Tanya Moiseiwitsch	Keith Michell ....*Proteus* Richard Gale ....*Valentine* Barbara Jefford ....*Julia* Ingrid Hafner ....*Silvia* Robert Helpmann....................*Launce*
1970	Royal Shakespeare Theatre, Stratford-upon-Avon	Robin Phillips	Daphne Dare	Ian Richardson ....*Proteus* Peter Egan ....*Valentine* Helen Mirren...............................*Julia* Estelle Kohler............................*Silvia* Patrick Stewart ....*Launce*
1971	Delacorte Theatre, New York Shakespeare Festival	Mel Shapiro	Ming Cho Lee	Raul Julia.................................*Proteus* Clifton Davis ....*Valentine* Carla Pinza ....*Julia* Jonelle Allen................................*Silvia* Jerry Stiller................................*Launce*
1975	The Shakespearean Festival Theatre, Stratford, Ontario	Robin Phillips, David Toguri	Molly Harris Campbell, Daphne Dare	Nicholas Pennell ....*Proteus* Stephen Russell....................*Valentine* Mia Anderson ....*Julia* Jackie Burroughs ....*Silvia* Eric Donkin ....*Launce*
1981	Royal Shakespeare Theatre, Stratford-upon-Avon	John Barton	Christopher Morley	Peter Land...............................*Proteus* Peter Chelsom.....................*Valentine* Julia Swift....................................*Julia* Diana Hardcastle.......................*Silvia* Geoffrey Hutchings ....*Launce*
1983	BBC-tv	Don Taylor	Barbara Gosnold	Tyler Butterworth...................*Proteus* John Hudson........................*Valentine* Tessa Peake-Jones ....*Julia* Joanne Pearce ....*Silvia* Tony Haygarth ....*Launce*
1991	Swan Theatre, Stratford-upon-Avon	David Thacker	Shelagh Keegan	Barry Lynch............................*Proteus* Richard Bonneville ....*Valentine* Clare Holman ....*Julia* Saskia Reeves ....*Silvia* Richard Moore ....*Launce*

'NEVER FORTUNE DID PLAY A SUBTLER GAME'

The Early Production History of *The Two Noble Kinsmen*

When it was first published in 1634, *The Two Noble Kinsmen* was stated to be 'by the memorable worthies of their time, Mr John Fletcher, and Mr William Shakespeare'. Although most recent scholarship endorses this ascription, the question of Shakespeare's participation in the authorship of the play has been the central issue and seems to have had a crucial influence on the evaluation of the play as theatre.

The Two Noble Kinsmen has a thin performance history. The first performance of the play probably took place sometime between 20 February 1613 and 31 October 1614. The clue to the earliest date of composition lies in the morris dance in III.5. which the King's Men seem to have borrowed from Francis Beaumont's *Masque of the Inner Temple and Gray's Inn*, presented at Whitehall on 20 February 1613. It seems likely that *Kinsmen* was still in the repertory at least until 31 October 1614 when a dramatic character named Palamon was mentioned in the first performance of Ben Jonson's *Bartholomew Fair*. *Kinsmen* was under consideration for presentation at Court

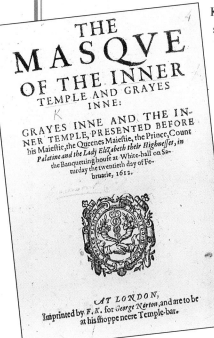

around 1619-20, and it was revived around 1625-26. There is no record of production after the Jacobean performances until the twentieth century, except for William Davenant's adaptation of the play entitled *The Rivals* in 1664. Charles II probably saw Mary Davis in the part of Celania, a shepherdess mad for love, in the 1667 revival.

Modern revivals began with the Old Vic production during its 1927-28 season. Ernest Milton's Palamon in a grotesquely bright orange wig exploited the comic possibilities of the rôle with a success that must have been achieved at the play's expense. After this production, there were no further professional performances of *Kinsmen* until the 1970s.

Top: Ernest Milton, who played Palamon in 1927
Left: Playbill for Beaumont's masque which, it is presumed, predates Shakespeare's play
Right: Mary Davis, actress and King's mistress, fl. 1669

THE TWO NOBLE KINSMEN

*Rivalry in love for a woman tests male friendship
and the play's resolution questions the nature of winning.*

Two productions of *The Two Noble Kinsmen* in the 1970s provoked a wide range of reactions from reviewers, although the quality of performances and the success of the interpretations varied. Having produced the play for the York Theatre Royal Company in 1973, Mervyn Willis mounted a second production in the following year, with the New Shakespeare Company in Regent's Park, London. It would seem that Willis was unable to overcome the difficulties of the play's structure, but compounded the problems posed by the double plot and dual authorship by introducing eccentrically costumed dance routines and some rather incongruous spectacle into the text. In 1979 a troupe called the Cherub Company staged their all-male production at the Edinburgh International Festival. No scenery was used and the cast wore black leather trousers and went bare-chested. Their sexual distinctions were stylised: painted faces and painted circles round the left breasts for the female characters, protuberant codpieces for the male characters. Nearly a third of the text was cut, which apparently made the narrative line compelling for the audience. The production was lucid and frequently exciting, and the two kinsmen Arcite and Palamon were effectively differentiated. Palamon was intense and suspicious, Arcite was open and rational. The main plot was full of erotic tension: the kinsmen's love for one another and their love for Emilia had the same romantic quality.

The Royal Shakespeare Company chose *The Two Noble Kinsmen* to open the Swan Theatre

Above: *… give us the bones
Of our dead kings, that we may chapel them*
The opening scene, 1974

in 1986. The play's potential for performance has long been questioned, mainly because of the evident stylistic difference in writing between the two authors. Another major difficulty in mounting any production is finding a setting which will consolidate the main and sub-plots. The director Barry Kyle believed that the play's wordiness made it necessary to edit the text, but he exploited the intrinsic contrast of the structural rhythm between the

two plots. *Kinsmen* is a Jacobean play which presents medieval chivalric values against the background of ancient Greece. Kyle transposed the setting of the play to feudal Japanese society, so that war, ritual and chivalric honour codes within the play would

make sense to a modern audience. This setting helped to create the sense of an alien and mysterious culture, thus giving the audience an appropriate remoteness from the play's ideology. There was no set or scenery, except for the prison cage suspended from the ceiling.

Kyle took the main plot scene by scene through a very stylised variety of settings and costumes, accompanied by kabuki-like choreography. Theseus' defeat of Hippolyta in the Amazonian war was enacted in the opening dumb show. Theseus held still to shoot Hippolyta who assumed a frozen posture with drawn sword held high. As she began to fall, blood-red rose petals were released from her bodice, thus symbolizing Theseus' conquest of her in battle and in love. This surrealistic stage rendering effectively illustrated Theseus' speech in *A Midsummer Night's Dream*: 'Hippolyta, I wooed thee with my sword, / And won thy love doing thee injuries' [I.1.16-17].

This scene was followed by their wedding ceremony, where Hippolyta was wound up with a very long white swathe of silken material, which stretched down from the upper gallery. The production made impressive use of long swathes of cloth. In the burial ceremony of the kings, the three widowed Queens lay across black lengths of cloth and then rolled themselves up into cocoons. Silver curtains streaked with green suggested Emilia's garden, and red rope stretched across the back of the stage symbolized the battlefield on which Theseus defeated Creon.

Compared with the highly stylised design for the main plot, the sub-plot of frustrated love was presented with more naturalism and vitality. The Gaoler's Daughter, who loves Palamon 'beyond love, and beyond reason, / Or wit, or safety' [II.5.11-12], defies Duke

Above left: Rehearsing the morris dance, 1986
Above: Imogen Stubbs, 1986

Theseus, sacrifices her father by releasing his prisoner, then runs away from home to meet Palamon in the woods. The Swan Theatre production placed a great deal of emphasis on the sexual connotations of the morris dance to explore visually the Gaoler's Daughter's desperate love for Palamon. The climax of the May fertility dance scene had Imogen Stubbs jump on top of a gigantic leather phallus carried by all the morris dancers. She was harnessed with a bridle, reins and blinkers, thus representing a hobby horse. The dance culminated with her hobby horse phallus collapsing after a mimed ejaculation of white silk directed at the female members of the royal hunting party.

Above: Anna Nygh as Hippolyta, 1986
Above right: Richard Moore as the Schoolmaster and Imogen Stubbs, 1986
Right: Imogen Stubbs at the climax of the morris dance, 1986

In *The Two Noble Kinsmen*, love is presented as a destructive passion which drives the Gaoler's Daughter into madness and leads Arcite to death. The kinsmen's mutual affection and admiration change instantly into rivalry and enmity with the appearance of Emilia. The only solution for their rivalry is fighting each other to the death and it is not until the moment of one's death that the other recognises the value of their friendship. Gerard Murphy's Palamon was passionate and intense, whereas Hugh Quarshie's Arcite was cooler and more rational. They maintained just the right degree of tension between hostility and affec-

NOTABLE PRODUCTIONS OF *THE TWO NOBLE KINSMEN*

	THEATRE	DIRECTOR	DESIGNER	PRINCIPALS
1974	New Shakespeare Company, Regent's Park	Mervyn Willis	Charles Dunlop	Philip Bowen ....*Palamon* Martin Potter ....*Arcite* Lea Dregorn ....*Emilia* Frances Jean Viner.................*Gaoler's Daughter*
1986	Swan Theatre, Stratford-upon-Avon	Barry Kyle	Bob Crowley	Gerard Murphy ....*Palamon* Hugh Quarshie ....*Arcite* Amanda Harris........................*Emilia* Imogen Stubbs ......*Gaoler's Daughter*

tion in the scene where they armed each other for the duel, conducting a dialogue which alternated between chivalry and absurdity. The philosophy of the swordsmanship embodied in kendo, the ideal that honour outweighs life and death, worked well and prevented the scene from becoming farce. Palamon's 'I would have nothing hurt thee but my sword' [III.6.87], as he gently avoided over-tightening Arcite's kendo armour, raised a kind and sympathetic laugh.

The presentation of Emilia in the RSC production explored the disadvantaged status of women, subjected to the kind of masculine control represented by Theseus. Emilia has been seen as an insipid character with little dramatic credibility, which is partly due to the discordant effects of the dual authorship. Shakespeare's Emilia desires to remain in pre-pubescent virginity but is reluctantly forced into marriage, while Fletcher's Emilia with a streak of sensuality grows increasingly interested in her two suitors. Kyle removed those inconsistencies from the text, and gave her psychological validity. As a result, Amanda Harris' Emilia was dramatised as a strong-minded individual in her own right. She made it clear that Emilia consented to marriage not from affection or any desire for a husband but out of pity, and in order to save at least one valuable life. Her resentment at being 'the treasure' [V.3.31] to be won by bloodshed was evident in her adamant refusal to watch the tournament. The helplessness of her situation culminated in the capriciously fatalistic ending of the play when she was awarded to Palamon on Arcite's deathbed. Emilia did not speak to Palamon but her last words were to promise 'tears':

I'll close thine eyes, prince; blessèd souls be
** with thee!**
Thou art a right good man, and while I live
This day I give to tears.

[V.4.96-8]

Imogen Stubbs surprised and delighted the audience with her extraordinary athletic enactment of the Gaoler's Daughter's emotional vulnerability. Especially touching was the episode in which she shinned up a tall pole that she imagined as the mast of a ship; crouched at the top she set sail in search of Palamon whilst her friends and relations played out the parts of kindly sailors. Her passionate freedom and boldness contrast with Emilia's passive and non-erotic interest in either of her suitors. The resolution of her madness, through her acceptance of the Wooer in Palamon's disguise, parallels the ending of the main plot where Palamon supplants Arcite as Emilia's husband. Being mistaken for Arcite by the Gaoler's Daughter, the Doctor expresses his delight in her marriage to the Wooer: 'I am glad my cousin Palamon / Has made so fair a choice' [V.2.89-90]. The most innovative aspect of the RSC production was its exploration of the similarity between the two heroines' distress. Prior to the tournament, a Messenger and Pirithous tied red swathes of silken material around Emilia's wrists. It implied that she was condemned to be a pawn in the two rival kinsmen's obsession with her. As she left, she passed the Gaoler's mad daughter, whose arms were bound into a white straitjacket. The production ended with them facing each other, one on each side of the stage.

Kyle's production was a clear attempt to give authoritative sanction for the play's acceptance into the Shakespeare canon. Although the authorship question prompted some reviewers to be conventionally negative in response to the text, most audiences and critics appreciated its excellence in performance. It remains to be seen whether the play will continue to attract directors and designers eager to take up the challenge of reinterpreting this many-faceted and intriguing work.

Etsuko Fukahori

THE WINTER'S TALE

*Tragedy seems certain if that which is lost be not found, but
a happy ending is compounded by the most remarkable theatrical surprise.*

'A sad tale's best for winter' observes Mamillius, King Leontes' young son, early in the play as he sits listening to stories with his mother, Hermione, and her women [II.1.25]. Like the tragedies, *The Winter's Tale* shows us how terrible is the human capacity to destroy. The play is not a tragedy, however, for it gives as much emphasis to healing and renewal as it does to destruction. It displays the power of Faith and asserts its marriage with Art. If we are moved by humanity, we can rehearse our compassion in the theatre. *The Winter's Tale* also gives us wonderful opportunities for laughter.

The play begins with a family idyll. King Leontes of Sicilia and Queen Hermione are delighting in their young son, Mamillius, who is the joy and hope of the whole court. Their pleasure is shared by an honoured guest of nine months, Polixenes, boyhood friend of the King. The circle of love and friendship is secure and deep. The first half of the play takes place in the cold winter of Sicilia and in Terry Hands' production, the court, all in white, was mirrored by a glassy backdrop and posed on a massive polar bear rug. The scene was somehow too white, too fragile in its glassy purity: one felt that something must be stained, must break. A warmer, general joy and confidence during these opening moments of the play were shown lightly, easily in Adrian Noble's production in 1993. There was mirth and laughter while above the celebration, brightly coloured balloons danced and jostled. Abruptly into this idyll bursts Leontes' jealousy of Polixenes and his wife. The fissure in family happiness was brilliantly evoked in Trevor Nunn's 1969 production. The action began in an exaggeratedly white and substantial playroom with shapes and structures you could trust: the King and his son rode a rocking horse, watched in pleasure by Hermione and Polixenes. Soon, as Leontes' neurosis took hold, the scene froze and was chilled with blue light. The words and movements of Hermione and Polixenes were deformed – becoming an imitation of the malicious imaginings of Leontes' mind.

Polixenes' flight from court with Camillo, the man Leontes hires to poison him, makes the King turn all his malice against Hermione and his tiny baby, born in prison. Here, the spirited Lady Paulina enters the play as their fearless defender. With audacity and defiance, she challenges the King's accusations – 'Good queen, my lord, good queen, I say good queen' [II.3.59] – and puts the case for the honour of the mother and the beauty and innocence of the child. Paulina is a wonderful part. Brenda Bruce, Elizabeth Spriggs and Gemma Jones have each brought out the integrity, wit and stalwart championing of Hermione's cause. One can almost hear an audience's relief when the character first enters: at last here is someone not afraid to expose Leontes' foolishness and they can laugh at the teasing humour with which she does so. Sheila Hancock's Paulina, observed how the baby had her father's features, including 'his smiles' – a double take by the courtiers drew attention to the King's glowering stare [101]. Paulina fails, and Hermione

Above: *Go together,
You precious winners all*
Patrick Stewart, Gemma Jones and Leonie Mellinger, 1981

is dragged from her childbed to face a gruelling public trial in the open air, knowing her baby has been taken to barren, foreign lands by Antigonus.

We become witnesses and see a woman of integrity, honesty and love forced:

'STRIKE ALL THAT LOOK UPON WITH MARVEL'

The Early Production History of *The Winter's Tale*

The Winter's Tale is first recorded in performance in May 1611 and was probably written a year or two earlier. It was based on Robert Greene's prose story, *Pandosto* (1588). Shakespeare introduced significant new characters, among them one who must 'Exit, pursued by a bear' [III.3.57], which has become a notorious and much loved stage direction. He also radically changed the ending. The play was liked by the early seventeenth century court but with changing tastes in the years after the English Civil War, *The Winter's Tale* became unpopular and remained in hibernation for nearly a century.

It is next recorded in performance at Giffard's theatre in Goodman's Fields, London, in 1741. A chequered history of adaptations, embellishments and mutilations of the text began which continued until the twentieth century. The 1741 performance was flanked by two halves of a concert and the following year ran briefly at Covent Garden embellished by a 'Grand Ballet'. The play's major eighteenth century successes were in adaptations by Macnamara Morgan (1754) and David Garrick (1756); both ignored the Sicilian scenes of the first half and presented the pastoral romance that takes place sixteen years later between Florizel and Perdita, daughter of King Leontes.

In the early nineteenth century, John Philip Kemble presented a much fuller version of the story but he too transposed and adapted scenes, sacrificing much to clarity and pace. Charles Kean's 1856 production went for Grecian spectacle: elaborate stage business, processions, animals, dances and crowds. The poetry, where it survived, came a poor second. This production did, however, include an eight-year-old Ellen Terry, who movingly acted Mamillius. In September 1887 at the Lyceum, Mary Anderson's production set the precedent of doubling the rôles of Hermione and Perdita. Notable productions this century were those of Harley Granville-Barker (1912) and Peter Brook at the Phoenix Theatre in 1951 with John Gielgud as Leontes.

Top: Ellen Terry as Mamillius, painted by Sir William Nicholson
Left: Goodman's Fields Theatre, c.1810
Right: Harley Granville-Barker

To prate and talk for life and honour 'fore
Who please to come and hear.

[III.2.40-1]

Samantha Bond gave touching detail to her characterisation. While everyone awaited the messengers from Apollo's Oracle, she was scarcely able to stand and rested for a moment on the arm of the guard nearby. She spoke her words about her father 'the Emperor of Russia' [118] and how he would pity her plight, only to the guard. The reflection became more private, more touching.

The trial scene has wonderful speeches for Hermione, thrilling, eloquent responses to Leontes' tyranny. These were beautifully expressed by Judi Dench. She moved between manifest dignity and blamelessness to justifiable anger. One was affected by those slight catches in the voice when she came close to tears but defied them. This scene builds to a tremendous climax and we are given an explicit and powerful indictment of wilful patriarchy and masculine error, and of a mentality that mistrusts, constrains and destroys feminine elements. In the theatrical moment, we feel those age-old and rigorous emotions, pity and terror. The absolute verdict of the Oracle is declared:

Hermione is chaste; Polixenes blameless;
Camillo a true subject; Leontes a jealous tyrant;
his innocent babe truly begotten; and the King
shall live without an heir, if that which is lost be
not found.

[131-4]

There is relief, relaxation as Hermione is vindicated, but the thrust of Leontes' delusion defies the god's authority:

Above right: Nathaniel Parker, Jeremy Irons, Gillian Barge and Penny Downie here as Perdita, 1986
Right: Joe Melia, 1986

There is no truth at all i'th'oracle
The sessions shall proceed: this is mere
falsehood.

[138-9]

Only Apollo has power to convince and does so through a devastating and irremediable blow; a servant rushes in with the news that Mamillius is dead. This moment of horror and compassion was powerfully attenuated in 1969. On hearing the news, Hermione (Judi Dench), fell into a slow-motion faint. In those everlasting seconds we had time to register fully these terrible events. We grieve and feel a world lost. The queen is carried off-stage. When Paulina returns it is to utter a fierce indictment of Leontes' crimes, culminating in the dreadful announcement that Hermione is dead. He is penitent and makes one of the most poignant acknowledgements in the theatre:

Go on, go on:
Thou canst not speak too much; I have deserved
All tongues to talk their bitt'rest.

[212-14]

A winter of unceasing penance and continuing grief begins.

Here, the play starts to turn. The action moves to Bohemia where we are soon to see elements of spring and summer burgeoning. The baby, abandoned on Bohemia's seacoast, is found by an old shepherd: the moment is a marvellous turning point. The old man tells his son, who has just seen Antigonus torn to pieces by a bear:

But look thee here, boy. Now bless thyself: thou met'st with things dying, I with things newborn.

[III.3.109-10]

Right: *O grave and good Paulina*
Ian McKellen and Barbara Leigh-Hunt, 1976

The cold, destructive shadow of Sicilia melts away and we are warmed by the earthy and accommodating humanity of the old shepherd and his son.

The passing of sixteen years is marked by Time's speech. In production, Time has appeared as a kind of witchdoctor or as a feathered figure fluttering above the stage. The most urbane and minimalist 'appearance' of Time came in 1992. A stray balloon drifted down, carrying a scroll from which

Camillo read Time's speech. He then popped the balloon with a pin.

The second half of the play throbs with the energy, song and dance of the sheep-shearing festival. For this, the Sicilian princess, Perdita (named by Hermione in a vision to Antigonus) serves as hostess for her 'father', the old shepherd. It also beats time to the songs and tricks of Autolycus, a rogue and 'snapper up of unconsidered trifles' [IV.3.25-6] who makes his way to the festival to fleece the human flock. In Noble's production, making his first entry as Autolycus on a tree of green balloons, and looking like a very down at heel jazz musican, Richard McCabe gave music-hall zest to the character's songs and routines. In this production, the sheep-shearing turned out to be a Thirties street party: band, bunting, church hall tables and chairs; characters clad in an extraordinary plethora of clothes – caps, cardigans, check jackets, striped waistcoats, floral dresses, Shetland pullovers, plaid skirts, plus fours – the whole event an exuberant reminiscence of community and family gatherings in a very English village. The balloons again came into their own, decoratively and, to the audience's great amusement, in pairs, as part of the sexual equipment of those who performed the satyrs' dance earnestly and with great concentration. The scene was a wonderful jamboree on a rural theme.

Years earlier, Derek Smith's effervescent Autolycus had also delighted audiences, sauntering, stealing and singing beguilingly and with gusto, Shakespeare's lyrics to Guy Woolfenden's Sixties 'pop' music. He established a dynamic and exuberant rapport with the audience, coming close to stealing the show. The show is in fact brutally ruptured by Polixenes' disgust and jealousy when, spying in disguise on his son, Florizel, he learns of his intention to marry Perdita. As a result of Camillo's machinations, the young couple flee to Sicilia to seek Leontes' support, followed by Polixenes, Camillo, the two shepherds and Autolycus.

There is a deeply affecting meeting between Leontes, Florizel and Perdita. In the 1993 production we moved from the busy abundance of visual image at the sheep-shearing to moments of stillness here: the clothes regained classical lines. Florizel wore vivid green, Perdita a dark, deep burgundy, reminiscent of her mother's gown in the early scenes. Contemplating the bright optimism and life-affirming presence of the young couple and remembering his own lost children, it was little wonder Leontes greeted them with sorrow and joy:

> **Welcome hither**
> **As is the spring to th'earth!**
>
> [V.1.150-1]

With the arrival of Polixenes, all identities are revealed and Leontes is reunited with his daughter, Polixenes and Camillo.

The final scene of the play is 'a sight which [is] to be seen, cannot be spoken of.' [V.2.41-2]. Paulina, who for sixteen years has been Leontes' guide and mentor, stage-manages an extraordinary transformation. She proves to be, like Shakespeare himself, a dramatist. The heartbeat of this final sequence is magical and, as with all the best magic:

> **It is required**
> **You do awake your faith.**
>
> [V.3.94-5]

We are invited to share in the creation of a wonderful imaginative reality, one which has the power to initiate and transfigure emotion. We hold our breath and watch a miracle, that of warm humanity living again before our eyes.

Susan L. Powell

NOTABLE PRODUCTIONS OF *THE WINTER'S TALE*

	THEATRE	DIRECTOR	DESIGNER	PRINCIPALS	
1969	Royal Shakespeare Theatre, Stratford-upon-Avon	Trevor Nunn	Christopher Morley	Barrie Ingham	*Leontes*
				Judi Dench	*Hermione*
				Richard Pasco	*Polixenes*
				Brenda Bruce	*Paulina*
				David Bailie	*Florizel*
				Judi Dench	*Perdita*
				Derek Smith	*Autolycus*
1976	Royal Shakespeare Theatre, Stratford-upon-Avon	John Barton	Di Seymour	Ian McKellen	*Leontes*
				Marilyn Taylerson	*Hermione*
				John Woodvine	*Polixenes*
				Barbara Leigh-Hunt	*Paulina*
				Nickolas Grace	*Florizel*
				Cherie Lunghi	*Perdita*
				Michael Williams	*Autolycus*
1981	Royal Shakespeare Theatre, Stratford-upon-Avon	Ronald Eyre	Chris Dyer	Patrick Stewart	*Leontes*
				Gemma Jones	*Hermione*
				Ray Jewers	*Polixenes*
				Sheila Hancock	*Paulina*
				Peter Chelsom	*Florizel*
				Leonie Mellinger	*Perdita*
				Geoffrey Hutchings	*Autolycus*
1986	Royal Shakespeare Theatre, Stratford-upon-Avon	Terry Hands	Gerard Howland	Jeremy Irons	*Leontes*
				Penny Downie	*Hermione*
				Paul Greenwood	*Polixenes*
				Gillian Barge	*Paulina*
				Nathaniel Parker	*Florizel*
				Penny Downie	*Perdita*
				Joe Melia	*Autolycus*
1992	Royal Shakespeare Theatre, Stratford-upon-Avon	Adrian Noble	Anthony Ward	John Nettles	*Leontes*
				Samantha Bond	*Hermione*
				Paul Jesson	*Polixenes*
				Gemma Jones	*Paulina*
				Alan Cox	*Florizel*
				Phyllida Hancock	*Perdita*
				Richard McCabe	*Autolycus*

Appendix I: *The lineal state and glory of the land*

When we go to the theatre, or indeed when we use the word 'drama', we generally expect action, excitement and suspense. By turning to relatively recent English history as the source-material for ten of his plays, Shakespeare dispensed with the last ingredient and offered his audience plays in which the outcome was not only well known but com-plicated by the force of contemporary events.

Both *King John* and *Richard II* examine the legitimacy and pressures of kingship. The resonance of a play that deals with the deposition of a monarch proved particularly powerful when rebellion threatened.

Elizabethan playgoers could enjoy *Henry IV* knowing that Hal would become the greatest King that England had ever known – and they could do so without disloyalty since a virgin queen was on the throne. Indeed, an audience's anxieties about the political and military complications of succession had been reflected in the turmoil of the earlier *Henry VI* plays. Just as a theatre company dependent upon patronage and box-office receipts might stage *Richard III* in which the last of the Plantagenet kings is vilified, so could *Henry VIII* exploit a mood of patriotic pride and fervour.

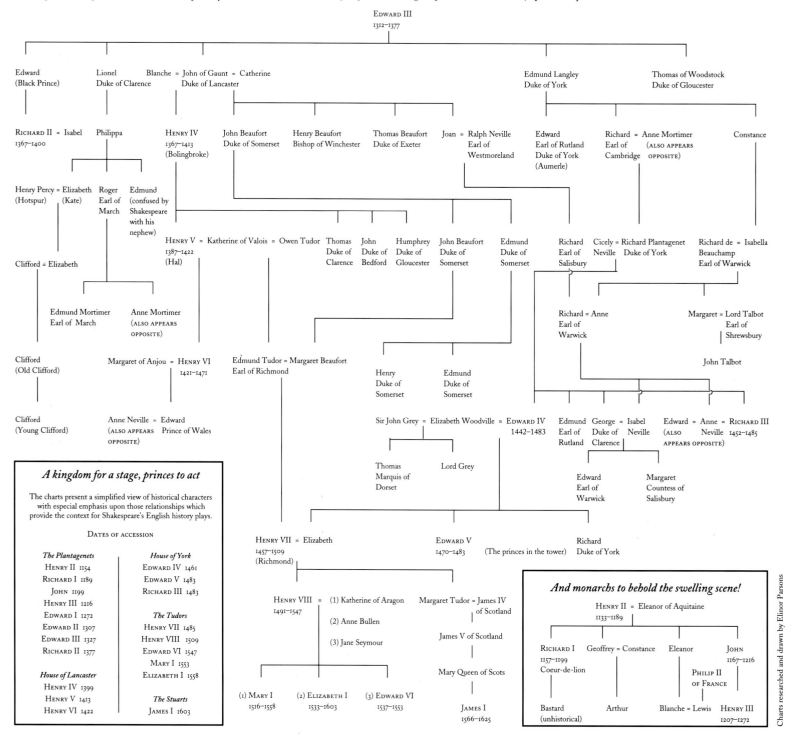

Charts researched and drawn by Elinor Parsons

Appendix II: *Shadows*

If we shadows have offended,
Think but this, and all is mended:
That you have but slumbered here
While these visions did appear.

1600

William Davenant 1606–1668

Thomas Killigrew 1612–1683

John Dryden 1631–1700

Thomas Betterton 1635–1710

Thomas Shadwell 1642–1692

Nahum Tate 1652–1715

1700

James Quin 1693–1766

Charles Macklin c.1697–1797

David Garrick 1717–1779

Sarah Siddons 1755–1831

John Philip Kemble 1757–1823

1800

Charles Kemble 1775–1854

Edmund Kean 1787–1833

William Charles Macready 1793–1873

Samuel Phelps 1804–1878

Edwin Forrest 1806–1872

Charles Kean c.1811–1868

Henry Irving 1838–1905

Ellen Terry 1848–1928

William Poel 1852–1934

Beerbohm Tree 1853–1917

1900

Harley Granville-Barker 1877–1946

Bertolt Brecht 1898–1956

Tyrone Guthrie 1900–1971

John Gielgud 1904–

Laurence Olivier 1907–1989

The course of Shakespearean production has been shaped by actors, theatre managers, adapters and directors. The listing complements the chapter entitled *The Changing Stage.*

Appendix III: *Goodly transformation*

Evidence of the sustained and continuing vitality of Shakespeare's work is found not only in its inspirational power for artists and poets as diverse as Dadd and Millais, Tennyson and Auden, but also in the fact that his plays are so frequently and so enthusiastically translated into different media. Something of the power of dance to explore the subtext of innermost thoughts and feelings, and to express the sublime aspiration that goes beyond words, has been discussed in the appropriate chapters with reference to Frederick Ashton's *The Dream* and Kenneth MacMillan's *Romeo and Juliet.* Setting classical ballet against modern dance helps define the rôle of Irek Mukhamedhov's 'extravagant and wheeling stranger' in Kim Brandstrup's *Othello.*

Shakespeare himself recognised 'the sweet power of music', and from Robert Johnson to Gerald Finzi and John Dankworth there have been settings of his songs in abundance. He has inspired orchestral composers such as Edward Elgar and Jean Sibelius, but opera has proved itself able to explore the emotional intensity of tragedy and to provide the degree of detachment for comic commentary on larger-than-life characters. Masterpieces such as Giuseppe Verdi's *Otello* and *Falstaff* are firmly established within the standard repertoire.

In one way or another screen adaptations have needed to embrace Shakespeare's essential theatricality. Olivier recognised that the plays must be reshaped to exploit the intimacy and boldness of film and he coped with the big Shakespearean moment such as 'Once more unto the breach…' before the assault on Harfleur (*Henry V,* III.1) not by zooming in but by tracking back. His use of cinematic devices such as crane-shots and deep-focus photography in *Hamlet* and of shadow in *Richard III* created a vocabulary that has been developed by Orson Welles, Grigori Kozintsev and Franco Zeffirelli – all of whom have been cited extensively in the articles on individual plays.

Shakespeare has been less well served by television. The BBC-tv Shakespeare productions generally suffer from a dead weight of worthiness, but there are some adventurous exceptions such as *Cymbeline, Henry VIII* and *Titus Andronicus.* The problem would seem to be in the rehearsal process rather than the medium, for the different ways in which Trevor Nunn's Royal Shakespeare Company productions of *Antony and Cleopatra, The Comedy of Errors* and *Macbeth* were transferred to a domestic frame indicate what can be achieved. Similarly, if the constraints of time and budget are recognised, there can only be gratitude that something of the intense theatricality of the English Shakespeare Company's *The Wars of the Roses* has been preserved for future generations.

The listing is an eclectic and personal selection of some of the more interesting adaptations which the reader may find worth exploring. Preference has been given to versions that are in current repertories somewhere in the world or are readily available as sound or video recordings. The list does not repeat those ballets and films which have been listed in the display panels of NOTABLE PRODUCTIONS for individual plays.

ANTONY AND CLEOPATRA
Antony and Cleopatra Opera by Samuel Barber. Deserving more widespread attention, it was first presented in a production by Franco Zeffirelli at The Metropolitan Opera House, New York, 16 September, 1966.

Carry on Cleo Feature film 'from an original idea by William Shakespeare' offering cringingly awful puns and very British humour. It used sets built for the Taylor-Burton *Cleopatra* and was directed by Gerald Thomas with Sidney James as Mark Antony and Amanda Barrie as Cleopatra, 1964.

HAMLET
Hamlet Dramatic ballet in one act with music by Peter Ilyich Tchaikovsky. Choreography by Robert Helpmann. Dream and flashback show Hamlet's confusion of affection for Gertrude and Ophelia. First presented with Robert Helpmann as Hamlet and Margot Fonteyn as Ophelia by the Sadler's Wells Ballet at the New Theatre, London, 19 May, 1942.

HENRY IV, V, VI, ETC.

The Wars of the Roses Video versions of the English Shakespeare Company's remarkable cycle of seven history plays recorded in the last week of a theatrical life which had begun in 1986. Theatre and television direction by Michael Bogdanov with Michael Pennington as Hal and Buckingham, Barry Stanton as Falstaff, Paul Brennen as Henry VI and Andrew Jarvis as Richard III, 1989.

KING LEAR

King Lear Television production directed by Michael Elliott. After playing Lear on stage when he was 39, Laurence Olivier returned to the part in the studio at the age of 75. Surrounded by a galaxy of theatrical talent, his performance is intensely moving, 1983.

Ran Film directed by Akira Kurosawa with Tatsuya Nakadai as a 16th century samurai king, Hidetori, who has three sons. Its title translates as *Chaos* and we see how man's hunger for power denies a rôle for compassion, 1985.

LOVE'S LABOUR'S LOST

Love's Labour's Lost Orchestral suite by Gerald Finzi. Strongly motivated by character and situation, the music was originally composed for a BBC broadcast in 1946 and then developed for use in open-air performances before being worked into a suite, 1955.

MACBETH

Macbeth Opera by Giuseppe Verdi. It provides psychological insight and a superlative rôle for a *prima donna* as Lady Macbeth, being memorable especially for her sleep-walking scene. First presented in 1847 and extensively revised in 1865.

Kumonosu-Jo Film directed by Akira Kurosawa with *Throne of Blood* as its English title. Toshiro Mifune as Washizu, strongly influenced by an older wife, becomes Lord of Cobweb Castle and in a thrilling climax is shot by the arrows of his own men, 1957.

THE MERCHANT OF VENICE

Serenade to Music Setting by Ralph Vaughan Williams of 'How sweet the moonlight sleeps upon this bank' achieves a sublime harmony of words and music, 1938.

THE MERRY WIVES OF WINDSOR

Die Lustigen Weiber von Windsor Comic opera by Otto Nicolai. The energy and invention of the women are at the heart of a version in which the farcical aspects of the play are given full weight without sacrificing a warm humanity. First presented in Berlin, 1849.

Falstaff Comic opera by Giuseppe Verdi. The love between Nannetta (Anne Page) and Fenton counterbalances a degree of pathos in an affectionate portrait of the fat knight whose character is shaped by the interpolation of his speech on 'honour' from *Henry IV*. First presented at the Teatro alla Scala, Milan, 9 February, 1893.

Sir John in Love Opera by Ralph Vaughan Williams. The text is taken from *Merry Wives* with the addition of some Elizabethan lyrics and the romantic

freshness of the music is influenced by English folk tunes. First presented at the Royal College of Music, London, March 1929.

A MIDSUMMER NIGHT'S DREAM

A Midsummer Night's Dream Feature film directed by Max Reinhardt and William Dieterle with scenes of shimmering magic and balletic realisation of Mendelssohn's music. Victor Jory as Oberon, Anita Louise as Titania, James Cagney as Bottom and Mickey Rooney as Puck, 1935.

A Midsummer Night's Dream Opera by Benjamin Britten. He sets Shakespeare's words making Oberon a rôle for a counter-tenor and Tytania for a coloratura. First presented at Aldeburgh, Suffolk, 1960.

A Midsummer Night's Dream Ballet in two acts with music by Felix Mendelssohn. Choreography by George Balanchine with the second act devoted to *divertissements*. First presented with Edward Villella as Oberon and Melissa Hayden as Titania by the New York City Ballet at the City Center, New York, 17 January, 1962.

MUCH ADO ABOUT NOTHING

Béatrice et Bénédict Opera in two acts by Hector Berlioz with spoken dialogue from Shakespeare. Conventional love is contrasted with the melodic development of a vigorous relationship. First presented at Baden-Baden, 9 August, 1862.

OTHELLO

Othello Ballet in one act. Choreographed by Kim Brandstrup to music by Ian Dearden. Created on Irek Mukhamedhov, who showed Othello's otherness by being the single classical dancer in a modern dance company. First presented with Leesa Phillips as Desdemona at Sadler's Wells, 9 February, 1994.

Otello Tragic opera in four acts by Giuseppe Verdi which follows Shakespeare's play closely except that it omits the first act and begins with the arrival at Cyprus. First presented at the Teatro alla Scala, Milan, 5 February, 1887.

ROMEO AND JULIET

I Capuleti e i Montecchi Opera in two acts by Vincenzo Bellini. Only loosely based on Shakespeare with Giulietta betrothed to Tebaldo (Tybalt). First presented at La Fenice, Venice, 1830.

Roméo et Juliette Dramatic symphony by Hector Berlioz. Seeking 'another mode of expression', the composer has three soloists, three choruses and full orchestra for a full-bloodedly romantic treatment derived from Garrick's version of the play. First presented at the Paris Conservatoire, 24 November, 1839.

Roméo et Juliette Tragic opera in five acts by Charles François Gounod in which Juliet wakes just before Romeo dies. First presented at the Théâtre Lyrique, Paris, 27 April, 1867.

Romeo and Juliet Feature film directed by George Cukor with Norma Shearer and Leslie Howard as older lovers (he was 49), but the film is characterised by grace and sensitivity, 1936.

Romeo and Juliet Ballet in three acts with music by Serge Prokofiev. Choreography by Leonid Lavrovsky. First presented with Galina Ulanova

and Konstantin Sergeyev at the Kirov State Theatre, Leningrad, 11 January, 1940.

West Side Story Stage musical conceived and choreographed by Jerome Robbins with music by Leonard Bernstein. Shakespeare's 'two households' become warring gangs of Jets and Sharks in Manhattan. First presented at the Winter Garden, New York, 26 September, 1957, and then filmed by Robert Wise and Jerome Robbins with Natalie Wood as Maria (Juliet), Richard Beymer as Tony (Romeo) and George Chakiris as Bernardo (Tybalt), 1960.

THE TAMING OF THE SHREW

The Taming of the Shrew Feature film directed by Sam Taylor 'by William Shakespeare with additional dialogue by Sam Taylor'. It starred Douglas Fairbanks and Mary Pickford who signalled her attitude towards Katherine's capitulation by winking at the camera, 1929.

Kiss Me Kate Stage musical by Cole Porter based on the legendary backstage conflict between Alfred Lunt and Lynn Fontane. It opened at the New Century Theatre, New York, on 20 December, 1948. Feature film directed by George Sidney with Kathryn Grayson as Lilli Vanessi (Katherine), Howard Keel as Fred Graham (Petruchio) and Ann Miller as Lois Lane (Bianca), 1953.

McLintock! Feature film directed by Andrew V. McLaglen in which John Wayne as a cattle-baron wrangles with the social aspirations of an untamed Maureen O'Hara as Katherine, his wife, 1963.

The Taming of the Shrew Ballet in two acts after Shakespeare by Kurt-Heinz Stolze after Domenico Scarlatti. Choreography and production by John Cranko. Petruchio and Katherine row in a carnival atmosphere in which Gremio and Hortensio are duped into marrying streetwalkers. First presented with Marcia Haydée and Richard Cragun by the Stuttgart Ballet at the Wurttembergische Staatstheater, 16 March, 1969.

Bronco Billy Feature film directed by Clint Eastwood. He plays a circus performer whose kindly-meant rough treatment rescues Sondra Locke as spoilt, rich bitch Antoinette Lily both from the world she lives in and from herself, 1980.

THE TEMPEST

The Tempest Feature film directed by Derek Jarman with Heathcote Williams as a brooding, introverted Prospero and Toyah Wilcox as a spirited Miranda. The text is reconstructed to exploit notions of dream and vision, 1979.

The Tempest Feature film directed by Paul Mazursky with John Cassavetes as Philip (Prospero). An architect abandons a corrupt society, escapes with his daughter to a Greek island inhabited by Kalibanos and on the way discovers a mistress in Susan Sarandon as Aretha (Ariel), 1982.

PLAYS AND POEMS

The Compleat Works Setting by John Dankworth, sung by Cleo Laine, in which Shakespeare's plays and poems are listed in 1 minute and 10 seconds, 1974.

Keith Parsons and Pamela Mason

Index of Names

Mention within captions is presented in **bold** type and subsumes any textual reference on the same page. Inclusion in the display panels of Notable Productions is indicated in *italic*.

William Shakespeare and the characters in his plays are not indexed.

A

Abbott, Tony *105, 181, 213*
Ackland, Joss 58, *60*, 80, *81*
Adams, John Cranford **21**
Adomaitis, Regimastas *116*
Adrian, Max *226*
Akalaitis, JoAnne 61, *66*
Alexander, Bill 61, *66, 142*, 147, 148, *148, 155*, 184, *187*, 189, 190, *194*, 197, 198, 200, *201, 232*
Alexander, Bruce *36*, **46**, *66*, **98, 148**, *232*
Allam, Roger 132, *135, 187*, **230**, 231
Allen, Jonelle *237*
Allen, Patrick 63, *66, 226*
Allen, Sheila 61, *110*
Allio, René *66*
Ananiashvili, Nina *194*
Anderson, Justine *148*
Anderson, Mary 244
Anderson, Mia *237*
Andrews, Harry *135*
Andrews, Paul *194*
Annis, Francesca *51*, 126, *129*
Apsion, Annabelle 184, **186**, *187*
Arden, Mary **13**
Armfield, Neil 229, 232, *232*
Armstrong, Alun *226*
Arne, Thomas 62
Arnold, Robert **63**
Ashcroft, Peggy 7, 34, *36*, **38**, 44, **62, 63**, 90, **95**, 98, *99*, 156, **184**, *187*, **188**
Asherson, Renée *88*
Ashton, Frederick 31, 152, 153, 154, *155*, 249
Atkins, Eileen *219*
Atkins, Robert 214
Auden, W.H. 249
Audley, Maxine *219*
Aylmer, Felix 71, *72*

B

Baddeley, Angela 114
Badel, Sarah *201*
Baillie, David *247*
Bainbridge, Martyn *66, 110*
Baker, Sean *135*, 164
Balanchine, George 250
Banham, Teresa **134**
Banks, Leslie *88*
Bannerman, Celia *49*
Barber, Frances 229, **231**, *232*
Barber, Samuel 249
Bardon, Henry *155*

Barge, Gillian **245**, *247*
Barrie, Amanda 249
Bartenieff, George *66*
Barton, John 61, 65, 66, *66*, 70, 71, *72*, 76, 90, 106, 110, *110*, 119, *123*, 135, *135*, 142, *142*, 157, 160, 161, *161*, 177, 178, 179, 180, 181, *181, 206*, 220, 223, *226*, 230, *232, 237, 247*
Bates, Alan *73*, **74**
Baxter, Keith *81*
Bayldon, Oliver *93*
Baylis, Nadine *43*
Beale, Simon Russell 115, **122**, *123*, 183, 184, 185, **186**, *187*, **208**, 222, **226**, *226*
Bean, Sean *192*, *194*
Beaumont, Francis **238**
Beavis, Ivan *161*
Beckett, Samuel 212, 223
Beckinsale, Kate **160**
Bedford, Brian **63**
Beevers, Geoffrey **98**
Bell, Duncan **204**
Bellini, Vincenzo 250
Bennent, David 205, *207*
Bennett, Rodney 72
Benson, Frank 32, **82**, 90, 120, 176, **210**
Benson, Peter **91**, *93*
Benson, Susan *201*
Benthall, Michael 62, 210
Benton, Mark *49*
Benyon, Johanna **205**
Berger, Sarah 97, *99*
Berlioz, Hector 250
Bernard, Antony 50
Bernstein, Leonard **190**, 250
Berri, Duc de 85, **178**, 180
Berriman, Diana *142*
Bertish, Suzanne *54*
Betterton, Thomas **24**, 25, 68, 76, 100, 136, 150, 162, 249
Beymer, Richard **190**, 250
Bidmead, Stephanie 114
Billington, Kevin *99*
Bjørnson, Maria *135, 206*
Blakely, Colin *43*
Blakiston, Caroline **59**, *60*
Bland, Joyce 112
Bland, Marjorie 137, 138, 142, *142*
Blane, Sue *43, 110*, **152**, *155*
Bloom, Claire 63, 71, *72, 99, 187*
Boccaccio, Giovanni 33
Bogdanov, Michael 55, 59, *60*, 75, 77, 78, *81, 88*, 92, *93*, 125, *129*, 183, 187, *187*, 189, 191, *194, 194*, 198, 199, *201*
Bond, Samantha **48**, *49*, 158, **159**, *161*, **245**, *247*
Bondarchuk, Sergei *165*, 166, *169*
Bonham-Carter, Helen *73*
Bonneville, Richard *237*
Booth, Barton 100
Booth, Edwin 68
Booth, James *116*
Booth, Junius Brutus 182
Bowe, John *142*
Bowen, Philip *175, 242*
Bowman, James *232*

Boxer, Stephen *187*
Bradley, David **65**, 66, *66, 73*, 114, 117, *117, 142*, **147, 148, 208, 230**
Braid, Hilda *110*
Branagh, Kenneth **57**, 59, *60*, **69**, 70, **71**, *73*, 74, 84, 85, 86, **87, 88**, *88, 123*, 157, 158, **159**, *161*, 230, 232
Brando, Marlon **101, 102**, *105*
Brandstrup, Kim 249, 250
Brecht, Bertolt 30, **31**, **56**, 91, 152, 183, 249
Bremmer, Richard **109, 110**, *110*
Bremner, Ewen *49*
Brennen, Paul **92**, *93*, 250
Brett, Jeremy *142*
Briers, Richard *60, 161*, 227, **231**, 232, *232*
Britten, Benjamin 250
Britton, Tony *99*
Brook, Peter 39, 41, *43*, 106, 111, 113, 116, *116*, 118, 119, 120, **130**, 132, 133, *135*, 151, 155, *155*, 205, *206, 207*, 209, *213*, 216, *219*, 244
Brooke, Arthur 188
Brooke, Paul *36*
Brown, Antony **93**
Brown, Bille *148*
Bruce, Brenda *72*, **143, 145**, *148*, 243, *247*
Bry, Theodore de **202**
Bryant, Michael *43, 73*, 203, **205**, *206*, 207, 208
Buchell, Arend van 16, **17**
Buller, Francesca *142*
Burbage, James 15
Burbage, Richard 68, **82**, 182
Burge, Stuart *169*
Burgess, John *60*
Burke, David *73*, **223**, *226*
Burns, Martha *66*
Burrough, Tony *219*
Burroughs, Jackie *237*
Burton, Richard **82**, **197, 198**, 200, 201, *201*, 249
Bury, John *72, 99, 187*
Butterworth, Tyler *237*
Byrne, Allie *232*
Byrne, Michael *73*
Byron, George 28, 235
Bywater, Isabella *219*

C

Cadman, Michael **138**
Cagney, James 250
Caird, John *43, 155*
Calder, David *93*, 118, **141**, *142*
Calder-Marshall, Anna *219*
Caldwell, Zoe 114
Calhern, Louis **101**, *105*
Campbell, Cheryl 33, *36*, 126, **128**, *129, 129*
Campbell, Molly Harris *237*
Cant, Richard 47, *49*
Carey, Elizabeth 150
Carey, Henry *17*
Carfagno, Edward *105*
Cariou, Len *201*

Carlisle, John 137, 138, **139**, 142, *142, 155*, **159**
Carson, Avril *142*
Carter, Fred *129*
Carteret, Anna *142*
Cassavetes, John 250
Castle, John 40, *43, 73, 93*
Castro, Fidel 212
Cecil, Robert 16
Cellan-Jones, James *54*
Chakiris, George **190**, 250
Charles I 18, 23, 62, **156**
Charles II 62, 238
Charleson, Ian *36, 43*
Chaucer, Geoffrey 150
Chelsom, Peter **236**, *237, 247*
Chendrikova, Valentina **115**
Chettle, Henry 15
Chitty, Alison *43*, 64, *66, 206*
Christie, Bunny 60
Church, Tony *52, 66*, 71, *72*, 117, *161, 181*
Cibber, Colley 106, 182
Cibber, Theophilus 90, 188
Cinthio, Giraldi 162
Clancy, Deirdre *232*
Clarke, Lynn *232*
Cleese, John 200, *201*
Clifford, Richard *161*
Clint, George 100
Close, Glenn *73*, **74**
Cloutier, Suzanne *163*, 164, *169*
Clunes, Alec **103**, *105*
Cobham, Lord **12**
Coe, Peter *213*
Coffey, Denise 229, *232*
Coffin, C. Hayden **228**
Coleridge, Samuel Taylor 28
Coles, Dick *60*
Colicos, John *213*
Collier, John **144**
Collier, Patience **114**
Collings, David *105*
Colverd, Susan **174**
Compton, Fay *169*
Condell, Henry 8, 9, **10**, 11
Cook, Ron **89**, 93, *93*
Cooke, William 26
Coward, Noel 235
Cowley, Richard 11
Cox, Alan *247*
Cox, Brian 215, **217, 218**, *219*
Cragun, Richard 250
Craig, Russell *99*
Cranko, John 250
Croft, Emma 46, *47, 49*
Cronin, Michael *60*
Cross, Henri 119
Crowley, Bob 46, *49, 73, 81, 93, 117*, 119, *123, 135, 169, 242*
Crowne, John 90
Cryer, Andrew *49*
Cukor, George 250
Cumberland, Richard 26
Cummins, Peter *232*
Cumpsty, Michael *66*
Curry, Julian **211**
Curtis, Ann *105, 110, 206*

253

PICTURE ACKNOWLEDGEMENTS

AKG, London: 31 left.

BBC Photo Library: 53,89 both, 91 all, 166 both.

Birmingham Central Library: 32 bottom left,61,112 bottom right, 196 bottom left.

Bridgeman Art Library: 10 top right and 84 right British Library, London; 18,19 and 76 bottom right Guildhall Library, Corporation of London; 23 left The Trustees of the Weston Park Foundation; 27 top left and 30 centre Stapleton Collection; 29 right and 150 bottom right Courtesy of the Board of Trustees of the Victoria and Albert Museum; 68 bottom left Museum of London; 120 top and 150 top Private Collection; 124 bottom left National Trust, Petworth House, Sussex; 156 top Philip Mould Historical Portraits Ltd; 176 top Westminster Abbey, London; 176 bottom right Yale Center for British Art,Paul Mellon Centre; 178 right Giraudon/Musee Conde, Chantilly.

British Library: 9 right,10 top left, top centre and bottom,13 bottom, 15 top, 220 bottom left, 238 bottom left.

Dominic Photography: 119 and 140 right Richard Smith; 157, 189 and 208 Catherine Ashmore.

Dulwich Picture Gallery: 82 bottom right.

ET Archive: 12 left and 156 bottom right V & A Museum; 12 top right Marquess of Bath; 13 top left College of Arms; 17 right; 23 right; 24 left Army and Navy Club; 25 left, 27 top right, 124 top, 136 top, 144 bottom right, 182 top and bottom left The Garrick Club; 120 bottom left Covent Garden Library; 202 bottom right New York Public Library.

Mary Evans Picture Library: 22, 124 bottom right, 170 bottom right, 238 bottom right, 244 bottom left.

Fotomas Index: 11 top right, 12 bottom, 17 left.

Andy Fulgoni Photography: 21 left.

The Ronald Grant Archive: 31 right, 67, 69 top left and top centre left, 75, 83, 84 left, 87 bottom right, 88, 101, 102 all, 125, 160 both, 161, 163, 183, 190, 191 right, 195, 197 both, 198 top left and top right.

Robert Harding Picture Library: 11 top centre Adam Woolfitt; 13 top right Roy Rainford; 13 centre Philip Craven; 14 left and right, 21 right.

The Illustrated London News Picture Library: 202 bottom left.

The Kobal Collection: 39, 47 top, 69 bottom centre right, 74, 115 both, 127 bottom, 164, 165, 184 left, 191 left.

Angus McBean photograph; Harvard Theatre Collection; The Houghton Library: 31 centre, 62 top and bottom right, 63, 111, 113 both, 114 both, 126, 131, 144 top, 162 top and bottom right, 215, 216 all.

Reproduced by permission of the Marquess of Bath, Longleat House, Warminster, Wiltshire, Great Britain: 214 bottom left.

Mander and Mitchenson Theatre Collection: 25 centre right, 27 bottom, 28 right, 38 bottom left, 44 top and bottom right, 50 bottom left, 56 top and bottom left, 68 top and bottom right, 82 top, 94 all, 100 top, 106 all, 112 top and bottom left, 130 top and bottom right, 136 bottom right, 156 bottom left, 182 bottom right, 196 bottom right, 214 top and bottom right, 233 Houston Rogers, 234 top, 238 top.

The Mansell Collection: 14 centre, 196 top, 228 bottom left.

Museum of London Picture Library: 16, 188 bottom left.

National Portrait Gallery,London: 8, 62 bottom left, 202 top, 210 top, 220 top, 244 bottom right © DACS, London, 1995.

National Trust Photo Library: 244 top Derrick Witty/Desmond Bankes and Co.

Oxford Stage Company: 174 all.

Performing Arts Library: 104 both, 105, 134 all Clive Barda; 151 top Fritz Curzon.

Photostage/Donald Cooper: 33, 34, 35, 36, 40, 41 both, 42, 43, 45, 46, 47 bottom, 48 both, 51, 55, 57 both, 58, 59 both,60, 65, 66, 69 bottom centre left and bottom, right, 70, 71, 77, 78, 79 both, 80, 81, 85 both, 86, 87 top and bottom left, 92 both, 93, 96, 97 both, 98, 107, 108 both, 109 both, 110, 121 top, 122 both, 128 all, 129, 137, 138, 139 all, 140 left, 141 all, 144 bottom left, 146, 147 both, 148, 149, 151 bottom, 153 both, 158 both, 159 both, 167 both, 168 both, 173 all, 177, 179 both, 180, 185 bottom left, 186 both, 192 top and bottom left, 193 right, 194, 198 bottom, 199 all, 200, 203, 204 all, 205 all, 206, 207, 209, 211 both, 212, 213, 217 both, 218 both, 219, 223 both, 224 centre and right, 225, 226, 227, 229 both, 230 all, 231 both, 232, 235 left, 236 all, 240 right, 241 top right.

RSC Collection: 56 bottom right, 100 bottom left, 120 bottom right, 188 top.

The Shakespeare Centre Library, Stratford-upon-Avon: 9 left, 15 bottom, 25 centre left, 25 right, 28 left, 32 top and bottom right, 37, 38 top and bottom right, 44 bottom left, 50 top and bottom right, 52, 64, 69 top centre right, top right and bottom, 73, 76 bottom left, 82 bottom left, 90 top and bottom left, 95 both , 99, 103, 117, 118, 121 bottom, 127 top, 130 bottom left, 132 both, 133, 143, 145 both, 150 bottom left, 151 centre, 152 both, 154, 170 top and bottom left, 171, 172 both, 178 left, 184 right, 185 top and bottom right, 192 bottom right, 193 left, 210 bottom left and bottom right, 220 bottom right, 221, 222, 224 left, 228 top, 234 bottom left and bottom right, 235 right, 240 left, 241 top left and bottom, 243, 245 both, 246.

John Timbers: 239.

University of Bristol Theatre Collection: 100 bottom right.

Courtesy of the Board of Trustees of the Victoria and Albert Museum: 24 right, 29 left, 30 left and right, 136 bottom left, 162 bottom right Angus McBean, 162 left, 188 bottom right, 228 bottom right.

John Vickers Theatre Collection: 76 top.

Geoffrey Wheeler: 90 bottom right BBC, 176 bottom left.

DUST JACKET – FRONT:

Main picture: Ronald Grant Archive/Renaissance Films.

Montage in descending order: Dominic Photography/Catherine Ashmore
Kobal Collection
Shakespeare Birthplace Trust
Shakespeare Birthplace Trust
Victoria and Albert Museum
Geoffrey Wheeler

DUST JACKET – BACK:

Top left: Mander and Mitchenson Theatre Collection; **Top centre:** Bridgeman Art Library/National Gallery,London; **Top right:** Bridgeman Art Library/Philip Mould Historical Portraits Ltd; **Bottom:** Martin Charles.

ILLUSTRATIONS:

Hugh J.Dixon: 20,21.
Vana Haggerty: Half-title page.